The Origins of Islamic Law

If the Qur'an is the first written formulation of Islam in general, Malik's *Muwaṭṭa'* is arguably the first written formulation of the 'Islam-in-practice' that becomes Islamic law. This book considers the methods used to derive the judgements of the law from the Qur'an, demonstrating in detail the various methods used, both linguistic and otherwise, in interpreting the legal verses. In many respects, this book is more about the history and development of Islamic law than it is about the science of Qur'anic interpretation. It questions hitherto accepted frameworks of both the classical Muslim view and the current revisionist western view on the development of Islamic law and is the first study in a European language to deal specifically with the early development of the Maliki school of jurisprudence.

'A significant contribution that sheds important light on the origins of Islamic law. Dutton represents a new generation of Islamic legal scholarship and makes a significant contribution to a more sophisticated understanding of early Islamic jurisprudence. His book should be read by all specialists in Islamic law.'

Khaled Abou El Fadl, International Journal of Middle East Studies

Yasin Dutton is Senior Lecturer in Arabic and Islamic Studies at the University of Edinburgh.

CULTURE AND CIVILIZATION
IN THE MIDDLE EAST

Series Editor:

Ian R. Netton
University of Leeds

This series studies the Middle East through the twin foci of its diverse cultures and civilisations. Comprising original monographs as well as scholarly surveys, it covers topics in the fields of Middle Eastern literature, archaeology, law, history, thought, science, folklore, art, architecture and language. While there will be a plurality of views, the series presents serious scholarship in a lucid and stimulating fashion.

The Origins of Islamic Law

The Qurʾan, the *Muwaṭṭaʾ* and Madinan *ʿAmal*

Yasin Dutton

RoutledgeCurzon
Taylor & Francis Group

First published 1999 by Curzon Press

Second edition first published 2002
by RoutledgeCurzon
11 New Fetter Lane, London EC4P 4EE

Simultaneously published in the USA and Canada
by RoutledgeCurzon
29 West 35th Street, New York, NY 10001

RoutledgeCurzon is an imprint of the Taylor & Francis Group

Typeset in Baskerville by LaserScript Ltd, Mitcham, Surrey
Printed and bound in Great Britain by
TJ International, Padstow, Cornwall

British Library Cataloguing in Publication Data
A catalogue record of this book is available from the British Library

Library of Congress Cataloguing in Publication Data
A catalogue record for this book has been requested

ISBN 0–7007–1669–6

Bismillāhi l-raḥmāni l-raḥīm
wa-ṣallā llāhu ʿalā Sayyidinā Muḥammadin
wa-ʿalā ālihi wa-ṣaḥbihi ajmaʿīn

Contents

Acknowledgements xi

Conventions xiii

INTRODUCTION 1
A note on sources 6
A further note 6

PART ONE
THE MADINAN BACKGROUND

CHAPTER ONE: Mālik and Madina 11
His family 11
Mālik's early life 12
His teachers 12
Mālik's reliance on Madinan sources 13
The importance of Madina 14
Mālik as teacher and scholar 15
Mālik the scholar of *ḥadīth* 16

CHAPTER TWO: The *Muwaṭṭa'* 22
The different transmissions (*riwāyāt*) of the text 22
The authenticity of the text 26
The arrangement of the text 27
The reason for its compilation 28
Other works by Mālik 31

CHAPTER THREE: The *ʿAmal* of the People of Madina 32
Mālik's *madhhab* 32
The nature of Madinan *ʿamal* 33

The authority of Madinan *ʿamal* 37
ʿAmal versus ḥadīth 41

PART TWO
MĀLIK'S USE OF THE QUR'AN IN THE *MUWAṬṬA*ʾ

CHAPTER FOUR: Textual Considerations 55
Mālik and the reading of Madina 55
Mālik and the *shādhdh* variant readings 57

CHAPTER FIVE: The Qurʾan as a Source of Judgements in the *Muwaṭṭa*ʾ 61
Qurʾanic reference in the *Muwaṭṭa*ʾ 61
The problems of Qurʾanic interpretation 63
Ẓihār 65
The inheritance due to children 72
Tadbīr versus debts 74

CHAPTER SIX: Techniques of Qurʾanic Interpretation in the *Muwaṭṭa*ʾ 78
The assumption of inclusion (*ʿumūm*) and literal meaning (*ẓāhir*) 79
The assumption that commands indicate obligation 88
Exceptions to the *ʿumūm* (*takhṣīṣ al-ʿumūm*) 90
Paired chapters 91
Iḥṣār 92
Qurʾan by Qurʾan: the assumption of 'one word, one meaning' 96
Deduction from juxtaposition 100
Ḥaml al-muṭlaq ʿalā l-muqayyad 104
Exceptions to Qurʾan by Qurʾan 105
Kalāla 106
Implication (*al-mafhūm*) 114
Mafhūm al-muwāfaqa 114
Mafhūm al-mukhālafa 115

CHAPTER SEVEN: Chronological Considerations 120
Naskh 121
Asbāb al-nuzūl 125
The Umayyad contribution 130
1. The meaning of the word *qar*ʾ 132
2. The inheritance of a grandfather 135
3. *ʿAmd versus khaṭa*ʾ in cases of homicide 135

4. The indemnity (*ʿaql*) for molars 137
5. *Īlāʾ* 139
6. 'Irrevocable' divorce (*al-batta*) 140
7. Triple divorce in *tamlīk* 141
8. The rights due to a *mabtūta* divorcee 142
9. *Zakāt* on horses 146
10. The prohibition against *ribā* 149
11. The *ʿidda* of *umm walads* 151
12. The penalty for *qadhf* 151

PART THREE
IMPLICATIONS

CHAPTER EIGHT: Qurʾan and *Sunna* 157
The Qurʾan in Islamic law 157
The importance of the Qurʾan in the *Muwaṭṭaʾ* 161
The *sunna* 161
The continuity of the *sunna* 164

CHAPTER NINE: *Sunna versus Ḥadīth* 168

CONCLUSIONS 178

Notes 181

Glossary 230

Biographical Notes 236

Bibliography and Bibliographical Abbreviations 245
Arabic 245
European 252

Indexes 256
Index of Legal Precepts 256
Index of Legal Principles 258
Index of Persons 260

Acknowledgements

This book began life as a dissertation which was accepted for the degree of D.Phil. in Oxford in 1992. My sincere thanks go to the many people who helped in its inception and in its eventually, after much revision, seeing the light of day as a published work. First and foremost I owe a particular debt of gratitude to Shaykh Abd al-Qadir al-Murabit, not only for introducing me to the significance of Mālik's *Muwaṭṭaʾ* and Madinan *ʿamal* but also for encouraging me to return to the world of formal learning after a long absence; also to Alan Jones, who made the path of that return so easy. I have also benefited considerably from the comments and advice of many people, among whom particular mention should be made not only of the above-mentioned persons but also of Lawrence Conrad, Michael Cook, Wilferd Madelung, Farhan Nizami, Jamil Qureshi and Iftikhar Zaman, all of whom gave up considerable portions of their time to read through parts, if not all, of earlier drafts of the book; also Umar Abd-Allah and ʿAbdallāh al-Shaʿlān, whose responses to my queries helped clarify a number of points.

This book would not have been possible either without financial assistance from several quarters: primarily a British Academy grant, but with support also from Mr. ʿAbdallāh ʿAlī al-ʿĪsā and the *Jamʿiyyat al-Iṣlāḥ al-Ijtimāʿī* in Kuwait (this last through the good offices of Dr. ʿAjīl Jāsim al-Nashmī, who also helped in many other respects) and, later, from the James Mew Fund of the University of Oxford, the World of Islam Festival Trust and Jesus College, Oxford. To all of these I am very grateful.

An edited version of Chapter 3, 'The *ʿAmal* of the People of Madina', appeared in Yasin Dutton, '*Sunna*, *Ḥadīth* and Madinan *ʿAmal*', *Journal of Islamic Studies*, iv (1993), pp. 1–31. I am grateful for permission to reprint portions of that work.

Finally, I must thank my wife and children for their constant support and admirable patience in putting up with a largely absent husband and father for long periods of time.

Conventions

In general, Arabic words are transliterated and italicised: the main exception is the word 'Qur'an' which I have left unitalicised and without a macron. For personal names I have included macrons but for the commoner place-names I have not (hence 'Madina' and 'Kufa' rather than 'Madīna' and 'Kūfa'). The word *ḥadīth* I have used both as a collective noun and as a countable singular having the plural *ḥadīths*. Quotations from the Qur'an, which are given according to the Madinan reading of Nāfiʿ, are given in a fully vocalised transliteration, reflecting more closely the way in which they would normally be said. For quotations from other sources, and for individual words and phrases, I have used a looser form of transliteration, although occasionally retaining the fully vocalised form where it has seemed appropriate. I have also used the now conventional 'al-' to indicate the Arabic definite article, regardless of whether it comes in front of a 'sun' or a 'moon' letter.

Because of the technical nature of this study and the specialised vocabulary that has developed in order to discuss these matters, many terms are retained in their Arabic form. These have either been glossed in the main text where they first occur, or, in the case of the most frequently used ones, explained in the Glossary, or, sometimes, both.

One translated term, however, needs special mention: for *ḥukm* I have consistently used the English word 'judgement', following the sense in which this word is used in the Authorised and Revised Versions of the Bible to translate the Hebrew *mishpaṭ(im)* (e.g. *Exod.* 21.1, 24.3, *Deut.* 4.1, 5.1, 6.1, and many other instances). The somewhat restricted meaning that this word seems to have acquired in contemporary usage has led some writers to suggest other translations, such as 'ruling', 'determination', and 'assessment'.[1] Nevertheless, 'judgement' is the word I use in my own idiolect and the word I have used here.

[1] See, for example, Reinhart, 'Islamic Law as Islamic Ethics'.

As far as possible, I have tried to abbreviate all bibliographical references. Where a source is commonly known by the name of its author, I have given just the name of the author; where it is commonly known by its title, I have usually given an abbreviated form of the title: otherwise, I have made my own choice between these two possibilities. Fuller details, along with the abbreviations used, will be found in the Bibliography.

Biographical details, including death-dates, have in general been left to the Biographical Notes at the end of the book, except in a few cases where it seemed appropriate to include them. Where dates are given in the text, only the Hijrī date is given; in the case of death-dates and dates of reigns, etc., the Christian equivalent will be found in the Biographical Notes. Dates in the first and second centuries of the Muslim era are notoriously difficult to pinpoint accurately, and often two, three or more conflicting dates are given for a particular event: in cases of uncertainty I have tried where possible to arrive at a reasonable compromise or simply left the problem unresolved.

For converting dates from the Hijrī to the Christian calendar I have either relied on the bibliographical works of Brockelmann and Sezgin and the *Encyclopaedia of Islam*, or used the tables given in Bacharach's *Near East Studies Handbook*. Obviously there are many instances where a year in the Hijrī calendar spans the end of one Christian year and the beginning of another: in such instances I have tried to use commonsense to determine which of the two dates is more likely, or simply taken the first date. The reader should therefore exercise due caution.

Introduction

This book is about the application of the Qurʾan as law. It considers the methods used by Mālik in his *Muwaṭṭaʾ* to derive judgements from the Qurʾan and is thus concerned on one level with the finer details of Qurʾanic interpretation. However, since any discussion of the Qurʾan in the context of the *Muwaṭṭaʾ* must necessarily include consideration of the terms *sunna*, *ḥadīth*, *ijtihād* and *ʿamal*, these terms – or at least the concepts behind them – also receive considerable attention. Indeed, the argument of this book has more bearing on the history and development of Islamic law – of which the above terms are the expression – than on the science of Qurʾanic interpretation.

There are at present two main views on the origins of Muslim jurisprudence: that of the 'classical' (i.e. post-Shāfiʿī) Muslim scholars, and that of the revisionist school of most modern Western scholarship associated in particular with the views of Goldziher and Schacht.[1] The classical picture shows Islamic law as deriving from two main sources, preserved as the texts of the Qurʾan and the *ḥadīth* of the Prophet (referred to as 'the *sunna*'), in addition to certain other acceptable sources such as *ijmāʿ* (consensus) and *qiyās* (analogy), all of which derive their ultimate authority from the texts themselves. Although it acknowledges that in the initial period the *ḥadīth* circulated in primarily oral transmissions, and the Qurʾan in an oral as much as a written form, this view is nevertheless essentially text-based, since the material, whether oral or written, depends for its authority on its fixed form. It culminates in the later view that a knowledge of Islam, and thus also of Islamic law, is effectively restricted to a knowledge of the texts of the Qurʾan and the *ḥadīth*, in particular the collections of al-Bukhārī and Muslim, although with some recognition of the other four of the 'Six Books', i.e. the collections of al-Tirmidhī, Abū Dāwūd, al-Nasāʾī and Ibn Mājah, which are what are most commonly seen today as the main sources of Islamic law.

The dominant paradigm in modern Western scholarship, however, although basically accepting the early origin of the Qurʾan, sees the vast majority of the *ḥadīth*-material as apocryphal, having been back-projected as sayings of the Prophet only at a much later date. This, it is said, was done in order to invest what was originally the local practice of individual centres of learning in the Muslim world with the authority of the Prophet himself in an attempt to accord legitimacy to their own views. The evidence adduced for this view is, very briefly, the relatively rapid appearance of a large body of *ḥadīth*-material where previously, it is claimed, none, or very little, had existed; and, also, the presence of numerous anomalies and contradictions both in the texts themselves and in their chains of authority (*isnāds*), all of which casts doubt on the authenticity of this material and points to its having been fabricated at a much later date than is usually claimed. This alleged wholesale fabrication of *ḥadīth* is seen as the result of the activities of an initially small group of scholars who, in opposition to what they considered to be on the one hand the godless, irreligious nature of the Islamic state at that time, and on the other hand the widely divergent and randomly derived local practice of the various legal schools of the time, aimed to impose some kind of unity and overall authority by developing the idea of a '*sunna* of the Prophet' which it was incumbent on all the Muslims to follow. Most Western scholars thus hold that the idea of the *sunna* of the Prophet as a normative model did not exist before this time. Instead, they argue, the word *sunna* referred variously to the consensus of opinion of the different local schools. The collocation '*kitāb* and *sunna*', and even the expression '*sunna* of the Prophet', is held to have been in use right from the earliest times, but only in the vague, general, sense of what was considered right or just by the particular group using it, as when used by the different political groups calling each other to 'the Book of Allah and the *sunna* of His Prophet'.[2]

It is the contention of the present study that there is a third view which has not yet been sufficiently examined (if even recognised) by modern scholars, whether Muslim or otherwise. This third view is one which, although in many respects highly traditional, nevertheless diverges from the 'classical' view on a number of important points, and which, although essentially opposed to the Western revisionist position, nevertheless agrees with it – against the 'classical' view – on a number of key issues. This third view is that offered by Mālik's *Muwaṭṭaʾ*.

This study is not constructed as a refutation of either of the two views outlined above. The intention is to point out that this third view exists in the sources but has not been adequately described, let alone adequately considered, by present-day scholarship, and that it has great bearing on our understanding of the nature and development of Islamic law. For whereas the first two views, although opposed to each other, are essentially similar in that they are both text-based – the one from a positive, the other from a negative, standpoint – this third view allows us a fundamentally different perspective on Islamic legal history where the true expression of the law is seen as being preserved not in a corpus of texts but in the actions, or *ʿamal*, of men.

This third view agrees with the traditional view – against the revisionists – in seeing Islamic law as based on Qurʾan and *sunna* from the beginning, but it disagrees with the traditional position with regard to how this *sunna* is defined. For whereas *sunna* in the traditional, 'classical', sense refers almost invariably to *ḥadīth* (as Schacht points out), in its Muwattan, 'pre-classical', sense it is by no means co-terminous with *ḥadīth* (as Schacht again points out), but is, rather, intimately linked with the idea of *ʿamal*, or 'practice' (Schacht also uses the expression 'living tradition' to cover this concept).[3] That is, *ḥadīth* refers to texts whereas *sunna* refers to action. However, not only must *sunna* be distinguished from *ḥadīth*, but – and this is where the Muwattan view diverges from the Schachtian – *sunna* must also be distinguished from *ʿamal*, though not in the same way. For whereas *sunna* in its Muwattan sense refers to a practice originating in the practice, or *sunna*, of the Prophet, *ʿamal* is a broader concept which includes not only the *sunna* established by the Prophet but also the *ijtihād* of later authorities. Thus all *sunna* is *ʿamal*, but not all *ʿamal* is *sunna*; indeed, as we shall see, Mālik typically differentiates those parts of *ʿamal* that contain elements of later *ijtihād* in addition to a base in Qurʾan and/or *sunna* by using the word *amr* rather than *sunna*.

What the *Muwaṭṭaʾ* shows most clearly is that these elements – Qurʾan, *sunna* and *ijtihād* – are seen as inextricably bound together into one whole, namely, the *ʿamal* of the people of Madina. Thus although the *Muwaṭṭaʾ* is seen by both traditional and revisionist scholars as an early book of *ḥadīth*, representing for the first group a kind of prototype *ṣaḥīḥ ḥadīth* collection with its *isnāds* not yet sufficiently elaborated and its *raʾy* not yet excised, and representing for the second a relatively similar picture of a midway stage where there is still considerable reliance on the opinions of early authorities rather than on the *ḥadīth* of the Prophet alone, it is in fact neither of these. Rather, it presents a composite picture of what Mālik considered to be the essential aspects of the *dīn* in action. The Qurʾan is there – in very large measure, as we shall see – and so too is the *sunna* of the Prophet; but so too are the judgements and *ijtihād* of the caliphs, governors and scholars (including Mālik himself) right through from the time of the Rightly-Guided Caliphs to when Mālik was compiling his material in the first half of the 2nd century AH, and none of these elements can ultimately be separated from the others. A particular practice may ostensibly derive from the Qurʾan, or from the *sunna* of the Prophet, or from later authorities, but it is seen as part of a whole – the existential, lived, reality that Mālik found himself in, so that he could describe it by saying, for example, '[This is] the *sunna* here and [this is] what I found the people of knowledge in our city doing . . .', or, 'This is the position that the people of knowledge have always held to here.'[4] What Mālik effectively presents us with is a package, and this package, although reaching us in the textual form of the book entitled 'the *Muwaṭṭaʾ*', was essentially one of *ʿamal*, i.e. action, rather than texts, hence the constant reference throughout to what people were actually doing.

What we further see suggested by the *Muwaṭṭaʾ* is a process whereby the original picture of *ʿamal* – intimately linked, as we have said, with the idea of *sunna* but by no means synonymous with it – gradually becomes replaced outside Madina, first in Iraq and then later practically everywhere else, by *ḥadīth*, which is then called *sunna* but may in fact not represent *sunna* at all. Thus what begins in Madina as an *ʿamal*-based *dīn* (represented by Mālik) becomes partially systematised in Iraq (represented by Abū Ḥanīfa, or, more correctly, his pupils Abū Yūsuf and al-Shaybānī) and then even more so by al-Shāfiʿī, so that by the time we come to Aḥmad ibn Ḥanbal, who effectively preferred weak *ḥadīths* to no *ḥadīths* at all,[5] and Dāwūd al-Ẓāhirī, for whom even *qiyās* was out of the question,[6] we have reached an almost totally *ḥadīth*-based, i.e. text-based, religion. This was clearly not Mālik's view of Qurʾan and *sunna*, for whom *ʿamal*, i.e. 'action', was paramount.

The particular importance of the *Muwaṭṭaʾ*, then, lies in its being not only our earliest formulation of Islamic law, but also our earliest record of that law as a lived reality rather than the theoretical construct of later scholars. In it we see judgements being handed down and precedents being created not only by the Prophet, the Rightly-Guided Caliphs and other senior Companions, but also by later caliphs, governors and scholars in a continuous extension of the initial Qurʾanic impulse as and when circumstances demanded. Furthermore, it represents Islamic law and legal literature *before* the major change of methodology propounded by al-Shāfiʿī, with his insistence on the overriding authority of Prophetic *sunna* as preserved by *ḥadīth* rather than the old idea of Prophetic *sunna* as preserved by *ʿamal*, was to transform it radically and lead to the great upsurge in the importance given to *ḥadīth* in the third and fourth centuries AH. Indeed, one of the dominant themes of the *Muwaṭṭaʾ* in its portrayal of the legal practice of the 'ancient' (to use Schacht's epithet) school of

Madina is precisely that of *sunna* being preserved by *ʿamal* rather than *ḥadīth*.

This study, then, is an attempt to go back before the time of al-Shāfiʿī and reconstruct a picture of how the most 'ancient' of the 'ancient' schools, i.e. that of Madina, approached the question of applying the Qurʾan as law. As Brunschvig suggested as long ago as 1950 (the year in which Schacht published his *Origins*): 'If we could free ourselves from the hold of al-Shāfiʿī, whose ingenious synthesis has falsified our perspectives for a long time indeed ... we would perhaps be able to see the origins of *fiqh* with new eyes.'[7] This study aims to do precisely that.

To investigate adequately every aspect of the *Muwaṭṭaʾ* would obviously be beyond the scope of a single volume. Instead, I have chosen to concentrate upon the specifically Qurʾanic element in it, for two main reasons: firstly, because of the importance of this element within the framework of Islamic law, and, secondly, because it has been almost totally neglected by modern Western scholarship.

This study divides naturally into three parts. The first gives the general contextual background of Madina which is essential if one is to place Mālik and his *Muwaṭṭaʾ* in their proper Madinan setting: Chapters One and Two therefore give a brief coverage of this setting and the Madinan character of the man and his book. Furthermore, since Mālik was an exponent – perhaps we should say *the* exponent – of Madinan *ʿamal*, and acceptance of this *ʿamal* is, in effect, the real point of difference between the 'ancient' Madinan school and all other schools, it is important to understand what he understood by *ʿamal*: Chapter Three is therefore devoted to this question and in particular the relationship between it and *ḥadīth* as a source of law in Islam, which is crucial to an understanding of the rest of the book.

Part Two concerns the more specifically Qurʾanic element in the *Muwaṭṭaʾ*. Chapter Four deals briefly with textual aspects of the Qurʾan in the *Muwaṭṭaʾ* and includes a survey of the *shādhdh* variants found therein and their value for exegesis. Chapters Five and Six cover the more technical aspects of Mālik's use of the Qurʾan in the *Muwaṭṭaʾ*, although always against the contextual background of *ʿamal*. Chapter Seven deals with more chronological considerations, namely, the value on the one hand of *naskh* and *asbāb al-nuzūl* for Qurʾanic interpretation in the context of *ʿamal*, and, on the other, of the Umayyad contribution to the development of Islamic law from its basis in Qurʾan and *sunna*.

Part Three (Chapters Eight and Nine and the Conclusion) is in the nature of a conclusory section where the commonly accepted axiom that Islamic law is based on the two-fold source of Qurʾan and *sunna* is re-examined in the light of the preceding chapters.

A note on sources

Mālik's own work and words naturally provide the basic data for this study, but clearly any full understanding of his ideas is not possible without reference to the ideas of his contemporaries. Later appreciations of his position are also helpful in determining his method, although one must be cautious of subsequent impositions of structure where none necessarily existed.

The main sources for this analysis are the *Muwaṭṭa'* and the Qur'an and the commentaries on them both. For the *Muwaṭṭa'* I have used in particular the commentaries of al-Bājī, al-Suyūṭī and al-Zurqānī, and for the Qur'an the *Tafsīrs* of al-Ṭabarī, Ibn Juzayy and 'al-Jalālayn' and the '*Aḥkām*' works of al-Jaṣṣāṣ and Ibn al-ʿArabī. Also important for the views of Mālik himself are the *Mudawwana* of Saḥnūn and the *ʿUtbiyya* (or *Mustakhraja*) of Muḥammad al-ʿUtbī. As for general works on *fiqh*, I have relied particularly on Ibn Rushd's *Bidāyat al-mujtahid* and Ibn Juzayy's *al-Qawānīn al-fiqhiyya* for an initial appraisal of points of difference between the *madhhabs*. For the specifically Ḥanafī position I have relied predominantly on al-Sarakhsī's *Mabsūṭ*, al-Jaṣṣāṣ's *Aḥkām* and al-Shaybānī's transmission of the *Muwaṭṭa'*, and, for the Shāfiʿī position, on al-Shāfiʿī's *Umm*. No systematic attempt has been made to collect data on any other of the main *madhhabs* – whether Sunnī or otherwise – although occasional reference has been made to them.

Two further points: firstly, although some of these sources are considerably later than the men whose opinions they purport to contain, there are hardly any discrepancies – and even then not serious – between the picture they give and that found in the earliest sources; I therefore consider them to be generally accurate presentations of earlier views. (Where I have noted a discrepancy I have indicated it). Secondly, I have not attempted to be strictly accurate in my reference to non-Mālikī views. Sometimes, for instance, I have referred to the 'Iraqi' or the 'Kufan' view when it could be argued that there was not necessarily consensus on the point in either Iraq or Kufa; nevertheless, for the purposes of this study, and especially as a foil to Mālik's view, I believe these designations to be essentially correct.

A further note

Those subscribing to the Goldziher/Schacht thesis are wont to cast doubt on the authenticity of early texts such as the *Muwaṭṭa'*. Suffice it to say here that the evidence at our disposal is overwhelmingly in favour of a text that must be attributed to Mālik himself, despite recent asseverations to the contrary. (The reader will find more on this topic in Chapter Two.)

As for Mālik's accuracy and honesty, it is enough that all the Muslims are agreed on his exceptionally high standards of transmission whether or not they always accept his judgements of *fiqh*. As al-Dhahabī put it: 'The *Muwaṭṭa'* inspires a confidence and respect which is unparalleled (*inna li-l-Muwaṭṭa' la-waqʿan fī l-nufūs wa-mahābatan fī l-qulūb lā yuwāzinuhā shay'*).'[8] Furthermore, one who would undergo severe physical punishment rather than suppress or misrepresent a recognised *ḥadīth* is not the sort of man to have lightly invented his material.[9]

I leave the reader to his own final judgement.

PART ONE

The Madinan Background

CHAPTER ONE

Mālik and Madina

Mālik ibn Anas al-Aṣbaḥī, after whom the Mālikī school of jurisprudence takes its name, was born in or near Madina,[1] probably in the year 93/711.[2] He was known as the '*ᶜālim* of Madina' and the appellation is fitting, for he grew up in Madina, studied there under predominantly Madinan teachers, and spent the greater part of his life there teaching and giving *fatwās* according to the Madinan tradition. Indeed, unlike many of his contemporaries who travelled widely in search of knowledge, Mālik is said to have only ever left Madina to go on *ḥajj* to Makka.[3] He died in Madina in 179/795, and was buried there in the graveyard of al-Baqīᶜ.

His family

Mālik's family were not originally from Madina but had moved north to settle there from the Yemen during the time of either his great-grandfather, Abū ᶜĀmir, or his grandfather, Mālik ibn Abī ᶜĀmir.[4] Abū ᶜĀmir transmitted *ḥadīths* from ᶜUthmān, the third caliph, and is said by some to have been a Companion.[5] His son, Mālik ibn Abī ᶜĀmir, i.e. our Mālik's grandfather, was one of the older Successors and a well-respected man of learning who related *ḥadīths* from various Companions including ᶜUmar, ᶜUthmān and Abū Hurayra.[6] He is also credited with having been one of those who copied out the Qurᵓan during the time of ᶜUthmān.[7] His connection with ᶜUthmān is further emphasised by reports that he was involved in the conquest of North Africa under the direct orders of ᶜUthmān and that he was one of the four who, when ᶜUthmān died, attended to the funeral arrangements.[8] One of Mālik's uncles, Abū Suhayl Nāfiᶜ ibn Mālik ibn Abī ᶜĀmir, was also a well-respected man of learning and transmitter of *ḥadīth* and, like his father, figures as an authority in the *Muwaṭṭaᵓ*.[9] Another uncle, al-Rabīᶜ ibn Mālik, is also known as a transmitter of *ḥadīth*,[10] and it is said that his father, Anas ibn Mālik, was one also.[11] With such a family background it was not, therefore, surprising that Mālik should have taken an interest in learning.

Mālik's early life

Very little is known about Mālik's early life. One report says that he helped his brother sell cloth before taking to a life of learning,[12] while another speaks of him keeping company with singers and wanting to be one himself until persuaded by his mother to study *fiqh* instead.[13] However, reports that speak of his mother dressing him up in 'the clothes of learning' (*thiyāb al-ᶜilm*) before he went out to study suggest that he was still only a young boy when he began studying.[14] Indeed, one report specifies that he began studying when he was eleven.[15] Whatever the case may be, he must have begun studying at an early age and been a particularly able student, since he was already a well-established and respected teacher by his late twenties, if not considerably earlier.[16]

His teachers

Mālik studied under many teachers, but the man said to have had the most influence on him was the younger Successor ᶜAbdallāh ibn Yazīd ibn Hurmuz.[17] Very little is known about Ibn Hurmuz, except that he was considered to be one of the great men of learning of his generation in Madina,[18] and that Mālik's association with him was likely to have been long and close.[19] There is no mention of Ibn Hurmuz as an authority in the *Muwaṭṭa*ʾ, but this is explained by him being said to have required from Mālik on oath not to mention his name in any *ḥadīth* he transmitted from him.[20]

Another teacher with great influence on Mālik was the older Successor Nāfiᶜ, the *mawlā* (freed slave) of ᶜAbdallāh ibn ᶜUmar. Nāfiᶜ's standing was such that Mālik said that if he had heard a *ḥadīth* from Nāfiᶜ from Ibn ᶜUmar he did not mind if he had never heard it from anyone else,[21] while the *isnād* 'Mālik – Nāfiᶜ – Ibn ᶜUmar' was considered by al-Bukhārī and later scholars of *ḥadīth* to be the 'golden chain' of authority (*silsilat al-dhahab*) because of the excellence of each individual link.[22]

Nāfiᶜ is in fact the only older Successor whose name figures prominently as a direct authority in the *Muwaṭṭa*ʾ. Most of Mālik's immediate teachers were younger Successors of the generation of Ibn Hurmuz, such as Ibn

Shihāb al-Zuhrī, Rabīʿa ibn Abī ʿAbd al-Raḥmān ('Rabīʿat al-raʾy'), Abū l-Zinād ibn Dhakwān and Yaḥyā ibn Saʿīd al-Anṣārī. These men in turn, although having met Companions, had for the most part gained their knowledge from older Madinan Successors such as Saʿīd ibn al-Musayyab, ʿUrwa ibn al-Zubayr, al-Qāsim ibn Muḥammad ibn Abī Bakr, Khārija ibn Zayd ibn Thābit, Sulaymān ibn Yasār, ʿUbaydallāh ibn ʿAbdallāh ibn ʿUtba ibn Masʿūd, Abū Bakr ibn ʿAbd al-Raḥmān ibn al-Ḥārith ibn Hishām, Abū Salama ibn ʿAbd al-Raḥmān ibn ʿAwf and Sālim ibn ʿAbdallāh ibn ʿUmar.

The first seven of these – Saʿīd ibn al-Musayyab, ʿUrwa, al-Qāsim ibn Muḥammad, Khārija, Sulaymān ibn Yasār, ʿUbaydallāh ibn ʿAbdallāh and Abū Bakr ibn ʿAbd al-Raḥmān – are the names most often grouped together under the honorific title of the 'Seven *Fuqahāʾ*' of Madina.[23] We need not assume the number 'seven' to be strictly accurate,[24] but, whatever the actual number, it does suggest that there was a consolidated body of opinion on matters of *fiqh* in Madina during the latter part of the first century AH. Thus we read that these 'seven' would gather together to solve the legal problems that were put to them and that judges would not give their verdict until they had consulted them and seen what their opinion was.[25] Similarly, when ʿUmar ibn ʿAbd al-ʿAzīz was appointed governor of Madina in 87 (or 86) AH he is said to have called together ten scholars (most of whom figure in the above-mentioned list) and made it clear to them that he did not wish to issue any orders without first consulting at least some, if not all, of them.[26]

Mālik's reliance on Madinan sources

The frequency with which Mālik cites the *ḥadīths* and legal opinions of these authorities indicates both the high regard that Mālik had for them as representatives of and authorities for the Madinan tradition of learning and the extent of his reliance on that tradition. Indeed, as Abd-Allah has pointed out, Mālik agrees with their consensus well over ninety per cent of the time, which also indicates a strong continuity between the *fiqh* of the 'Seven *Fuqahāʾ*' and that of Mālik.[27]

This overwhelming reliance on the Madinan tradition is reflected in the *isnāds* of the *Muwaṭṭaʾ*. According to al-Ghāfiqī there are 95 sources from whom Mālik directly transmits *musnad ḥadīths* in the *Muwaṭṭaʾ*, 'all of whom', he says, 'are from Madina except six'.[28] From these six non-Madinans Mālik transmits a total of only twenty-two *ḥadīths* from the Prophet[29] compared with a total of 822 (600 *musnad* and 222 *mursal*) in the *Muwaṭṭaʾ* as a whole,[30] i.e. less than three per cent of the total, which indicates how extensively he relied on Madinan sources.[31]

However, despite these figures, and the many reports that indicate Mālik's doubts about the reliablility of *ḥadīths* from non-Madinan, particularly Iraqi, sources,[32] the presence of such *ḥadīths* in the *Muwaṭṭa'*, albeit in such small numbers, does show that he was not averse on principle to transmitting from non-Madinans. Indeed, one key reason for his preferring Madinan sources would seem to have been not merely the high esteem in which he held the Madinan *ᶜulamā'* of his time, but the simple fact that he knew the people of his native city much better than he did the people of other places, and was thus more likely to be able to make a correct judgement as to their reliability. Furthermore, although he himself rarely travelled outside Madina, other Madinans such as Saᶜīd ibn al-Musayyab and Ibn Shihāb al-Zuhrī had done so,[33] and through these men – especially Ibn Shihāb, who was probably his main source of *ḥadīth*[34] – he had access to other non-Madinan material in addition to that which he gained from those that he himself met in Madina. Nevertheless, to judge from the *Muwaṭṭa'*, his use of outside sources was minimal, and his overwhelming preference for Madinan authorities, while not inflexible, is immediately evident from his book.

The importance of Madina

Despite the early shifts in political authority first from Madina to Kufa (in the time of ᶜAlī [r. 35–40]), then to Damascus (with the Umayyads) and then later to Baghdad (with the ᶜAbbāsids), Madina retained its importance throughout the first and second centuries as one of the foremost centres – if not *the* foremost centre – of learning in the lands of Islam. There was no disagreement that Madina had been paramount in this respect until the death of ᶜUthmān, and even then it was only the Kufans who, after the collapse of the Madinan caliphate and ᶜAlī's move to Kufa, ever seriously disputed the claim of Madinan supremacy, and even they only claimed equality and never superiority.[35]

Madina retained its importance for two main reasons: firstly, its greater number of scholars and, secondly, its historical associations with the Prophet and the Companions, especially the Rightly-Guided Caliphs. It was the city to which the Prophet and his Companions had emigrated, where the majority of the legal verses of the Qur'an had been revealed and first put into practice, and where, for the first time, an Islamic polity had been successfully established and maintained for at least thirty-five years.

Many learned Companions had, it is true, left Madina to settle in the newly-conquered territories of Islam, taking their knowledge with them, but far more had remained in Madina than had ever left it.[36] Furthermore, because of the religious merit of visiting its mosque, Madina continued to attract people – both scholars and others – from all over the Muslim world, especially in conjunction with the *ḥajj* to Makka, which would nearly always be an occasion to visit both cities.

Thus Madina retained its centrality and, as a result, the scholars of Madina not only had a greater collective knowledge and experience of matters of the *dīn* but also a greater access to the ideas and intellectual currents of the rest of the Muslim world than the scholars of any other centre at that time. For this reason the Madinan *ʿulamāʾ* – and Mālik with them – felt that the knowledge and experience that they could pass on to others far exceeded the knowledge and experience that others could pass on to them. As Mālik is reported to have said to a prospective student: 'If you want knowledge, take up residence here (i.e. in Madina), for the Qurʾan was not revealed on the Euphrates.'[37]

Mālik as teacher and scholar

There was widespread agreement on Mālik's pre-eminence in learning during his lifetime, especially in Madina, where by the end of his life he was the undisputed authority on matters of knowledge. When Ḥammād ibn Zayd visited Madina, he heard an announcement to the effect that no-one should give legal judgements (*fatwās*) or teach *ḥadīths* in the mosque of the Prophet except Mālik ibn Anas,[38] which has since become enshrined in the often quoted phrase *lā yuftā wa-Mālik fī l-Madīna* ('No-one should give *fatwās* while Mālik is in Madina').

His reputation was early established in his native Madina where, as we have seen, he already had his own circle of students while still a young man.[39] His fame soon spread and students came to study under him from every corner of the Muslim world. Indeed, he is said to be the one referred to in the *ḥadīth* 'The time is nigh when people will strike the livers of their camels (i.e. urge them on) in search of knowledge, but they will not find any *ʿālim* more knowledgeable than the *ʿālim* of Madina.'[40]

An eloquent testimony to Mālik's standing among his contemporaries is the quantity and quality of those who studied under him. ʿIyāḍ, in his *Madārik*, says that he knows the names of at least 1,300 people who transmitted from Mālik, while his list of 'the *fuqahāʾ* among them' covers over twenty-five pages of printed text.[41]

A number of Mālik's teachers themselves transmitted from him. Yaḥyā ibn Saᶜīd, for instance, transmitted many of the *ḥadīths* of Ibn Shihāb from Mālik,[42] while Ibn Shihāb himself is said to have transmitted from Mālik the *ḥadīth* of al-Furayᶜa bint Mālik about where a widow should spend her *ᶜidda* period.[43] Of the great *fuqahā*ᵓ and *ḥadīth*-scholars of his time, the following were among his students: al-Layth ibn Saᶜd, al-Awzāᶜī, Sufyān al-Thawrī, Sufyān ibn ᶜUyayna, Ibn al-Mubārak, Shuᶜba ibn al-Ḥajjāj and ᶜAbd al-Razzāq al-Ṣanᶜānī.[44] Abū Ḥanīfa, after whom the Ḥanafī *madhhab* is named, is also said to have transmitted from him, although there is some doubt about this.[45] Of the two main students of Abū Ḥanīfa, Abū Yūsuf and al-Shaybānī, who together were effectively responsible for founding the 'Ḥanafī' *madhhab*, al-Shaybānī spent three years studying under Mālik and related the *Muwaṭṭa*ᵓ from him,[46] while Abū Yūsuf, although not transmitting the *Muwaṭṭa*ᵓ directly from Mālik, nevertheless did so *via* an intermediary.[47] Al-Shāfiᶜī, the founder of the third of the 'orthodox' Sunnī *madhhabs*, was one of Mālik's main students and also transmitted the *Muwaṭṭa*ᵓ from him,[48] while Aḥmad ibn Ḥanbal, the fourth of the four 'orthodox' *imāms*, although effectively too young to have met Mālik,[49] nevertheless transmitted the *Muwaṭṭa*ᵓ from al-Shāfiᶜī (and other sources) and was thus a student of a student of Mālik.[50] Thus all the *madhhabs* were, in a sense, dependent on Mālik, and, through him, on the Madinan tradition of learning of which he was the acknowledged master in his time.[51]

Mālik the scholar of *ḥadīth*

In Mālik's time the formal transmission of knowledge was still largely an oral process consisting of the transmission of '*ḥadīth*', which still referred, as the word implies, to primarily verbal reports, and, moreover, reports from various earlier authorities rather than reports specifically from, or about, the Prophet (although these were always an important element). Mālik was renowned for his knowledge of *ḥadīth*, particularly of the Madinan tradition, and this knowledge gained for him the unreserved praise of the *ḥadīth* scholars of his own time and later, as well as earning for him the title of *amīr al-mu*ᵓ*minīn fī l-ḥadīth* ('the commander of the faithful with regard to *ḥadīth*').[52] His *musnad ḥadīths* (i.e. those with complete chains of authority going back to the Prophet) were held in the highest regard by all scholars. We have already seen how al-Bukhārī, whose *Ṣaḥīḥ* is probably the most famous collection of *ḥadīth*, considered the *isnād* 'Mālik – Nāfiᶜ – Ibn ᶜUmar' to be the most accurate *isnād* of all,[53] to which Abū Dāwūd, whose *Sunan* is another major collection of *ḥadīth*, added, 'then "Mālik, from al-Zuhrī, from Sālim, from his father (i.e. Ibn ᶜUmar)", then "Mālik, from Abū l-Zinād, from al-Aᶜraj, from Abū Hurayra"', without mentioning anything from anyone other than Mālik.[54] Another of the famous third-century scholars of *ḥadīth*, al-Nasāʾī, said of Mālik, 'There is no-one in my opinion after the Successors who is better or more excellent than Mālik, nor anyone who is more reliable and trustworthy with regard to *ḥadīth* than him.'[55] Indeed, it is said that his *Muwaṭṭaʾ* was the model on which all the later compilers of *ḥadīth* based their work.[56]

His *mursal ḥadīths* (i.e. those with incomplete chains of authority, especially when the Companion link is missing) were considered by most to be just as authentic. Abū Dāwūd said, 'If Mālik says, "I have heard (*balaghanī*)", that is an authentic chain of authority',[57] while Ibn ᶜUyayna, a well-respected student and contemporary of Mālik, said, 'Mālik would only cite as *mursal* what was authentic, and would only transmit *ḥadīths* from men who were trustworthy.'[58] Many similar reports have come down from other authorities, such as ᶜAlī ibn al-Madīnī, Yaḥyā ibn Saᶜīd al-Qaṭṭān, and Ibrāhīm al-Ḥarbī, to note but a few.[59]

A particularly clear indication of Mālik's exacting standards with regard to *ḥadīth* is that even those who disagreed with his *fiqh* nevertheless wholeheartedly trusted him as a *muḥaddith*. Thus al-Shāfiᶜī, who often disagrees fundamentally with Mālik on the interpretation of *ḥadīths*, nonetheless relies on him heavily as an authority for his material throughout his *Kitāb al-Umm*, and had such a high opinion of him as a *muḥaddith* that he could say, 'If *ḥadīths* (*al-khabar*) come to you, Mālik is the star',[60] while his view on the *Muwaṭṭaʾ* was that it was the most accurate book on the face of the earth after the Qurʾan.[61] Similarly, al-Shaybānī, whose criticism of Mālik and the Madinans is at times quite severe,[62] nevertheless trusts his transmission of *ḥadīths* and, indeed, relates, as we have seen, a version of the *Muwaṭṭaʾ* (albeit highly edited) from him.[63]

The great respect that Mālik's contemporaries had for him as a scholar and transmitter of *ḥadīth* was to a large extent based on his rigorous standards in selecting his sources. Numerous reports indicate that there were four categories of people from whom Mālik would not transmit *ḥadīths*: those who were incompetent (*sufahāʾ*); those who were known to lie in ordinary discourse even if they did not do so when teaching; heretics; and people who, although of great piety, did not have a sufficient understanding of what they were passing on.[64] Thus honesty, accuracy and sincerity – even piety – were only minimal criteria: Mālik demanded something else. As one report from him says:

> This knowledge is a *dīn*, so think carefully about who you take your *dīn* from.[65] I have met by these pillars (i.e. the pillars of the mosque in

> Madina) many (lit. 'seventy') of those who say 'The Messenger of Allah, may Allah bless him and grant him peace, said . . .', but I have never taken anything from them, even though if one of them were to be entrusted with a treasury he would fulfil that trust. This is because they were not people of this business. Then Ibn Shihāb came to us and we used to crowd around his door.[66]

In another report expressing the same idea he elaborates on what he means by 'people of this business':

> During my lifetime I have come across people in this city who, if they had been asked to pray for rain, would have had their prayers answered. But, although they had heard much by way of knowledge and *ḥadīth*, I never transmitted anything from any of them. [This is] because they concerned themselves with fear (*khawf*) of Allah and asceticism, whereas this business, that is, teaching *ḥadīth* and giving legal decisions, needs men who have awareness (*tuqā*) of Allah, scrupulousness, steadfastness, exactitude (*itqān*), knowledge, and understanding, so that they know what comes out of their heads and what the result of it will be tomorrow. As for those who do not have this exactitude and understanding, no benefit can be derived from them, nor are they a conclusive proof, nor should knowledge be taken from them.[67]

These reports indicate the importance that Mālik attached to this knowledge and the consciousness he had of his responsibility as a teacher in passing it on. This knowledge was the knowledge of a *dīn*, of how to live one's life with a view to what was correct both in terms of this life and the hereafter, and the *ʿulamāʾ*, as inheritors of the prophets, considered it their obligation to pass on this knowledge as faithfully and accurately as possible.[68] There were, nevertheless, important criteria for deciding what knowledge would be of direct benefit to particular people at a particular time, and what, if necessary, should be withheld, and it is this understanding of the relative value of the material being transmitted and its position in the overall context of the *dīn* that is referred to in the term *fiqh*, which means, literally, 'understanding'.[69] This was the quality that Mālik required in his sources, for he considered it essential that for a man to transmit *ḥadīth* he should not only be accurate in his transmission, but also one who understood his material.

Mālik himself combined both these qualities. He is described by Aḥmad ibn Ḥanbal as 'an *imām* in *ḥadīth* and *fiqh*',[70] while the famous *ḥadīth* scholar Ibn Mahdī put the same idea in the following terms: 'Al-Thawrī is an *imām* with regard to *ḥadīth* but not an *imām* with regard to the *sunna*; al-Awzāʿī is an *imām* with regard to the *sunna*, but not an *imām* with regard to *ḥadīth*. Mālik, however, is an *imām* with regard to both.'[71] Being an *imām* with regard to both meant, firstly, that he knew the context in which to evaluate the normative value of *ḥadīths*; secondly, that he knew the opinions of his predecessors on points arising from, but not necessarily covered by, these *ḥadīths*; thirdly, that he knew how to derive his own secondary judgements from this primary material. That is, he had an understanding (*fiqh*) of the *dīn* and its normative form (*sunna*). Without this understanding, *ḥadīths*, however authentic they were, could easily be a source of misguidance and error rather than a source of knowledge and enlightenment. Thus we find Ibn Wahb saying, 'Anyone who knows a *ḥadīth* but does not have an *imām* in *fiqh*, is astray (*ḍāll*); and if Allah had not saved us through Mālik and al-Layth, we would have gone astray',[72] and Ibn ʿUyayna saying, '*Ḥadīths* are a source of misguidance (*maḍalla*) except for the *fuqahāʾ*',[73] while Mālik himself said that he would be consciously misleading people (*uḍilluhum*) if he were to transmit everything he knew,[74] and, in another version, 'I would be a fool if I were to pass on everything I knew.'[75]

Mālik was thus concerned about what knowledge he would pass on to others. We know from numerous reports that there were many *ḥadīths* that he chose not to pass on to others, such as the many *ḥadīths* from Ibn Shihāb that he neither taught nor intended to teach,[76] and the knowledge he gained from Ibn Hurmuz which he considered unsuitable for passing on to others.[77] When he died it is said that several chests of books (*kutub*) were found in his house containing *ḥadīths* which none of his students had ever heard him mention.[78] Indeed, the *Muwaṭṭaʾ* itself is said to have originally consisted of several thousand *ḥadīths* (variously described as 'ten' or 'four' thousand)[79] which he then edited down until only some thousand or so remained, according to what he saw as being most beneficial (*aṣlaḥ*) for people and the best example for them to follow with regard to their *dīn* (*amthal fī l-dīn*),[80] and even then he is said to have regretted not having excised more.[81]

The literature on Mālik suggests that there were two types of *ḥadīth* in particular that he considered should not be generally transmitted even though they were authentic because of the danger that they might mislead others. Firstly, there were those *ḥadīths* which might mislead people with regard to matters of belief, such as those containing anthropomorphic descriptions of Allah, e.g. the *ḥadīths* referring to Allah creating Adam in His form (*ʿalā ṣūratihi*), or exposing His leg on the Day of Resurrection, or putting His hand into Jahannam and taking out of it whomsoever He wishes, the transmission of which Mālik specifically forbade; or the *ḥadīth* that refers to the Throne shaking at the death of Saᶜd, about which Mālik said, 'What makes a man tell these *ḥadīths* when he can see how they are likely to mislead people (*wa-huwa yarā mā fī-hi min al-taghrīr*)?'[82]

The second type, and of more interest to us here, are those *ḥadīths* that deal with legal matters which did not represent the normative practice in Madina, i.e. were not in accord with *ᶜamal*. Indeed, it is stated in the literature that there were many *ḥadīths* that Mālik would not pass on for precisely this reason.[83] Sometimes, however, he relates a *ḥadīth* which is not in accord with *ᶜamal* precisely in order to make it clear that, although known, it is not acted upon.[84]

Similarly, he deplored the tendency in some students to ask questions merely for the sake of asking questions and to seek knowledge as a purely intellectual indulgence. He is reported to have said:

> I do not like over-mention (*ikthār*) of questions (*masāʾil*) and *ḥadīths*, and I found the people of this city disapproving of what people do today. The first [members] of this community were not given to asking this many questions, nor to delving into such [unnecessary] details (*lam yakun awwal hādhihī l-umma bi-akthar al-nās masāʾil wa-lā hādhā l-taᶜammuq*).[85]

Just as a teacher should only teach what would be of benefit to his students, so too should a student only ask about what would be of benefit to him.[86] For this reason, contrary to the tendency evident in Iraq, he disliked hypothetical reasoning and cautioned people against asking about situations that not only had not happened but were also not likely to arise.[87] It was not, of course, wrong to ask questions, but asking about a genuine problem that had arisen so that one knew how to act in that situation was very different from indulging one's intellectual curiosity by postulating unreal situations merely in order to know what the judgement might be if such-and-such were to happen. It was the latter tendency, which would (and did) lead to the creation of trained specialists whose expertise was intellection rather than action and which would thus create a split between the two, that Mālik discouraged. As he once said, when asked about a highly theoretical and improbable legal problem, 'Ask about what happens and not about what doesn't happen.'[88]

Similarly, he disliked argument about the *dīn*. The central body of knowledge was clear, and it was enough for people to get that right and put that into practice without getting side-tracked into unnecessary and irrelevant details. As one report from him puts it:

> Follow what is clear of the *dīn* (*al-dīn al-maḥḍ*) and be careful not to be side-tracked (*iyyāka wa-bunayyāt al-ṭarīq*). Follow what you know and leave aside what you do not know.[89]

Arguing about this knowledge, which was essentially about how to behave correctly, was only to encourage its opposite. Mālik was once asked whether someone who knew the *sunna* should argue on behalf of it and he said: 'No. He should inform [the other man] what the *sunna* is, and, if he accepts it, that's fine; if not, he should keep quiet.'[90] On another occasion, he mentioned Ibn ᶜUmar's reply to just such a man: 'As for me, I'm on a clear path from my Lord.[91] As for you, go and argue with a doubter like yourself.'[92]

Mālik shared this certainty about the basics of the *dīn*, both in terms of beliefs and legal judgements. He was confident about the rightness of the path he was on, which was the 'well-trodden' (*muwaṭṭaʾ*) path of the great Madinan scholars before him, and concerned not to let that central picture become blurred. The Qurʾan had been revealed, the *sunna* of the Prophet had been instituted, and what Allah and His Messenger had made *ḥalāl* or *ḥarām* was clear. As for the details where no judgement had been specified, people should avoid what they had doubt about in favour of what they had no doubt about, and, if absolutely necessary, go for what they considered to be the closest to what they knew to be true.[93] They should certainly be extremely cautious about declaring something *ḥalāl* or *ḥarām* without sufficient knowledge to do so, since to give the wrong decision would be tantamount to making up lies (*iftirāʾ*) about Allah and His Prophet.[94] For this reason we find Mālik exercising the utmost restraint when answering questions or giving legal judgements, so much so that he is famous for the response 'I do not know' (*lā adrī*) which he is said to have given on one day to thirty-two out of forty-eight questions put to him[95] and about which one of his students said that if he wanted to fill a whole page (*ṣaḥīfa*) with Mālik's saying '*lā adrī*' he would be able to do so before Mālik had given an answer to even one point.[96]

In Mālik, then, we have a man whose knowledge of Madina and its tradition of learning was unparalleled and whose authority as a teacher of it was unquestioned. His conscious identification of himself with this tradition, his certainty about it and the concomitant reluctance to make any final judgements about unclear details, are all reflected in his book the *Muwaṭṭaʾ*, which is his summation of all that he considered important in this Madinan tradition, which, in his view, saw its expression not only as a body of knowledge handed down from one generation of scholars to the next, but as a continuous lived reality in the city where it had begun from the time it had begun. It is to this book that we now turn.

CHAPTER TWO

The *Muwaṭṭa'*

The *Muwaṭṭa'* is one of the earliest – if not *the* earliest – formulation of Islamic law that we possess,[1] as well as being one of the earliest major collections of *ḥadīth*.[2] But, although it contains both *ḥadīths* and legal judgements, the *Muwaṭṭa'* is neither simply a book of *ḥadīth* nor a book of *fiqh*. It is, rather, a book of *ʿamal*, that is, a record of the accepted principles, precepts and precedents which had become established as the *ʿamal* of Madina. This is implied in the name *Muwaṭṭa'* – which Mālik himself gave to the work[3] – which means 'the well-trodden [path]',[4] i.e. the path followed and agreed upon by the scholars of Madina up to and including his own time, expressed as the *ʿamal*, or practice, of the people of his native city. The word *muwaṭṭa'* also carries the idea of having been smoothed out and made ready and, thus, made easy. This path, then, was not only one that was well-known and agreed upon, but also one that had been made easy for people to follow, both by the efforts of past scholars and then by Mālik himself in his presentation of it.

The different transmissions (*riwāyāt*) of the text

The *Muwaṭṭa'* in its final form is the result of a lifetime spent by Mālik in gathering and disseminating this knowledge of Madinan *ʿamal*, of which it is the distillation. The basic text was in place by around the year 150 AH,[5] but underwent various editorial changes over the next thirty years which are reflected in the different transmissions that have survived to this day.

Although over ninety people are recorded as having transmitted the *Muwaṭṭa'* in its entirety directly from Mālik,[6] the number of transmissions known to us either through existing texts or the quotations of other authors is considerably less. Iyāḍ personally knew of twenty or so versions, although he says that others at his time put the figure at thirty.[7] Al-Ghāfiqī mentions twelve, to which al-Suyūṭī adds another two,[8] while modern editors of the *Muwaṭṭa'* mention between fourteen and sixteen transmissions.[9] At the present time, to the best of my knowledge, only nine of these are known to exist, either in complete form or as fragments. These nine are the transmissions of:

1. Yaḥyā ibn Yaḥyā al-Laythī (d. 234). Yaḥyā studied the *Muwaṭṭa'* under Mālik during the last year of Mālik's life (i.e. 179 AH)[10] and his transmission therefore represents the text as Mālik was teaching it at the end of his life. It is by far the best known transmission and is the one that is generally meant when reference is made to 'the *Muwaṭṭa'*'. It has been published many times.
2. al-Shaybānī (d. 189). This transmission, which differs markedly from the others,[11] has also been published several times.[12]
3. Ibn Bukayr (d. 231). This transmission was published under the title *Muwaṭṭa' al-imām al-mahdī* by the Gouvernement Général de l'Algérie (Algiers, 1323/1905).[13]
4. ʿAlī ibn Ziyād (d. 183). This is one of the earliest known transmissions, having been transmitted from Mālik before 150 AH.[14] An early parchment fragment of this transmission (dated 288 AH) containing chapters on game and slaughtered animals (*al-ṣayd wa-l-dhabā'iḥ*) has recently been edited and published.[15]
5. al-Qaʿnabī (d. 221). This is said to be the longest (*akbar*) transmission.[16] A number of chapters of this transmission, corresponding to the initial portion of Yaḥyā ibn Yaḥyā's transmission up to and including the section on *iʿtikāf* as well as a few chapters from the section on business transactions (*buyūʿ*), have recently been edited and published.[17]
6. Abū Muṣʿab al-Zuhrī (d. 242). Abū Muṣʿab is said to have been the last to have related the *Muwaṭṭa'* from Mālik and, indeed, his transmission is very close to that of Yaḥyā ibn Yaḥyā. A manuscript of this transmission in Hyderabad, India, has recently been edited and published.[18]
7. Suwayd al-Ḥadathānī (d. 240). The incomplete, but substantial, fragment of this transmission in the Ẓāhiriyya library in Damascus has recently been edited and published.[19] This transmission is close to that of Yaḥyā ibn Yaḥyā, but not as close to it as those of al-Qaʿnabī and Abū Muṣʿab, there being a greater divergence of wording and also a seeming omission of several reports contained in the other three.
8. Ibn al-Qāsim (d. 191). Fragments of this transmission, including a large part of the section on business transactions (for which knowledge Ibn al-Qāsim was famous),[20] exist in manuscript form in Tunis and Qayrawān.[21] Al-Qābisī's *Mulakhkhaṣ* (or *Mulakhkhiṣ),* which contains all the *musnad ḥadīths* from this transmission, has recently been published under the title *Muwaṭṭa' al-Imām Mālik ibn Anas riwāyat Ibn al-Qāsim wa-talkhīṣ al-Qābisī.*[22]

9. Ibn Wahb (d. 197). According to Schacht, the published fragments of al-Ṭabarī's *Kitāb Ikhtilāf al-fuqahā*ʾ contain 'fairly comprehensive' extracts from the transmission of Ibn Wahb on the subjects of *jihād* and *jizya*, and this transmission 'follows that of Yaḥyā ibn Yaḥyā quite closely.'[23]

Schacht also considered the manuscript fragment in Qayrawān entitled *Kitāb al-muḥāraba min Muwaṭṭa*ʾ *ʿAbdallāh ibn Wahb* to be part of Ibn Wahb's transmission of Mālik's *Muwaṭṭa*ʾ.[24] However, it now seems clear from the recent edition of this fragment published by Muranyi that it is part of Ibn Wahb's own '*Muwaṭṭa*ʾ' rather than his transmission of Mālik's book,[25] for this text, as well as containing distinctively 'Muwattan' material – such as reports containing expressions relating to Madinan *ʿamal*[26] – also contains extensive material now recorded specifically in either the *Mudawwana*[27] or the *ʿUtbiyya*.[28] Indeed, much of the material is closer textually to the *Mudawwana* than to the *Muwaṭṭa*ʾ.[29] Given the basic similarity between the known transmissions of the *Muwaṭṭa*ʾ – including, according to Schacht, the other fragments of Ibn Wahb's transmission available – one has to conclude, with Muranyi, that this particular text is not part of Ibn Wahb's transmission of the *Muwaṭṭa*ʾ of Mālik but rather of his own '*Muwaṭṭa*ʾ'.[30]

There is also a fragment of the *Muwaṭṭa*ʾ on papyrus which Abbott discusses and which would seem, from the small but significant variations between it and the Yaḥyā ibn Yaḥyā transmission, not to be of the latter, despite Abbott's statement that it is.[31] From similar textual variations it can also be said that it is not of the transmissions of Suwayd or Abū Muṣʿab (the only other published fragments containing the relevant section).[32] Which transmission it does represent, though, is not clear.

Apart from Ibn Wahb's '*Muwaṭṭa*ʾ', these transmissions are for the most part remarkably similar, differing only in small details such as the order of the contents, the titles of the chapter-headings, and the inclusion or exclusion of small amounts of material. None of these differences is surprising when we bear in mind the fact that although we now know the *Muwaṭṭa*ʾ in the fixed form of a 'book', for Mālik it was primarily a text for teaching which he used for that purpose for some thirty years or so, during which it was not unreasonable for him to have made small editorial changes.[33] Indeed, the overall similarity between the different transmissions speaks highly for the authenticity of the text and its attribution to Mālik.[34]

Of the published transmissions (again, ignoring Ibn Wahb's '*Muwaṭṭa*ʾ'), the transmission that shows the most marked differences from the others is undoubtedly that of al-Shaybānī. Firstly, the order, chapter divisions and titles used for his material are very different from those of the other versions that we know. Secondly, and more importantly, al-Shaybānī consistently excludes Mālik's own comments and references to Madinan *ᶜamal* (as well as excluding other reports, especially from the Successors, but also, on occasions, *ḥadīths* from the Prophet) and, instead, includes his own references to the views of Abū Ḥanīfa and the *fuqahā*ʾ of Kufa, often adding his own *ḥadīths*. Thus in the transmissions of Yaḥyā, al-Qaᶜnabī, Abū Muṣᶜab and Suwayd for instance, the various sections on *tayammum* and reciting when praying behind an *imām* (to take random examples) are almost identical in content (although that of Suwayd somewhat less so than the others),[35] whereas al-Shaybānī, although retaining the Prophetic and Companion *ḥadīths*, excludes all the comments by Mālik, adds his own comments, and, in the case of the second section mentioned, adds thirteen more *ḥadīths* from various authorities (including the Prophet).[36] In his chapter on *liᶜān*, al-Shaybānī only relates one short Prophetic *ḥadīth* from Mālik, to which he adds a comment that this is in accord with the Kufan position, whereas Yaḥyā's and Abū Muṣᶜab's transmissions contain, in addition to the short *ḥadīth*, another much longer one about the *sabab al-nuzūl* of the *liᶜān* verses (which does not accord with the Kufan position), a quotation from Mālik of the verses in question, and numerous reports from him concerning details arising from the same.[37] Al-Shaybānī's editing is even more evident when we consider ᶜAlī ibn Ziyād's transmission, which, although some thirty years earlier than Yaḥyā's, is nevertheless remarkably similar to it (although perhaps not quite as much as those of al-Qaᶜnabī, Abū Muṣᶜab, and, to a lesser extent, Suwayd): the chapters on 'Game of the Sea' (*ṣayd al-baḥr*) and 'The *ᶜAqīqa* Sacrifice', for instance (to take random examples), are very similar to those in the other transmissions (although Ibn Ziyād includes some extra comments from Mālik).[38] Al-Shaybānī, on the other hand, excludes most of the later – i.e. post-Companion – material and again adds his own comments.[39] It would seem clear that the difference is that whereas Yaḥyā, al-Qaᶜnabī, Suwayd, Abū Muṣᶜab and ᶜAlī ibn Ziyād agreed with Mālik's *madhhab* and method – or at least with the presentation of his material – al-Shaybānī did not, but chose rather to include in his version only that material which he considered useful for his own teaching purposes, i.e. which accorded with what was taught in Iraq. This is particularly clear from the chapters on *iḥṣār* (i.e. being prevented from reaching Makka while in *iḥrām* for *ḥajj* or *ᶜumra*): in the transmissions of Yaḥyā, Suwayd and Abū Muṣᶜab, Mālik makes a clear distinction between *iḥṣār* by an enemy and *iḥṣār* by some other cause, both of which scenarios are highlighted by separate chapter-headings and supported by *ḥadīths* and references to *ᶜamal*;[40] al-Shaybānī, however, excludes the majority of this material, mentioning only one *ḥadīth* from Ibn

ʿUmar, after which he adds a comment about the Kufan position.[41] In other words, although he trusted Mālik as a transmitter of *ḥadīth*,[42] he remained firmly committed to Kufan *fiqh*.

Al-Shaybānī's transmission is thus very much, as Goldziher puts it, 'a revision and critical development of Mālik's work',[43] and clearly his choice of what material to transmit was occasioned by the theoretical concerns of the Kufans, who preferred *ḥadīths* from the Prophet and the Companions to the opinions of later authorities and/or the *ʿamal* of the people of Madina.[44]

The authenticity of the text

At this point a short digression is necessary. Calder has recently expressed doubt as to the second century nature of what is normally considered to be Mālik's *Muwaṭṭaʾ*, suggesting that it is a Cordoban production of the latter part of the third century.[45] It will be clear from the above that my own view is that the *Muwaṭṭaʾ* is not only a product of Mālik in Madina before his death in 179 AH, but was also substantially in place before the year 150 AH, thus making it our earliest extant text of this nature.[46] Let us briefly review the evidence for this, which is fourfold:

Firstly, there is the papyrus fragment of the text referred to above[47] which Abbott dates by textual evidence – particularly the characteristics of the script, the absence of glosses, and, most significantly in her opinion, the consistent use of *ʿan* in the *isnāds* together with the absence of any initial transmission formula such as *qāla*, *akhbaranī*, *ḥaddathanī*, etc – to Mālik's own day in the second half of the second century AH.[48]

Secondly, we possess the parchment fragment of ʿAlī ibn Ziyād's transmission, dated 288 AH, referred to above.[49] This fragment was transmitted by a certain Ḥasan ibn Aḥmad[50] from Jabala ibn Ḥammūd (d. 299) from Saḥnūn (d. 240) from ʿAlī ibn Ziyād, who was Saḥnūn's main teacher.[51] As mentioned above, Ibn Ziyād, who is credited with being the first to introduce the *Muwaṭṭaʾ* into Ifrīqiyā, returned to Tunis in around the year 150 AH, which period his transmission must therefore predate.[52] (We are also told that Ibn Ziyād was teaching the *Muwaṭṭaʾ* to Saḥnūn before the latter's departure for Egypt at the beginning of the year 178 AH.[53] If we bear in mind that this is the same Saḥnūn who was responsible for transmitting the *Mudawwana* from Ibn al-Qāsim – himself another transmitter of the *Muwaṭṭaʾ*, as we have seen[54] – it is clear that there are problems with Calder's claim that the *Mudawwana* is the earlier of the two books[55] if in fact they are both related by and/or from the same person, i.e. Ibn al-Qāsim.)

Thirdly, a comparison of Ibn Ziyād's and the other transmissions currently available either wholly or partly in printed form, in particular those of Yaḥyā ibn Yaḥyā al-Laythī, al-Shaybānī, al-Qaᶜnabī, Suwayd and Abū Muṣᶜab, shows, as mentioned above, that all six are remarkably similar in their basic content and thus clearly represent one text.[56] We might also mention in this context the evidence of the *Umm* of al-Shāfiᶜī, who, according to our sources, is another transmitter of the *Muwaṭṭa*ʾ from Mālik:[57] in his sustained argument against Mālik and the Madinans, he quotes extensively from 'Mālik's book',[58] and his quotations reflect a text almost identical with that of Yaḥyā ibn Yaḥyā's transmission, both in the wording and the order of the reports quoted.[59] Since, when they were transmitting this text, Ibn Ziyād was in Tunis,[60] Yaḥyā in Cordoba,[61] al-Shaybānī in various parts of Iraq, Syria and Khurāsān,[62] al-Qaᶜnabī in Basra (or perhaps Makka),[63] Suwayd in northern Iraq (al-Ḥadītha),[64] Abū Muṣᶜab in Madina,[65] and Ibn Bukayr, Ibn al-Qāsim, Ibn Wahb and al-Shāfiᶜī (if we include them) in Egypt,[66] the only common link from which these transmissions could reasonably have derived is precisely that which is claimed in the sources to be the case, i.e. Mālik in Madina.

Fourthly, we have the secondary evidence of the biographical literature which tells us, as we have seen, of numerous individuals transmitting the *Muwaṭṭa*ʾ directly from Mālik,[67] and also of several commentaries being written on it before Calder's proposed date of *c.* 270 for the book's emergence, e.g. those of Ibn Wahb (d. 197),[68] al-Akhfash (d. before 250),[69] Ibn Muzayn (d. *c.* 259) – this latter itself compiled from the commentaries of ᶜĪsā ibn Dīnār (d. 212), Yaḥyā ibn Yaḥyā al-Laythī (d. 234), Muḥammad ibn ᶜĪsā (d. *c.* 218) and Aṣbagh ibn al-Faraj (d. 225)[70] – and others.[71] These transmissions and commentaries would not of course have been possible had the text not existed.[72]

The arrangement of the text

Like most of the other *ḥadīth*-works of its time, the *Muwaṭṭa*ʾ contains sayings of the Companions and the Successors as well as *ḥadīths* of the Prophet, but, unlike them, it also contains reports of the *ᶜamal* of the people of Madina. There are also a number of the personal opinions of Mālik but these are relatively few since it is the author's intention to present the agreed upon opinions of his predecessors rather than his own opinions.[73] The book is arranged according to subject-matter, dealing first with the Five Pillars, and then with family law, economic activity, criminal law, etc. Each major section (*kitāb*) is sub-divided into chapters (*abwāb*), each of which deals with a specific topic usually indicated by the chapter-heading.[74] Within any one chapter the usual arrangement is for *ḥadīths* of the Prophet to be mentioned first, then the sayings of Companions and/or Successors, and then, finally, comments by Mālik himself, including illustrations of *ʿamal*. Often one or more of these categories is missing, so that individual chapters may contain, for example, only *ḥadīths* of the Prophet,[75] or only statements of *ʿamal*,[76] but where there is more than one category, as is usually the case, the above-mentioned order is almost invariably adhered to.[77] Thus, although Prophetic *ḥadīths* are given pride of place, the book contains much more than simply *ḥadīths*, and often the last word is, as it were, given to *ʿamal*.

One characteristic feature of the *Muwaṭṭaʾ* is the inclusion of 'miscellaneous' (*jāmiʿ*) chapters which contain general material which does not easily come under any of the specific chapter headings and yet does not warrant a chapter by itself. Such chapters come especially at the end of main sections of the text, e.g. '*Jāmiʿ al-ṣiyām*' at the end of the Book of Fasting[78] and '*Jāmiʿ al-ḥajj*' at the end of the Book of *Ḥajj*,[79] or at the end of a topic within a section, e.g. the five '*jāmiʿ*' chapters within the Book of *Ḥajj*.[80] Indeed, the last third of the *Muwaṭṭaʾ* bears the title '*Kitāb al-jāmiʿ*' (Miscellany) and includes various points of law and behaviour that do not come under the major headings already dealt with. This again gives us an indication of how Mālik graded his material, with the major points of law highlighted by separate chapter-headings and the more general material left to the end of the relevant section.[81]

The reason for its compilation

The first half of the second century AH saw the beginning of the widescale compilation of *ḥadīth*. Abū Bakr ibn Ḥazm, a *qāḍī* and, later, governor of Madina, and Ibn Shihāb had already been instrumental in collecting *ḥadīth* at the request of the caliph ʿUmar ibn ʿAbd al-ʿAzīz (r. 99–101), who was concerned that knowledge of the *sunna* might be lost if it were not collected and recorded in writing.[82] This project seems to have been mainly concerned with those parts of the *sunna* that dealt with the economic life of the community, but after ʿUmar's death, and particularly in the time of Hishām (r. 105–125), it was expanded by Ibn Shihāb to include a much more substantial collection of *ḥadīth* to the extent that it is Ibn Shihāb who is credited with being the first person to make a comprehensive collection of *ḥadīth* (*awwal man dawwana l-ʿilm*, or, in another version, *al-ḥadīth*).[83] Despite this '*tadwīn*', however, Ibn Shihāb seems not to have organised this more comprehensive material into a book, which is what Mālik and contemporaries of his, such as Ibn Jurayj and Maᶜmar ibn Rāshid, began doing.[84] Indeed, from this time onwards the writing down of *ḥadīth* takes on a new importance, with the productions of this period, among which the *Muwaṭṭa'* is arguably the most important, marking the transition between the more traditional oral methods of transmission and the newer method of recording everything in writing.[85]

There are several reports that associate Mālik's compilation of the *Muwaṭṭa'* with the caliph Abū Jaᶜfar al-Manṣūr (r. 136–158). Al-Manṣūr is said to have requested Mālik to collect his knowledge (in some versions it says 'his books') into one book which he would then make everyone in the empire follow, if necessary by force. Mālik refused this, giving as his reason the fact that many of the Companions had spread out into various lands and each of them had taught and given judgements according to his own knowledge and *ijtihād*; every place therefore had its own way of doing things and it would thus be unreasonable, if not impossible, to force everyone to adhere to one view.[86] Mālik's refusal would thus seem to have been not because he did not want to see everyone follow the the *ᶜamal* of the people of Madina – we know that he held that all people *should* follow it[87] – but this was not something that could be imposed by a formal pronouncement of the state: rather, it had to be transmitted by, and accepted from, the men who knew it. Furthermore, as has been noted by more than one contemporary scholar, there would seem to have been a clear political element to Mālik's refusal: to accede to the caliph's request would be to allow the possibility of Mālik's legal and spiritual authority being misused by the caliph to back unacceptable policies and actions, when the knowledge that the book contained was itself the unchanging critique of any regime.[88]

It is also said that ᶜAbd al-ᶜAzīz ibn al-Mājishūn, one of the most important second century Madinan *fuqahā'*, was the first to compile a '*muwaṭṭa'*', but that he did so mentioning only judgements and not including any *ḥadīths*. When Mālik saw it he is said to have been impressed by the work but felt that it would have been better if the *ḥadīths* had been mentioned first and then the judgements, after which he resolved to compile his own version, which is the *Muwaṭṭa'* that we now know.[89]

These reports may seem mutually contradictory, but it is possible to partially harmonise them if we assume that Mālik had compiled 'books' (*kutub*) on various subjects after seeing Ibn al-Mājishūn's '*muwaṭṭa'*' and that al-Manṣūr then later spoke to him about his idea of unifying the *umma* on one code of law (which would presumably have been in or shortly after the year 147 AH, when al-Manṣūr is said to have visited Madina).[90] This would then accord with al-Manṣūr's reference in Ibn Saᶜd's version of their conversation to 'these books (*kutub*) of yours', which Ibn Saᶜd specifically says refers to the *Muwaṭṭaʾ*,[91] thus presupposing the existence of the *Muwaṭṭaʾ* in at least some form at that time. That some such chronology is indeed the case is further bolstered by a report that Mālik began writing down 'books' (*kutub*) at the time when he 'retreated into his house' (*iᶜtazala wa-lazima baytahu*),[92] i.e. at the time of the uprising of Muḥammad ibn ᶜAbdallāh ('al-Nafs al-Zakiyya') in 145 AH,[93] and, more especially, by our knowledge that ᶜAlī ibn Ziyād had already learnt the *Muwaṭṭaʾ* from Mālik before his return to Tunis in 150 AH.[94]

Whatever the immediate reason for Mālik's compiling the *Muwaṭṭaʾ*, it would seem that his intention was, like that of ᶜUmar ibn ᶜAbd al-ᶜAzīz before him, to record the knowledge that he felt to be essential for a correct understanding and practice of the *dīn* lest it should disappear along with those who knew it. However, Mālik's choice of material and his method of arrangement suggest that there may have been another, rather more subtle, motive for his work. Knowledge of *ḥadīths* was obviously important for any scholar of the *dīn*, whatever school he belonged to, and that it was valuable to record them in writing was no longer in dispute. But simply to write something down was to fix it and to expose it to a certain kind of abuse: while such knowledge remained oral the teacher always had the chance of explaining what he was teaching and placing it in its proper context, but once it was committed to paper that link between teacher and taught was considerably weakened. The existence of written texts of *ḥadīth* outside of their context of *ᶜamal* would thus fuel both the tendency expressed by the term *aṣḥāb al-ḥadīth* ('the people of the *ḥadīth*'), referring to those who gave overwhelming authority to *ḥadīths per se* and thus put too much reliance on texts divorced from action, and that expressed by the term *aṣḥāb al-raʾy* ('the people of opinion'), referring to those who allowed full rein to their deductive powers in deriving judgements from limited textual sources and thus put too much reliance on intellect divorced from action. Indeed, Mālik's method of arrangement in the *Muwaṭṭaʾ* shows how conscious he was of the importance of retaining the context of *ᶜamal* in order to keep to a balanced way between these two extremes: *ḥadīths* are given pride of place, but they are continually placed within their context of *ᶜamal*.

The aim of the *Muwaṭṭaʾ* then, would seem to have been twofold: firstly, Mālik was concerned not so much to preserve the *ḥadīths* as to preserve the 'well-trodden path' indicated by these *ḥadīths*; secondly, he was concerned to protect this path, with all its inherent anomalies, from any excessive systematisation by the intellect. We have already noted Ibn ᶜUyayna's comment that '*ḥadīths* are a source of misguidance (*maḍalla*) except for the *fuqahā*'",[95] and Mālik's dislike of people taking an over-indulgently intellectual approach to matters of the *dīn*.'[96]

Other works by Mālik

The *Muwaṭṭa'* is undoubtedly Mālik's most important work but it is not the only source of either his *ḥadīths* or his opinions. We have seen how, by its very nature, it contains only a selection of the *ḥadīths* he knew, and *ḥadīths* recorded from him that do not appear in the *Muwaṭṭa'* may be found in other major collections.[97]

We have also noted that the *Muwaṭṭa'* contains very little of Mālik's own personal opinions since his intention was to record what was agreed upon by his predecessors rather than simply his own personal view.[98] However, other works containing his own opinions do exist, the most important of which are: the *Mudawwana* of Saḥnūn (d. 240), which includes Ibn al-Qāsim's record of the opinions of Mālik; the *Mustakhraja* of al-ʿUtbī (d. 255), also known as the *ʿUtbiyya*;[99] the *Wāḍiḥa* of Ibn Ḥabīb (d. 238);[100] the 'Mawwāziyya' of Ibn al-Mawwāz (d. 269);[101] the 'Mukhtaṣar al-kabīr fī l-fiqh' of Ibn ʿAbd al-Ḥakam (d. 214);[102] the 'Mukhtaṣar fī l-fiqh' of Abū Muṣʿab (d. 242);[103] and the 'Kitāb al-Nawādir wa-l-ziyādāt' of Ibn Abī Zayd al-Qayrawānī (d. 386).[104]

Other writings attributed to Mālik are extant, but of these only one is relevant to our present concerns, and that is his letter to al-Layth ibn Saʿd about Madinan *ʿamal*, which we shall have occasion to refer to below.[105]

CHAPTER THREE

The ᶜAmal of the People of Madina

Mālik's *madhhab*

According to Ibn al-Madīnī, Mālik followed the opinion (*qawl*) of Sulaymān ibn Yasār, who followed the opinion of ᶜUmar ibn al-Khaṭṭāb.[1] Mālik's *madhhab* then, as has been frequently noted, was the *madhhab* of ᶜUmar.[2] Indeed, Ibn Taymiyya states that the judgements of ᶜUmar form the second major source of the *ᶜamal* of the Madinans after the *sunna* of the Prophet,[3] and this is immediately evident from the large number of judgements from ᶜUmar recorded in the *Muwaṭṭaʾ*.[4]

ᶜUmar's importance as an authority is a reflection of the circumstances prevailing during his caliphate (13–23 AH). Before him, Abū Bakr's short caliphate (11–13 AH) had seen a preoccupation with the wars of the *Ridda* and was a time of consolidation rather than expansion. As a result, there are very few judgements recorded from that period.[5] ᶜUmar's caliphate, on the other hand, was not only considerably longer, but also witnessed a period of major expansion outside Arabia and relative stability inside Arabia which allowed for, as it indeed also necessitated, the development of legal activity on a much larger scale than had previously been the case as new situations arose and people needed to know how to deal with them in the light of the Qurʾan and the *sunna*. This development is reflected in the large number of judgements from ᶜUmar referred to above.

Mālik obviously had a high regard for ᶜUmar. He considered his reign to be a reign of justice in practice, which was the prime goal of the *sharīᶜa*, and he saw ᶜUmar's judicial activity as a genuine extension of the Prophetic *sunna*.[6] It thus seems fitting that when Mālik taught in the mosque in Madina he is said to have consciously chosen the place where ᶜUmar used to sit, which was also the place where the Prophet used to put his bedding when doing *iᶜtikāf*.[7]

After the *ḥadīth* of the Prophet and the judgements of ᶜUmar, two other sources are particularly prominent in the *Muwaṭṭaʾ*: the opinions of ᶜUmar's son, ᶜAbdallāh ibn ᶜUmar, and the opinions of the great Madinan

Successors, such as the 'Seven *Fuqahā'*' referred to above.[8] ʿAbdallāh ibn ʿUmar is said to have been the most like ʿUmar of all ʿUmar's sons.[9] He was also one of the longest-lived of the Companions and by the end of his life had acquired considerable knowledge not only of the *sunna* of the Prophet but also of the judgements of his father and others since that heyday of the Madinan caliphate.[10] Indeed, Mālik relates that Ibn Shihāb told him not to deviate from the opinion of Ibn ʿUmar because Ibn ʿUmar had lived for sixty years after the death of the Prophet and there was nothing about the Prophet that had escaped him.[11]

Of the Successors, Ibn ʿUmar's knowledge was transmitted in particular by his son Sālim (who, in turn, is said to have been the most like Ibn ʿUmar of Ibn ʿUmar's sons)[12] and his *mawlā* Nāfiʿ, who, as we have seen, was one of Mālik's main teachers.[13] The importance of all three men as authorities of knowledge has already been mentioned.[14]

There are other Successors who are particularly associated with the *madhhab* of ʿUmar and feature prominently in the *Muwaṭṭa'*: Sulaymān ibn Yasār's connection has already been noted,[15] while Saʿīd ibn al-Musayyab, described by Mālik as the most learned man in Madina in his time,[16] is also said to have been the most knowledgeable (*aḥfaẓ*) with regard to the judgements of ʿUmar.[17] Mention should also be made here of ʿUmar ibn ʿAbd al-ʿAzīz, whose judgements in his capacity both as governor of Madina and, later, caliph of the Muslims, figure prominently in the *Muwaṭṭa'*.[18] This ʿUmar was particularly impressed by his predecessor of the same name and keen to emulate him,[19] and Mālik was in turn particularly impressed by ʿUmar ibn ʿAbd al-ʿAzīz.[20]

The nature of Madinan *ʿamal*

Schacht points out that the *madhhab* of the Madinans, and thus that of Mālik, is based on a combination of *ʿamal* and *ra'y*.[21] *ʿAmal* was the established practice of the people of Madina, and *ra'y* ('opinion') was the necessary exercise of independent reasoning (*ijtihād*) in the absence of any clear precedent in the existing *ʿamal*. As we have commented above, it is in the nature of the *Muwaṭṭa'* that it contains little of Mālik's own personal *ra'y*, since in it he was concerned not so much with presenting his own opinions as with presenting the agreed position of those before him.[22] Indeed, as Mālik is reported to have said when asked about the terms that he uses in the *Muwaṭṭa'*:

> Most of what is in the book is my opinion (*ra'yī*),[23] but, by my life, it is not so much my opinion as that which I have heard from more than

> one of the people of knowledge and excellence and the *imāms* worthy of being followed from whom I took my knowledge – and they were people who feared God (*kānū yattaqūna*) – but in order to simplify matters I have said it is my opinion (*fa-kathura ʿalayya fa-qultu raʾyī*). This [I have done] when their opinion was the same as that which they found the Companions following, and which I then found them [i.e. the Successors] following. It is thus an inheritance which has been passed down from one generation to another down to our present time. So when I say 'I am of the opinion (*arā*)', it is really the opinion of a large group of the *imāms* who have gone before.[24]

In other words, it is his opinion, i.e. the view to which he gives his assent, but only by virtue of the fact that a large number of scholars before him in Madina had also held it. A little later he says:

> Where I have heard nothing from them, I have used my own judgement (*ijtahadtu*) and considered the matter according to the way (*madhhab*) of those I have met, until I felt that I had arrived at the truth, or near to it, so that it would not be outside the way (*madhhab*) of the people of Madina and their opinions, even though I had not heard that particular [judgement] directly.
>
> I have thus said that it is my opinion after having considered the matter deeply in relation to the *sunna* and what has been endorsed by the people of knowledge who are worthy of being followed (*mā maḍā ʿalayhi ahl al-ʿilm al-muqtadā bi-him*), and what the practice here has been (*al-amr al-maʿmūl bi-hi ʿinda-nā*) from the time of the Messenger of Allah, may Allah bless him and grant him peace, and the Rightly-Guided Caliphs, along with what those I have met in my life-time [have said]. It is thus their opinion, and I have not gone outside it for anyone else's.[25]

Raʾy is, of course, a composite term, and includes various methods of legal reasoning. Foremost among these we can identify the concepts of *qiyās* (analogical reasoning), *istiḥsān* (considerations of equity), *sadd al-dharāʾiʿ* (lit. 'blocking the means', i.e. preventing the use of lawful means to achieve unlawful ends) and *al-maṣāliḥ al-mursala* (considerations of public good), the last two of which are particularly associated with the Mālikī *madhhab*, although by no means exclusive to it.[26] The referent of Mālik's *raʾy* is, however, in all cases, as is evident from the above quotations, the *ʿamal* of the people of Madina,[27] and it is this concept of *ʿamal* that provides the key to understanding Mālik's legal reasoning. Indeed, it is his reliance on Madinan *ʿamal* that differentiates his *madhhab* from all the other *madhhabs*, as it is also the point on which the proponents of all the other *madhhabs* disagreed with him.

ᶜAmal also is a composite term. Its basic constituents are '*kitāb*' and '*sunna*', dating from the time of the Prophet, but there is also the additional element of the *raʾy* of later authorities as this *raʾy*, in turn, becomes incorporated into the existing *ᶜamal*.[28] This basic chronological distinction between *ᶜamal* deriving from the Prophet and *ᶜamal* deriving from later authorities is evident from Mālik's letter to al-Layth ibn Saᶜd (which we shall look at shortly), where he speaks of the Companions and the Successors following the Prophet's *sunna* where the Prophet had established a *sunna*, and exercising their own *ijtihād* where there was no established precedent.[29] The same distinction is well reflected in the writings of later theorists, foremost among whom we may mention ᶜIyāḍ and Ibn Taymiyya, both of whom divide *ᶜamal* (although they speak specifically of Madinan *ijmāᶜ* rather than of *ᶜamal* in its broader sense) into two broad categories: what derives from the time of the Prophet (*ijmāᶜ naqlī*) and what derives from later authorities (*ijmāᶜ ijtihādī*).[30]

The first of these two categories, which is referred to as one general category by Ibn Taymiyya, is subdivided by ᶜIyāḍ into four types: things which the Prophet said (*qawl*); things which the Prophet did (*fiᶜl*); things which the Prophet affirmed in others (*iqrār*); and things which the Prophet consciously avoided doing (*tark*).[31] As examples of the first two types, ᶜIyāḍ mentions the measures of the *ṣāᶜ* and the *mudd* and the fact that the Prophet collected *zakāt* from people using these measures;[32] the way of calling the *adhān* and the *iqāma*;[33] reciting the *Fātiḥa* in the prayer without saying '*bi-smi llāhi l-raḥmāni l-raḥīm*';[34] and the question of the binding nature of endowments.[35] As an example of the third type he cites the question of liability for defects in slaves (*ᶜuhdat al-raqīq*).[36] As for the fourth type, he gives the example of the Prophet not taking *zakāt* from fresh fruit and vegetables despite the fact that these items were well known to the Prophet and important in the local economy.[37]

ᶜIyāḍ remarks that all these matters were common knowledge to the Madinans, having been transmitted by great numbers of people from great numbers of people (*al-jumhūr ᶜan al-jumhūr*) since the time of the Prophet. Such knowledge was definitive (*qaṭᶜī*) and a conclusive proof (*ḥujja*) which should be followed, regardless of any contradictory isolated *ḥadīths* (*akhbār al-āḥād*) or judgements arrived at by analogy (*qiyās*). Such *mutawātir* transmission (i.e. *via* many separate authorities at each level back to the original source) was incontrovertible and, indeed, was what caused Abū Yūsuf, for instance, to accept the Madinan specifications for the *ṣāᶜ* and the *mudd* when he saw for himself how knowledge of them had been preserved and handed down from generation to generation in Madina.[38] Nevertheless, despite the strength of this argument in the eyes of the Madinans, people from other cities still often preferred to follow their own local traditions, on the basis that learned Companions had spread out into various parts of the new Muslim lands, taking their knowledge with them, and that it was as legitimate to follow any of these as it was to follow the Madinan *ʿulamāʾ*, with some of them even claiming the status of *tawātur* for their own local transmissions. ʿIyāḍ's answer to this is that one of the conditions for *tawātur* is that both 'ends' of the line of transmission should be equal, i.e. that many people should have transmitted the knowledge in question from many Companions, from the Prophet. This situation, he claims, only existed in Madina, where a whole generation were able to transmit from a whole generation who had been alive at the time of the Prophet, whereas in all other cities the lines of transmission ended only with individual Companions, however great their level of learning: such transmissions were therefore in fact *akhbār al-āḥād* rather than *mutawātir*. Even, for instance, in the case of the *adhān* in Makka, for which one could possibly claim *mutawātir* transmission from the time of the Prophet, the different *adhān* in Madina had the advantage of being the later of the two and the one that was being done when the Prophet died. This is why, he says, when Mālik was asked about this point, he said: 'I do not know about the *adhān* of a day and a night. Here is the mosque of the Messenger of Allah, may Allah bless him and grant him peace, where the *adhān* has been done [continuously] from then until now and no-one has ever recorded any objection (*inkār*) to the way the *adhān* has been done here.'[39]

Ibn Taymiyya also regards this first category of *ʿamal* as a conclusive proof and claims that all the Muslims do too, citing the instance of Abū Yūsuf accepting the Madinan position on the *ṣāʿ* and the *mudd*, the fact that no *zakāt* is taken from green vegetables and fruit, or from less than five *wasqs*, and that endowments, once made, are irrevocable.[40] However, in view of the fact that differences remained between the *madhhabs* as to how, for example, the *adhān* should be done, or whether or not the *basmala* should be recited at the beginning of the prayer, this claim of Ibn Taymiyya's is, as ʿIyāḍ's comments on the non-Madinans preferring to follow their own local traditions plainly indicate, not wholly correct.[41]

The second main category is where the *ʿamal* derives from the *ijtihād* of later authorities. Ibn Taymiyya draws a distinction between *ʿamal* that was instituted before the death of the third caliph ʿUthmān (35 AH), which he terms *ʿamal qadīm* ('early *ʿamal*'), and *ʿamal* that was instituted after the death of ʿUthmān, which he terms *ʿamal mutaʾakhkhir* ('later *ʿamal*'). The first type, he holds, is a conclusive proof (*ḥujja*) which ought to be followed (*yajib ittibāᶜuhā*), supporting his view by quoting the *ḥadīth* 'You must hold to my *sunna* and the *sunna* of the rightly-guided caliphs after me' (these 'rightly-guided caliphs' then being defined by another *ḥadīth* as those of the first 30 years, i.e. up to and including the caliphate of ᶜUthmān).[42] The second type, *ᶜamal muta'akhkhir*, is not, according to Ibn Taymiyya, generally held to be a conclusive proof, although, he says, some Mālikīs in the Maghrib consider it so.[43]

ᶜIyāḍ draws no such distinction between *ᶜamal qadīm* and *ᶜamal muta'akhkhir*, but notes three different opinions among the Mālikīs on whether or not post-Prophetic *ᶜamal* is a conclusive proof that others should follow. Most, he says, do not hold that it is a conclusive proof, nor that it can be used to give preference to one person's *ijtihād* over another's, this being particularly the view of the Baghdadi followers of Mālik. Others, he says, are of the view that although it is not a conclusive proof it can be used to give preference to one person's *ijtihād* over another's. There are also some, he says, who hold that where there is consensus among the Madinans on a practice arrived at by *ijtihād*, this is also a conclusive proof. This third view, he says, is that of Abū l-Ḥusayn ibn Abī ᶜUmar in particular among the Baghdadis, and also of a number of Maghribis, who consider that such *ᶜamal ijtihādī* should be given preference over *akhbār al-āḥād*. It is also, he says, what all the opponents of Mālik think is Mālik's view, although this is not actually the case.[44]

The authority of Madinan *ᶜamal*

Mālik clearly saw Madinan *ᶜamal* as authoritative. Perhaps the best expression of his view on this matter is his letter to al-Layth ibn Saᶜd on precisely this point. In this letter we learn that al-Layth has been giving *fatwās* contrary to the *ᶜamal* of Madina, and that Mālik is writing to him to counsel him never to go against this *ᶜamal*. After a short introduction, he says:

> All people are subordinate (*tabaᶜ*) to the people of Madina. To it the Hijra was made and in it the Qur'an was revealed, the lawful (*ḥalāl*) made lawful and the forbidden (*ḥarām*) made forbidden. The Messenger of Allah, may Allah bless him and grant him peace, was living amongst them and they were present during the very act of revelation. He would tell them to do things and they would obey him, and he would institute *sunnas* for them and they would follow him, until Allah took him to Himself and chose for him what is in His presence, may Allah bless him and grant him peace.

> Then there rose up after him those who were put in authority after him and who, of his community, were the ones who followed him most closely. When matters arose about which they had knowledge, they put that knowledge into practice. If they did not have [the requisite] knowledge, they would ask [others] and would go by what they considered to be the most valid opinion according to their own personal reasoning (*ijtihād*) and their recent experience [of when the Prophet was alive] (*ḥadāthat ʿahdihim*). If someone disagreed with them, or said something that was more valid and more worthy of being followed, they would leave aside their own opinion and act according to the other, stronger opinion. After them the Successors trod the same path and followed the same *sunnas*.
>
> So, if there is something which is clearly acted upon in Madina (*idhā kāna l-amr bi-l-Madīna ẓāhiran maʿmūlan bi-hi*), I am not of the opinion (*lam ara*) that anyone may go against it, because of this inheritance that [the Madinans] have which it is not permissible for any others to ascribe to, or claim for, themselves. Even if the people of other cities were to say, 'This is the practice (*ʿamal*) in our city', or 'This is what those before us used to do (*wa-hādhā lladhī maḍā ʿalayhi man maḍā minnā*)', they would not have the same authority for that, nor would it be permissible for them in the way that it is for [the people of Madina].[45]

Mālik's position on the matter would thus seem to be unequivocal: *all* people are subordinate to the people of Madina, by virtue of the Madinans' greater direct experience and collective knowledge which the people of no other city can lay claim to despite the high level of learning of individuals amongst them. This was Mālik's argument against Iraq and the other centres of learning of the Muslim world at his time. He acknowledged that they had received learning from individual Companions of great stature who had settled there, and he allowed that people in the outlying provinces were free to follow their own men of knowledge,[46] but Madina was the origin of that knowledge, and the primary source was always preferable to the secondary. We find Mālik illustrating this by reference to an incident where Ibn Masʿūd, the most learned of the scholars of Kufa in his time, gave a judgement to someone in Kufa on a detail of law and then later went to Madina only to find that the position in Madina on that point was different, whereupon the first thing he did on returning to Kufa was to go to the man and tell him what the correct, i.e. Madinan, judgement was.[47]

Al-Layth's reply to Mālik has been preserved for us both by al-Fasawī (from whom Ibn Taymiyya's student, Ibn Qayyim al-Jawziyya, also transmits it), and, in a shortened form, by ᶜIyāḍ.[48] What is of particular interest in al-Layth's reply is that he makes a distinction between Madinan *ᶜamal* on which there was consensus (*ijmāᶜ*) and Madinan *ᶜamal* on which there was not consensus. He says: 'I do not think there is anyone to whom knowledge is ascribed who has more dislike for isolated opinions (*shawādhdh al-futyā*), or more respect for the scholars of Madina who have gone before, or who is more receptive to their opinions *when they are agreed on a matter* than I am.'[49] Thus what he disagrees with is that Madinan *ᶜamal* should be binding in instances where the Madinan *ᶜulamāʾ* themselves were not agreed. His point, and it was the point most commonly raised against the Mālikīs on this issue, is that the Companions had spread out throughout the new lands of Islam, taking with them their knowledge of the Book and the *sunna*, and exercising their best judgement (*yajtahidūna bi-raʾyihim*) when they knew of no specific guidance on a matter. Furthermore, the first three caliphs had been concerned to avoid dispute among the Muslim troops and had sent directives to them on even relatively unimportant matters (*al-amr al-yasīr*) in order to establish the *dīn* and prevent dispute over the Book and the *sunna*, but they had never told anyone to go against the practice of any of the Companions, whether in Egypt, Syria or Iraq, if this had been the constant practice of these Companions up until their death. In other words, the Companions had come to different decisions on various matters but they had had a right to do so, and if the first three caliphs had not forced people to follow the Companions of a particular place, why should anyone else? This applied even more so in the time of the Successors, whose sharp disagreements, says al-Layth, are as well known to Mālik as to anyone else. Finally, al-Layth illustrates his argument by citing a number of examples of where he feels justified in accepting an opinion contrary to the *ᶜamal* in Madina precisely because the practice based on the contrary opinion had been instituted by one or more worthy Companions.[50]

Did Mālik, then, hold that all *ᶜamal* was equally authoritative? We have seen how, in his letter to al-Layth, Mālik says, 'If there is something which is clearly acted upon in Madina, I am not of the opinion that anyone may go against it',[51] and this, together with the implications of al-Layth's objections to having to follow *ᶜamal* on which there was not consensus, would suggest that Mālik did indeed hold the view, as his opponents claimed, that all Madinan *ᶜamal* should be followed whatever its origin, the only proviso being that it should be 'clearly acted upon in Madina'. However, Abd-Allah's recent studies on Mālik's terminology suggest that this is not entirely the case, and that Mālik drew clear distinctions between different types of *ᶜamal* and the degree to which they were binding.

Abd-Allah demonstrates how Mālik's terminology refers to a number of different categories of *ʿamal*, indicating not only its date of origin but also the degree of consensus in Madina that it represents, which, as we have seen, was not one of the considerations of either ʿIyāḍ or Ibn Taymiyya who were both concerned primarily with Madinan *ijmāʿ*.[52] Mālik frequently uses terms such as *al-sunna ʿindanā* ('the *sunna* here'), *al-sunna llatī lā khtilāfa fī-hā ʿindanā* ('the *sunna* about which there is no dispute here'), *al-amr ʿindanā* ('the practice here'), *al-amr al-mujtamaʿ ʿalayhi ʿindanā* ('the agreed practice here'), and *al-amr alladhī lā khtilāfa fī-hi ʿindanā* ('the practice about which there is no dispute here'), and until recently these terms have been either undiscussed by most scholars or considered to be interchangeable.[53] Abd-Allah's analysis, however, has shown that there is a clear distinction between Mālik's *sunna* and *amr* terms: *sunna* refers to *ʿamal* that derives from a normative practice of the Prophet (or sometimes a pre-Islamic Madinan custom endorsed by the Prophet) without any element of later *ijtihād*, whereas *amr* refers to *ʿamal* that, although often originating in the practice of the Prophet, nevertheless contains at least some element of later *ijtihād*.[54] These two terms thus indicate a distinction comparable to that between *ʿamal naqlī* and *ʿamal ijtihādī* referred to above.[55] Furthermore, both these terms are often qualified by expressions indicating different degrees of consensus. Where any difference of opinion in Madina is specifically denied (such as in the formula *alladhī lā khtilāfa fī-hi*) we are dealing with points upon which there was complete consensus in Madina and which thus come under the categories discussed by ʿIyāḍ and Ibn Taymiyya. The qualifying phrase *al-mujtamaʿ ʿalayhi ʿindanā*, however, does not necessarily indicate complete consensus, but rather a predominant consensus where there were differences of opinion in Madina but not such as constituted any significant breach of the view of the great majority.[56] When the terms are not qualified at all, such as *maḍat al-sunna* ('the *sunna* has been established'), *al-sunna ʿindanā* or *al-amr ʿindanā*, there were often (but not necessarily) significant differences of opinion in Madina on the points in question.[57] Thus there were clearly different levels of consensus for both *ʿamal naqlī* and *ʿamal ijtihādī*.

It would seem, therefore, that Mālik was aware of differing degrees of authoritativeness for different kinds of *ʿamal*, and, although he favoured the preponderant *ʿamal* in Madina, he would not have held that all types of *ʿamal* were equally authoritative.[58] This is particularly evident in cases of what Abd-Allah calls 'mixed *ʿamal*', such as in the question of how to wipe over leather socks (*khuffs*), where different, and equally prestigious, Madinan authorities held differing views.[59] Indeed, the whole question of when it was permissible to wipe over *khuffs* at all was something on which

Mālik appears to have changed his mind during his life, which suggests that no particular practice had gained predominance in Madina by that time.[60]

Furthermore, as we have seen with Mālik's response to al-Manṣūr's suggestion that all the *umma* should be made to follow the knowledge of the people of Madina, although Mālik was positive about the *ᶜamal* of the Madinans he was not negative about the knowledge of other cities, however much he may have considered it to be a deviation from the clear path of the Madinans.[61]

ᶜAmal versus ḥadīth

The opposition to Madinan *ᶜamal* centred not so much on objections to Madinan *ijtihād* as opposed to the *ijtihād* of others, as on the relationship between *ᶜamal* and *ḥadīth*, particularly those *ḥadīths* that went back to only one or a very few Companions (*akhbār al-āḥād*, sing. *khabar al-wāḥid*). (One should note that *ḥadīths* are commonly divided into two types, namely *akhbār al-āḥād*, i.e. those going back to single authorities among the Companions, and *mutawātir ḥadīths*, i.e. those going back to a large number of Companions, and the vast majority of *ḥadīths* are, technically speaking, *akhbār al-āḥād*.)[62] *Mutawātir ḥadīths*, on the other hand, were not only much fewer in number but were also, in the very nature of things, unlikely to contradict *ᶜamal*, itself *mutawātir*, since it is practically impossible to conceive of two *mutawātir* transmissions being both authentic *and* contradictory (although al-Qāḍī ᶜAbd al-Wahhāb allows that, if this should occur, they should be considered as two contradictory *ḥadīths*).[63]

ᶜIyāḍ discusses this point in some detail, saying that *ᶜamal* must relate to such isolated *ḥadīths* in one of three ways: either (i) the *ᶜamal* in question will accord with the *ḥadīth*, in which case it will serve as a support for the validity of the *ḥadīth*; or (ii) the *ᶜamal* will accord with one *ḥadīth* but be contradicted by another, in which case the *ᶜamal* is one of the strongest arguments for preferring the first *ḥadīth* to the second; or (iii) the *ᶜamal* will contradict the *ḥadīth* (or *ḥadīths*). If in this last instance the *ᶜamal* is *ᶜamal naqlī*, i.e. derives from the time of the Prophet, it is to be preferred to the *ḥadīth*, because this type of *ᶜamal* is definitively authoritative (*qaṭᶜī al-thubūt*) whereas the *khabar al-wāḥid* is only presumptively authoritative (*ẓannī al-thubūt*). If, however, it is *ᶜamal* based on *ijtihād*, then the predominant view is that *akhbār al-āḥād* are given preference over it, though there is dispute on this point, as mentioned earlier.[64]

ᶜIyāḍ also discusses a fourth possibility, which is if there is a *ḥadīth* on a point but no *ᶜamal*. In this case, he says, there is of course no conflict and the *ḥadīth* is followed, providing it is authentic and that there is no contradictory *ḥadīth*. If there is, and one of the *ḥadīths* is related through Madinan sources while the other is not, then, according to Abū Isḥāq al-Isfarāyīnī, preference is given to the *ḥadīth* with the Madinan credentials.

Al-Shāṭibī, however, disagrees with ʿIyāḍ on this last point and suggests that the absence of *ʿamal* is itself an indication that the contents of such a *ḥadīth* are not to be considered normative, since if they were there would have been some *ʿamal* instituted in its favour (assuming that the matter in question was one that would be expected to have occurred in the lives of the first community).[65] He illustrates this by a report from Mālik regarding the question of the 'prostration of thankfulness' (*sajdat al-shukr*). Mālik was asked about whether someone who has heard some good news should prostrate to Allah out of gratitude and he said that this should not be done and that it was not part of people's general practice (*laysa mimmā maḍā min amr al-nās*). When the fact that Abū Bakr had made such a prostration after the battle of Yamāma was mentioned to him, he said:

> I have not heard about this, and I consider it a lie against Abū Bakr. It is a type of misguidance that someone should hear something and then say 'This is something about which we have heard nothing contradictory.' ... Many victories came to the Messenger of Allah, may Allah bless him and grant him peace, and to the Muslims after him, but have you heard that any of them made such a prostration? When you hear this sort of report about something that would have happened in their midst and been part of their general experience and yet nothing else has been heard about it, then let that (i.e. what you already know) be enough for you. If such a thing had happened, it would have been mentioned, because it would have been part of their direct experience (*li-annahu min amr al-nās alladhī kāna fī-him*). But have you heard that anyone made such a prostration? This, then, is a point of general consensus (*ijmāʿ*). If you hear something [like this] which you do not know about, leave it (*idhā jāʾaka amr lā taʿrifuhu fa-daʿhu*).[66]

Mālik's attitude on this point is well documented and many reports show that he held *ʿamal* to be more reliable (*athbat*) than *ḥadīth*. There is a long report in the *Madārik* concerning his meeting with Abū Yūsuf and their discussions about the *adhān* and the measures of the *ṣāʿ* and the *mudd*. ʿIyāḍ reports:

> Abū Yūsuf said [to Mālik], 'You do the *adhān* with *tarjīʿ*,[67] but you have no *ḥadīth* from the Prophet about this.' Mālik turned to him and

said, '*Subḥāna llāh!* I have never seen anything more amazing than this! The call to the prayer has been done [here] every day five times a day in front of witnesses, and sons have inherited it from their fathers since the time of the Messenger of Allah, may Allah bless him and grant him peace. Does this need "So-and-so from so-and-so"? This is more accurate (*aṣaḥḥ*) in our opinion than *ḥadīth*.'

Abū Yūsuf also asked him about the *ṣāᶜ* and Mālik said, 'Five and one-third *raṭls*.' Abū Yūsuf said, 'What's your basis for saying that?' Mālik said to some of the people with him, 'Go and fetch the *ṣāᶜs* that you have.' So many of the people of Madina, both Muhājirīn and Anṣār, came, and every one of them brought a *ṣāᶜ* [with him] and said, 'This is the *ṣāᶜ* which I inherited from my father, who inherited it from *his* father who was one of the Companions of the Messenger of Allah, may Allah bless him and grant him peace.' Mālik said, 'This sort of widespread knowledge (*hādhā l-khabar al-shāʾiᶜ*) is more reliable (*athbat*) in our opinion than *ḥadīth*.' So Abū Yūsuf accepted Mālik's opinion.[68]

ᶜIyāḍ devotes an entire chapter to comments by earlier authorities on the superiority of *ᶜamal* over *ḥadīth*. It is worth quoting in full, since it gives a very clear picture of Mālik's view[69] on the matter:

On What Has Been Related from the First Community and the Men of Knowledge Regarding the Obligation of Going Back to the Practice (*ᶜamal*) of the People of Madina, and Its Being a Conclusive Proof (*ḥujja*) in Their Opinion, even if It is Contrary to *Ḥadīth* (*al-athar*)[70]

It is related that ᶜUmar ibn al-Khaṭṭāb, may Allah be pleased with him, once said on the *minbar*: 'By Allah, I will make things difficult for any man who relates a *ḥadīth* which is contrary to *ᶜamal*.'

Ibn al-Qāsim and Ibn Wahb said: 'I saw that with Mālik *ᶜamal* was stronger than *ḥadīth*.'[71]

Mālik said: 'There were people among the men of knowledge of the Successors who would narrate certain *ḥadīths*, and hear other *ḥadīths* from others, and they would say, "We are not ignorant of this, but the *ᶜamal* that has come down to us is different."'[72]

Mālik said: 'I once saw Muḥammad ibn Abī Bakr ibn ᶜAmr ibn Ḥazm, who was a *qāḍī*, being reproached by his brother ᶜAbdallāh, who was an honest man with an extensive knowledge of *ḥadīth*, for giving a judgement on a case about which there was a *ḥadīth* giving a different judgement. ᶜAbdallāh said, "Hasn't such-and-such a *ḥadīth* come down about this?" Muḥammad replied, "It has." ᶜAbdallāh said, "Then why don't you give your judgement according to it?" Muḥammad replied, "But what is the position of the people with regard to it?" – i.e. the agreed *ᶜamal* in Madina, by which he meant that the *ᶜamal* of Madina was stronger than *ḥadīth*.'[73]

Ibn al-Muᶜadhdhal said: 'I once heard someone ask Ibn al-Mājishūn, "Why do you transmit a *ḥadīth* and then not act upon it?", and he replied, "So that it be known that it is with full knowledge of it that we do not act upon it."'[74]

Ibn Mahdī said: 'The established *sunna* of the people of Madina is better than *ḥadīth*.'[75] He also said: 'Often I will have numerous *ḥadīths* on a subject, but will find the people who teach in the mosque (? – *ahl al-ᶜarṣa*) following something contrary to them, and so those *ḥadīths* will become weak in my opinion' – or words to that effect.[76]

Rabīᶜa said: 'One thousand from one thousand is preferred by me to one from one. One from one would tear the *sunna* right out of your hands.'

Ibn Abī Ḥāzim said: 'Abū l-Dardā' would be asked questions and would give answers and if someone said, "But such-and-such has reached us", contrary to what he had said, he would reply, "I too have heard that, but I have found the practice (*al-ᶜamal*) to be different."'

Ibn Abī l-Zinād said: 'ᶜUmar ibn ᶜAbd al-ᶜAzīz used to gather the *fuqahā'* together and ask them about the *sunnas* and the judgements which were acted upon (*yuᶜmalu bi-hā*). These he would then affirm, whilst those that were not acted upon he would discard, even though their source was absolutely trustworthy.'[77]

Mālik said: 'The Messenger of Allah, may Allah bless him and grant him peace, came back after such-and-such a *ghazwa* with so many thousands of the Companions. Some ten thousand of them died in Madina and the rest of them spread out in various places. So which of them are more worthy of being followed and having their opinions (*qawl*) accepted, those among whom the Prophet, may Allah bless him and grant him peace, and those Companions whom I have just mentioned died, or those among whom one or two of the Companions of the Prophet, may Allah bless him and grant him peace, died?'

ᶜUbaydallāh ibn ᶜAbd al-Karīm said: 'When the Messenger of Allah, may Allah bless him and grant him peace, died, there were twenty thousand weeping eyes.'[78]

This view is thus seen as going back to at least the time of ʿUmar. Particularly significant is the comment of Rabīʿa, one of Mālik's main teachers. 'One thousand from one thousand' means a large number of Successors, for example, taking directly from a large number of Companions, which was only possible in Madina, where there were some ten thousand Companions ('twenty thousand weeping eyes') at the time of the death of the Prophet. 'One from one', however, was the situation in the rest of the Muslim world, where individual Successors took their knowledge from individual Companions.[79] Thus this directly-received knowledge of the Madinans of how the *sharīʿa* was put into practice automatically had higher authority in their view than most *ḥadīths*, since it had the status of what was *mutawātir* – i.e. what had been related by so many Companions that there could be no reasonable doubt about its authenticity – whereas most *ḥadīths*, as we have seen, were not *mutawātir*.[80]

It is important to emphasise that *ʿamal* and *hadith* are not, of course, mutually exclusive, as ʿIyāḍ's analysis indicates.[81] *ʿAmal* may, or may not, be recorded by *ḥadīth*; and *ḥadīth* may, or may not, record *ʿamal*. Where they overlap they are a strong confirmation of each other; but where there is contradiction, *ʿamal* is preferred to *ḥadīth* by Mālik and the Madinans, even when the sources of these *ḥadīth* are completely trustworthy, as indicated in the comment of Ibn Abī l-Zinād in the above passage. Thus, for example, the standard *adhān* in Madina, or the way of standing for the prayer with one's hands by one's sides (*sadl*, or *irsāl al-yadayn*), or reciting in the prayer without beginning with '*bi-smi llāhi l-raḥmāni l-raḥīm*', or the size of the *ṣāʿ* and the *mudd*, were matters that were not recorded initially in the form of *ḥadīth* but were nevertheless known generally amongst the people and understood to have originated in the time of the Prophet.[82] Other practices, however, although recorded in authentic *ḥadīths* and even transmitted, for example, in the *Muwaṭṭaʾ*, were not acted upon by their transmitters precisely because they did not represent the *sunna*. In other words, they were either exceptional instances or earlier judgements that had later been changed, or otherwise minority opinions that held little weight, and which, even though they derived from the Prophet, were nevertheless outweighed by other judgements also deriving from the Prophet. It was for this reason that Ibn ʿUyayna could say that *ḥadīths* were a source of misguidance except for the *fuqahāʾ*,[83] and Mālik that *ʿamal* was a more reliable source than *ḥadīth*.[84]

There are a number of striking examples in the *Muwaṭṭaʾ* of *ʿamal* being preferred to *ḥadīth*, even though the *ḥadīths* in question are considered completely trustworthy. The following examples, where Mālik transmits *ḥadīths* which he does not consider should be acted upon, serve to illustrate the point:

1. Mālik relates two *ḥadīths* whose overt import is that the prayer should be done with the right hand holding the left at the wrist (*qabḍ*).[85] He makes no comment on this in the *Muwaṭṭa*ʾ, but in the *Mudawwana* Ibn al-Qāsim records him as saying: 'I do not know of this practice as far as obligatory prayers are concerned (*lā aʿrifu dhālika fī l-farīḍa*), but there is no harm in someone doing it in voluntary prayers (*nawāfil*), if he has been standing for a long time, in order to make things easier for himself.'[86] The transmitter of the *Mudawwana*, Saḥnūn, also records a *ḥadīth* to the effect that a number of the Companions had reported seeing the Prophet doing the prayer with his right hand placed over his left. Despite this *ḥadīth* and the similar reports in the *Muwaṭṭa*ʾ, the *madhhab* of the *Mudawwana*, which became the major source for later Mālikīs as summarised in Khalīl's *Mukhtaṣar*,[87] was that it was preferable in all circumstances to pray with one's hands by one's sides, since this was the predominant *ʿamal*. This way of doing the prayer was also preferred by al-Layth ibn Saʿd, accepted by Ibrāhīm al-Nakhaʿī, ʿAṭāʾ ibn Abī Rabāḥ and al-Awzāʿī, and recorded from other important authorities such as Saʿīd ibn al-Musayyab, Saʿīd ibn Jubayr, al-Ḥasan al-Baṣrī, Ibn Sīrīn and Ibn Jurayj.[88] It is, furthermore, interesting to note that this practice, although rejected by all the other surviving Sunnī *madhhabs*, is nevertheless that of the Zaydīs, the Ithnā ʿAsharī Shīʿa, the Ismāʿīlīs and the Ibāḍīs,[89] thus bolstering the argument for the 'ancient' (i.e. Prophetic) origin of this *ʿamal*, since the differences between these groups and the main body of the Muslims arose at a very early date and on questions of belief and political authority rather than on points of *fiqh*. There can have been no reason for them inventing such a detail of *fiqh*, and the obvious inference is that they were merely continuing an established practice.[90]

2. Another example of where Mālik seemingly goes against a *ḥadīth* is the question of *rafʿ al-yadayn* ('raising the hands') during the prayer. In the chapter 'What Has Come Down About Beginning the Prayer', Mālik relates one report, *via* Sālim and Ibn ʿUmar, to the effect that the Prophet used to raise his hands when saying '*Allāhu akbar*' both at the beginning of the prayer and when coming up from *rukūʿ*, and another, *via* Nāfiʿ, to the effect that Ibn ʿUmar used to do the same.[91]

Despite recording no *ḥadīths* in the *Muwaṭṭa*ʾ overtly to the contrary, Mālik's view, according to Ibn al-Qāsim in the *Mudawwana*, was that one only raised one's hands at the beginning of the prayer, that is, when doing the initial *takbīr* (*takbīrat al-iḥrām*). Again, as in the above instance, Mālik uses the phrase 'I do not know of this [practice] (*lā aʿrifu dhālika*)', adding the exceptive clause 'except in the *takbīrat al-iḥrām*.'[92]

Although Abū Ḥanīfa and the Kufans held the same view as the Madinans on this point, basing their argument on reports to that effect from ᶜAlī and Ibn Masᶜūd *via* Ibrāhīm al-Nakhaᶜī,[93] al-Shāfiᶜī held the contrary view that one should raise one's hands both before and after each *rukū*ᶜ as well as at the beginning of the prayer, basing his argument on the above-mentioned *ḥadīths* and at the same time accusing the Madinans of inconsistency in relating these *ḥadīths* and yet not acting upon them.[94]

This would therefore seem to be a clear case, as Ibn Rushd indicates, of where Mālik relates a *ḥadīth* but rejects its import because it is not in accord with ᶜ*amal*.[95]

3. Under the heading 'Doing *Ḥajj* for Someone Else', Mālik relates a *ḥadīth* about a woman who came to the Prophet and asked whether she could do *ḥajj* on behalf of her father who was too weak through old age to do so himself and the Prophet said that she could.[96]

Despite relating this *ḥadīth*, Mālik held that no-one should normally do *ḥajj* for anyone else. The Qurᵓan clearly states that *ḥajj* is an obligation only for those who are able to do it (Q 3: 97: '*mani staṭāᶜa ilayhi sabīlan*'), and, if a man was no longer physically able to do *ḥajj*, it was no longer an obligation for him, even if he had the money to get someone else to do it for him.[97] In this respect, Mālik considered *ḥajj* to be essentially a 'bodily' (*badanī*) obligation, like doing the prayer and fasting, rather than a financial (*mālī*) one, like paying the *zakāt*, and in his opinion such 'bodily' obligations, if they could not be done by a particular individual, never devolved on anyone else.[98] The only exception he made to this rule with regard to *ḥajj* was if someone made a bequest that someone else should go on *ḥajj* for him, in which case Mālik held that the bequest should be carried out, although he disliked the practice.[99]

Mālik thus saw this *ḥadīth* as a special exception for this particular woman which had no normative value for people in general. In particular, there was no indication that her doing *ḥajj* for her father would in any way count for him as his obligatory *ḥajj*: she had merely asked whether it was permissible for her to do *ḥajj* on his behalf and whether there would be any reward (*ajr*) in it for him if she did so, and she had been told there would be.[100] Thus, at best, the *ḥadīth* was about merit, and said nothing about obligation.

Al-Shāfiᶜī, however, considered this *ḥadīth* (and others to the same effect) to be evidence that a person could do *ḥajj* for someone else who was too old or weak to do so himself, commenting that this was the view of 'all the people of *fiqh* – whether from Makka, the East, or the Yemen – except the people of Madina'.[101] In fact, although Abū Ḥanīfa and the Iraqis allowed this practice, they did not go as far as al-Shāfiᶜī in their assessment of it: they only held that it was acceptable, rather than obligatory, for someone with enough money to get someone else to go on *ḥajj* for him,[102] whereas al-Shāfiᶜī held that someone in this situation (or even someone who, though he did not have the money, nevertheless had the authority to get someone else, such as a close relative, to go for him) was still 'able' (*mustaṭīᶜ*) and therefore still under the obligation to do *ḥajj* if he had not already done so.[103] Thus al-Shāfiᶜī and the Iraqis, contrary to the Madinans, envisaged *ḥajj* more as a financial obligation than as a bodily one.

4. There are a number of instances in the *Muwaṭṭaʾ* where Mālik relates a *ḥadīth* and then specifically states that the *ᶜamal* is contrary to the suggestion in the *ḥadīth*. One of the best examples of this is the *ḥadīth* about *khiyār al-majlis* (the right to withdraw from a sale while the two parties to it are still together) that he relates from Nāfiᶜ from Ibn ᶜUmar – the 'golden chain' of authority[104] – in which the Prophet says, 'The two parties to a sale have the right to withdraw as long as they have not parted company (*mā lam yatafarraqā*), except for *bayᶜ al-khiyār*,'[105] after which Mālik comments, 'There is no fixed limit for this here, nor any established practice regarding it (*laysa li-hādhā ᶜindanā ḥadd maᶜrūf wa-lā amr maᶜmūl bi-hi fī-hi*).'[106] Al-Shāfiᶜī, going by this *ḥadīth*, held that sales only became binding when one or both of the parties had left the place where the contract was made, rather than at the actual time of the contract, whereas Mālik and Abū Ḥanīfa held that the general Qurʾanic injunctions to honour one's contracts[107] overruled such isolated *ḥadīths* (*akhbār al-āḥād*), however strong their *isnāds*.[108]

5. Another instance where both the Madinans and the Iraqis rejected a *ḥadīth* which al-Shāfiᶜī chose to follow is ᶜĀisha's report of a Qurʾanic verse – which, she says, 'was still being recited at the time of the death of the Prophet' – which indicates that foster relationship is established by a minimum of five sucklings rather than an original ten.[109] Mālik cites this *ḥadīth* (along with others indicating that either five or ten sucklings establish foster relationship, although he also includes reports indicating that ᶜĀisha's view was the exception) but then adds that the *ᶜamal* in Madina is not in accord with this. Rather he held, along with the Iraqis, that even one suckling brought about foster relationship (as long as the child was under two years of age), thus preferring, along with many earlier authorities, the general meaning (*ᶜumūm*) of the relevant Qurʾanic judgement – i.e. Q 4: 23's 'And [forbidden in marriage for you are] your mothers who have suckled you (*wa-ummahātukumu llātī arḍaᶜnakum*)' – to what was an isolated report (*khabar al-wāḥid*) not supported by *ᶜamal*.[110] Moreover, the report was ambiguous: it was possible to take ᶜĀisha's claim that the verse was still

being recited as part of the Qurʾan at the time of the death of the Prophet as meaning that it had not been abrogated, but it could also mean that it *had* been abrogated but that not everyone had heard by that time that it had been abrogated and so were still reciting it.[111] Furthermore, the Qurʾan could only be established by *tawātur*, and this was only an isolated report. The *ẓāhir* (apparent, overt meaning) of the report was thus misleading, and Mālik's comment 'This is not what is done here (*wa-laysa ᶜalā hādhā l-ᶜamal*)' was a simple way of warning people against going only by the *ẓāhir*.[112]

6. Mālik relates that ᶜUmar ibn al-Khaṭṭāb wrote to one of his military commanders saying: 'I have heard that some of your men have been pursuing an enemy into the mountains, and then, when he has found a safe refuge, one of them will say to him "*ma-tars*",[113] meaning "Don't be afraid", and then kill him when he reaches him. By Him in whose hand my self is, if I learn of the whereabouts of anyone doing this, I will put him to death.' Mālik then comments: 'This *ḥadīth* is not one that is generally agreed upon, nor is the *ᶜamal* in accordance with it (*laysa hādhā l-ḥadīth bi-l-mujtamaᶜ ᶜalayhi wa-laysa ᶜalayhi l-ᶜamal*)', meaning that, although it is agreed that it is forbidden for a Muslim to break his pledge of safe conduct to an enemy soldier, it is not the accepted practice to kill an offending Muslim for so doing.[114]

7. One of the clearest statements of this attitude is that by Mālik's student, Ibn al-Qāsim, in the chapter in the *Mudawwana* on marriage without a legal guardian. Ibn al-Qāsim's interlocutor, Saḥnūn, mentions a *ḥadīth* from ᶜĀisha according to which she had acted as the guardian for Ḥafṣa bint ᶜAbd al-Raḥmān in her marriage to al-Mundhir ibn al-Zubayr while the girl's father was away travelling. Ibn al-Qāsim does not deny the authenticity of the *ḥadīth*, but says, 'We do not know what the explanation (*tafsīr*) of this is, except that we assume that she appointed someone else to actually contract the marriage.' Saḥnūn then raises the point that, according to Mālik, such a marriage would be invalid even if she had appointed someone else and even if the girl's father had agreed. Ibn al-Qāsim replies:

> This *ḥadīth* has come down to us. If it had been accompanied by continuous *ᶜamal* up until the time of those we met and from whom we took [knowledge], and they likewise from those *they* had met, it would be correct to follow it. But in fact it is like other *ḥadīths* which are not accompanied by *ᶜamal*, such as what has been related from the Prophet, may Allah bless him and grant him peace, regarding using perfume while in *iḥrām*, and the report that has come down from him

> where he said, 'A fornicator is no longer a believer when he fornicates, nor [is a thief] a believer when he steals', whereas Allah has revealed the punishment [for fornication] and [the punishment of] cutting off the hand [for stealing] only for believers. Various things have been related from the Companions which have not been bolstered [by anything else] or been considered strong enough [to put into practice] (*lam tashtadda wa-lam taqwa*), while other things have been put into practice and been followed by most people and most of the Companions.
>
> This *ḥadīth* thus remains neither rejected as inauthentic nor acted upon (*ghayr mukadhdhab bi-hi wa-lā maᶜmūl bi-hi*). Rather, other *ḥadīths* that were accompanied by practice have been acted upon and transmitted by the Successors of the Companions of the Prophet, may Allah bless him and grant him peace, from the Companions, and have then been transmitted from these Successors in the same way, without them either rejecting them as inauthentic or denying what has been transmitted. What was not acted upon is left aside without rejecting it as inauthentic, and what was acted upon is acted upon and accepted as authentic (*yuṣaddaqu bi-hi*).
>
> [In this case] the *ᶜamal* which is well attested to and accompanied by practice is [the judgement indicated by] the statement of the Prophet, may Allah bless him and grant him peace, 'A woman should not be married without a legal guardian', and the statement of ᶜUmar, 'A woman should not be married without a legal guardian', and the fact that ᶜUmar separated a man and a woman who had married without a legal guardian.[115]

The important conclusion to be drawn from these examples (and there are many others) is that although for Mālik the textual sources of the Qurᵓan and the *ḥadīth* are treated with the utmost respect, they are, as Abd-Allah has observed, 'dependent or ancillary sources in that they are evaluated against the semantic context of *ᶜamal*'.[116] Thus it is the non-textual source of *ᶜamal* that constitutes the basic source, and, indeed, carries the greater authority.[117] Again, as Abd-Allah has pointed out, Mālik studies *ḥadīth* against the background of Madinan *ᶜamal*, while those who disagreed with him (particularly the Iraqis – represented by Abū Yūsuf and al-Shaybānī – and al-Shāfiᶜī) study Madinan *ᶜamal* against the background of *ḥadīth*,[118] and the two, as is clear from the above, not infrequently contradict each other.

ᶜAmal, then, was preferred to *ḥadīth* by the Madinans. The following passage by Ibn Qutayba in his *Kitāb Taᵓwīl mukhtalif al-ḥadīth* gives a comprehensive summary of why:

> In our opinion the truth is more likely to be established by *ijmāᶜ* than by the transmission of *ḥadīth* (*al-riwāya*). *Ḥadīth* may be subject to forgetfulness, error, uncertainties, different possible interpretations, and abrogation; someone trustworthy may transmit from someone who is not; there may be two different commands, both of which are possible, such as making either one or two *taslīms* [at the end of the prayer]. Similarly, a man may have been present when the Prophet, may Allah bless him and grant him peace, gave a certain command and then been absent when he told [people] to do something different: he will then transmit the first command and not the second, because he does not know it. *Ijmāᶜ*, however, is free from such vicissitudes. This is why Mālik, may Allah have mercy on him, sometimes transmits a *ḥadīth* from the Messenger of Allah, may Allah bless him and grant him peace, but then says, 'The *ᶜamal* in our city is such-and-such', mentioning something that is different to the *ḥadīth.* [This is] because his city was the city of the Prophet, may Allah bless him and grant him peace, and if the *ᶜamal* in his time had included such-and-such a practice, that would have become the *ᶜamal* of the following generation, and the generation after them, and the generation after them – and it is not possible that all the people would have stopped doing something that they were all doing in his city at his time and then done something else instead – and one generation from one generation is a much greater number than one from one. Indeed, people have related many *ḥadīths* with complete chains of authority (*muttaṣila*) and then not acted according to them.[119]

Ibn Rushd (al-Jadd) makes a similar comment in his commentary on the *ᶜUtbiyya*:

> It is a well-known part of the *madhhab* of Mālik that continuous *ᶜamal* in Madina is given preference over isolated *ḥadīths* related by trustworthy transmitters (*akhbār al-āḥād al-ᶜudūl*). [This is so] because Madina was the place where the Prophet, peace be upon him, lived and where he died, and there were many Companions there [with him]. It is therefore highly unlikely that a *ḥadīth* should be unknown to them, just as it is not possible that there should be a practice of the Companions which was continued by those afterwards which contradicts a *ḥadīth* unless they knew that [the *ḥadīth*] had been abrogated. Similarly, *qiyās* is given preference in Mālik's view over isolated *ḥadīths* if it is not possible to reconcile the two. The proof for

this is that isolated *ḥadīths* may be subject to abrogation, error, forgetfulness, mistakes, or may relate only to particular instances, whereas there can only be doubt about *qiyās* from one angle, which is, whether or not the basis for the *qiyās* [between the two situations] is really the same. It is therefore considered stronger than isolated *ḥadīths* and is given preference over them.[120]

Mālik and the Madinans thus held that *ʿamal* was the better indication of the *sunna*, whereas the Iraqis and, later, al-Shāfiʿī, held that the authentic *sunna* was that which was supported by authentic reports and that *ʿamal* was not acceptable unless it was supported by such reports. In other words, they considered that a textual source whose origin was known for certain should be given preference over a non-textual source whose origin could not be known for certain. For Mālik, however, it is not *ḥadīth* but *ʿamal* that is the primary source of normative *sunna*. Indeed, as we have said, he judges *ḥadīth* against the criterion of *ʿamal*, which is to say that he judges *ḥadīth* by reference to the *sunna* rather than judging *sunna* by reference to the *ḥadīth*. The *ʿamal versus ḥadīth* argument is thus really an extension of the argument about the meaning of the word *sunna*, to which we shall return in Part Three of this study.

PART TWO

Mālik's Use of the Qurʾan in the *Muwaṭṭaʾ*

CHAPTER FOUR

Textual Considerations

In the foregoing sections we have seen how complete was Mālik's reliance on the *ʿamal* of the people of Madina as a normative model for putting into practice the principles and precepts of the *dīn* of Islam. We have also seen that, although being one of the greatest *ḥadīth*-scholars of his day – indeed of all time – he nevertheless gives preference to *ʿamal* over *ḥadīth*, that is, he interprets *ḥadīth* against the contextual background of *ʿamal*. We shall see that it is against the same contextual background of *ʿamal* that Mālik interprets the Qurʾan.

Before looking in detail at Mālik's interpretation of the Qurʾan as evinced in the *Muwaṭṭaʾ*, we shall briefly consider what he would have been familiar with as the Qurʾan in Madina and the nature of the Qurʾanic text as it appears in the *Muwaṭṭaʾ*.

Mālik and the reading of Madina

The Qurʾan-reader *par excellence* in Madina during the greater part of Mālik's life was Nāfiʿ ibn ʿAbd al-Raḥmān ibn Abī Nuʿaym (d. 169) (not to be confused with Nāfiʿ the *mawlā* of Ibn ʿUmar) and it is Nāfiʿ's reading that became accepted as the standard reading in Madina.[1] Mālik himself studied the Qurʾan under Nāfiʿ (as Nāfiʿ studied *ḥadīth* under Mālik),[2] and his great respect for him as a scholar of Qurʾan recitation is reflected in his comment, when asked about a technical detail of recitation, 'Ask Nāfiʿ, for every branch of learning has its people to whom such questions should be put, and Nāfiʿ is the *imām* of all with regard to Qurʾan recitation.'[3]

Mālik considered Nāfiʿ's reading to be *sunna* and thus to be the preferred way of reciting the Qurʾan.[4] Indeed, the two main transmissions from Nāfiʿ, i.e. those of Qālūn (d. 220) and Warsh (d. 197), have always been closely associated with the Mālikī *madhhab*, and to this day are the prevalent readings in the region extending from Upper Egypt and northern Sudan to

North and West Africa, throughout all of which the Mālikī *madhhab* is dominant. It is thus reasonable to assume that when Mālik recited or quoted the Qur'an it was the Madinan reading that he used, and we would expect the Qur'anic quotations in the *Muwaṭṭa'* to accord with the reading of Nāfiᶜ. This, however, is not usually the case, since modern editors, under the influence of the now prevalent Ḥafṣ from ᶜĀṣim recension,[5] have frequently edited out what must have originally been the Madinan reading and replaced it with the (to them) more familiar Kufan reading of Ḥafṣ,[6] although occasionally Madinan variants or other indications of the Madinan reading survive in the printed text.[7]

As far as Mālik's attitude to the non-Madinan readings is concerned, there is an interesting report in the *ᶜUtbiyya* of him showing some of his students a copy of the Qur'an that his grandfather had written out during the caliphate of ᶜUthmān.[8] In it they noticed the following thirteen variant readings:

1. *wa-awṣā* rather than *wa-waṣṣā* in Q 2: 132
2. *sāriᶜū* rather than *wa-sāriᶜū* in Q 3: 133
3. *yaqūlu* rather than *wa-yaqūlu* in Q 5: 53
4. *man yartadid* rather than *man yartadda* in Q 5: 54
5. *alladhīna* rather than *wa-lladhīna* in Q 9: 107
6. *minhumā* rather than *minhā* in Q 18: 36
7. *li-llāhi* rather than *allāhu* in Q 23: 87 and 89
8. *fa-tawakkal* rather than *wa-tawakkal* in Q 26: 217
9. *wa-an* rather than *aw an* in Q 40: 26
10. *fa-bi-mā* rather than *bi-mā* in Q 42: 30
11. *mā tashtahī* rather than *mā tashtahīhi* in Q 43: 71
12. *fa-inna llāha huwa l-ghaniyyu* rather than *fa-inna llāha l-ghaniyyu* in Q 57: 24
13. *wa-lā yakhāfu* rather than *fa-lā yakhāfu* in Q 91: 15.

The first nine of these accord with the standard Madinan reading as opposed to the Iraqi (Basran?) reading (which is mentioned second), whereas the last four represent the Iraqi (Basran?) reading as opposed to the Madinan reading (which is mentioned second).[9] Al-Dānī, after mentioning the same report, further relates that Nāfiᶜ said: 'In the *imām* [i.e. master-copy of the Qur'an] it has *huwa l-ghaniyyu* with the addition of the *huwa* in *Sūrat al-Ḥadīd* (Q 57) and *wa-lā yakhāfu* instead of *fa-lā yakhāfu* in *Sūrat al-Shams* (Q 91).'[10]

These comments are interesting in that they imply that what became known as the reading of Nāfiᶜ was indeed the norm in Madina at that time and that such non-Madinan variants were considered exceptions to it, even though they were well known and well substantiated. As with the *ḥadīth versus ʿamal* debate, we have here a situation where readings, although known about and accepted as authentic, were not used because the *ʿamal* that had become established was based on other readings which better represented the normative *sunna* of Qurʾanic recitation.[11]

Mālik and the *shādhdh* variant readings

So far we have mentioned only those variants that are accepted by all Sunnī scholars as valid elements of the Qurʾanic corpus because of their *mutawātir* status, and it is obvious from the foregoing that, like them, Mālik accepted all these variants as permissible (even though they might not all be *sunna*). The question arises, however, as to his attitude to the *shādhdh* ('irregular', 'non-canonical') readings recorded (mostly) only from individual Companions, the transmission of which was on a par with *akhbār al-āḥād* rather than *mutawātir ḥadīths*.

There are six overt references in the *Muwaṭṭaʾ* to *shādhdh* readings, namely:

1. that ʿUmar used to read (*kāna yaqraʾ*) ***fa-mḍū*** *ilā dhikri llāh* ('go to the remembrance of Allah') in Q 62: 9;[12]
2. that ʿĀisha and Ḥafṣa both specified the inclusion of ***wa-ṣalāti l-ʿaṣri*** ('and the afternoon prayer') in Q 2: 238 when having a *muṣḥaf* copied out;[13]
3. that in Ubayy's reading (*fī qirāʾat Ubayy*) Q 5: 89 was read *thalāthati ayyāmin* ***mutatābiʿātin*** ('three consecutive days');[14]
4. that Ibn ʿUmar read (*qaraʾa*) *fa-ṭalliqūhunna li-****qubuli*** *ʿiddatihinna* ('so divorce them at the beginning of their *ʿidda*') in Q 65: 1;[15]
5. ʿĀisha's reference to a verse about suckling – ***ʿashru raḍaʿātin maʿlūmātin yuḥarrimna*** ('ten known sucklings make *ḥarām* [i.e. constitute a barrier to marriage]') – which had been part of the Qurʾan (*fī-mā unzila min al-Qurʾān*) but had then been abrogated (*nusikhna*) by ***khams(in) maʿlūmāt(in)*** ('five known [sucklings]'), which was 'part of what was recited as Qurʾan' (*fī-mā yuqraʾu min al-Qurʾān*) at the time of the death of the Prophet;[16]
6. ʿUmar's reference to the stoning verse (*āyat al-rajm*) – ***al-shaykhu wa-l-shaykhatu fa-rjumūhumā l-batta*** ('mature men and mature women, stone them completely') – which, he says, they had certainly recited (*fa-innā qad qaraʾnāhā*).[17]

It is important to note here that although Mālik does not himself use the term *shādhdh*, his use of the verb *qaraʾa* (to read or recite) rather than a variant of the *qāla llāhu* ('Allah says') formula, which is what he usually uses when citing established Qurʾanic text, indicates that he recognised a clear distinction between the two. Indeed, we know that Mālik did not accept such readings as valid for the prayer,[18] which means that he did not accept them as part of the Qurʾan. However, the question remains of whether or not such readings could be used for purposes of *tafsīr*. Both Ibn ʿAbd al-Barr and al-Bājī hold that this was indeed what Mālik was doing in mentioning ʿUmar's reading of ***fa-mḍū*** instead of the normative *fa-sʿaw* in Q 62: 9's *fa-sʿaw ilā dhikri llāh* ('make effort [to go] to the remembrance of Allah'), referring to the Jumuʿa prayer.[19] *Fa-sʿaw* was ambiguous: it could refer to a light run, as in the *ḥadīth* 'When the *iqāma* is called for the prayer, do not run to it (*lā taʾtūhā wa-antum tasʿawna*), but come to it with composure',[20] and as in the *saʿy* that forms part of the rites of *ḥajj*;[21] or it could refer to making effort and striving in a more general sense, as in the Qurʾanic passages that Mālik cites immediately after mentioning ʿUmar's reading,[22] and as he himself uses the term to indicate the ability of a slave to work and earn money for his master.[23] As far as the Qurʾan is concerned, Mālik is clearly of the opinion that *saʿy* is used in this more general sense of striving, and only that. He also clearly endorses the judgement in the above-mentioned *ḥadīth* that one should not run to the prayer, although he allows that it is permissible to speed up one's pace a little as long as one does not break into a run (*mā lam yasʿa aw yakhubba*).[24] It would seem, therefore, that he accepts the validity of ʿUmar's reading as an indication of the meaning here, although of course not accepting it as Qurʾan.

The same applies to Ubayy's reading of *thalāthati ayyāmin* ***mutatābiʿātin***. The question here was whether the three days' fasting in expiation of a broken oath should be done consecutively or not. Q 4: 92 and 58: 4 specified that the two months' fasting in expiation for accidental killing or breaking an oath of *ẓihār* should be consecutive. It was further specified in the *ḥadīth* that the two months' fasting in expiation for breaking the fast in Ramaḍān should be consecutive.[25] In the received text of Q 5: 89 consecutiveness was not specified: but should it be understood as applying here also, in view of the reading recorded from Ubayy, and since this was also an instance of *kaffāra* (expiation)?[26]

Mālik's view is clear: 'What I prefer (*aḥabbu ilayya*) is that everything that Allah mentions in His Book should be fasted consecutively.'[27] In other words, he does not see the word ***mutatābiʿātin*** as being part of the Qurʾan, since that would then mean that the judgement was obligatory. He only holds that it is preferable, as with other types of fasting where consecutiveness is not specified, such as making up days missed in Ramaḍān (as in Q 2: 184, 185), or fasting three days during *ḥajj* and seven on one's return if one cannot manage to sacrifice a *hady* (as in Q 2: 196), which are best done as soon as possible – which means consecutively – partly because that means discharging one's responsibilities sooner (*taᶜjīlan li-barāʾat al-dhimma*), partly in order to avoid matters about which there is dispute, and partly because (in the case of Ramaḍān at least) the original days are done consecutively and so it is good to make them up in the same way too.[28] So Ubayy's reading is accepted as having some validity, but not as definitive Qurʾan that would necessitate obligation.[29]

Mālik's citation of Ibn ᶜUmar's reading *fa-ṭalliqūhunna li-**qubuli** ᶜiddatihinna* comes in the 'Miscellaneous Chapter on Divorce' (*Jāmiᶜ al-ṭalāq*). It is obviously intended as a corroboration of the judgement that divorce should take place during a woman's period of purity (*ṭuhr*) and not while she is menstruating, with the further condition that the husband should not have had intercourse with her during this period of purity. This is the import of a *ḥadīth* recorded in an earlier chapter to the effect that the same Ibn ᶜUmar divorced his wife while she was menstruating whereupon he was told by the Prophet to take her back and wait until she had finished her next menstrual period and then, when she was pure again, either keep her or divorce her before having had intercourse with her, this being 'the *ᶜidda* at which Allah has commanded that women should be divorced (*fa-tilka l-ᶜidda llatī amara llāh an yuṭallaqa lahā l-nisāʾ*)',[30] referring to Q 65: 1's *fa-ṭalliqūhunna li-ᶜiddatihinna* ('divorce them at [the time of] their *ᶜidda*)'. In other words, Ibn ᶜUmar's reading (which is also related from the Prophet)[31] indicates that the standard reading of *li-ᶜiddatihinna* (lit. 'at their *ᶜidda*') is best taken to mean 'at the beginning of their *ᶜidda*',[32] i.e. at the beginning of the time when their *ᶜidda* may correctly begin, namely, when a woman has become pure again after menstruation, providing that her husband has not had intercourse with her during this period of purity. This reading, then, like the readings of ᶜUmar and Ubayy, is denied as Qurʾan but accepted as corroboration of a judgement.

As for ᶜĀisha's and Ḥafṣa's reading of *wa-l-ṣalāti l-wusṭā* ***wa-ṣalāti l-ᶜaṣr***, Mālik is firmly of the opinion that *al-ṣalāt al-wusṭā* does not refer to the prayer of *ᶜaṣr*.[33] As to what it does refer to, he makes it clear in the *Muwaṭṭaʾ* that he prefers the view of Ibn ᶜAbbās and ᶜAlī that it refers to the *ṣubḥ* prayer.[34] This view is in fact supported by ᶜĀisha's and Ḥafṣa's reading if the *wa-* ('and') is taken to indicate another, separate, item after *al-ṣalāti l-wusṭā*, as Ibn Rushd (al-Jadd) and al-Bājī both point out,[35] but obviously many felt that it indicated that the two were one and the same, as if the phrase *wa-ṣalāti l-ᶜaṣr* was an explanation of *wa-l-ṣalāti l-wusṭā*, and this indeed was the preferred view of Abū Ḥanīfa and several others, who considered this interpretation to be bolstered by the *ḥadīth* in which the Prophet referred to the *ᶜaṣr* prayer on the Day of the Trench as *al-ṣalāt al-*

wusṭā.[36] Mālik and al-Shāfiʿī, however, preferred the interpretation that *al-ṣalāt al-wusṭā* was the *ṣubḥ* prayer, partly because (for them) it was the prayer in which the *qunūt* supplication was made (the verse ends with *wa-qūmū li-llāhi qānitīn*), partly because the *ṣubḥ* prayer was the most difficult for people and the one with the highest reward and thus the most excellent of the prayers and the most worthy of being singled out for special mention, and partly because it was the most 'central' (*wusṭā*) of the (obligatory) prayers in that it came between the two night-time prayers of *maghrib* and *ʿishāʾ* and the two day-time prayers of *ẓuhr* and *ʿaṣr*, in addition to which, unlike these others, it did not share its time with any other prayer and thus could be singled out as being different from them and central with respect to them.[37] In this instance, therefore, Mālik is not so much using a reading to explain a meaning as clarifying the potentially misleading implications of that reading. He does not say definitively that it refers to *ṣubḥ*, only saying 'That is what I prefer most out of what I have heard',[38] but he feels strongly that ʿĀisha's report should not be taken to mean that *al-ṣalāt al-wusṭā* refers to *ʿaṣr*.

Similarly, he rejects the implicit judgement in ʿĀisha's reading of ***ʿashru raḍaʿātin maʿlūmātin yuḥarrimna*** that was then abrogated by ***khams(in) maʿlūmāt(in)*** by saying, 'This is not what is done here (*wa-laysa ʿalā hādhā l-ʿamal*).'[39] He accepts, however, the judgement of the stoning verse and ʿUmar's report that it used to be part of the Qurʾan, although not of course accepting that it is any longer part of the Qurʾan.[40]

We have noted that when Mālik mentions such 'non-canonical' variants he uses the verb *qaraʾa*, whereas when he introduces established Qurʾanic text he uses some variation of the formula *qāla llāhu*.[41] The clear implication of Mālik's treatment of the two types of 'Qurʾanic' citations is that there is a major difference between the two: although he might accept the judgements recorded in the *shādhdh* variants, these variants are not (or are no longer) part of the text that is to be preserved, recited and acted upon as the Qurʾan by the Muslims.

Malik's view then on the text of the Qurʾan was, as we might expect, the traditional Madinan one. What was normally recited in Madina was *sunna*, and thus preferred. Certain variants were acceptable, but only those that had the backing of *tawātur* and were in accordance with the ʿUthmānī *muṣḥafs*, such as the four non-Madinan consonantal variants in his grandfather's *muṣḥaf*. *Shādhdh* readings, though, however authentic their individual chains of authority, were not acceptable as Qurʾan and thus could not make a judgement obligatory any more than they could be used, for instance, for the obligatory recitation of the Qurʾan required in the prayer. They could, however, be cited as corroborative evidence for meaning, but by themselves they had no authority.

CHAPTER FIVE

The Qur^ʾan as a Source of Judgements in the *Muwaṭṭaʾ*

Qurʾanic reference in the *Muwaṭṭaʾ*

There are numerous references to the Qurʾan throughout the *Muwaṭṭaʾ*, both explicit and implicit. Most of these deal with the *tafsīr* of individual words or phrases but there are also several sections that deal with the Qurʾan in a more general way, and in particular with how it should be handled in formal acts of devotion such as the prayer, of which Qurʾanic recitation forms an essential part. Thus we find chapters on whether or not one must be in *wuḍūʾ* to touch or recite the Qurʾan;[1] how the Qurʾan should best be divided up in order to recite a portion every day;[2] where the verses of prostration occur;[3] how the recitation in the prayer should be done;[4] what *sūras* may be used for what prayers;[5] and so on. On a more general level, we find material on how, when and in what context the revelation took place;[6] on the excellence of certain *sūras*;[7] and the *ḥadīth* about the seven *aḥruf* according to which the Qurʾan was revealed.[8] There are, furthermore, several instances of where Companions are reported to have used specific Qurʾanic *duʿāʾs* or to have responded to particular situations by quoting relevant passages from the Qurʾan: these have no direct bearing on our subject except that they do help to confirm firstly, the form of the text at that time, and secondly, the effect that the message of the Qurʾan had on the lives of the people who first heard it.[9]

In the following chapters we shall be concerned primarily with the main bulk of references that relate to the *tafsīr* of *āyas* seen as having legal significance and which thus illustrate how Mālik derives his judgements (*aḥkām*) from the Qurʾan. In other words, we shall be looking at Mālik as *mufassir*, or interpreter, of the verses of legal import (the '*āyāt al-aḥkām*'); or, to put it another way, we shall be looking at the overlap between *tafsīr* and what later became known as *uṣūl al-fiqh* ('the principles of jurisprudence'), which is effectively the systematisation of the methods used for resolving ambiguity in, and deriving judgements from, the two-fold source of Qurʾan and *sunna*.

On a formal level, Malik's use of the Qurʾan in the *Muwaṭṭaʾ* in the sense just indicated can be broadly divided into three main types. Firstly, there are his direct citations of the Qurʾan, of which there are over fifty instances in the book. These are usually prefaced by some variant of the *qāla llāhu* ('Allah says') formula, such as *li-anna llāha tabāraka wa-taʿāla qāla* ('because Allah, the Blessed and Exalted, says'), or *dhālika anna llāha tabāraka wa-taʿāla qāla* ('that is because Allah, the Blessed and Exalted, says'), etc. In addition to these there are over thirty-five citations of this nature attributed to earlier authorities.

Secondly, and much less frequently (with some twenty or so instances altogether), there are various direct references to the Qurʾan without any actual citation of a Qurʾanic text. These are usually introduced by a formula such as *ka-mā qāla llāh* ('as Allah says'), or *ka-mā amarahu llāh* ('as Allah has told him'), or *fī kitābi llāh* ('in the book of Allah'), etc. The verses to which these phrases refer are usually self-evident from the context and would certainly have been apparent to anyone familiar with the Qurʾan, as we may assume that most of Mālik's students were.

The third type of use is that of implicit reference, where Qurʾanic phrases and concepts are freely and frequently incorporated into the text, usually without any direct acknowledgement of their source. Thus we find, for example, chapters such as 'What Has Come Down About the Two Arbiters' (*Mā jāʾa fī l-ḥakamayn*) and 'What Has Come Down About *Aqrāʾ*' (*Mā jāʾa fī l-aqrāʾ*), which clearly refer to particular words in the Qurʾan;[10] chapters such as 'What Has Come Down About the "Lowering of the Sun" and the "Darkening of the Night"' (*Mā jāʾa fī dulūk al-shams wa-ghasaq al-layl*) and 'Whatever Sacrificial Animal Is Easy' (*Mā staysara min al-hady*), which directly echo Qurʾanic phrases;[11] and chapters dealing with subjects such as inheritance, or the various types of *ʿidda*, or the prohibition against usury (*ribā*), all of which clearly deal with subjects that are mentioned because of their inclusion in the Qurʾan.[12] This type of use is extremely widespread and occurs throughout the book.

The first two types are of particular interest in that they illustrate specific details of Mālik's method in Qurʾanic interpretation. The third type, though, is by far the most pervasive, and also the most indicative of the Qurʾanic element in Islamic law. Indeed, most of the basic section- and chapter-headings into which the *Muwaṭṭaʾ* is divided come under this last type, since in the majority of instances, as we shall see in some detail in the following chapters, their subject-matter derives either directly or indirectly from the Qurʾan.

All three types of reference are also found attributed to the Prophet, the Companions and the Successors, thus providing an important chronological layering to the material. Such references may not, strictly speaking, be Mālik's own direct use of the Qur'an, but, to the extent that he has chosen to incorporate them into his book, they can also be said to be part of his use of the Qur'an in the *Muwaṭṭa'*.

In the following sections we shall, firstly, consider the problems associated with Qur'anic interpretation, and then, using examples from all three types of reference outlined above, illustrate the way in which Mālik resolves these problems of interpretation of the Qur'an in the *Muwaṭṭa'*.

The problems of Qur'anic interpretation

It is obvious from the frequency of reference to the Qur'an in the *Muwaṭṭa'* that for Mālik the Qur'an was an important source for the judgements of the law. However, it is equally obvious from the manner of treatment of these Qur'anic topics that there were major problems in using this Qur'anic material, for while some of these judgements are given in some detail, many, if not most, are referred to only in general terms, such as the obligations of doing the prayer and paying the *zakāt*[13] or the prohibition against usury,[14] or only indicated indirectly, such as the prohibition against *gharar* (transactions involving uncertainty).[15] Furthermore, although the Qur'an's language is 'clear' – it is described as being 'in a clear Arabic tongue (*bi-lisānin 'arabiyyin mubīn*)'[16] and 'a clarification of everything (*tibyānan li-kulli shay'*)'[17] – it is nevertheless in the nature of any text, indeed of language in general, to contain inherent ambiguities: it was the task of the *fuqahā'* to resolve such ambiguities in the Qur'an so that the Qur'anic commands could be put into practice as faithfully as possible.

Certain Qur'anic judgements were considered to be unambiguous and to present no particular problems of interpretation: such explicit texts were later categorised under the term *naṣṣ*, which simply means 'text'.[18] (In this and the following paragraphs the later terminology of the *uṣūlīs* is employed as a convenient framework within which to discuss this material.)

More often, however, a text would involve some sort of ambiguity. It could be that the general meaning of a word was clear, but its exact meaning in the context was not: such texts became known as *mujmal* (i.e. stated in general terms). It could be that an individual word had two or more equally plausible meanings, or an individual phrase or grammatical construction two or more equally plausible interpretations: such words or phrases became known as *mushtarak* (i.e. having more than one meaning). Where a text had one obvious meaning, although others were possible, it was said to be *ẓāhir* (lit. 'apparent', 'overt', 'obvious'); if, for good reasons, a less obvious meaning was preferred, the text was said to be *muʾawwal*, i.e. it had been subject to *taʾwīl* (interpretation).

There were also the implications (*mafhūm*) of a text: it could be that because an expressly mentioned judgement applied in certain circumstances, it would apply equally, or even more so, in similar circumstances (this became known as *mafhūm al-muwāfaqa*, or *al-mafhūm bi-l-awlā*);[19] or that because an expressly mentioned judgement applied in certain circumstances, it would not apply in the absence of those circumstances (this became known as *mafhūm al-mukhālafa*, or *dalīl al-khiṭāb*).[20]

Furthermore, there were chronological considerations: not only was it important to distinguish between the interpretations of the Prophet, the Companions, the Successors, and their Successors (the earlier source generally having the greater authority), but it was also important to distinguish, if possible, the relative chronology of the actual revelations, for which purpose the separate sciences of *naskh* ('abrogation') and *asbāb al-nuzūl* ('the occasions of revelation') came into being.

Lastly, but by no means least, were considerations of context: not merely the linguistic context of neighbouring verses, or even the complete text of the Qurʾan, but the whole context of how the Qurʾanic message was lived out in the lives of men from the time of the Prophet right up until Mālik's own day, that is, the context of *ʿamal*. Indeed, we shall see that, although Mālik deals with the problems raised by the above-mentioned systematisation (i.e. questions of *ijmāl*, *ishtirāk*, implication, etc), he does so, as with *ḥadīth*, against the ever-present background of Madinan *ʿamal*, which was clearly for him the single most important consideration in deciding exactly how the Qurʾan should be interpreted, and thus acted upon.

Given the inherent element of ambiguity in language, we must expect all texts to contain at least some degree of ambiguity, and in this respect the Qurʾan is no exception. Indeed, despite the many instances when Mālik cites what are technically *naṣṣ* texts in the sense used by the *uṣūlīs*, on only two occasions in the *Muwaṭṭaʾ* do we find Mālik citing a Qurʾanic text in such a way as to suggest that it contains a clear illustration of a judgement and that no further comment is necessary. The first is in the chapter on *ẓihār*[21] where Mālik, in order to explain the *kaffāra* (expiation) for breaking such an oath, mentions the relevant parts of Q 58: 3–4 without adding any further comment.[22] The second is in the chapter on *liʿān*[23] where, again, he cites the relevant verses (Q 24: 6–9) without any comment.[24] In both instances one has to assume that Mālik considered the verses clear enough by themselves not to warrant any comment.

However, that even such 'unambiguous' *naṣṣ* texts were in need of considerable interpretation if they were to be effectively applied in practice is amply illustrated by the same two chapters on *ẓihār* and *liʿān*. In both instances the (relatively) clear Qurʾanic provisions are cited (and are indeed the initial reason for these chapters), but in both instances the chapters contain far more material than could be derived directly from the Qurʾanic text, from which there has thus been a marked extension. By way of illustration we shall consider the first of these two examples in some detail.

Ẓihār

With regard to *ẓihār*, the Qurʾan says the following:

> Those who make an oath of *ẓihār* against their women (*wa-lladhīna yaẓẓahharūna min nisāʾihim*) and then go back against what they have said (*thumma yaʿūdūna li-mā qālū*) should free a slave before they [i.e. the husband and wife] may touch each other (*min qabli an yatamāssā*) [again] ... and whoever cannot manage to do so should fast for two consecutive months before they may touch each other [again]; and whoever is not able to do so should feed sixty poor people.[25]

This raised a number of issues for the *fuqahāʾ*. In the chapter on *ẓihār* Mālik deals with the following ten questions:

1. The basic form of the oath of *ẓihār* (which was a well-known form of divorce in the Jāhiliyya)[26] consisted of the expression *anti ʿalayya ka-ẓahri ummī* ('You are to me like my mother's back'), but did it have to include the word *umm* ('mother'), or would reference to any equivalent female relative also be considered *ẓihār*? Similarly, did it have to include the word *ẓahr* ('back'), or would reference to any equivalent part of the body be considered the same? In the *Muwaṭṭaʾ* Mālik makes it clear that reference to any female relative whom it is forbidden for the husband to marry is the same as reference to his mother;[27] while in the *Mudawwana*, Ibn al-Qāsim deduces from other judgements of Mālik that the judgements for other parts of the body would indeed be the same as for the back.[28] Both these judgements were also held by Abū Ḥanīfa and al-Shāfiʿī, but not by all authorities.[29]

2. The phrase *min nisāʾihim* obviously included wives, but was it restricted to them, as, by *ijmāʿ*, in Q 2: 226's *wa-lladhīna yuʾlūna min nisāʾihim* ('Those who make an oath of *īlāʾ* against their wives'), since *īlāʾ*[30] was a kind of divorce and thus could only apply to wives, or did it also include slave-girls? Mālik, taking the idea of *ẓihār* as a type of oath rather than a type of divorce and thus preferring the general meaning (*ʿumūm*) of the word *nisāʾ* in Q 58: 3 to *qiyās* with Q 2: 226, held that it included all women over

whom a man had sexual rights,[31] whereas Abū Ḥanīfa, al-Shāfiʿī and others held that *ẓihār* was a type of divorce, like *īlāʾ*, and thus only related to wives.[32]

3. Was *ẓihār* effective only against present wives (and slave-girls, assuming their inclusion), or against future wives as well? Mālik cites three reports to the effect that such an oath did indeed apply to the future.[33] This was also the view of Abū Ḥanīfa, but not of al-Shāfiʿī, who held that rather than being a condition that the man had imposed on himself and should thus fulfil (following the general principle that people should abide by their conditions – '*al-Muslimūna ʿalā shurūṭihim*'),[34] *ẓihār*, like *ṭalāq*, should only apply to women that a man has immediate rights over, based on a *ḥadīth* to that effect about divorce.[35]

4. Did divorce break the effect of *ẓihār* or not, so that if after doing *ẓihār* and then divorcing his wife he married her again he would have to do the *kaffāra* for *ẓihār* before consummating the second marriage? Mālik held that he should, as long as the divorce was not irrevocable,[36] whereas al-Shāfiʿī, in one view (his other view being the same as Mālik's), held that this only applied during her *ʿidda*, and that if he remarried her after her *ʿidda* was over he did not have to do the *kaffāra*,[37] while Abū Ḥanīfa held that *ẓihār* applied in any remarriage whatsoever.[38] The question here was therefore whether divorce rescinded all the judgements pertaining to the couple's married state or not: Abū Ḥanīfa was of the view that no divorce broke all such ties; Mālik was of the view that irrevocable divorce broke such ties but anything short of that did not; al-Shāfiʿī held that once any *ʿidda* period was over such ties were broken; while others (Ibn Rushd assumes them to be the Ẓāhirīs) held that any type of divorce broke such ties.[39]

5. Did the phrase *thumma yaʿūdūna li-mā qālū* refer to repeating the oath a second time, as Dāwūd and the Ẓāhirīs held, or to breaking it, as the majority said?[40] And, if the latter, what was the *ʿawd* being referred to that constituted breaking the oath? Mālik cites the relevant Qurʾanic passage and then explains that it refers to when a man makes an oath of *ẓihār* against his wife and then decides to keep her and resume full marital relations with her, at which point it is obligatory for him to do the requisite *kaffāra* before he can touch her, since he has now broken his oath. (Intention was sufficient to break this oath because actual intercourse was forbidden by the Qurʾan until the *kaffāra* had been done and thus could not be a prerequisite of the *kaffāra*). If, on the other hand, having done *ẓihār* he then divorced his wife and had no intention of taking her back again, he would not have to do any *kaffāra*, since he had not broken his oath.[41] This was also the view of Abū Ḥanīfa, who, like Mālik, based his judgement on

the fact that *ẓihār* was, in effect, a type of oath (*yamīn*) and thus needed no expiation unless it was actually broken.[42] Al-Shāfiʿī's view differed only slightly: he said that the *kaffāra* became obligatory if the man did not actually divorce his wife after doing *ẓihār*, since if he did not he was effectively accepting his married status with her, and that was tantamount to resuming sexual relations.[43] Since all the main *madhhabs* were agreed on this interpretation of the *ʿawd* being referred to, Mālik's inclusion of this explanation in the *Muwaṭṭaʾ* is presumably directed at those who might, like the Ẓāhirīs, take the phrase *yaʿūdūna li-* to indicate going back to, i.e. repeating, what they had said, rather than the less obvious meaning of going back to, i.e. doing again, what they had said they would not do, which thus meant breaking their oath.

6. If someone made an oath of *ẓihār* against more than one wife at one and the same time, did he have to do more than one *kaffāra*? Mālik held that this was only one oath, and so breaking it entailed only one *kaffāra*.[44] Abū Ḥanīfa's view, however, and that of al-Shāfiʿī, was that the man had to do a separate *kaffāra* for each wife.[45] Mālik thus likened the situation to an oath of *īlāʾ*, which was considered as only one oath regardless of how many wives were involved, whereas the other two likened it to an oath of *ṭalāq*, in which all the judgements applied for every wife divorced.[46]

Mālik similarly held that repeating an oath of *ẓihār* against the same wife also needed only one *kaffāra* (as long as the repeated oaths were repetitions of the same intention), unless the man repeated his oath after already having done the *kaffāra*, in which case he needed to do a *kaffāra* for the second oath as well, since it was a new one.[47] Again, as in the above-mentioned instance, Abū Ḥanīfa and al-Shāfiʿī said that he had to do a separate *kaffāra* for each *ẓihār*.[48]

7. If a man took back his wife and had intercourse with her before doing the *kaffāra*, did he have to do a second *kaffāra*? Mālik said that although this was a wrong action, since the Qurʾan says the *kaffāra* must be done *min qabli an yatamāssā* ('before they may touch each other'), it did not entail a second *kaffāra* since the *kaffāra* was specifically for breaking the oath of *ẓihār* and not for going against the injunctions of the Qurʾan with regard to the *kaffāra*.[49] On this point all the main *madhhabs* were agreed, because of a Prophetic directive specifying this judgement in such a situation.[50]

8. Did *ẓihār* apply to women? That is, could women make such oaths against their husbands? Mālik said that they could not, because only the husband had the right to make such a declaration, as with divorce.[51] Both al-Shāfiʿī and Abū Ḥanīfa agreed with Mālik that *ẓihār*, like *ṭalāq*, was the

prerogative of men not women, but others said that if a woman made such an oath she had to do the *kaffāra* for *ẓihār*, since *ẓihār* was a type of oath (*yamīn*) and the judgements about broken oaths applied equally to women; a few also said that she only had to do the ordinary *kaffāra* for breaking an oath (which is, by Q 5: 89, either feeding ten poor people, or clothing them, or freeing a slave, or, failing that, fasting for three days), on the basis that *ẓihār* did not apply to women whereas ordinary oaths did.[52]

9. Would the judgements for *īlā᾽* also apply in cases of *ẓihār*? In other words, was there the same four-month time limit (i.e. within which the man had to choose whether he was going to keep his wife as wife or divorce her) as there was with *īlā᾽*? Abū Ḥanīfa and al-Shāfiᶜī said that the two situations were separate,[53] whereas Mālik held that although they were normally separate, *īlā᾽* nevertheless applied if the man was intending harm to his wife by deliberately not doing the *kaffāra* even though he was in a position to do so.[54]

10. Did *ẓihār* also apply to slaves? Mālik said that it did, but that the judgements regarding the *kaffāra* were necessarily more limited. Since a slave was technically someone else's wealth[55] and so any wealth he might have was ultimately the responsibility – and property – of his master, he was not free to dispose of any wealth he might have without the permission of his master, nor could he, as a slave owned by someone else, have the *walā᾽* of any slave he might free if he could free one. He was therefore not in a position to be able to free a slave or, for that matter, feed others for the *kaffāra*; instead, his *kaffāra* was limited to fasting two consecutive months.[56] (This was also the position held by Abū Ḥanīfa and al-Shāfiᶜī, although there was a small difference between them in that Mālik – although with some reservations and only under certain circumstances – allowed a slave to feed poor people if his master allowed it, whereas the other two did not.)[57] This, however, meant that *ilā᾽* could not apply to slaves in cases of *ẓihār*, since, according to Mālik (but not Abū Ḥanīfa or al-Shāfiᶜī) the *īlā᾽* of a slave was only two months rather than four (by *qiyās* with the *ḥadd* punishments for *qadhf* and *zinā* which were reduced to half for slaves by virtue of Q 4: 25 – *fa-ᶜalayhinna nisfu mā ᶜalā l-muḥṣanāti mina l-ᶜadhāb* ['for them is half the punishment that there is for free women]'),[58] and so the end of his *īlā᾽* would come upon him before he had finished fasting the two months for his *kaffāra*.[59]

These are merely the topics mentioned in the chapter on *ẓihār* itself. Elsewhere in the *Muwaṭṭa᾽* Mālik refers to other problems connected directly with the verses in question:

11. In the chapter entitled 'Slaves Not Permitted to Be Freed for Obligatory *Kaffāras*' (*Mā lā yajūzu fī l-riqāb al-wājiba*) he points out that only

Muslim slaves should be freed for obligatory *kaffāras* (thus including the *kaffāra* for *ẓihār*). The reason usually given for this by later authorities (including as al-Shāfiʿī) is that Q 4: 92 (referring to the *kaffāra* for accidental killing) gives the same alternatives of freeing a slave or fasting for two consecutive months as do the verses detailing the *kaffāra* for *ẓihār* but specifies that the slave should be 'believing' (*raqaba mu'mina*), i.e. Muslim, and therefore one should assume that the 'slave' (*raqaba*) referred to in Q 58: 3 should also be a believing one, on the basis that if a word is unqualified in one place but qualified in another, the qualification is assumed to apply to both instances (this principle being known as *ḥaml al-muṭlaq ʿalā l-muqayyad*).[60]

However, in the immediately preceding chapter ('What Is Permissible with Regard to the Obligation of Freeing a Slave') Mālik cites a *ḥadīth* to the effect that the Prophet allowed a slave-girl to be freed for a *kaffāra* (the reason for which is not specified but which would seem by the context to be for some sort of oath) after he had verified that she was a believer (*mu'mina*), thus suggesting that the real reason for Mālik's judgement was the *sunna* rather than any linguistic technique of *ḥaml al-muṭlaq ʿalā l-muqayyad.* A further reason, which becomes clear at the end of the second of these two chapters, is that it is Muslims rather than non-Muslims who should benefit from the wealth given away in such acts of obedience to God: thus not only should slaves to be freed in such situations be Muslims, but so too should those who are to be fed, as with the recipients of *zakāt.*[61]

Al-Shāfiʿī agreed with Mālik that only Muslim slaves should be freed for *kaffāras* (although basing it on the parallel with Q 4: 92).[62] Abū Ḥanīfa, however, said that it was permissible to free any slave, whether Muslim or not, for the *kaffāra* of *ẓihār*, taking the *āya* at its face value and rejecting the validity of *ḥaml al-muṭlaq ʿalā l-muqayyad* where two different situations were involved.[63]

12. The judgement that only Muslims should be the recipients of food given away for the purposes of *kaffāra* was also shared by al-Shāfiʿī, who, like Mālik, considered the situation to be equivalent to *zakāt*, which the majority agreed should normally only be given to Muslims.[64] It was also the preferred view of Abū Ḥanīfa, although he also allowed that food for a *kaffāra* could be given to non-Muslims living within the Muslim community (i.e. the *ahl al-dhimma*), since the important thing was that the man doing the *kaffāra* fed someone, and the Qur'an did not forbid acts of kindness (*mabarra*) towards non-Muslims in general but only to those who were at war with the Muslims (*ahl al-ḥarb*).[65]

13. In the chapter on 'How *Zakāt al-Fiṭr* is Measured', Mālik states that, contrary to the practice with the other types of *kaffāra* and the *zakāt*

on foodstuffs, the *kaffāra* for *ẓihār* should be measured using the larger *mudd*, or *mudd* of Hishām,[66] this usually being considered equivalent to either one and two-thirds or two *mudds* going by the smaller *mudd*, or *mudd* of the Prophet.[67] According to al-Bājī, this did not mean that a different type of *mudd* was being used just for this one particular judgement, but that the amount for the *kaffāra* was two (or one and two-thirds) *mudds* per person if going by the smaller *mudd*.[68] This was different to the amount for the *kaffāra* for a broken oath (*kaffārat al-yamīn*) because the latter is mentioned in the Qur'an with the specific wording that the amount be average, i.e. *min awsaṭi mā tuṭʿimūna ahlīkum* ('from the average of that with which you feed your family') (Q 5: 89), whereas the *kaffāra* for *ẓihār* is mentioned unconditionally, and should therefore be greater than the average amount (*awsaṭ*) to ensure that enough food is given to each person to satisfy his hunger.[69]

Al-Shāfiʿī held that the amount should be one *mudd* per person, while Abū Ḥanīfa held that it should be two *mudds*, each going by what he considered to be the correct measurement for the *kaffārat al-yamīn*,[70] the difference in these judgements being the result of a difference in interpretation of the *awsaṭ* phrase mentioned above: did it refer to an average meal (one *mudd*) or an average day's food, i.e. a morning meal and an evening meal (two *mudds*)?[71] There were other reasons for these judgements: equating the *kaffārat al-yamīn* with the *kaffāra* for breaking the fast in Ramaḍān would suggest one *mudd* per person, while equating it with the *kaffārat al-adhā* for shaving the head, etc, during *ḥajj* would suggest two *mudds* per person.[72]

Finally, there were certain points raised directly by the *āya* which Mālik does not mention in the *Muwaṭṭa'* but does refer to elsewhere. Among these we may briefly mention the following three issues:

14. The Qur'an says that both freeing a slave and fasting for two consecutive months by way of *kaffāra* for *ẓihār* should be done *min qabli an yatamāssā* ('before they touch each other'). For both Mālik and Abū Ḥanīfa any type of sexual contact was considered to be included under *yatamāssā*, whereas for al-Shāfiʿī the meaning was restricted solely to sexual intercourse; indeed, Mālik even held that the man should avoid lying in the same bed as his wife until he had done the *kaffāra*, this being an example of going by *sadd al-dharā'iʿ* as well as by the *ʿumūm*.[73]

15. The Qur'an specifies that if someone cannot either free a slave or fast two months, he should feed sixty poor people. Mālik and al-Shāfiʿī, going by the *ẓāhir* of the *āya*, held that this number was essential, whereas Abū Ḥanīfa, allowing *qiyās*, said that it was enough to feed a single individual sixty times.[74]

16. Although the Qur'an specifies that both freeing a slave and fasting two consecutive months should be completed 'before they touch each other', the option of feeding sixty poor people is mentioned in an unqualified way. Did, therefore, the option of feeding have to be completed before the couple resumed normal marital relations or did it not matter when the feeding took place? Most of the *fuqahā'*, including Mālik, Abū Ḥanīfa and al-Shāfiʿī, said that this feeding should be completed before the resumption of marital relations, like the other two options (i.e. by *ḥaml al-muṭlaq ʿalā l-muqayyad*), whereas some authorities, such as the 5th-century Ẓāhirī scholar Ibn Ḥazm, said that if someone was doing the *kaffāra* of feeding it did not matter whether he had intercourse with his wife before completing his *kaffāra* or not.[75]

Of all the *naṣṣ* texts in the Qur'an, perhaps none are considered more detailed and thus less ambiguous than the verses on inheritance, and Mālik's method of interpretation, showing the link between the Qur'an and the judgements of *fiqh*, is nowhere better illustrated than in the section on inheritance. The first five chapters of this section deal specifically with details of the law of inheritance that derive directly from the Qur'an, covering the inheritance due to children, husbands and wives, parents, uterine brothers and sisters, and full brothers and sisters respectively. In each of these chapters Mālik follows the same format: he first announces the nature of the *ʿamal* on the particular point, then states in detail what that *ʿamal* is, and then ends each chapter by quoting the relevant Qur'anic *āya* as justification for what he has said, using the formula *wa-dhālika anna llāha tabāraka wa-taʿālā qāla/yaqūlu fī kitābihi* ... ('This is because Allah ... says in His Book ...').[76]

This formula suggests at first glance that the foregoing material derives directly from the verse in question. However, this is true only up to a certain point: not only do the texts themselves present certain ambiguities, but there are gaps that need to be filled in since the verses only cover the basic rules. What this claim of Qur'anic justification must mean therefore is that the judgements have been worked out in this way not so much because of the details of the verses as because of their very existence. In other words, once the basic judgements of the verses are put into practice, the details necessarily have to be worked out.

The first of these five chapters, that of the inheritance of children of the deceased, will serve as an illustration of Mālik's method.

The inheritance due to children

Q 4: 11 states: 'Allah commands you with regard to your children: a male has the same as the portion of two females (*li-l-dhakari mithlu haẓẓi l-unthayayn*). If they [i.e. the children] are women, [and there are] more than two, they have two-thirds of what he [i.e. their father] leaves; if there is only one, she has half.' Mālik begins his chapter by echoing this *āya*, saying that 'if a man or a woman dies, leaving both male and female children, a male has the same as the portion of two females. If they are women, [and there are] more than two, they have two-thirds of what he leaves; if there is only one, she has half.'[77]

From this point on, he goes beyond the text. Firstly, he explains that proportional shares due to the presence of a son are always distributed after any fixed shares (such as those of a parent, husband or wife), if these apply. Secondly, he points out that if there are no immediate sons, grandchildren through a son are treated as sons and inherit accordingly, but if there is an immediate son, grandchildren do not inherit. Thirdly, he points out that if there are no sons but there are two or more daughters, grand-daughters through a son may inherit (along with the daughters) as long as they have a brother with them, in which case anything that is left over after the fixed shares have been apportioned is divided between them on the basis of Q 4: 11's 'a male has the same as the portion of two females'; if, however, there is nothing left over, they receive nothing. If, on the other hand, there is only one daughter among the immediate children, she receives a half, and any grand-daughters through a son receive a sixth if they have no brother with them (thus completing the two-thirds due to two or more daughters);[78] if they have a brother with them, they do not receive a fixed portion but share between them any excess on the basis of 'a male has the same as the portion of two females'. Finally, he concludes the chapter by saying that all of the above judgements are 'because Allah ... says in His Book: "Allah commands you with regard to your children ... etc."'

We can thus see how a number of extensions have been made from the text: firstly, there is the principle that fixed shares are apportioned first; secondly, that grandchildren through a son are considered the same as immediate children in the absence of any immediate children; thirdly, there are the ramifications of who inherits what when the deceased leaves both children and grandchildren.

The basic Qurʾanic judgements were agreed upon by all the *fuqahāʾ*, precisely because of their being mentioned unambiguously in the Qurʾan. So too was the principle that fixed shares should be apportioned before proportional shares, because of a Prophetic directive to that effect.[79] The judgement that only grandchildren through a son (and not through a daughter) could inherit in the absence of any immediate children, however, was a point of dispute. The Madinans, following the view attributed to Abū Bakr and Zayd ibn Thābit (and followed by both Mālik and al-Shāfiʿī), held that only grandchildren through the male line could inherit, whereas the Iraqis, following the view attributed to ʿAlī and Ibn Masʿūd (and followed by Abū Ḥanīfa), considered that grandchildren through both the male and female line could inherit.[80] The reasoning behind the Madinan position was said to be the fact that there was no clear indication of such a judgement in either the Qur'an, the *sunna* or *ijmāʿ*, and judgements about inheritance, for which there were such detailed provisions, should not be subject to *qiyās*, and while all agreed on the inclusion of a son's children, not all agreed about a daughter's children.[81] The Iraqis for their part held that the verse *wa-ulū l-arḥāmi baʿḍuhum awlā bi-baʿḍ* ('Those related by blood are nearer to one another') (Q 8: 75) indicated that blood relatives of whatever sort had a right to inheritance;[82] there was also a *ḥadīth* to the effect that a maternal uncle could inherit when there was no other inheritor, as well as the consideration that two connections – blood relationship and Islam – gave more right to inheritance than simply the single connection of Islam (in the absence of any relatives to inherit from him, a dead man's estate would, according to Mālik, go to the *bayt al-māl*, i.e. to the Muslims in general).[83]

There were other, less widespread, disagreements: Abū Thawr and Dāwūd were of the opinion that if the deceased left daughters and grandchildren but no immediate sons, the daughters received two-thirds and the rest went to the grandsons only and not the grand-daughters, on the basis of the *ḥadīth*, 'Divide up property between the rightful heirs (*ahl al-farā'iḍ*) according to the Book of Allah, and whatever is left over should go to the nearest male relative.'[84] There was also the problem of whether grandsons would affect others' inheritance in the same way as sons: thus while the majority, as we have seen, considered that in the absence of sons grandsons through a son were like sons and could thus reduce the portion due to a husband or wife, Mujāhid is reported to have held that the presence of a grandchild did not have this effect.[85]

Even these points did not exhaust the ambiguities of the verse: both a single daughter and three or more daughters are mentioned in the Qur'an, but what if there were only two daughters? Would they take two-thirds, as would three or more daughters, or a half, as would a single daughter? Ibn ʿAbbās is recorded as having said that two daughters receive only a half, while the majority held that they should share two-thirds, partly because two sisters would share two-thirds between them by Q 4: 176 (*fa-lahumā l-thuluthāni mimmā tarak* – 'the two of them have two-thirds of what he leaves'), partly because a single daughter alongside a single son would receive a third and so should have even more right to a third with a second daughter, and partly because two uterine sisters would receive the same portion as three or more by Q 4: 12 (*wa-in kāna rajulun yūrathu kalālatan awi mraʾatun wa-lahu akhun aw ukhtun fa-li-kulli wāḥidin minhumā l-sudus; fa-in kānū akthara min dhālika fa-hum shurakāʾu fī l-thuluth* – 'If a man is inherited from by way of *kalāla*[86] – or a woman – and he has a brother or a sister, each of them has a sixth; if there are more than that, they share a third between them'), and so two or more daughters should be treated in the same way; there was, furthermore, a *ḥadīth* to the same effect.[87]

The latter judgement is not mentioned in the *Muwaṭṭaʾ*, but we find a similar ambiguity dealt with in the third of the five above-mentioned inheritance chapters. There was general agreement that if a man died leaving brothers and/or sisters, his mother's portion would be reduced from a third to a sixth because of the verse *fa-in kāna lahu ikhwatun fa-li-ummihi l-sudus* ('If he has brothers, his mother has a sixth') (Q 4: 11). However, since Arabic has a dual, and the word *ikhwa* is a plural, did the word *ikhwa* indicate that there needed to be a minimum of three brothers and/or sisters before the mother's portion was reduced, or would two also have the same effect? The majority held that *ikhwa* could be used for two or more, rather than necessarily three, which later became standardised as the principle that 'the least plural is two' (*aqall al-jamᶜ ithnān*). Once again, it is Ibn ᶜAbbās who is said to have opposed this view and held that the minimum for a plural was three.[88] Mālik's inclusion of this judgement shows that he was aware of dispute on the matter, but he clearly upholds the dominant view, saying, 'The *sunna* has been established (*maḍat al-sunna*) that *ikhwa* refers to two or more.'[89] Al-Qarāfī states that according to Mālik the 'least plural' is two, whereas Abū Ḥanīfa and al-Shāfiᶜī say it is three.[90] Nevertheless, all three agreed on the above judgement that two brothers reduce the mother's share to a sixth.[91]

Tadbīr versus debts

Another instance where a number of detailed judgements are justified by a verse of very general import even more clearly demonstrates the place that *ᶜamal* took in Mālik's interpretation of the Qurʾan. In the chapter entitled 'Injury Caused by a *Mudabbar*' (*Jirāḥ al-mudabbar*),[92] Mālik mentions a decision (*qaḍāʾ*) of ᶜUmar ibn ᶜAbd al-ᶜAzīz that if a *mudabbar* slave causes an injury for which blood-money is due, the slave's master may, if he wants, allow the slave to work for the victim (*ṣāḥib al-jarḥ*) until he has paid off the blood-money that is owed, whereupon he returns to his master as before.[93] (The other option is that the master pays off the blood-money owed and retains his slave. He may not sell the slave to pay off the debt because a *mudabbar* slave cannot be sold.)[94] Mālik then explains that the practice in Madina (*al-amr ʿindanā*) is that if a *mudabbar* slave causes an injury for which blood-money is due, and his master then dies leaving no wealth other than that slave, only a third of the slave is considered free by virtue of the *tadbīr* arrangement (whereas normally a *mudabbar* slave would, by definition, become free on his master's death), since *tadbīr* is considered a type of bequest (*waṣiyya*) and, by the *sunna*, bequests can only ever take up a maximum of a third of a man's estate.[95] The responsibility for paying the blood-money then devolves partly on the slave, who is resposible for a third since he is now a third free, and partly on the inheritors, who still own two-thirds of the slave and are thus responsible for two-thirds of the blood-money. If the inheritors want, they can, as in the first instance, allow the victim to benefit from the labour of the slave until their two-thirds portion of the blood-money is paid off, or, if they want, they may pay off what they owe and retain the use of their portion in the slave. This, Mālik says, is because the injury is a crime committed by the slave and not a debt owed by the master, and therefore does not affect the *tadbīr* arrangement that the master has made. It is not the master's direct responsibility and therefore should not affect his *waṣiyya*, which remains valid up to a third of his estate.

If, however, in addition to the blood-money that is owed the master owes a debt, the situation is different, since debts are to be paid off before any bequests come into effect, but the blood-money takes precedence over any debts. Accordingly, the slave is sold to the extent that is necessary to pay off first the blood-money (owed by the slave) and then the debt (owed by his master), after which whatever is left of the value of the slave is divided up between the slave and the inheritors, a third of it representing the master's *waṣiyya*, to which extent the *mudabbar* is now free, and the other two-thirds being the portion of the inheritors.

Mālik illustrates this by the following example: if a man dies leaving a *mudabbar* slave worth 150 dinars who has inflicted a *mūḍiḥa* (head) wound on a free man – for which the blood-money is 50 dinars – and the master also owes a debt of 50 dinars, 50 dinars' worth of the slave should be sold to pay off the blood-money and another 50 dinars' worth sold to pay off the master's debt. Of the remaining third of the slave's value, one third (i.e. one-ninth of the total value) becomes free while the other two-thirds (i.e. one-sixth of the total value) goes to the inheritors. Mālik explains:

> Thus the blood-money owed by the slave takes precedence over the debt owed by his master, and the debt owed by his master takes precedence over the *tadbīr* arrangement, which is considered as a bequest (*waṣiyya*) and is thus subject to the limit [for bequests] of one-third of the dead man's estate. It is not correct (*lā yanbaghī*) for any *mudabbar* slave to become free while there is still a debt owed by his master that has not been paid. This is because Allah, the Blessed and Exalted, says: 'After a bequest that he makes (*yūṣī bi-hā*), or a debt.'[96] If one-third of the master's estate encompasses the value of the *mudabbar* slave, the slave becomes free and the blood-money for the injury he has caused becomes a debt which, as a free man, he is then responsible for, even if it is a question of paying the full blood-money, as long as his master does not owe any money.[97]

Thus, although *tadbīr* is a special type of *waṣiyya* that cannot normally be altered,[98] nevertheless it is still a *waṣiyya* and so can never exceed one-third of the dead man's estate, this third being calculated, as Mālik makes clear, *after* any debt that is owed by his master has been paid off. The difference between the two situations was thus that if the master died leaving no debts, the payment of the indemnity for the injury caused by the slave devolved on the slave and the inheritors, i.e. with the dead man's *waṣiyya* (in this case, the *tadbīr*) having come into effect, whereas if the master died leaving a debt, the payment of the blood-money devolved on the master rather than the slave and the inheritors, because his *waṣiyya* – which would result in the slave being partly free and partly owned by the inheritors – could not come into effect until the master's debt was paid off, which is why Mālik connects the whole situation to the Qurʾanic *āya* 'after a bequest that he makes, or a debt'. However, although Mālik justifies these judgements by quoting this *āya*, we can see that there are a number of details that have been supplied between the text and the judgements that it is being used to justify. Again, as in the case of inheritance due to children, this was a necessary corollary of putting the verse into practice. In this instance, the priority between the various claims on the master's wealth obviously had to be established, especially since *tadbīr* was normally an irreversible arrangement. Since the master's *tadbīr* agreement with his slave was his own personal arrangement regarding his own wealth, and thus was in the nature of a bequest even if it did not share all the characteristics of ordinary bequests (which are reversible), and since debts always took precedence over bequests (since bequests related to what a man wished to do with his own wealth, assuming he had it, while what he owed was not his to do with as he pleased), so too did they take precedence over the 'bequest' of *tadbīr*.

All of this was, for Mālik, clearly subsumed, by his knowledge and experience of the *ʿamal* on this point, under the phrase 'after a bequest that he makes, or a debt', even though the phrase itself did not contain these details.

These three examples – of *ẓihār*, the inheritance due to children and *tadbīr versus* debts – demonstrate the considerable ambiguity and need for interpretation even in the most seemingly straightforward texts. We now turn to a more detailed consideration of the various techniques used to resolve these ambiguities, some of which have already been alluded to in the above-mentioned examples.

CHAPTER SIX

Techniques of Qur᾿anic Interpretation in the *Muwaṭṭa᾿*

We have seen in the last chapter how Mālik's interpretation of the Qur᾿an is very much tempered by Madinan *ʿamal*. Nevertheless, despite this reliance on *ʿamal*, it is possible to identify a number of techniques that Mālik uses to interpret the Qur᾿an. In particular we may note the following two major assumptions:

Firstly, words are understood initially in their most inclusive sense (*ʿumūm*). In other words, all items subsumed under the class indicated by a particular word or phrase are understood to be included in that word or phrase, unless there is clear evidence to the contrary. Since this attitude also implies taking the overt, literal (*ẓāhir*) meaning of a word or phrase as the intended meaning, we find later theorists equating the *ẓāhir* of the Qur᾿an with its *ʿumūm*.[1]

Secondly, words are understood initially to have the same meaning in one place of the Qur᾿an as in another. In other words, there is an assumed underlying unity to the vocabulary of the Qur᾿an. This assumption is reflected in the prevalent tendency to explain the Qur᾿an by the Qur᾿an (*tafsīr al-Qur᾿ān bi-l-Qur᾿ān*), which we find used not only to define the meanings of particular words but also to derive judgements by deduction.

To both these assumptions there were, of course, many exceptions. Exceptions to the first category come under the (albeit later) headings of *takhṣīṣ al-ʿumūm*, i.e. restriction of the general sense, and *ta᾿wīl al-ẓāhir*, i.e. preferring a less obvious meaning, while exceptions to the second come under considerations of *ijmāl* and *ishtirāk*, i.e. the acknowledgement of more than one possible meaning to a single term. Furthermore, it was of course possible not only to make exceptions to these rules but also to make extensions from them, in particular by *qiyās* (analogy) and the techniques of *mafhūm al-muwāfaqa* and *mafhūm al-mukhālafa*, i.e. considerations of the implications of the text.

Using examples from the *Muwaṭṭa᾿*, we shall both illustrate these assumptions and consider the means by which either exceptions and/or extensions were made to the basic Qur᾿anic texts.

The assumption of inclusion (*ʿumūm*) and literal meaning (*ẓāhir*)

1. The assumption of inclusion is overtly expressed in the *Muwaṭṭa'* in the section on *iʿtikāf*. Mālik points out that it is acceptable to do *iʿtikāf* in any mosque – and not just a Jumuʿa mosque – provided that the intended period does not include a Jumuʿa prayer since that would then mean having to break the *iʿtikāf* in order to be present elsewhere for the Jumuʿa prayer. He says:

> The position here about which there is no dispute (*al-amr ʿindanā lladhī lā khtilāfa fī-hi*) is that there is no disapproval of anyone doing *iʿtikāf* in a mosque in which the Jumuʿa is done. And in my opinion the only reason why *iʿtikāf* is disapproved of in mosques where the Jumuʿa is not done is that it is disapproved of both for a man to leave the mosque where he is doing *iʿtikāf* in order to go to the Jumuʿa, and for him to forego the Jumuʿa. If the mosque is one where the Jumuʿa is not done, and there is no obligation for the man to go to the Jumuʿa in another mosque, I see no harm in him doing *iʿtikāf* there, because Allah, the Blessed and Exalted, says, 'While you are doing *iʿtikāf* in mosques (*fī l-masājid*).'[2] Allāh has thus included all mosques (*fa-ʿamma llāh al-masājid kullahā*) and not specified any particular type (*wa-lam yakhuṣṣa shay'an minhā*). For this reason it is permissible for someone to do *iʿtikāf* in a mosque where the Jumuʿa is not done as long as he does not have to leave it in order to go to another mosque where it is done.[3]

Thus the initial assumption, going by the *ʿumūm* of the *āya*, is that *iʿtikāf* can be done in any mosque; this *ʿumūm* is then restricted by the command to go to the Jumuʿa (Q 62: 9).

That *iʿtikāf* could be done in any mosque was also the view of the majority of the *fuqahā'*, including Abū Ḥanīfa and al-Shāfiʿī, but whereas al-Shāfiʿī said that *iʿtikāf* in a non-Jumuʿa mosque should not include a Jumuʿa, since leaving for the Jumuʿa prayer would in his view break *iʿtikāf*, Abū Ḥanīfa held that leaving such a mosque in order to go to the Jumuʿa did not break *iʿtikāf* and was thus permissible.[4] Some earlier authorities – among them the Madinan Saʿīd ibn al-Musayyab – even restricted *iʿtikāf* to the two mosques of Makka and Madina or the three mosques of Makka, Madina and Jerusalem,[5] but this view was never generally accepted and did not survive long, and is thus an instance of later agreement on a point where earlier there had been dispute.

2. In the chapter on *liʿān*, Mālik states the Madinan position that a wife of unequal legal status to her husband nevertheless has the right to do *liʿān* against him:

> A Muslim slave-girl or a free Christian or Jewish woman may do *liʿān* against a free Muslim man if he is married to such a woman and has consummated his marriage with her. This is because Allah, the Blessed and Exalted, says, 'And those who accuse their wives (*azwājahum*) . . .'[6] and these women are wives. This is the position here (*wa-ʿalā hādhā l-amr ʿindanā*).[7]

The *ʿamal* is thus that 'wives' includes all wives, whatever their legal or religious status. He also clarifies in the same chapter that it does not matter either whether the husband is of free or slave status (although he would have to be Muslim since Muslim women could not be married to non-Muslim men and cases between non-Muslims fell outside the jurisdiction of the *sharīʿa*).[8] Thus, for Mālik, *liʿān* is a valid procedure between any married couple.[9]

Al-Shāfiʿī agreed with this judgement, but Abū Ḥanīfa held that only those acceptable as witnesses, i.e. free, *ʿadl*, Muslims, could participate in *liʿān*, since the verse in question (Q 24: 6) refers to the participants as having to bear witness (*fa-shahādatu aḥadihim arbaʿa shahādātin* . . . – 'one of them should bear witness four times . . .') and thus *liʿān* is a type of *shahāda* rather than merely an oath (*yamīn*).[10] Furthermore, he held that *liʿān* should only apply between couples whose accusations would otherwise be considered *qadhf*, i.e. who were both free and Muslim, since the *liʿān* verses (Q 24: 6ff – 'those who accuse their wives (*wa-lladhīna yarmūna azwājahum*) . . . etc') were a specific exception for married couples to the verses detailing the penalty for *qadhf* (Q 24: 4f – 'those who accuse *muḥṣanāt* women (*wa-lladhīna yarmūna l-muḥṣanāt*) . . . etc'), and it was universally agreed that *muḥṣanāt* in this instance referred to free, Muslim, women – and by extension free, Muslim, men – thus excluding slaves and non-Muslims.[11] The majority, however, held to the *ʿumūm* of the *āya*: 'wives' meant what it said. As for the claim that *liʿān* was a type of *shahāda*, that was seen as invalidated by the Qurʾan itself: in Q 63: 1 the hypocrites are referred to as 'bearing witness' only to be followed in the next verse by a description of their words as 'oaths' (*aymān*), thus disproving the '*shahāda*' argument.[12]

However, although slave-girl wives were definitely included in the word 'wives' (*azwāj*) by the Madinans, there was some dispute among them as to the position of *umm walads*[13] in this respect. There is a report in the *Muwaṭṭaʾ* that al-Qāsim ibn Muḥammad, when he heard that the caliph Yazīd ibn ʿAbd al-Malik had ordered that *umm walads* whose masters had died should observe the four-month ten-day *ʿidda* that the Qurʾan prescribes for widows, said: '*Subḥāna llāh!* Allah says in His Book, "Those among you who die and leave wives (*azwājan*) . . . ."[14] These are not wives!'[15] Thus the word *azwāj* was understood in its general meaning to include all wives, but extension from it (by *qiyās*) to include *umm walads*, who, although free after their master's death, were nevertheless not his wives, was rejected. However, despite this majority judgement (it is ascribed to Mālik, al-Shāfiʿī, Ibn Ḥanbal, al-Layth and Abū Thawr, and, before them, to al-Shaʿbī, Abū Qilāba and Ibn ʿUmar, as well as al-Qāsim ibn Muḥammad),[16] certain Madinan authorities, notably Saʿīd ibn al-Musayyab and Ibn Shihāb (as also ʿUmar ibn ʿAbd al-ʿAzīz, whose Madinan connections are well known),[17] are said to have held that the *ʿidda* of an *umm walad* whose master has died is four months and ten days, like that of a free widow.[18] The generally held Iraqi view (ascribed to Abū Ḥanīfa, al-Thawrī and, before them, to Ibrāhīm al-Nakhaʿī, ʿAlī and Ibn Masʿūd) was that, since the *umm walad* is now free but not a wife, she should observe neither the four-month ten-day *ʿidda* of a free woman whose husband has died nor the *istibrāʾ* (waiting-period) of one menstrual period of a slave-girl whose master has died, but, rather, the ordinary *ʿidda* of a free divorcee, i.e. three menstrual periods (*qurūʾ*).[19] There was also the view that since her original status was that of a slave-girl but her situation after her master's death was in many respects similar to that of a wife whose husband has died, she should observe the *ʿidda* of a widowed slave-wife, which was half that of a free widow, i.e. two months and five days.[20] The existence in Madina of more than one opinion on this point – even if not all of the above-mentioned possibilities – would seem reflected in Mālik's description of al-Qāsim's judgement as '*al-amr ʿindanā*',[21] which, as we have noted above, is an expression which generally indicates a dominant position among other possibilities.[22]

Similarly, the word *nisāʾ* in the verse on *ẓihār* (Q 58: 3 – *wa-lladhīna yaẓẓahharūna min nisāʾihim*) was, as we have seen, understood by Mālik to include slave-girls as well as wives, since for him *ẓihār* was a type of oath *vis-à-vis* a man's sexual rights rather than a type of divorce, and thus a general interpretation of the word *nisāʾ* to include anyone over whom a man had sexual rights was more appropriate in this instance than the specific meaning of 'wives' in Q 2: 226's *wa-lladhīna yuʾlūna min nisāʾihim*; whereas Abū Ḥanīfa, al-Shāfiʿī and others held that *ẓihār*, like *īlāʾ*, was a type of divorce, and thus related only to wives.[23]

However, although for *ẓihār* Mālik takes the word *nisāʾ* to refer to women in general, elsewhere he does seemingly understand it to refer specifically to wives. He speaks, for instance, of how if a man marries a woman and then also marries her mother and consummates that marriage with her, both marriages are null and void and both women are from then on *ḥarām* for him for ever (by Q 4: 23 – *wa-ummahātu nisāʾikum wa-rabāʾibukumu llātī fī ḥujūrikum min nisāʾikumu llātī dakhaltum bi-hinna*).[24] Furthermore, not only are both women *ḥarām* for him, but they are also *ḥarām* for his father (by Q 4: 23 – *wa-ḥalāʾilu abnāʾikumu lladhīna min aṣlābikum* ['and the wives of sons from your own loins']) and for his sons (by Q 4: 22 – *wa-lā tankiḥū mā nakaḥa ābāʾukum mina l-nisāʾ* ['Do not marry those women your fathers have married']).[25] None of these prohibitions apply, however, to illicit liaisons outside marriage (i.e. *zinā*) because, Mālik says,

> Allah, the Blessed and Exalted, says, *wa-ummahātu nisāʾikum* [lit. 'and the mothers of your women'] and has thus only made *ḥarām* what occurs through marriage (*mā kāna tazwījan*) without mentioning *zinā* ... This is what I have heard, and this is the practice of people here (*hādhā lladhī samiʿtu wa-lladhī ʿalayhi amr al-nās ʿindanā*).[26]

Thus the word *nisāʾ* here is taken to refer specifically to wives rather than to women in general.

This was also the position of the majority of the rest of the *fuqahāʾ* but not that of Abū Ḥanīfa, who held that *nakaḥa* in Q 4: 22 referred not so much to marriage, and thus to *ḥalāl* intercourse within marriage, as to intercourse in general (*al-waṭʾ*), whether *ḥalāl* or otherwise, thus preferring, as Ibn Rushd puts it, the basic meaning (*dalāla lughawiyya*) of the word rather than its usual meaning in the *sharīʿa* (*dalāla sharʿiyya*).[27]

Mālik goes on to expand upon the Madinan view using another verse from the Qurʾan to support his argument:

> If a man commits *zinā* with a woman and is punished accordingly, he may marry her daughter, and his son may marry the woman herself, if he wants. This is because he has had intercourse with her in a *ḥarām* way and Allah has only forbidden marriage [i.e. of a man to his father's wife or her mother or daughter, or to his son's wife or her mother or daughter] where the man has had intercourse with the woman within a correct, or seemingly correct, marriage (*mā uṣība bi-l-ḥalāl aw ʿalā wajh al-shubha bi-l-nikāḥ*). Allah, the Blessed and Exalted, says: 'Do not marry those women your fathers have married (*wa-lā tankiḥū mā nakaḥa ābāʾukum mina l-nisāʾ*).'[28]

Thus the word *nisāʾ* is taken in this instance also to refer to wives, and *nakaḥa* to marriage.

However, it is clear from the prohibition in the chapter entitled 'The Prohibition Against a Man Having Intercourse with a Slave-Girl that Used to Belong to His Father' that the *mā nakaḥa ābāʾukum mina l-nisāʾ* phrase, although not extended to include *zinā*, was understood to refer equally, by *qiyās*, to a man's slave-girls, regardless of whether or not they were also his wives.[29] Thus, even though *nisā'* is glossed as 'wives', the distinction is not so much between wives as opposed to all other women, as between women over whom a man has sexual rights and those over whom he does not.[30]

The similarity between free women and slaves in this respect is further apparent in the chapter entitled 'What Has Come Down About Having Intercourse with Two Slave-Girl Sisters, or a Mother and Her Daughter, by Virtue of Ownership' where Mālik clearly supports the view that slave-girls are like free women with respect to the combinations of women that a man may be married to at any one time, the only difference being that whereas he is restricted to only four wives, there is no restriction on the number of slave-girls he may have.[31]

3. 'Killing game' in Q 5: 95 – *lā taqtulū l-ṣayda wa-antum ḥurum* ('Do not kill game while you are in *iḥrām*') – is taken in a general sense to refer to any killing of game by a *muḥrim*, regardless of whether he hunts it and kills it himself, or buys it and then kills it, or catches it while he is *ḥalāl* and then kills it after going into *iḥrām*. Mālik says:

> Allah, the Blessed and Exalted, says: 'O you who believe, do not kill game while you are in *iḥrām*. Whoever among you kills it deliberately [must pay] a recompense of the like of what he has killed in domestic livestock, which two just men among you should decide, as a sacrificial offering (*hady*) to reach the Kaᶜba, or [make] an expiation of feeding poor people, or the equivalent of that in fasting, so that he may taste the evil of his doing (*wabāla amrihi*).'[32] Thus someone who hunts game while he is *ḥalāl* and then kills it while in *iḥrām* is like someone who buys it while he is in *iḥrām* and then kills it: Allah has prohibited its being killed, and so he has to pay a recompense.[33]

Similarly, the word *ṣayd* ('game') in Q 5: 94 – *la-yabluwannakumu llāhu bi-shay'in mina l-ṣaydi tanāluhu aydīkum wa-rimāḥukum* ('Allah will most surely test you with a certain amount of game that you will take with your hands and your spears') – is interpreted broadly as anything that is caught and killed in any way, regardless of the animal's size and regardless of the weapon used to kill it – as long as the weapon penetrates one of the animal's vital organs (*maqātil*) so that Q 5: 3's prohibited category of *al-mawqūdha* ('that which is killed by a blow') is avoided. Mālik says:

> I see no harm in eating what has been killed by a throwing-stick (*miᶜrāḍ*) if it penetrates and reaches one of the vital organs. Allah, the Blessed and Exalted, says, 'O you who believe, Allah will surely test

> you with a certain amount of game that you will take with your hands and your spears', and so everything that a man takes either with his hand or his spear or with any other weapon – as long as it penetrates a vital organ – is game, as Allah says.[34]

Thus the word 'game' includes anything that is hunted and caught, regardless of the weapon and/or method used, as long as the animal is killed in a correct manner.[35]

This judgement also shows well the connection between the *ʿumūm* of a phrase and the extension from it by *qiyās*: the *ʿumūm* is indicated by the word 'everything' in the phrase 'everything that a man takes either with his hand or his spear', while the extension by *qiyās* is in the addition of the words 'or with any other weapon'.

4. The word 'horses' (*khayl*) as it occurs in the Qurʾan is taken to include mixed-breed horses (*al-barādhīn wa-l-hujun*) as well as thoroughbred Arab horses (*al-ʿirāb*); such horses are therefore due the same portion as thoroughbreds when the spoils of war are divided up. Mālik says:

> Non-thoroughbred horses (*al-barādhīn wa-l-hujun*) are considered horses (*khayl*) because Allah, the Blessed and Exalted, says in His Book, 'And horses, mules and donkeys, for you to ride and as an adornment',[36] and He, the Noble and Majestic, also says, 'And prepare for them what you can of force and tethered horses to frighten thereby the enemy of Allah and your enemy',[37] and so I think (*arā*) that non-thoroughbred horses are included in [the word] *khayl*, if the governor (*wālī*) allows them [i.e. to be used for *jihād*]. Furthermore, Saʿīd ibn al-Musayyab said, when asked whether there was any *zakāt* on mixed-breed horses (*barādhīn*), 'Is there any *zakāt* on horses (*khayl*)?'[38]

In other words, since mules and donkeys are mentioned alongside *khayl* in the first *āya*, one can assume a general meaning of *khayl* to cover any type of horse. Therefore, on the assumption of underlying unity to the vocabulary of the Qurʾan, the *khayl* in the second *āya* may also be assumed to refer to all types of horses, and, accordingly, mixed-breeds should receive the same share as thoroughbreds when they are used for the same purpose in *jihād*. This, again, was the view of the majority, although there were some dissenters who felt that this was not a fair comparison, since the performance of *barādhīn* was not up to that of pure Arab horses and that their share should therefore be less.[39]

There is further confirmation of this 'general' interpretation of the term *khayl* as it occurs in the second *āya* in the section entitled 'The

Encouragement to Do *Jihād*' where Mālik mentions a *ḥadīth* in which the Prophet speaks of the different merits of horses with regard to *jihād* and is then asked about donkeys, to which he replies, 'Nothing has been revealed to me about them except this unique, all-inclusive *āya*: "Whoever does an atom's weight of good will see it, and whoever does an atom's weight of evil will see it".'[40] Thus the Prophet himself is going by the *ʿumūm* of the verse to include any good or evil that is done, in this instance by using donkeys rather than horses for *jihād*.[41]

5. In the chapter on 'Retaliation for Murder', Mālik points out that it is possible for a free man to be killed in retaliation for murdering a free woman and *vice versa*, his justification for this being the verse 'And We prescribed for them in it [i.e. the Torah] "A life for a life (*al-nafsa bi-l-nafsi*), an eye for an eye, a nose for a nose, an ear for an ear, a tooth for a tooth, and, for wounds, retaliation (*qiṣāṣ*)."'[42] Allah, he says, mentions a life for a life, and so the life of a man can be taken in retaliation for the life of a woman and a man can be injured in retaliation for injuring a woman.[43] In other words, the word *nafs* is taken here in a general sense to include both men and women, who are thus considered equal with regard to retaliation for pre-meditated acts of murder or injury, even though the full blood-money for a woman is only half that for a man.[44] Not only was this Mālik's view, but it was also that of the overwhelming majority of the *fuqahā᾿*, with only a few dissenting voices.[45]

[NOTE: This judgement is said by some to be an example of going by the *sharīʿa* of previous communities (*sharʿ man qablanā*) – in this instance the Jews – which most *ʿulamā᾿*, including Mālik, considered a valid source of judgements as long as such judgements had come down to the Muslims in their own sources, were mentioned in an affirmatory way, and had not been abrogated.[46] However, although Mālik ostensibly uses this principle as the basis for this and other judgements (e.g. that a father can arrange the marriage of a virgin daughter of his without asking for her consent, and that a contract of hire (*ijāra*) is acceptable as a dowry, both of which judgements were seen as being derived from Q 28: 27 – *inniya urīdu an unkiḥaka iḥdā bnatayya hātayni* ('I wish to marry you to one of these two daughters of mine') – where the reference is to the contract of marriage that Moses made with the father of the two girls that he had helped by 'the water of Madyan'),[47] he does not do so consistently, and other judgements on this basis are rejected. Thus, for example, the fat of animals slaughtered by Jews, although *ḥarām* for them according to Q 6: 146, was not considered by Mālik to be *ḥarām* for Muslims, although it seems that whereas he had initially considered eating such fat to be perfectly acceptable for Muslims – in the transmission of Ibn Ziyād it is permitted precisely because the Qurʾan mentions it as something that was forbidden to the Jews rather than the Muslims[48] – towards the end of his life he clearly disapproved of the practice although not categorically forbidding it,[49] presumably since it involved condoning disobedience to God on the part of those doing the slaughtering.]

However, although Mālik allowed retaliation between men and women, this judgement was restricted by considerations of legal status, i.e. whether the murderer and/or victim were free or slaves, again on the basis of a Qurʾanic *āya*. As he says:

> The best I have heard about the *āya* where Allah, the Blessed and Exalted, says, 'A free man for a free man and a slave for a slave' – these being males – 'and a female (*unthā*) for a female'[50] is that retaliation takes place between females as it takes place between males: that is, a free woman may be killed for [killing] a free woman, just as a slave-girl may be killed for [killing] a slave-girl. Retaliation between women [thus] takes place in the same way as it does between men.[51]

In this way the judgement about 'females' is understood to be restricted by the immediately preceding distinction between free men and slaves. Since slaves were considered lower in their status than free men and since retaliation between men is mentioned only between those of equal status ('a free man for a free man and a slave for a slave'), the obvious inference was that retaliation did not apply between those of unequal status. That is, a free man could not be killed in retaliation for killing a slave since the free man's life was worth more than the slave's and to take a free man's life in return for a slave would therefore be an unjust retaliation.

Again, Mālik's use of the phrase 'the best that I have heard' indicates that other opinions were also prevalent. Indeed, although this free/slave distinction was also accepted by al-Shāfiʿī and others, Abū Ḥanīfa, going by the *ʿumūm* of the '*al-nafsa bi-l-nafsi*' *āya* rather than the implications of Q 2: 178, and, according to Ibn Rushd, a *ḥadīth* to the effect that the blood of all Muslims is of equal value (*al-Muslimūna tatakāfaʾu dimāʾuhum*),[52] did not accept it and held that a free man could be killed for killing a slave (as long as it was not the free man's own slave, in which case there was a complication engendered by the fact that the slave was, from one point of view, the free man's property, although certain other Iraqis, notably Ibrāhīm al-Nakhaʿī, even included a man's own slave in the *ʿumūm* of this verse).[53] There was no disagreement, however, that a slave could be killed for killing a free man.[54]

6. An early example of conflict between the *ʿumūm* of a verse and a more restrictive interpretation occurs in the chapter entitled 'What Has

Come Down About Cutting off the Hand of a Runaway Slave Who Steals'.[55] Mālik mentions two *ḥadīths*, both relating to the Umayyad period, to the effect that, contrary to the view of some, a runaway slave who steals *is* subject to the general *ḥadd* punishment for stealing in Q 5: 38 – *wa-l-sāriqu wa-l-sāriqatu fa-qṭaʿū aydiyahumā* ('Men and women who steal, cut off their hands'). In the first, Saʿīd ibn al-ʿĀṣ, a governor of Madina under Muʿāwiya, refuses to punish a runaway slave of Ibn ʿUmar for stealing, whereupon Ibn ʿUmar takes it upon himself to carry out the punishment; in the second, Zurayq ibn Ḥakīm (or Ruzayq ibn Ḥukaym), the governor of Ayla under ʿUmar ibn ʿAbd al-ʿAzīz, writes to ʿUmar on the same issue and ʿUmar writes back to him telling him to carry out the punishment, basing his judgement overtly on Q 5: 38 which he quotes in his letter. Mālik then adds the comment that 'this is the practice about which there is no dispute among us (*wa-dhālika l-amr alladhī lā khtilāfa fī-hi ʿindanā*).'[56]

The reason for the earlier, contrary view is not given but would seem to be either that a runaway slave might well be prompted by hunger to steal and it was accepted that this penalty was not applied if the reason for the stealing was hunger,[57] or that the slave was effectively on a journey and there was a prohibition against cutting off the hand of someone who stole while on a journey (although in one version this is restricted to someone on *jihād*).[58] Ibn Rushd even mentions the possibility that some people felt that a slave should only receive half the penalty for a free man, as with *zinā*, and that this meant that his hand should not be cut off, although he himself does not consider this to be a very convincing argument.[59] However, despite this earlier element of uncertainty about the judgement, the more general interpretation of the *āya* became universally accepted in later times, and is thus another example, like *iʿtikāf* above (p. 79), of where an earlier disputed point was replaced by a unanimous later judgement.[60]

7. Mālik takes the Qurʾanic command to 'complete *ḥajj* and *ʿumra* for Allah (*wa-atimmū l-ḥajja wa-l-ʿumrata li-llāh*)' (Q 2: 196) in an inclusive sense to apply equally to voluntary as well as obligatory *ḥajjs* and *ʿumras*, and, indeed, to all similar acts of worship, such as the prayer, fasting, *ṭawāf*, etc. As he says:

> It is not correct (*lā yanbaghī*) for a man to begin any act of worship, such as the prayer, fasting, *ḥajj* and other such actions which people may do voluntarily, and then stop doing it before completing it in the way it should be done (*ʿalā sunnatihi*). If he says '*Allāhu akbar*' (i.e. at the beginning of the prayer) he should not stop until he has done two

> *rakʿas*; if he is fasting he should not break his fast until he has completed a whole day; if he goes into *iḥrām* [for *ḥajj*] he should not come out of it until he has completed his *ḥajj*; and if he starts doing *ṭawāf* he should not stop until he has completed seven circuits. It is not correct for him to stop doing any of these actions once he has begun it until he has finished it, unless it is because of something which occurs to people unexpectedly, such as illness and other matters for which people are excused. This is because Allah, the Blessed and Exalted, says in His Book, 'And eat and drink until the white thread [of day] becomes clear to you from the black thread [of night] at dawn and then complete (*atimmū*) the fast until the night',[61] and so a man must complete the fast, as Allah says. Allah also says, 'And complete (*atimmū*) *ḥajj* and *ʿumra* for Allah', and so if a man goes into *iḥrām* for a voluntary *ḥajj*, having already done his obligatory one, he does not have the right to stop his *ḥajj* once he has started it and go away having come out of *iḥrām*. Everyone who begins a voluntary act (*nāfila*) should complete it once he has started it just as he would complete an obligatory act (*farīḍa*). This is the best that I have heard.[62]

This passage occurs in the chapter called 'Making Up Voluntary Fasting Missed (*Qaḍāʾ al-taṭawwuʿ*)', where Mālik uses this argument to support the judgement that voluntary fasting, if broken, should be made up, unless the reason for doing so was unavoidable, in which case *qaḍāʾ* is no longer obligatory.[63] This same judgement about voluntary fasting was shared by Abū Ḥanīfa who, like Mālik, extended it also to voluntary prayers, but, unlike him, required *qaḍāʾ* whether the fast was broken avoidably or not; al-Shāfiʿī, for his part, although considering it recommended for someone not to break a voluntary fast, nevertheless did not consider any *qaḍāʾ* to be necessary, basing his judgements on other *ḥadīths* ostensibly to that effect.[64] There was no disagreement, however, that *ḥajj* and *ʿumra*, once begun, should be completed, except for a *shādhdh* view recorded by Ibn Rushd that a voluntary *ḥajj* did not have to be made up.[65]

The assumption that commands indicate obligation

This last example raises another issue which is considered by al-Bājī to come under the heading of what is *ẓāhir*, and that is the question of commands.[66] It was of course recognised that what are grammatically speaking commands may be merely recommendatory or even rhetorical and indicate, for example, guidance or warning, but the initial assumption was that commands were to be taken as obligatory unless there was clear evidence to the contrary.[67] Thus, in the above-mentioned instance, *atimmū* ('finish') was taken to indicate obligation: both *ḥajj* and *ʿumra*, once started, must be finished, because the command says 'finish'.

Commonsense, however, demanded that certain Qurʾanic commands be taken merely in the sense of permissibility (*ibāḥa*) rather than obligation. The two prime examples of this in the Qurʾan are Q 5: 2 – *wa-idhā ḥalaltum fa-ṣṭādū* ('When you come out of *iḥrām*, [you may] hunt') – which allows, rather than obligates, hunting when people finally come out of *iḥrām*, and Q 62: 9 – *fa-idhā quḍiyati l-ṣalātu fa-ntashirū fī l-arḍi wa-btaghū min faḍli llāh* ('When the prayer is finished, spread out in the land and seek the bounty of Allah') – which similarly allows people to 'spread out in the land' and 'seek the bounty of Allah' rather than obligating them to do so.

Mālik refers to both these instances in order to clarify a third instance of the same phenomenon. He says:

> The position here (*al-amr ʿindanā*) is that the master of a slave is not under any obligation to come to a *kitāba* agreement with him if the slave asks him for one. I have never heard of any of the people of knowledge (*aʾimma*) considering it obligatory for a man to come to a *kitāba* agreement with his slave, and I have heard some of the people of knowledge, when asked about the verse *fa-kātibūhum in ʿalimtum fī-him khayran* ('Then make a *kitāba* agreement with them if you know there to be good in them'),[68] read out these two *āyas*: *wa-idhā ḥalaltum fa-ṣṭādū* and *fa-idhā quḍiyati l-ṣalātu fa-ntashirū fī l-arḍi wa-btaghū min faḍli llāh*. This is simply a matter that Allah has allowed people to do (*adhina . . . fī-hi li-l-nās*) and is not obligatory for them (*wa-laysa bi-wājib ʿalayhim*).[69]

This was also the position of Abū Ḥanīfa, al-Shāfiʿī and the majority of the *fuqahāʾ*, although the contrary view, that such an arrangement was obligatory for the master, is recorded in particular from ʿAṭāʾ (and, later, the Ẓāhirīs) and is the overt import of a report that ʿUmar made Anas enter into a *kitāba* arrangement with a slave of his called Sīrīn.[70]

The same verse – Q 24: 33 – also provided another instance in the phrase *wa-ātūhum min māli llāhi lladhī ātākum* ('And give them some of the wealth that Allah has given you'). Was it obligatory to give *mukātab* slaves money and thus make it easier for them to pay their instalments and achieve their freedom, or was it merely a recommendation? What form should this 'giving' take? And who were those addressed by the command?

Mālik took this command as a recommendation only, as did Abū Ḥanīfa and the Iraqis generally, whereas al-Shāfiʿī held that it was an obligation.[71] As for what this 'giving' consisted of and who the command was addressed to, Mālik says clearly that it refers to a master making a *kitāba* arrangement with a slave of his and then reducing the full payment by a certain amount towards the end, saying that this is what he had heard from the people of knowledge and what he had found the practice of the people (*ʿamal al-nās*) to be in Madina. He then supports this view by citing a report to the effect that this was what Ibn ʿUmar had done, making a *kitāba* arrangement with a slave of his for 35,000 dirhams and then reducing it by 5,000 towards the end of the man's *kitāba*.[72]

Mālik does not claim *ijmāʿ* in Madina for this interpretation, and indeed there are reports of different interpretations from earlier Madinan authorities. Al-Bājī, for instance, records that both ʿUmar and (later) Zayd ibn Aslam held that such money should come from the *zakāt* (i.e. under the category of Q 9: 60's *wa-fī l-riqāb*) rather than be the responsibility of the master.[73] Nevertheless, the interpretation in the *Muwaṭṭaʾ*, by virtue of its being described there as 'the practice of the people', can be accepted as the dominant *ʿamal* on this point, thus further illustrating interpretation of the Qurʾan by *ʿamal*, as Abd-Allah has observed.[74]

Exceptions to the *ʿumūm* (*takhṣīṣ al-ʿumūm*)

There were, of course, as noted above, many exceptions to the *ʿumūm*; indeed, it is often said that there is hardly a general statement to which there is not an exception.[75] We have already noted several examples of this as, for instance, when Mālik takes the word *nisāʾ* to refer primarily to 'wives' rather than simply to 'women', this being an example of *takhṣīṣ* by *ʿurf* (i.e. 'custom', in this case *ʿurf sharʿī*, or customary meaning according to the *sharīʿa*, to use the later terminology).[76] Similarly, although we saw that *al-nafsa bi-l-nafsi* was taken to refer generally to men and women, the phrase *al-unthā bi-l-unthā* was not understood in its general sense to include 'any female for any female' but presumed rather to maintain the distinction between free and slave of the preceding *al-ḥurru bi-l-ḥurri wa-l-ʿabdu bi-l-ʿabd*.[77] Other types of *takhṣīṣ al-ʿumūm* include where a Qurʾanic term is interpreted restrictively by reference to the same word elsewhere in the Qurʾan, and the related technique of *ḥaml al-muṭlaq ʿalā l-muqayyad*, both of which we shall consider shortly.[78]

Paired chapters

One particularly clear indication of the phenomenon of *takhṣīṣ al-ʿumūm* is the high incidence of chapters occurring in pairs, where the first one details what is permitted with regard to a certain subject and the second specifies what is not, thus defining exceptions to the general rule. We have already referred in the discussion on *ẓihār* above to the two chapters 'Slaves Permitted/Not Permitted to Be Freed for Obligatory *Kaffāras*'.[79] In the first Mālik makes the point that as long as a slave is Muslim, he or she may be freed for an obligatory *kaffāra*, even if he or she is illegitimate; while in the second he points out that although non-Muslim slaves may not be freed for such *kaffāras* they may be freed as a voluntary act, since the Qur'an says (referring to non-Muslim prisoners of war who would normally become slaves if kept by the Muslims), 'Then either [show] magnanimity (*mann*) afterwards or ransom them', and *mann*, he says, means 'to set free' (*ʿitāqa*).[80]

Such paired chapters occur very frequently, e.g. the pairs 'Game that a *Muḥrim* Is Permitted/Is Not Permitted to Eat',[81] 'Oaths for which *Kaffāra* Is/Is Not Obligatory'[82] and 'When the Hand Must Be/Is Not Cut Off',[83] to mention but a few that echo specifically Qur'anic themes. However, paired chapters are by no means the only manifestation of this phenomenon. Often the norm is assumed and only the exception mentioned. Thus we find chapters such as 'Women that One May Not Be Married to at the Same Time', which details an extension to the Qur'anic prohibition against marrying two sisters at the same time which is itself an exception to the general Qur'anic provisions for marriage;[84] or the chapter 'A Man's Marrying the Mother of a Woman He has Had Sexual Intercourse with in a Disapproved Manner', in which there is both an exception and an extension to the Qur'anic prohibition against marrying a wife's mother;[85] or the three chapters entitled 'The *ʿIdda* of a Woman Whose Husband Dies While She Is Pregnant', 'The *ʿIdda* of an *Umm Walad* Whose Master Dies', and 'The *ʿIdda* of a Slave-girl Whose Master or Husband Dies', which can be seen as exceptions to – or at least related judgements not included under – the Qur'anic prescription of a four-month ten-day *ʿidda* for a woman whose husband has died.[86] The first of these latter three chapters illustrates well how an exception to a Qur'anic verse is made by *sunna* – i.e. in this case the Prophet's judgement that Subayʿa al-Aslamiyya was free to remarry after she had given birth – which then becomes *ʿamal*, as indicated by Mālik's phrase, 'This is the position that the people of knowledge have always held to here (*wa-hādhā l-amr alladhī lam yazal ʿalayhi ahl al-ʿilm ʿindanā*).'[87] The second and third of these chapters illustrate exceptions to the same Qur'anic judgement by *qiyās*, based ultimately on the distinction in Q 4: 25 that slave-girls should receive half the punishment allotted to *muḥṣanāt* for *zinā* (i.e. fifty, instead of a hundred, lashes), *muḥṣanāt* being understood in this context, as at the beginning of the same verse and in Q 5: 5, to mean 'free women' (although further restricted in Q 4: 25, by the *sunna* of *rajm* for free, married, women, to 'free, unmarried, women').[88] As in the first instance, the judgements in both are again endorsed by *ʿamal*, as shown by the expression 'And this is the practice here (*wa-huwa l-amr ʿindanā*)' at the end of both chapters.[89]

Iḥṣār

Many examples could be chosen to further illustrate the phenomenon of *takhṣīṣ* but one, which shows the particular importance of *ʿamal* in this respect, will suffice. In the 'Book of *Ḥajj*' Mālik includes a pair of complementary chapters about *iḥṣār* (i.e. being prevented from completing *ḥajj* or *ʿumra*). Mālik and the Madinans drew a distinction between on the one hand being prevented by an enemy and on the other hand being prevented by some other cause, such as sickness or a miscalculation of the date, this distinction being reflected in the two chapter headings '*Iḥṣār* by an Enemy' and '*Iḥṣār* by Something Other Than an Enemy'.[90] Someone who was prevented by an enemy merely had to come out of *iḥrām* where he was by sacrificing his sacrificial offering (*hady*) if he had one and then shaving his head, without needing to do anything else by way of reparation. If, however, he was prevented by sickness, he had to sacrifice a *hady* for not completing his *ḥajj* or *ʿumra* (or fast if he could not afford one) and then make up this *ḥajj* or *ʿumra* on a future occasion.

Abū Ḥanīfa and the Iraqis, however, held that both types of *iḥṣār* were essentially the same and that in both cases a *muḥṣar* (someone subject to *iḥṣār*) must (a) sacrifice a *hady* for not completing his *ḥajj* or *ʿumra* and (b) make up this *ḥajj* or *ʿumra* on a future occasion. Furthermore, he held that all *hadys* without exception must be sacrificed within the *ḥaram*, even if this meant sending someone else on to do so.[91]

Al-Shāfiʿī drew a similar distinction to Mālik between *iḥṣār* by an enemy and *iḥṣār* by some other cause. Like Mālik (but unlike Abū Ḥanīfa) he held that no *qaḍā'* was necessary for *iḥṣār* by an enemy; but, unlike Mālik (and like Abū Ḥanīfa), he held that it was obligatory for both types of *muḥṣar* to sacrifice a *hady*.[92]

These differences of opinion centred around interpretation of Q 2: 196: 'And complete *ḥajj* and *ʿumra* for Allah; and if you are prevented (*fa-in uḥṣirtum*), [you should sacrifice] whatever sacrificial animal is easy (*mā staysara mina l-hady*); and do not shave your heads until the sacrificial animal reaches its place of sacrifice (*maḥillahu*). And whoever among you is ill, or suffers harm (*adhā*) to his head, [should pay] a recompense (*fidya*) of fasting or almsgiving (*ṣadaqa*) or a sacrifice (*nusuk*). Then, when you are safe (*fa-idhā amintum*), whoever does *tamattuʿ* with an *ʿumra* until the *ḥajj* (*fa-man tamattaʿa bi-l-ʿumrati ilā l-ḥajj*)[93] [should sacrifice] whatever sacrificial animal is easy (*mā staysara mina l-hady*). And whoever does not have one should fast three days during the *ḥajj* and seven when you return; that is ten altogether. This is for those whose families are not present at the Sacred Mosque. And have fear of Allah, and know that Allah's punishment is severe.'

This verse is said to have been revealed on the occasion of Ḥudaybiya (in the year 6 AH) when the Prophet, along with some 1,400 of his Companions, set out from Madina to do *ʿumra* but was prevented from doing so by the Makkans and was thus obliged to turn back without having reached the House, this view being further bolstered by the agreement that the central portion of the *āya* – 'And whoever among you is ill . . . etc' – was revealed about Kaʿb ibn ʿUjra and the incident of the lice that were troubling his head, which occurred at Ḥudaybiya.[94] Indeed, al-Shāfiʿī states that he knows of no disagreement among the scholars of *tafsīr* that this verse was revealed at the time of Ḥudaybiya.[95]

It is for this reason that al-Shāfiʿī takes the verse to refer initially to *iḥṣār* by an enemy,[96] which leads him to the judgement that a *muḥrim* subject to *iḥṣār* by an enemy must sacrifice a *hady* before he can come out of *iḥrām*.[97] However, since there is no mention in the *āya* of *qaḍāʾ* (whereas other commmands are mentioned) and since it was known that many of those at Ḥudaybiya did not do *qaḍāʾ* in the following year when, according to those who held that *qaḍāʾ* was necessary, the Prophet made up his missed *ʿumra*, he does not hold *qaḍāʾ* to be necessary in such instances.[98] But, since he takes the command to 'complete *ḥajj* and *ʿumra*' to be general,[99] he takes the command to sacrifice a *hady* to apply to *iḥṣār* by other causes also. Furthermore, since the command is to 'complete' *ḥajj* or *ʿumra*, then, once started, such acts should be completed, by remaining in *iḥrām* until it is possible to get to the House and come out of *iḥrām* in the correct manner (i.e. having done *ṭawāf* and *saʿy*), and then repeating the missed *ḥajj* or *ʿumra* in a succeeding year, the only exception to this being *iḥṣār* by an enemy.[100]

Abū Ḥanīfa, although recognising the connection of the verse with Ḥudaybiya, nevertheless takes as his starting-point the ordinary linguistic meaning of *uḥṣirtum* as referring to a 'non-enemy' situation, and then extends it, by *qiyās*, to being blocked by an enemy.[101] Like al-Shāfiʿī, he holds that sacrificing a *hady* for *iḥṣār* is obligatory, but, unlike al-Shāfiʿī, he holds that, whatever the situation, this *hady* must always be sacrificed in the *ḥaram*, even if that means sending it on with someone else, and, again unlike al-Shāfiʿī, he holds that, whatever the situation, *qaḍā'* is necessary.[102] The reasons given for the first of these two differences are that the verse goes on to say *wa-lā taḥliqū ru'ūsakum ḥattā yablugha l-hadyu maḥillahu* ('Do not shave your heads until the sacrificial animal reaches its place of sacrifice'), this 'place of sacrifice' (*maḥill*) being interpreted as 'the *ḥaram*' by virtue of Q 22: 33's *thumma maḥilluhā ilā l-bayti l-ʿatīq* ('and then its place of sacrifice is to the Ancient House'), and that sacrificing a *hady* was a special act of devotion (*qurba*) and should, like the *hady* for *tamattuʿ* in the same verse, be sacrificed in a special place at a special time, i.e. in the *ḥaram* during the days of sacrifice, and that although it might have seemed from the Ḥudaybiya incident that the Prophet's *hady* was not sacrificed in the *ḥaram*, in fact half of Ḥudaybiya lies within the bounds of the *ḥaram* and his *hady* was sacrificed in that part which lies within the *ḥaram*.[103] The reasons given for the second are that not only was the Prophet's *ʿumra* in the following year an *ʿumra* of *qaḍā'*, but that also any *ḥajj* or *ʿumra*, once begun, should be finished, without exception.[104]

Thus we see Abū Ḥanīfa applying primarily linguistic considerations to an understanding of the Qur'an from which he then builds up his basic model for *iḥṣār* from which the judgements are then extended by *qiyās* to all other types, including *iḥṣār* by an enemy, with the *ḥadīths* being interpreted accordingly. Al-Shāfiʿī, conscious firstly of the *sabab al-nuzūl* of the *āya* and then of the linguistic necessities of the Qur'anic text, and at the same time aware of the basic distinction in the *ḥadīth*-material between the 'non-enemy' and 'enemy' scenarios, in a sense works in the opposite way to Abū Ḥanīfa, taking the 'enemy' scenario, i.e. the *ḥadīth*-material, as his basic model, and then interpreting the Qur'anic judgements accordingly, extending out by *qiyās* and a consideration of the other relevant *ḥadīths* to cover the 'non-enemy' situation.

Malik, however, in contrast to the above two approaches, bases his judgement firmly on *ʿamal*, this *ʿamal* being that there are two different scenarios, as indicated by the chapter titles in the *Muwaṭṭa'* referred to above. The first is that of the 'enemy' situation, illustrated by the actions of the Prophet at Ḥudaybiya, while the second is that of the 'non-enemy' situation, illustrated by a judgement of ʿUmar's regarding Habbār ibn al-Aswad (who missed the *ḥajj* by miscalculating the date) and Abū Ayyūb al-Anṣārī (who did so through losing his way) who were both told to come out of *iḥrām* after doing an *ʿumra* and then to do *ḥajj* again in the future and sacrifice a *hady* or, if they could not afford a *hady*, to fast three days during the *ḥajj* and seven when they got back home, in accordance with Q 2: 196, which was then extended out by *qiyās* in the judgements of several well-known Madinan Companions to the situation of being prevented by sickness.[105] Thus in the first scenario it is not obligatory to sacrifice a *hady*, nor is it necessary if one is sacrificed for it to be done in the *ḥaram*, nor is there any obligation to make up the uncompleted *ḥajj* or *ʿumra* at a later date. In the second, by contrast, it is necessary to sacrifice a *hady*, it is necessary for this to be done in the *ḥaram*, and it is necessary for the person to make up his uncompleted *ḥajj* or *ʿumra* at a later date.

It is thus clear that the first scenario, although it derives from the same historical incident that occasioned the revelation of the verse, diverges from the verse's overt meaning in three respects. Firstly, as we have seen, the command *wa-atimmū l-ḥajja wa-l-ʿumrata li-llāh* ('And complete *ḥajj* and *ʿumra* for Allah') indicates that, once begun, these rites should be completed, and Malik not only normally accepts this judgement for obligatory actions, but also applies it, by virtue of the *ʿumūm* of the command, to voluntary actions, citing this very *āya* about *ḥajj* to support his view.[106] *Iḥṣār* by an enemy, however, was an exception, because, says Mālik, 'since that time [i.e. Ḥudaybiya] there has been no knowledge (*thumma lam yuʿlam*) that the Messenger of Allah, may Allah bless him and grant him peace, told any of his Companions or those who were with him to make up anything or go back and do anything again.'[107]

Secondly, by the same assumption that commands are obligatory unless there is clear evidence to the contrary, the '*mā staysara mina l-hady*' injunction indicates that sacrificing a *hady* in cases of *iḥṣār* is obligatory and, indeed, this judgement is accepted by Mālik in general terms. But, again, *iḥṣār* by an enemy was an exception, and his view is that someone who is subjected to *iḥṣār* by an enemy only has to sacrifice a *hady* if he has one, and that there is no obligation otherwise.[108]

Thirdly, the Qur'an says *wa-lā taḥliqū ru'ūsakum ḥattā yablugha l-hadyu maḥillahu* ('And do not shave your heads until the sacrificial animal reaches its place of sacrifice'). Mālik uses this very *āya* elsewhere to indicate not only that people should not shave their heads until they have slaughtered their *hadys*, but also that this should be done (as far as *ḥajj* is concerned) in Minā,[109] this latter judgement being further supported by Q 22: 33's *thumma maḥilluhā ilā l-bayti l-ʿatīq* where the *maḥill* is identified as being 'the Ancient House', i.e. Makka and Minā (or, more generally, the *ḥaram*),[110] and also by a *ḥadīth* he relates that all of Minā is a valid place of sacrifice for someone doing *ḥajj*, and all of Makka a valid place of sacrifice for someone doing *ʿumra*, from which he concludes that any area outside these two places is unacceptable.[111] Indeed, he overtly states that all *hadys* should normally be sacrificed in Makka:

> If it is judged that someone should sacrifice a *hady* for killing game [while in *iḥrām*], or if he has to sacrifice a *hady* for any other reason, this

> *hady* must only be sacrificed in Makka, as Allah, the Blessed and Exalted, says: 'a *hady* that reaches the Kaʾba (*hadyan bāligha l-Kaʿba*).'[112]

Nevertheless, despite all this, Mālik quite clearly makes an exception to this general judgement in the instance of someone who is subjected to *iḥṣār* by an enemy, who, if he has a *hady*, simply has to sacrifice it where he is, without having to do so, or have someone else do so for him, in Makka.

Thus three major exceptions are made to the verse, but all with the complete confidence that this was, in his view, what the Prophet had done at Ḥudaybiya and what Ibn ʿUmar, following him, had done during 'the troubles' (*al-fitna*),[113] since which time it had remained the continuous *ʿamal* in Madina up to and including Mālik's own time.[114]

The second scenario, however – that of being prevented from completing *ḥajj* by illness or some comparable situation – accords exactly with the verse. Not only do the relevant judgements match those given in the verse, but the normal meaning of *fa-in uḥṣirtum* is preserved too. Thus, even though Mālik knows of the association of this *āya* with Ḥudaybiya, he considers the Ḥudaybiya type of incident to be an exception to it. The judgement about *iḥṣār* by an enemy is thus a clear instance of *takhṣīṣ al-Qurʾān* by *ʿamal*.

Qurʾan by Qurʾan: the assumption of 'one word, one meaning'

1. Reference has already been made to Mālik's discussion of the meaning of the word *fa-sʿaw* in Q 62: 9's *fa-sʿaw ilā dhikri llāh* ('Make effort [to go] to the remembrance of Allah').[115] The word *saʿy* was lexically ambiguous (*mushtarak*): it could refer to a light run, as in the *saʿy* between Ṣafā and Marwa and the *ḥadīth* about not running to the prayer; or it could refer to 'making effort' in a more general sense, including the specific meaning of a slave minor becoming old enough to work for his master (*bulūgh al-saʿy*), as in the chapter entitled '*Saʿy al-mukātab*', referring to a deceased *mukātab*'s children being old enough to work and thus pay off any instalments still owed by their father.[116] For the most part these usages were clearly distinct, but in the particular instance of Q 62: 9 Mālik clearly felt it necessary to dispel any ambiguity. We have already noted how he cites a *shādhdh* variant reading to support his view that the *saʿy* being referred to in Q 62: 9 is not that of 'hurrying', as might be expected from the use of the verb in conjunction with the preposition *ilā*, but rather the less obvious, but more suitable, meaning of 'making effort', i.e. in this case,

'making the effort to go', as suggested by ʿUmar's reading of ***fa-mḍū*** *ilā dhikri llāh.*[117]

Mālik's method in this instance is to appeal to an expectation of unity in the Qur'an, that is, that the word *saʿy* as used in the Qur'an consistently refers to 'making effort' rather than 'hurrying'. Having introduced this idea by mentioning ʿUmar's reading, he then backs it up by citing a number of verses which, in his opinion, reflect this meaning of 'making effort' and thus go to show that the same meaning is intended in the command *fa-sʿaw* in Q 62: 9. He says:

> The word *saʿy* in the Book of Allah refers to effort and action (*al-ʿamal wa-l-fiʿl*). Allah, the Blessed and Exalted, says, 'And when he turns away, he acts (*yasʿā*) in the land';[118] and He says, may He be exalted, 'And as for he who comes to you in earnest (*yasʿā*), fearing [Allah]';[119] and He says, 'And then he turns away in earnest (*yasʿā*)';[120] and He says, 'Surely your efforts (*saʿyakum*) are diverse.'[121] So the *saʿy* that Allah mentions in His Book does not refer to running or hurrying (*al-saʿy ʿalā l-aqdām wa-l-ishtidād*), but, rather, to effort and action (*al-ʿamal wa-l-fiʿl*).[122]

The idea behind this interpretation is clear: Mālik is affirming the ruling contained in the *ḥadīth* which we referred to above to the effect that one should not run to the prayer but, rather, approach it with dignity and composure, even if that means missing part of it.[123] Since there was no disagreement among the *fuqahā'* on this judgement,[124] one must assume that Mālik's inclusion of this point was aimed at preventing a possible misunderstanding that might arise in his students' minds or that they might encounter later on.

2. In the chapter on 'Standing (*al-wuqūf*) at ʿArafa and al-Muzdalifa' Mālik glosses the words *rafath* and *fusūq* in the phrase *fa-lā rafatha wa-lā fusūqa wa-lā jidāla fī l-ḥajj* ('Let there be no *rafath* nor *fusūq* nor argument during the *ḥajj*') (Q 2: 197) by reference to the same words elsewhere in the Qur'an. He says:

> *Rafath* means 'sexual intercourse' (*iṣābat al-nisā'*), and Allah knows best: Allah, the Blessed and Exalted, says, 'Intercourse (*al-rafath*) with your wives is permitted for you on the night of the fast';[125] and *fusūq* means 'sacrifices made to idols' (*al-dhabḥ li-l-anṣāb*), and Allah knows best: Allah, the Blessed and Exalted, says, 'or a sacrifice (*fisqan*) which has been made to other than Allah'.[126]

Both these terms were thus given a very restrictive interpretation by Mālik (as was also the third term *jidāl* ('argument'); see below, pp. 128ff). As regards *rafath*, the option was between taking it to refer generally to all behaviour with a sexual orientation, including lewd speech, or taking it in the more specific sense of sexual intercourse, as in the agreed instance of Q 2: 187.[127] Similarly, *fusūq* could be taken to refer generally to all acts of disobedience (*maʿāṣī*); or to bad speech (as in Q 49: 11's *biʾsa l-ismu l-fusūqu baʿda l-īmān* – 'what an evil name – bad speech after belief!'); or, with a more direct relevance to *ḥajj*, to those acts of disobedience that broke *iḥrām*; or, more specifically still, to sacrifices made to idols.[128] That Mālik should have opted for the specific interpretation in both instances is interesting, given, as we have seen, that in general he prefers the *ʿumūm*.[129] It would seem in this instance that the reason is that the restrictive interpretations accorded better with the limited judgements regarding these issues known to the *fuqahāʾ*. Thus *rafath* in the specific sense of sexual intercourse rather than the broader sense of lewd language and/or behaviour made better sense in terms of the judgements associated with the *āya*, since sexual intercourse was clearly forbidden for anyone on *ḥājj*, and, indeed, invalidated it, whereas the same could not be said for lewd speech. Similarly, *fusūq* in the specific sense of 'sacrificing to idols' was clearly forbidden during *ḥajj*, in which sacrificial rites play a major role, and was thus a more immediately relevant interpretation than the more general meaning of 'wrong action'.[130] Later scholars, however, were almost invariably to prefer broader interpretations.[131]

3. In the chapter entitled 'Marrying a Slave-girl When Already Married to a Free Woman', Mālik discusses the implications of Q 4: 25, saying:

> It is not correct (*lā yanbaghī*) for a free man to marry a slave-girl (*ama*) if he has the means (*ṭawl*) to marry a free woman (*ḥurra*), nor should he marry a slave-girl even if he does not have the means to marry a free woman unless he fears *ʿanat*. This is because Allah, the Blessed and Exalted, says in His Book, 'And those among you who do not have the means (*ṭawl*) to marry believing *muḥṣanāt* [may marry] from among those of your believing *fatayāt* whom your right hands possess . . . That is for those among you who fear *ʿanat*',[132] and *ʿanat* means *zinā* [i.e. illicit sexual intercourse].[133]

His use of the words *ama* and *ḥurra* clearly shows that he takes *fatayāt* to mean 'slave-girls' and *muḥṣanāt* to mean 'free women'. Indeed, the verse would not make sense if taken any other way: *fatayāt* clearly means 'slave-girls', as both the context of 'whom your right hands possess' and the use of the word elsewhere in the Qurʾan – e.g. Q 24: 33: 'Do not force your slave-girls (*fatayātikum*) to prostitution' – show. *Muḥṣanāt*, therefore, being contrasted here with the idea of slave-girls, must have the connotation of 'free women', the only other alternative; and, indeed, that meaning in this instance was universally accepted.[134]

Having established this meaning, Mālik then applies it to Q 5: 5, where the phrase *al-muḥṣanātu mina l-mu'mināt* ('*muḥṣanāt* from among the believers') is mentioned in conjunction with *al-muḥṣanātu mina lladhīna ūtū l-kitāba min qablikum* ('*muḥṣanāt* from among those who were given the Book before you'). He says:

> It is not permissible [for a Muslim] to marry a Jewish or Christian slave-girl because Allah, the Blessed and Exalted, says in His Book, 'And [permitted for you are] *muḥṣanāt* from among the believers and *muḥṣanāt* from among those who were given the Book before you',[135] these being free (*ḥarā'ir*) Jewish and Christian women; and Allah, the Blessed and Exalted, says, 'And those among you who do not have the means to marry believing *muḥṣanāt* [may marry] from among those of your believing *fatayāt* whom your right hands possess',[136] and *fatayāt* means 'slave-girls' (*imā'*). So in our view (*fī-mā nurā*) Allah has permitted marriage with believing [i.e. Muslim] slave-girls but has not permitted marriage with slave-girls of the People of the Book.[137]

Mālik thus deduces that a free Muslim may marry a Muslim slave-girl (although, in his view, only under the conditions mentioned in Q 4: 25, i.e. if he does not have the wealth (*ṭawl*) to marry a free woman, and if he also fears *zinā*),[138] but he may only marry a Christian or Jewish woman if she is free, since the permission in Q 5: 5 is restricted to *muḥṣanāt*, i.e. free women. Mālik goes on to point out that although a Muslim may not marry a Christian or Jewish slave-girl, he is permitted to have intercourse with such a woman by virtue of ownership; intercourse, however, with any woman outside these three religions is totally prohibited, even if they are his slave-girls,[139] the principle behind these judgements being that where marriage to free women is allowed, intercourse by virtue of ownership is also allowed, and where marriage to free women is prohibited, intercourse by virtue of ownership is also prohibited.[140]

The prohibition against marrying Christian and Jewish slave-girls, however, was not universally held. All the *fuqahā'*, as we have noted, agreed that Q 4: 25 refers to marrying Muslim slave-girls when free Muslim women are not available, as they also agreed (except Ibn ʿUmar) that it was permissible, by Q 5: 5, for a Muslim to marry a free Christian or Jewish woman.[141] The disagreement was on the unspecified category of Christian and Jewish slave-girls, who were not mentioned either in Q 4: 25

or Q 5: 5. Mālik, as we have seen, held that it was not permitted for a Muslim to marry them since only free (*muḥṣanāt*) women are allowed by Q 5: 5. Abū Ḥanīfa, however, held that such a lack of mention did not necessarily imply prohibition: rather, if marriage was permitted to both Muslim and Jewish or Christian free women, then, since it was permitted to marry Muslim slave-girls by Q 4: 25, so too, by *qiyās*, should it be permitted to marry Jewish or Christian slave-girls.[142] The conflict therefore was between *qiyās* on the one hand and the *ʿumūm* of the verse on the other: in other words, if one allowed the exception of Q 4: 25 to the *ʿumūm* of *al-muḥṣanātu mina l-muʾmināt* in Q 5: 5, should one also allow the same exception, by *qiyās*, to the *ʿumūm* of *al-muḥṣanātu mina lladhīna ūtū l-kitāba min qablikum*? Abū Ḥanīfa allowed this *qiyās*, whereas Mālik and al-Shāfiʿī rejected it, saying that the only exception to the general prohibition against marrying non-Muslim women in Q 2: 221 (*wa-lā tankiḥū l-mushrikāti ḥattā yuʾminna* – 'Do not marry idolatresses until they believe') was that of Q 5: 5, and that only allowed marriage to *muḥṣanāt*, i.e. free Christian and Jewish women, while marriage to Christian and Jewish slave-girls remained forbidden.[143]

Ibn Rushd mentions a further reason for conflict: since only Muslim slave-girls are specified in Q 4: 25 as an exception to the general rule, then, by *mafhūm al-mukhālafa*, non-Muslims are not included. If, however, one rejected *mafhūm al-mukhālafa* and preferred *qiyās* instead, as did Abū Ḥanīfa and the Iraqis,[144] non-Muslim slave-girls could be included and given the same judgement as Muslim slave-girls. This conflict can thus also be viewed as a conflict between *qiyās* and *mafhūm al-mukhālafa*.[145]

Deduction from juxtaposition

4. Sometimes, as in the above instance, it is not merely an individual word that is explained by the juxtaposition of two *āyas*, but rather a deduction that is made. Another particularly good example is where Mālik mentions the judgement that a pregnant woman in the final stages of pregnancy may not make decisions about her wealth beyond the third allowed for bequests, and that this final stage begins after six months of pregnancy have elapsed, this judgement being supported by a mixture of *qiyās* and the deductions derived from juxtaposing various Qurʾanic *āyas*. He says:

> The best that I have heard about the bequest of a pregnant woman and all her decisions concerning her wealth and what is permissible for her is that the same applies to her as applies to a sick man: if the

> sickness is not serious and there is no [real] fear for the sick man, he may do what he likes with his property, but if the sickness is serious it is not permissible for him to dispose of any of his wealth beyond the third [of his estate which he is allowed to bequeath].
>
> The same applies to a pregnant woman. The beginning of pregnancy is [a time of] good news and joy rather than illness and fear, because Allah, the Blessed and Exalted, says in His Book, 'And so We gave her the good news of Isḥāq, and, after Isḥāq, Yaᶜqūb',[146] and He also says, 'She bears a light burden, and moves about [easily] with it; but when she becomes heavy [with child], they call on their Lord, [saying], "If you give us a healthy (*ṣāliḥ*)[147] child, we will be among the thankful."'[148] So when a woman is heavy with child she may not make any decisions about her property beyond her third. The earliest possible complete term of pregnancy (*awwal al-itmām*) is six months. Allah, the Blessed and Exalted, says in His Book, 'Mothers may suckle their children for two whole years',[149] and He also says, 'His bearing and his weaning are [for] thirty months.'[150] So when six months have passed from the time of conception she may not make any decisions about her property beyond her third.[151]

Thus for Mālik there is a distinction between the early stages of pregnancy, which are considered a time of joy, and the later stages, when childbirth and therefore possibly death – since death in childbirth was a relatively frequent occurrence – could happen at any time. Her situation was thus analogous to that of a man in the last stages of a serious illness, or one about to go out to battle, since death in all these instances was a distinct possibility, and, although normally a man could dispose of his money more or less as he wished, someone on or near the point of death was only allowed to make bequests, and bequests, as we have noted above, could only be made up to a limit of a third of a man's estate.[152] Having made this *qiyās*, the question then was how to define when this last stage of pregnancy began. Mālik's deduction is that the minimum period for a complete pregnancy (*awwal al-itmām*) is six months, because, if the limit for weaning is two years, i.e. twenty-four months, and the limit for pregnancy and weaning together is thirty months, then clearly the pregnancy element in this last figure could be as little as six months.

It is interesting to note that although Mālik says that this judgement is the best that he has heard on the subject, thus presupposing that the problem had been addressed by others before him, the specific deduction from the Qurʾanic verses is not attributed here to any earlier authority and thus might be assumed to be Mālik's own. However, in the chapter on 'What Has Come Down About Stoning', we find exactly the same deduction attributed to ᶜAlī ibn Abī Ṭālib in the time of the third caliph ᶜUthmān. The transmitter, Yaḥyā, says:

> Mālik told me that he had heard that a woman who had given birth after only six months was once brought to ᶜUthmān ibn ᶜAffān, who ordered her to be stoned. ᶜAlī ibn Abī Ṭālib said to him, 'She is not liable for that (*laysa ᶜalayhā dhālika*). Allah, the Blessed and Exalted, says in His Book, "And his bearing and his weaning are [for] thirty months",[153] and He also says, "And mothers may suckle their children for two whole years, for those who wish to complete suckling",[154] so pregnancy may be for only six months, and therefore she should not be stoned.' ᶜUthmān ibn ᶜAffān accordingly sent someone after her but found that she had already been stoned.[155]

Thus what might appear at first sight to be Mālik's own deduction in one place is quite clearly attributed by him to a much earlier authority in another, thus providing indirect confirmation of the report from him referred to above in which he comments that 'his opinion' is in fact also the opinion of a large number of his predecessors.[156]

All the *fuqahāʾ* agreed, precisely because of these two verses, that the minimum period of pregnancy was six months,[157] but both Abū Ḥanīfa and al-Shāfiᶜī rejected the judgement that the restriction on bequests came into effect after six months of pregnancy and instead allowed her to dispose of her wealth as she felt fit except if there was any danger to her life actually at the time of delivery.[158]

5. We have seen above how Mālik uses an inclusive interpretation of 'horses' (*khayl*) in Q 16: 8 to explain the use of the word in Q 8: 60 where it occurs in the context of *jihād*, from which he then deduces that any type of horse used for *jihād*, whatever its breed, is entitled to the same portion of the spoils as thoroughbred horses.[159] He also uses the same verse (Q 16: 8) in conjunction with two others to support the judgement that horse-meat should not be eaten. As in the judgement above on the minimum length of pregnancy, he refers implicitly to a dispute on the matter after which he gives his own preferred interpretation, saying that the best that he has heard is that

> horses, mules and donkeys are not to be eaten, because Allah, the Blessed and Exalted, says, 'And [He has created] horses, mules and donkeys so that you may ride them and as an adornment',[160] whereas He, the Blessed and Exalted, says about camels (*anᶜām*),[161] 'so that you

> may ride on some of them, and from some of them you eat',[162] and He, the Blessed and Exalted, also says, 'so that they may mention the name of Allah over those domestic animals (*bahīmat al-anʿām*) that He has given them as provision ... So eat from them and feed the poor and visitors (*al-qāniʿ wa-l-muʿtarr*)'.[163] [...] So Allah mentions horses, mules and donkeys [only] for riding and adornment, whereas He mentions camels [both] for riding and eating.[164]

Thus horses, mules and donkeys are mentioned for riding and adornment but not for food, whereas camels are mentioned both for riding and food, the implication (*mafhūm*) being that if horses, etc, had also been intended for food that use would have been mentioned, but, as it is not, their meat should be avoided. 'This', Mālik adds in the transmission of Ibn Ziyād, 'is the position with us here (*wa-ʿalā dhālika l-amr ʿindanā*).'[165]

Abū Ḥanīfa took the same view as Mālik, and, it would seem, for very much the same reasons, but Abū Yūsuf and al-Shaybānī, along with al-Shāfiʿī, considered horse-meat to be acceptable (*mubāḥ*), giving preference to certain *ḥadīths* to that effect over other, contrary, reports, and rejecting, in the face of these reports, the deductions from the Qurʾanic evidence mentioned above and also any *qiyās* with donkeys and mules, which they agreed should not be eaten.[166]

6. A further illustration of this technique is in the chapter entitled 'The Command to Be in *Wuḍūʾ* to Touch the Qurʾan' where Mālik uses the undisputed reference to angels in Q 80: 15–16 (*bi-aydī safaratin kirāmin barara* – 'in the hands of noble, obedient recording [angels]') as evidence that the phrase *lā yamassuhū illā l-muṭahharūn* ('which only the purified touch') in Q 56: 79 refers to angels rather than people. He first mentions a *ḥadīth* to the effect that only a person in *wuḍūʾ* (*ṭāhir*) should touch the Qurʾan, adding the explanation that this judgement is not for any reason of physical uncleanliness but rather out of respect for the Qurʾan. He then says:

> The best I have heard about the *āya* 'which only the purified touch (*lā yamassuhū illā l-muṭahharūn*)'[167] is that it is like the *āya* in Sūrat ʿAbasa where Allah, the Blessed and Exalted, says, 'Nay, it is a reminder – and whoever wishes will remember it – in ennobled pages, raised, purified (*muṭahhara*), in the hands of noble, obedient recording [angels] (*bi-aydī safaratin kirāmin barara*)'.[168]

Mālik thus equates the *muṭahharūn* of Q 56 with the *safaratin kirāmin barara* of Q 80 and, in so doing, regards as secondary the interpretation that the *kitāb maknūn* ('hidden book') of Q 56: 78 refers to actual *muṣḥafs* and that the phrase *lā yamassuhū illā l-muṭahharūn* is a statement with the force of a prohibition with *muṭahharūn* referring to human beings, and that therefore only those who are purified by having done *wuḍū᾿* may touch the Qur᾿an. Mālik does not of course deny the judgement: the *ḥadīth* he has just mentioned makes that amply clear. Rather, he denies that the judgement derives directly from the verse, although this was to be a common assumption in later times[169] and had clear antecedents in, for example, the story of ᶜUmar's conversion to Islam where he finds his sister and others reading from pages containing Sūrat Ṭāhā and wants to see what is in them for himself but is told that he may not do so without first washing himself, since 'only someone who is pure may touch them (*lā yamassuhā illā l-ṭāhir*)'.[170] However, it is possible, as al-Bājī points out, to see these verses as support for Mālik's judgement in that they affirm the general meaning of the nobility of the Qur᾿an which should therefore be treated with the utmost respect.[171]

Both Abū Ḥanīfa and al-Shāfiᶜī held the same judgement as Mālik on this issue, though it is not clear whether they did so because of the *āya* (which is the suggestion of later representatives of their views) or for other reasons (e.g. the *ḥadīth* that Mālik relates).[172]

Ḥaml al-muṭlaq ᶜalā l-muqayyad

Another extension of the Qur᾿an by Qur᾿an principle was the application of *taqyīd al-muṭlaq*, or *ḥaml al-muṭlaq ᶜalā l-muqayyad*, i.e. assuming that an expression that is unqualified (*muṭlaq*) in one place will be qualified by the same qualification that it has in another place, provided the context is similar.[173] We have already noted two instances of this in the discussions on *ẓihār* above: firstly, the judgement that a slave being freed for the *kaffāra* of *ẓihār* in Q 58: 3 has to be a 'believing', i.e. Muslim, slave, as in Q 4: 92;[174] and, secondly, that the option of feeding sixty poor people for this same *kaffāra* should be completed 'before they touch each other (*min qabli an yatamāssā*)', as with the other two options of freeing a slave and fasting two consecutive months, although only in the latter two cases is this specified in the Qur᾿an.[175] A further instance occurs in the 'General Chapter on Sacrificial Offerings' (*Jāmiᶜ al-hady*) where Mālik says:

> If it is judged that someone should sacrifice a *hady* for killing game [while in *iḥrām*], or if he has to sacrifice a *hady* for any other reason, this *hady* must only be sacrificed in Makka, as Allah, the Blessed and Exalted, says: 'a *hady* that reaches the Kaᶜba (*hadyan bāligha l-Kaᶜba*)'.[176]

Thus the expression 'that reaches the Kaᶜba', which in this instance qualifies the *hady* that should be sacrificed by a *muḥrim* who kills game, is taken to refer also to the *mā staysara mina l-hady* ('whatever *hady* is easy') that according to Q 2: 196 must be sacrificed both by someone who is prevented from completing *ḥajj* and someone who does *tamattuᶜ*.[177]

There was general agreement that the sacrifices associated with *ḥajj* and *ᶜumra* should be sacrificed in or around Makka ('in the *ḥaram*'), not so much because of Q 5: 95's *hadyan bāligha l-Kaᶜba*, which, as we have just seen, was specifically about the *hady* for killing game while in *iḥrām*, as because of Q 22: 33's *thumma maḥilluhā ilā l-bayti l-ᶜatīq* ('and then its place of sacrifice is to the Ancient House').[178] While the Iraqis, however, said that *all* such sacrifices, without exception, had to be sacrificed in the *ḥaram*, Mālik excepted not only the *hady* of someone prevented from doing *ḥajj* by an enemy, which, as we have seen, he held should be sacrificed wherever the man is,[179] but also the sacrifice for the *fidyat al-adhā* (reparation for shaving the head, etc), which he held could be sacrificed anywhere,[180] because it is referred to in the Qurᵓan using the word *nusuk* rather than the word *hady*, thus indicating a distinction, and it is only *hadys* which have to 'reach the Kaᶜba'.[181] Al-Shāfiᶜī followed Mālik in that the *hady* of a man prevented from doing *ḥajj* (*muḥṣar*) could be sacrificed wherever the man was,[182] but not as regards the *nusuk* for the *fidyat al-adhā*, which, like Abū Ḥanīfa, he equated with *hadys* in general and said should be sacrificed in the *ḥaram*.[183]

Another difference was that Abū Ḥanīfa and al-Shāfiᶜī allowed *hadys* to be sacrificed anywhere within the bounds of the *ḥaram*,[184] whereas Mālik said that they had to be sacrificed actually within the settled area of Makka (or Minā) and not just in the *ḥaram* because of the *ḥadīth* that 'Marwa is a place of sacrifice (*manḥar*), all the ravines (*fijāj*) of Makka are a place of sacrifice, and its roads (*ṭuruq*) are a place of sacrifice.'[185] However, it is apparent from the frequent reference in the literature to 'Makka and/or Minā' as an alternative for 'the *ḥaram*' that the *maḥill* of Q 22: 33 (and also Q 2: 196 and 48: 25) was normally assumed by all to be either Minā (for *ḥajj*) or Makka (for *ᶜumra*), as it was in Mālik's view.[186]

Exceptions to Qurᵓan by Qurᵓan

In certain instances, however, two Qurᵓanic verses would give a seemingly different judgement on the same topic, thus making it impossible to interpret one by reference to the other. Thus, for example, when ᶜUthmān was asked whether a man who owned two slave-girls who were sisters was permitted to have sexual relations with both of them (it being forbidden to be married to two sisters at the same time by Q 4: 23 – *wa-an tajmaʿū bayna l-ukhtayn* – 'and that you should be married to two sisters at the same time'), he replied, 'One *āya* permits it, and another forbids it.'[187] The *āya* permitting it is said to be either Q 4: 24 – *wa-l-muḥṣanātu mina l-nisāʾi illā mā malakat aymānukum* ('and the *muḥṣanāt* among women, except what your right hands possess') – which, if one assumed the exceptive *illā mā malakat aymānukum* to relate back to all the preceding prohibitions, would thus also be an exception to Q 4: 23's *wa-an tajmaʿū bayna l-ukhtayn*, or Q 23: 6 – *wa-lladhīna hum li-furūjihim ḥāfiẓūna illā ʿalā azwājihim aw mā malakat aymānuhum* ('and those who protect their private parts, except with their wives or what their right hands possess') – while the *āya* prohibiting it is Q 4: 23's *wa-an tajmaʿū bayna l-ukhtayn.* However, although recognising this possibility, ʿUthmān himself (like the majority of the Companions, and all the later *fuqahāʾ*) disapproved of the practice.[188]

Another instance was the question of the *ʿidda* for a pregnant widow. Q 2: 234 states that a woman whose husband has died should observe an *ʿidda* of four months and ten days, while Q 65: 4 says that the *ʿidda* for a divorced woman who is pregnant is until delivery. What, then, should be the *ʿidda* for a woman who is both a widow, as in Q 2: 234, and pregnant, as in Q 65: 4? The majority, including all the later *fuqahāʾ*, held that her *ʿidda* should last until delivery, whether that was earlier or later, in particular because of the *ḥadīth* to that effect concerning Subayʿa al-Aslamiyya.[189] Ibn ʿAbbās, however, is said to have held initially that she should wait until the longest of the two periods was up (*ākhir al-ajalayn*), whichever that was,[190] the reason for this presumably being the feeling that if a woman gave birth soon after her husband had died and was free to marry again immediately afterwards, she would not have observed a waiting period proper for a widow, which Q 2: 234 suggested should be longer than that for an ordinary divorcee. The reason for Mālik's judgement is, once again, *ʿamal*, as he makes clear in his comment at the end of the chapter that 'This is the position which the people of knowledge have always held to here (*wa-hādhā l-amr alladhī lam yazal ʿalayhi ahl al-ʿilm ʿindanā*).'[191]

Kalāla

One particularly taxing task for the *fuqahāʾ* in this respect was the question of *kalāla*, i.e. inheritance in the absence of parents and/or children. The word itself occurs twice in the Qurʾan but with a different judgement in each case. The first instance, in Q 4: 12, says:

> And if a man is inherited from by way of *kalāla* (*kalālatan*)[192] – or a woman – and he has a brother or a sister, each one of them has a sixth. If there are more than that, they share a third between them.

The second, Q 4: 176, says:

> They will ask you for a ruling (*yastaftūnaka*). Say, Allah gives you a ruling about *kalāla*. If a man dies without a son (*laysa lahu walad*)[193] and he has a sister, she has half of what he leaves; and he inherits from her if she has no son (*walad*). If there are two sisters, they have two-thirds of what he leaves. If there are brothers and sisters, a male has the portion of two females. Allah clarifies [these matters] for you so that you do not go astray, and Allah has knowledge of everything.

Thus these two verses, although both clearly referring to '*kalāla*', contain very different judgements. In the first, there is no difference between males and females: a single brother or sister will take a sixth while two or more will share a third equally between them. In the second, however, both the judgements and the relative portions of males and females are different: a single sister will take half, while a single brother will take all; two sisters will share two-thirds; and in any combination of brothers and sisters the inheritance will be divided up between them on the basis of a male receiving twice as much as a female.

That the concept of *kalāla* was seen as problematic from the beginning is evident from a report in the *Muwaṭṭa᾿* that ᶜUmar asked the Prophet about *kalāla* and was told that Q 4: 176 was enough for him.[194] Despite this, however, *kalāla* remained a problem: Abū Bakr finally decided during his caliphate that it referred to all heirs except the father and any sons (*mā khalā l-wālid wa-l-walad*), although acknowledging that he might be wrong.[195] ᶜUmar was obviously still uncertain about the meaning during his own caliphate but decided to defer to Abū Bakr's judgement for want of any clearer indication of the meaning: indeed, *kalāla* is said to have been one of the three points that he wished the Prophet had given more details about before he died.[196]

Other views on the meaning included the view that *kalāla* referred to heirs other than children (*mā dūna l-walad*), regardless of whether the deceased's father was among them or not,[197] or that it referred to heirs other than the father (*mā dūna l-ab*), or to brothers and sisters, or uterine brothers and sisters, or agnatic cousins (*banū l-ᶜamm*), or to secondary agnatic relatives (*al-ᶜaṣaba*) in general.[198] However, the view that it referred specifically to when someone died leaving neither father nor son as an inheritor became the view of the majority of scholars from the time of the Companions onwards.[199]

As well as this discussion on the meaning there was also much discussion about the grammatical status of the word, especially as it occurs in Q 4: 12. Was it a verbal noun, as words of the pattern *faᶜāla* would normally be, indicating the situation of someone dying leaving neither father nor son (or any other of the above-mentioned options), or was it a substantive, indicating either the man who died in such a situation, or the people who would inherit from him, or even the inheritance itself?[200]

The word was thus both lexically and grammatically ambiguous: what is interesting though is that, despite the space devoted to these problems, neither of them seems to have been the main one, and certainly not the cause of ʿUmar's continued anxiety about the term. Effective agreement was soon reached, as we have seen, on Abū Bakr's preferred definition of the meaning, while the discussions on the grammatical status of the word were, from the point of view of the *fuqahā'*, basically irrelevant since it was the definition of the *kalāla* situation that mattered rather than the syntax of the sentence in which the word occurred, which did not affect any judgements. The real problem was, firstly, how to harmonise the two verses with their differing judgements on *kalāla*, and secondly, and more importantly, how to find a sound basis for resolving the conflicting claims arising from these verses between, on the one hand, collaterals (i.e. brothers and sisters) and, on the other, other heirs apart from the father and any sons (in particular, as we shall see, the grandfather on the father's side). In other words, as we saw with the verses regarding the inheritance of children referred to above (pp. 72ff), the problem was not so much about what the verses said, as how to fill in the gaps about what the verses did not say.

The first problem was solved relatively simply: Q 4: 176 reflected the ordinary agnatic type of inheritance ('to a male the portion of two females') and was therefore taken to refer to brothers and sisters who shared the same father as the deceased, while Q 4: 12 reflected a situation where males and females were treated equally and was therefore seen as referring to brothers and sisters who shared the same mother as the deceased, this interpretation being reflected in the *shādhdh* variant *wa-lahu akhun aw ukhtun* ***min ummin*** [or ***mina l-ummi***] ('and he has a brother or sister through the mother'), attributed to, amongst others, Ibn Masʿūd, Saʿd ibn Abī Waqqāṣ and Ubayy.[201]

The second problem was altogether more complicated. As far as Q 4: 12 was concerned, it was agreed that both the father and the grandfather (i.e. the father's father) as well as any children (or children of a son) of the deceased, whether male or female, would exclude uterine collaterals from inheritance: *kalāla* here referred to those other than a father or a child, with 'father' including 'father's father' and 'child' including immediate children and grandchildren through a son. However, in a case where the deceased had been survived by a daughter, a son's daughter and a (full) sister, the Prophet had judged that all should inherit, thus allowing a collateral to inherit when there was a daughter (and a son's daughter).[202] The *kalāla* of Q 4: 176, then, had to be interpreted differently from that of Q 4: 12: the phrase *laysa lahu walad*, which would normally mean 'without any child', had to be interpreted restrictively to mean 'without any son (or son's sons)', since the Prophet's precedent had shown that daughters of the deceased did not exclude a sister from inheriting.[203]

It had early been decided, as we have seen, that Q 4: 12 referred to uterine collaterals and Q 4: 176 to agnates. Thus, assuming there were no other heirs, uterines would receive up to one third of the estate and agnates would share the remainder between them on the basis of a male receiving twice the portion of a female. Conflict, however, could arise between the two groups necessitating a decision between the relative rights of the different types of 'brothers'. The most famous example of this is the so-called *Ḥimāriyya* case: in the time of ᶜUmar ibn al-Khaṭṭāb a woman died leaving her husband, her mother, two germane brothers and two uterine brothers. Going strictly by the Qur˒anic provisions of Q 4: 12, the husband would receive a half, the mother a sixth (because of the presence of more than one 'brother'; cf. above, p. 74) and the uterine brothers would share the remaining third between them, thus exhausting the estate and leaving nothing for the germanes. This was how ᶜUmar at first judged the case, but on appeal by the germane brothers he reversed his decision and allowed them to share in the third due to uterines since all of them shared the same mother. The germane brothers' argument, according to one version, was expressed in the words 'Consider our father a donkey', thus giving rise to the name *al-Ḥimāriyya*, or the Case of the Donkey.[204] This rule was accepted by Mālik and al-Shāfiᶜī, following ᶜUmar's decision, but was rejected by Abū Ḥanīfa who followed the principle 'once an agnate, always an agnate' and thus excluded all agnatic collaterals from inheritance in this instance.[205]

However, the greatest problems to arise out of the *kalāla* verses (and particularly Q 4: 176) concerned the inheritance due to collaterals alongside a grandfather (what is meant here, and throughout the discussion, is the father's father). As ᶜUmar is recorded to have said, 'If anyone wants to rush headlong into the depths of the Fire, let him judge between a grandfather and collaterals', and, 'The most daring of you in deciding a grandfather's portion is the most daring of you with regard to the Fire.'[206] Indeed, like *kalāla*, the inheritance due to a grandfather was one of the three problems which ᶜUmar wished there had been more guidance on while the Prophet was still alive.[207]

It was agreed that a grandfather excluded uterine collaterals (since it was agreed that he was subsumed under the term 'father' as far as Q 4:

12's 'uterine' *kalāla* inheritance was concerned and thus excluded uterines as did the father), but there was considerable disagreement about the relative rights of a grandfather alongside agnatic collaterals. Abū Bakr and Ibn ʿAbbās, following the principle that if a son's son was like a son in the absence of a son, then so too should the father's father be like the father in the absence of the father, said that the grandfather excluded all collaterals, including agnates, from inheritance, as would the father, and this was the view accepted by Abū Ḥanīfa (although not by either Abū Yūsuf or al-Shaybānī).[208] Mālik, on the other hand (and al-Shāfiʿī), followed the view of Zayd ibn Thābit, which was that both inherited together,[209] Zayd's view being seen as based on the argument that although the grandfather, as father of the father of the deceased, had a clear right to inheritance, the brothers, as sons of the father of the deceased, also had a clear right, with, if anything, priority being due to descendants rather than ascendants: everyone agreed, for instance, that a father inheriting alongside a son would take only one-sixth while the son would take the remaining five-sixths; similarly, there was universal agreement that a nephew (i.e. brother's son) was given preference to an uncle (i.e. grandfather's son), which again supported the general principle that descendants are given priority over ascendants.[210]

In the simple case of a grandfather surviving alongside a full brother, Zayd, following the decision of ʿUmar and ʿUthmān, held that both should inherit a half; if there were two brothers, each should receive a third; if there were more than two brothers, the grandfather should still receive a third and the brothers should divide the rest between them. In other words, he should be treated as equal to a brother as long as he received a minimum of a third of the estate, but never receive less than this in competition with collaterals. Accordingly, if competing with sisters, he should be treated like a brother as long as he received a third or more (i.e. alongside from one to four sisters) but never receive less than that.[211]

Consanguine collaterals were treated in exactly the same way as germanes in the absence of any germanes (except that, not sharing the same mother, they would never inherit as germanes would in the *Ḥimāriyya* situation). It was a special feature of Zayd's doctrine, however, that if both consanguines and germanes were present both would be 'counted' (*yuʿāddūna*) against the grandfather in determining the portion due to him, even though the consanguines would be excluded from inheritance by the germanes.[212] This, however, could lead to anomalies, such as if a grandfather were to inherit alongside a germane and a consanguine brother: the grandfather would be treated as one of three brothers and thus receive a third, but the germane brother would exclude the consanguine brother and thus take the remaining two-thirds rather than sharing the estate equally with the grandfather (or with both the grandfather and the consanguine brother). The only exception to the *muʿādda* doctrine was when a grandfather inherited alongside a germane sister and a consanguine brother and sister: 'counting' the two sisters and one brother against the grandfather would initially allow him and the brother, as males, a portion of two-sixths each, and the two sisters, as females, a portion of one-sixth each. The full sister, however, was due half of the inheritance as Qur'anic heir: her portion was therefore increased to that of one-half at the expense of the consanguines, who then divided the remainder of the estate (i.e. one-sixth, being the residue left after the full sister had taken her half out of the four-sixths due to the brothers and sisters by the *muʿādda* doctrine) between them on the basis of a male getting the same as the portion of two females (i.e. the brother would get two-thirds of the remaining sixth and the consanguine sister one-third of it), with the grandfather retaining his original third.[213]

So far we have spoken of a grandfather inheriting only alongside collaterals. When others with a fixed share, such as a mother and/or a spouse, were also present, the conflicting claims caused many problems and resulted in widely differing solutions. The case of 'The Tatters' (*al-Khuraqā'*), where the grandfather survived alongside the mother and a full sister, is a case in point. According to Abū Bakr and Ibn ʿAbbās, the mother would receive a third and the grandfather, excluding all collaterals, would receive the remaining two-thirds. According to Zayd, the mother would still receive her third, but, although he allowed the sister to inherit alongside the grandfather, her Qur'anic portion of one half as sole agnatic collateral did not make sense against what would then be only one-sixth remaining for the grandfather, considering that the grandfather as sole inheritor would be entitled to the whole estate as opposed to the sister's half. He therefore treated the grandfather and the sister as agnatic residuaries: the grandfather, as a male, would receive two-thirds of the remainder, and the sister, as a female, one-third. Others, such as Ibn Masʿūd and ʿAlī, allowed the sister her Qur'anic half first, but then differed: whereas ʿAlī also allowed the mother her Qur'anic third, thus leaving only the remaining sixth to the grandfather, Ibn Masʿūd felt that the grandfather should never get less than the mother (since a father would either get the same as a mother if inheriting alongside children, or get twice as much as her if there were no children) and therefore divided the remainder out between the grandfather and the mother on the Qur'anic 2:1 basis, thus giving the mother a sixth and the grandfather a third. (This last solution was also said to be that of ʿUmar).[214]

The conflict between the grandfather and collaterals was particularly evident in instances where a deceased woman left a mother and a husband as well as a grandfather and collaterals. In such cases the husband would automatically take a half and the mother (her portion reduced by the presence of more than one collateral)[215] would take a sixth, thus leaving only a third of the original estate to be divided between the remaining heirs, i.e. the grandfather and any collaterals. If the collaterals were all agnatic (i.e. germane and/or consanguine), recourse was had to the principles described above regarding agnatic collaterals, including the *muʿādda* doctrine when both germane and consanguine were present, with the additional proviso that the grandfather would never receive less than a sixth (his portion by *qiyās* with the minimum Qur'anic portion for a father).

If the collaterals were all uterine they would, as we have seen, be excluded by the grandfather,[216] who would thus take the whole of the remaining third.

If the collaterals included both consanguines and uterines, Mālik's position was that neither type should inherit and that the grandfather should again take the remaining third, his argument being that the grandfather excluded the uterines, but that if there were no grandfather the uterines would take a third at the expense of the consanguines: therefore the grandfather had more right to inheritance than the uterines, who in turn had more right than the consanguines. Consequently, if the uterines received nothing alongside the grandfather, nor too should the consanguines. This rule, which was specific to the Mālikīs, was known as *al-Mālikiyya*, or 'Mālik's rule'.[217]

If, on the other hand, there was a germane brother or brothers present with the uterines, Mālik followed the principle illustrated in the *Ḥimāriyya* case: since, in the absence of the grandfather, the germane brother or brothers would share in the inheritance with the uterines by virtue of having the same mother, they were to be considered as uterines in his presence as well, and thus be excluded by the grandfather and receive nothing. In other words, alongside their uterine brothers they could not be considered as uterines for one purpose and agnates for another. This rule was known as the *shibh al-Mālikiyya*, or 'the rule analogous to Mālik's rule'.[218]

A further situation which initiated much difference of opinion was when a woman died leaving her husband, her mother, a full sister and a grandfather. This case, known as *al-Akdariyya* ('The Confounding Case') is in fact the *Khuraqā'* case with the addition of the husband: accordingly, we find the same solutions as in the *Khuraqā'* case but with the necessary proportional reduction (*ʿawl*) of all shares after the apportionment of the agreed one-half to the husband.[219]

If we consider the complex problems and solutions that such combinations of collaterals and grandfather engendered (and we have by no means considered all the solutions proposed), it is hardly surprising that ʿUmar should have been so reluctant to come to any final decision as to the relative rights of a grandfather (with no overt Qurʾanic portion but with implicit rights as father of the father) inheriting alongside collaterals (with their overtly specified Qurʾanic portions). There were too many ambiguities and too many different ways of applying *qiyās*: indeed, as Ibn Rushd points out, the commonest causes for dispute on questions of inheritance were, firstly, the different ways that *qiyās* could be applied, and, secondly, the problem of *ishtirāk*, i.e. that words could be defined in more than one way (e.g. *walad* and *kalāla*).[220] Given this background, what is remarkable is how definite Mālik's treatment of this problem is. Indeed, for him it is as if there *is* no problem. He refers to the *kalāla* section of Q 4: 12 in the two chapters dealing respectively with uterine and germane collaterals, but also devotes an entire chapter specifically to *kalāla*.[221] What is noteworthy here is that, as with the chapters on inheritance referred to in the previous chapter, his reliance on *ʿamal* is absolute. After mentioning the *ḥadīth* about ʿUmar's uncertainty referred to above, he says quite simply, 'The agreed position here, about which there is no doubt, and which I found the people of knowledge in this city following, is that there are two types of *kalāla* …' He then goes on to explain that Q 4: 12 refers to the inheritance of uterine collaterals when there is neither child nor father to inherit (*ḥattā lā yakūna walad wa-lā wālid*), while Q 4: 176 refers to when collaterals inherit by virtue of their agnatic link with the deceased. Finally, he indicates what the essential problem must have been *vis-à-vis kalāla*, by discussing why the grandfather has precedence over collaterals in cases of *kalāla*, even though collaterals are afforded specific shares of inheritance in the Qurʾan while the grandfather is not.[222] In other words, the problem was about the relative rights of the grandfather alongside collaterals.

It would seem therefore that ʿUmar's uncertainty about *kalāla* was not so much an uncertainty about the basic meaning of the word, as about the specific implications of the two *kalāla* verses when applied in practice, which centred in particular on the rival claims of the grandfather alongside collaterals, with or without other inheritors.[223] In other words, as we noted above in the case of the inheritance due to children, the problems were raised, and therefore had to be solved, precisely because people were putting, or trying to put, the Qurʾanic injunctions into practice. By Mālik's time, if not considerably earlier, these problems had, as we have seen, been effectively solved, albeit according to different principles in the two main geographical centres of Iraq and the Ḥijāz. To repeat, what is remarkable is the degree of unanimity on these matters – at least in Madina – despite the problems, so that Mālik can say, 'The agreed position here, about which there is no doubt, and which I have found the people of knowledge in this city following, is that there are two types of *kalāla* ...', which once again illustrates his complete confidence and certainty in Madinan *ʿamal*.

Implication (*al-mafhūm*)

We have noted above several instances of where Mālik arrives at a judgement by juxtaposing two or more verses. It was of course also possible to arrive at a judgement by considering the implications (*mafhūm*, lit. 'what is understood') of a single verse.

This idea of the *mafhūm* later became discussed under the two headings of *mafhūm al-muwāfaqa* and *mafhūm al-mukhālafa* (other 'implications' being subsumed under the categories of *qiyās*, *ʿumūm*, etc). As mentioned earlier, *mafhūm al-muwāfaqa* – or *al-mafhūm bi-l-awlā* as it is also known – is the idea that because an expressly mentioned judgement applies in certain circumstances, it will apply equally or even more so in similar circumstances; while *mafhūm al-mukhālafa* – or *dalīl al-khiṭāb* as it is also known – is the idea that because an expressly mentioned judgement applies in certain defined circumstances, it will not apply in the absence of those circumstances.[224]

We shall briefly consider both of these techniques of interpretation as they occur in the *Muwaṭṭaʾ*.

Mafhūm al-muwāfaqa

In many respects *mafhūm al-muwāfaqa* is similar to *qiyās* in that if a certain judgement applies to X, then the same judgement is considered to apply to something similar to X. The classic example of this is Q 17: 23's *wa-lā taqul lahumā uffin* ('And do not say "Uff!" to them [i.e. one's parents]'), from which it was understood that similar or worse actions, such as swearing at them or hitting them, were equally forbidden, if not more so, which is why this principle is also known as *al-mafhūm bi-l-awlā*, i.e. *a fortiori* deduction.[225]

There are of course many examples of *qiyās* in the *Muwaṭṭaʾ*, but there is only one obvious example of *mafhūm al-muwāfaqa*, and that is in the chapter entitled 'What a Sick Man Should Do With Regard to His Fasting.' Mālik says:

> The position that I have heard from the people of knowledge (*al-amr alladhī samiʿtu min ahl al-ʿilm*) is that if a sick man is suffering from an

> illness which makes it difficult for him to fast and tires him out and exhausts him, he may break his fast. The same applies to a sick man when his sickness reaches the point where he finds it difficult to do the prayer standing up – and [only] Allah knows better than His servant when this is the case[226] – and sometimes it does not reach this point. If it does, he may pray sitting down, for the *dīn* of Allah is ease. Allah has made an allowance (*arkhaṣa*) for a traveller to break his fast while travelling, although he has more strength to fast than a sick man. Allah, the Exalted, says in His Book, 'So whoever among you is ill or on a journey [should fast] a number of other days',[227] so Allah has made an allowance for a traveller to break his fast while travelling, although he has more strength to fast than a sick man. This is what I like best out of what I have heard and this is the agreed position [here] (*fa-hādhā aḥabbu mā samiᶜtu ilayya wa-huwa l-amr al-mujtamaᶜ ᶜalayhi*).'[228]

Thus, if a traveller, who only experiences a limited amount of difficulty, may break his fast, then how much more so should a sick man, who experiences much greater difficulty, be allowed to do so.

Mālik's deduction and his comment that this is what he likes best out of what he has heard, which thus presupposes other opinions, is somewhat puzzling given that the *fuqahā᾿* were all agreed that a sick man could break his fast, precisely because of the very verse that Mālik mentions, and that some of them even allowed a broader definition of 'sickness' to include anything that could go under the name rather than just a sickness that was difficult to bear.[229] Al-Bājī points out that Mālik's argument is an argument against those who held that a sick man could only break his fast if he feared for his life and not just because he was experiencing great difficulty, but then acknowledges that he knows of no-one who ever actually held this opinion.[230] One can only assume either that Mālik had indeed heard such a view on this point and was responding to it, or that (as al-Bājī suggests) he was providing an answer to a possible future objection that his students might come across, rather in the way that we saw in the instance of *saᶜy* mentioned above.[231]

Mafhūm al-mukhālafa

We have already noted a number of examples of Mālik's employing the technique of *mafhūm al-mukhālafa*. It is particularly evident in the judgement that a Muslim may only marry a slave-girl if the two conditions mentioned in Q 4: 25 are met: by *mafhūm al-mukhālafa*, if the conditions are not met, the permission does not apply.[232] (This type is known as *mafhūm al-sharṭ*, lit. 'the implication of the conditional clause').[233] That this slave-girl must also be a Muslim is also based on *mafhūm al-mukhālafa* (in this case, *mafhūm al-waṣf*, lit. 'the implication of the adjective'): since the permission in the verse is restricted to 'believing', i.e. Muslim, slave-girls, the implication is that non-Muslim slave-girls are not acceptable.[234] Similarly, in the example mentioned earlier about the permissibility of eating horse-meat, horses, mules and donkeys are mentioned in Q 16: 8 only for riding and adornment and are therefore assumed not to be used for food since if this use had been intended it would have been mentioned, as it was in the case of camels.[235]

Another example that has been referred to is the judgement that *zinā* does not bring about the same prohibitions that marriage does, because, in Mālik's view, 'Allah, the Blessed and Exalted, says, "And the mothers of your wives" and has thus only made *ḥarām* what occurs through marriage without mentioning *zinā*.'[236] Thus because only wives are mentioned, the other category, i.e. non-wives, are assumed to be excluded (slave-girls, as we have seen, being considered to come under the category of wives, thus extending the idea of 'marriage' (*nikāḥ*) in the prohibitions of Q 4: 22–23 to 'licit intercourse').[237]

There were many exceptions, however, to this rule of *mafhūm al-mukhālafa*. In particular we may note the following instances:

1. Q 5: 95 declares that killing game while in *iḥrām* is forbidden and then says that whoever does so deliberately (*muta'ammidan*) must pay a recompense (*jazā'/kaffāra*) for his act.[238] By *mafhūm al-mukhālafa* one would expect accidental killing of game to be excluded from this judgement, or at least that the judgement for it would be different. In fact, the predominant majority (*jumhūr*) of the *fuqahā'* made no such distinction: killing game while in *iḥrām*, whether intentionally or otherwise, necessitated a recompense, since a life which should be protected had been unnecessarily destroyed and the killer was liable (*ḍāmin*) for such 'damage' (*itlāf*) whether his action was deliberate or accidental, the only difference being that deliberate killing involved a blameworthy action (*ithm*) whereas accidental killing did not.[239] As Mālik comments:

> I have heard some of the people of knowledge say that if a *muḥrim* throws [something] at something and thereby kills some game although not intending to do so, he must pay a recompense for it. Similarly, if a person not in *iḥrām* throws [something] at something in the *ḥaram* and thereby kills some game although not intending to do so, he must pay a recompense for it, since, as far as this is concerned, deliberate and accidental killing are alike.[240]

Indeed, it was only the Ẓāhirīs (Ibn Juzayy also attributes this view to the earlier authorities Ibn ᶜAbbās, Abū Thawr and Ibn al-Mundhir)[241] who excepted non-*mutaᶜammids* from this judgement, and they did so not because of *mafhūm al-mukhālafa*, which they did not accept, but because only the judgement for killing game deliberately appears in the Qur᾽an, and therefore only that judgement should be applied.[242]

2. A similar example occurs in the chapter 'What Has Come Down About the Two Arbiters (*al-ḥakamayn*)'.[243] Mālik reports the view of ᶜAlī that the 'two arbiters' referred to in Q 4: 35 – 'If you fear a breach between them [i.e. the husband and wife], then send an arbiter (*ḥakam*) from his family and an arbiter from her family: if they [i.e. the two arbiters] desire reconciliation, Allah will bring about agreement between them [i.e. the husband and wife]'[244] – have the authority to either reconcile or separate, although the verse suggests only reconciliation, adding his own comment that this opinion is the best that he has heard from the people of knowledge.[245] Abū Ḥanīfa for his part and al-Shāfiᶜī according to one opinion of his held that the 'two arbiters' did not have the authority to separate the couple unless the husband specifically allowed them to do so, since, in their view, divorce was always the sole prerogative of the husband.[246] Mālik, however, considered the 'two arbiters' to be representatives of the ruling authority (*sulṭān*) rather than agents (*wukalā᾽*) of the couple, and thus allowed them the right to separate the couple if they saw fit, as he also allowed the ruler the right to make a man divorce if he was causing harm (*ḍarar*) to his wife, as, for example, when a man refused to either divorce or return to his wife after the four months of *īlā᾽* were up (this latter judgement being an example of *al-maṣāliḥ al-mursala*, i.e. where a new judgement is arrived at on the basis of what is for the general good (*al-maṣlaḥa al-ᶜāmma*) even though it may go against an accepted general principle, i.e., in this case, that divorce is the sole prerogative of the husband).[247]

3. An interesting early example of how the *mafhūm* could mislead occurs in the 'General Chapter on *Saᶜy*' where there is a report from ᶜUrwa that when he was young he used to think that the Qur᾽anic verse 'Ṣafā and Marwa are among the outward signs (*shaᶜā᾽ir*) of Allah, so when someone goes on *ḥajj* to the House, or does *ᶜumra*, there is no harm in him going around them both (*fa-lā junāḥa ᶜalayhi an yaṭṭawwafa bi-himā*)' (Q 2: 158) implied that it did not matter if one did not go around them. However, when he mentioned this to his aunt ᶜĀisha she corrected him and said that if that had been the case the verse would have read '. . . there is no harm in him not going around them both', and then explained to him that the verse had come down about the Anṣār who, in the days before Islam, used to go

on *ḥajj* to the shrine of Manāt, near Qudayd, and would avoid doing *saʿy* between Ṣafā and Marwa. Then, when Islam came, they asked the Prophet about this and Q 2: 158 was revealed, saying that 'Ṣafā and Marwa are among the outward signs of Allah, so when someone goes on *ḥajj* to the House, or does *ʿumra*, there is no harm in him going around them both.'[248] ʿĀisha is thus pointing out that the contrast is not between options at the present time – as if it did not matter whether one did *saʿy* or not – but between the situation before Islam, when the Anṣār felt that it was blameworthy to do so, and the situation after Islam, when it was no longer blameworthy but, rather, an intrinsic part of *ḥajj* and *ʿumra*.

We thus have here (assuming the authenticity of the report) an early example of *tafsīr* by context, this context being two-fold: firstly, the knowledge that the Prophet and his Companions had done *saʿy* as part of the rites of *ḥajj* and *ʿumra*, and, secondly, the knowledge that the Anṣār had formerly avoided it but that they had lost any compunction that they might have had about it when Q 2: 158 was revealed. If this context were not known, it would be easy to completely misconstrue the verse, as did ʿUrwa in his youth; as it is, the context was known and thus the real contrast was clear. Nevertheless, some authorities (among them Ibn Masʿūd, Anas, ʿAṭāʾ, Ibn Sīrīn, and also ʿUrwa), presumably going by the *ẓāhir* implication of the text, are said to have held that *saʿy* was only voluntary, this being reflected in the variant reading *an* ***lā*** *yaṭṭawwafa bi-himā* ('... in him not going around them both') which overtly states that it is acceptable not to do *saʿy*.[249] However, the established *ʿamal* of the *saʿy* was so strong that the idea of it being merely voluntary was not preserved in any of the later *madhhabs*.[250]

Finally, it should be noted that universal agreement was reached that *mafhūm al-mukhālafa* did not apply in instances where (a) the qualification restricting the judgement is being used merely as a usual description, as in Q 4: 23's *wa-rabāʾibukumu llātī fī ḥujūrikum* ('and your step-daughters who are in your care') (rather, *all* step-daughters were included, not just those living in their step-father's house); or (b) where it is an exhortatory addition, as in Q 3: 130's 'Do not devour usury in multiplied multiples (*aḍʿāfan muḍāʿafa*)' (rather, *ribā* was considered *ḥarām* however much or little of it was involved); or (c) where a specific judgement is mentioned but *qiyās* is clearly valid, as in the *ḥadīth* about the five *fawāsiq* which a person in *iḥrām* is allowed to kill, which was extended to include all dangerous beasts;[251] or (d) where there is other evidence regarding the judgement, as, for example, in the instance of 'A free man for a free man and a slave for a slave and a female for a female' (Q 2: 178) where one would expect, by *mafhūm al-mukhālafa*, that a man should not be killed in retaliation for killing a woman, but where Q 5: 45's 'a life for a life' indicated that this could be done;[252] or (e) where the restricted judgement is the answer to a specific question or situation, as in the verse about *saʿy* just mentioned.[253]

The examples in this and the preceding chapters thus illustrate not only the extent of Qurʾanic reference in the *Muwaṭṭaʾ* but also the tendencies and techniques used by Mālik to derive judgements from the Qurʾan. However, since there are exceptions to all these techniques, it seems reasonable to suggest that there was a higher criterion governing Mālik's thinking, namely, Madinan *ʿamal*. Since the main arguments for or against this *ʿamal* hinge on its historical pedigree and the nature of its historical development, it is to such considerations that we now turn.

CHAPTER SEVEN

Chronological Considerations

It will be apparent from many examples in the previous chapters that the work of Qurʾanic interpretation was seen by Mālik as a continuing process: it had been begun by the Prophet and continued by the Companions and their Successors, and was still operative in his own time, since not only were new situations always arising, but so too were they always changing, however subtly, and even well accepted judgements might need to be revised in the light of new circumstances. Thus we find Mālik commenting that the verse *li-yastaʾdhinkumu lladhīna malakat aymānukum wa-lladhīna lam yablughū l-ḥuluma minkum thalātha marrātin* … ('Let those whom your right hands possess and those among you who have not reached puberty ask you for permission [to enter] at three times …') (Q 24: 58) no longer applies in the same way as it did before people began using doors and curtains, the implication being that when there were no doors and/or curtains there was no sign of whether or not the occupant of a room wanted to remain undisturbed and slaves and minors (who could normally come and go freely) would have to ask permission before entering at these three times, whereas once doors and curtains began to be used, a closed door or a let down curtain was sufficient indication that no one was to enter without permission.[1] Mālik's comment must therefore mean not that these people no longer had to ask permission before entering at these three times, but that with the use of doors and curtains there was no longer the same need to ask as there had been before.[2] Nevertheless, as will already be obvious from the discussions on Madinan *ʿamal* above, the overwhelming tendency in Mālik's case (and, indeed, the intention behind the *Muwaṭṭaʾ*) is to preserve the traditional picture with all its peculiarities rather than to try to change, adapt or systematise it in any way.

This chronological development results in a very definite 'layering' to the judgements in the *Muwaṭṭaʾ*, which finds expression in, for example, the ordering of the material in each chapter and the difference between Mālik's *sunna* and *amr* terms, the first indicating judgements deriving from the time of the Prophet, and the second indicating judgements containing a significant element of later *ijtihād*.[3] Indeed, what we find illustrated by the *Muwaṭṭa*ʾ is a continuous development of the details of the law, first of all by the Prophet, and then by the Companions, the Successors, and the Successors of the Successors (including Mālik). Furthermore, this development is not only the work of scholars, but is also, quite naturally, the work of those with political authority, and thus we find numerous references in the *Muwaṭṭa*ʾ to the judgements of various Umayyad caliphs and governors in addition to the well-known scholars of Madina. In the present chapter we shall look briefly at certain aspects of the chronology of this material, beginning with the inter-related sciences of *naskh* (abrogation) and *asbāb al-nuzūl* (the occasions of revelation), which relate specifically to judgements deriving from the time of the Prophet (i.e. Qurʾanic and *sunna* material), followed by a consideration of the *amr* material deriving from the time of the Companions and the Successors, and, in particular, the contribution of the caliphs and governors of the early Umayyad period, i.e. up to and including the reign of Yazīd ibn ʿAbd al-Malik (r. 101–5), who is the last caliph to whom there is specific reference in the *Muwaṭṭa*ʾ.

Naskh

Mālik records how Ibn ʿAbbās said that during the lifetime of the Prophet the Companions 'used to go by the most recent practice of the Messenger of Allah (*kānū yaʾkhudhūna bi-l-aḥdath fa-l-aḥdath min amr rasūl Allāh*)',[4] thus presupposing that certain judgements could be, and were, superseded by others. This was the phenomenon of *naskh*, or abrogation. That this could also apply to the Qurʾan is of course a standard element in traditional *fiqh* (although questioned at various times by various authorities, particularly those with Muʿtazilite tendencies).[5] The idea is clearly accepted by Mālik, who overtly refers to this concept in the chapter on 'Bequests to Heirs and the Right of Possession (*al-ḥiyāza*)' where he says that the verse 'It is prescribed for you [that] if one of you is at the point of death and leaves wealth, [he should make] a bequest (*al-waṣiyya*) to his parents and relatives' (Q 2: 180) was abrogated (*mansūkha*) by the verses detailing the specific shares of inheritance (i.e. Q 4: 11, 12 and 176).[6] Indeed, there was no disagreement among any of the *fuqahā*ʾ, both in the earliest period and later, that the judgement about bequests in Q 2: 180 had been at least partly superseded firstly by the inheritance verses, which gave specific shares to parents and (certain) relatives rather than allowing them a general right to receive bequests, and, secondly, by the Prophet's judgement that bequests were only allowed up to a maximum of one third of a man's estate, none of which could (normally) be given to someone who would otherwise be entitled to any of the inheritance.[7] The only disagreement was over whether bequests to those who were not otherwise entitled to inheritance should be restricted to relatives (thus retaining the general framework of Q 2: 180 and assuming *takhṣīṣ* rather than *naskh*), or be allowed to anybody (thus assuming complete abrogation of the verse's judgement). A few *ʿulamāʾ* (Ṭāwūs is given particular mention) took the first view, whereas the majority took the latter view, going by the *ḥadīth* that the Prophet had allowed only two out of six (i.e. the one-third maximum for bequests) of the slaves that a man had freed on his death to remain free when that was all the wealth the man had left, and the two who benefited from this decision were certainly not relatives of the dead man.[8]

The verb *nasakha* is also used in the technical sense of abrogation in the report from ʿĀʾisha referred to earlier concerning the minimum number of sucklings (*raḍaʿāt*) that brought about foster relationship and thus constituted a bar to marriage.[9] ʿĀʾisha's wording is:

> Part of what was revealed as Qurʾan was: 'ten known sucklings constitute a bar [to marriage] (*ʿashru raḍaʿātin maʿlūmātin yuḥarrimna*).' This was then abrogated by 'five known sucklings' (*thumma nusikhna bi-khamsin maʿlūmātin*), which was still part of what was recited as Qurʾan when the Messenger of Allah, may Allah bless him and grant him peace, died.[10]

Al-Shāfiʿī accepted the validity of this report and the implied judgement that a minimum of five sucklings was necessary before foster-relationship could be accepted (although not only because of this 'Qurʾanic' judgement but also because of various *ḥadīths* to the same effect),[11] but the earlier, 'ancient', position, shared by both the Madinans and the Iraqis (with some even claiming *ijmāʿ* for it),[12] was that, provided the suckling took place within the first two years of the child's life, even one suckling brought about foster relationship, and thus a bar to marriage.[13] The reason for this judgement was ostensibly the *ʿumūm* of the prohibition in Q 4: 23 – *wa-ummahātukumu llātī arḍaʿnakum wa-akhawātukum mina l-raḍāʿa* ('And [prohibited for you are] your mothers who have suckled you and your sisters by suckling') – and the *ʿumūm* of the *ḥadīths* on the same subject (e.g. *yaḥrumu min al-raḍāʿa mā yaḥrumu min al-nasab* – 'what is *ḥarām* by birth is *ḥarām* by suckling'),[14] but for Mālik, despite his preference for the *ʿumūm*, *ʿamal* was, once again, the decisive criterion, and ʿĀʾisha's judgement in this particular instance was not in accordance with *ʿamal* (*wa-laysa ʿalā hādhā l-ʿamal*).[15] Rather, her judgement was seen as being derived from the special indulgence (*rukhṣa*) allowed by the

Prophet in the case of Sahla bint Suhayl and her adopted son Sālim, which was understood by the other wives of the Prophet to have been specific to that case and not intended as a general rule.[16]

As for the validity of the Qurʾanic reading, ʿĀʾisha's words were not denied, but (the argument was later advanced) this reading was only known through ʿĀʾisha, and readings known only from single authorities were not accepted as Qurʾan; accordingly, judgements derived from them only had the authority of judgements derived from *ḥadīths* related from single authorities (i.e. *akhbār al-āḥād*) which, as we have seen, were not considered a strong enough argument against established *ʿamal*.[17] That this reading should have still have been 'part of what was recited as Qurʾan' was interpreted as meaning not that it was still genuinely part of the Qurʾan at that time, but that some of the Companions still did not know at the time of the Prophet's death that it had been abrogated.[18]

Similar in some respects to the instance of suckling was the stoning penalty for adultery. Mālik mentions a report from ʿUmar to the effect that the stoning penalty had been included in the Qurʾan but that the wording had later been abrogated although the judgement remained. ʿUmar says:

> *Sunnas* have been established for you and obligations (*farāʾiḍ*) have been laid down for you and you have been left on a clear path, unless you lead people astray to the right and the left ... Be careful lest you perish through [ignoring] the verse of stoning (*an tahlikū ʿan āyat al-rajm*) with somebody saying, 'We do not find two *ḥadds* in the Book of Allah.' The Messenger of Allah, may Allah bless him and grant him peace, carried out the stoning penalty, and so have we. By Him in whose hand my self is, if it were not that people would say, "ʿUmar ibn al-Khaṭṭāb has added to the Book of Allah, the Exalted', we would have written it – 'Mature men and mature women, stone them both absolutely (*al-shaykhu wa-l-shaykhatu fa-rjumūhumā l-batta*)' – because we have most certainly recited it.[19]

On a theoretical level this would thus have been, like al-Shāfiʿī's minimum of five sucklings referred to above, another example of where the words of the Qurʾan were abrogated but not the judgement (*naskh al-tilāwa dūna l-ḥukm*), but it is obvious that for Mālik such concerns are hardly a consideration. His position is, rather, that of ʿUmar's words, 'The Messenger of Allah, may Allah bless him and grant him peace, carried out the stoning penalty and so have we.' In other words, the stoning penalty for adulterers had the sanction of being a *sunna* which had been established by the Prophet and continued by the Rightly-Guided Caliphs. It was, therefore, the agreed *ʿamal* and needed no further justification. That it had also been in a verse of the Qur'an – and was in the Torah – is also accepted by Mālik, as the reports included in the chapter on stoning show, but these three elements – the *sunna* of the Prophet, the one-time stoning verse of the Qur'an and the judgement of the Torah – are not seen as three different possible alternatives for the source of the penalty (contrary to what Burton, for instance, has suggested), but, rather, as integral, even if not equally important, elements in a composite picture of 'What Has Come Down About Stoning' (the title of the chapter).[20] Furthermore, we may note that although for Mālik it is enough that the practice of stoning is endorsed by *ʿamal*,[21] he was obviously aware of the contrary opinion of those who denied it because it was not in the Qur'an (i.e. the opposition group implied by ʿUmar's comment, 'Let no-one say that are not two *ḥadds* in the Book of Allah', and identified by Ibn Ḥajar as the Khawārij and some of the Muʿtazila),[22] and the reports about the stoning verse in the Qur'an and the Torah can thus be seen to function as further evidence of (a) the penalty's validity and acceptability, and (b) of its divine credentials (albeit in an earlier dispensation).

Finally, note should be made of a third instance of actual mention of the word *naskh* that occurs in the transmission of al-Shaybānī, who records that Saʿīd ibn al-Musayyab said that the verse 'A fornicator (*al-zānī*) should marry only a fornicatress or an idolatress (*mushrika*), and a fornicatress should be married only to a fornicator or an idolater' (Q 24: 3) had been abrogated (*nusikhat*) by verse 32 in the same *sūra* which says, 'And help the unmarried among you to get married (*wa-ankiḥū l-ayāmā minkum*), and the righteous (*ṣāliḥīn*)[23] among your slaves and slave-girls', thus encouraging marriage between people in general, regardless of any considerations of earlier sexual impropriety.[24] This judgement was in fact shared by the majority of the *ʿulamā'*, including Mālik, because of reports indicating that it was condoned by both the Prophet and various Companions.[25]

It is thus obvious that for Mālik, as indeed for all those who accepted it, the phenomenon of *naskh* was not in question: they accepted it as fact. Furthermore, for Mālik, given the natural sifting influence of *ʿamal*, questions of what was *nāsikh* and what was *mansūkh* were almost an irrelevance: what was retained by *ʿamal* was obviously *nāsikh* and what was not retained was obviously *mansūkh*.

A certain amount of analysis has been done recently on *naskh* by Western scholars, particularly Burton and, to a lesser extent, Wansbrough and Powers. A recurrent theme in Burton's work (and, following him, that of the other two) is that the theories of *naskh* were one of a number of techniques invented by the *uṣūlīs* to explain 'embarassing' contradictions in *fiqh* and justify their own particular position, rather than being the later systematisation of a genuine, well-attested, phenomenon which was taken for granted by such as Mālik.[26] Here is not the place to go into the whole debate about *naskh*, beyond the simple reaffirmation that for the 'ancient' schools in general, and Mālik in particular, *naskh* was never in question; nor was it (for Mālik at any rate) particularly relevant to the problem of determining the *sharīʿa*, as is amply demonstrated by what we have seen of his almost complete lack of concern in the *Muwaṭṭaʾ* for the problems later to be associated with this topic.

Asbāb al-nuzūl

Associated with the discussions on *naskh* was the whole science of *asbāb al-nuzūl*, i.e. the knowledge of when particular parts or verses of the Qurʾan had been revealed. This had the function not only of enabling a more accurate dating of a particular verse and thus determining whether it might be abrogating or itself have been abrogated, but also of providing a context for understanding the wording of an *āya*. However, despite the value given to it by certain Muslim scholars (al-Suyūṭī, for instance, following al-Wāḥidī and others, regards it as one of the main branches of knowledge that an interpreter of the Qurʾan must know),[27] its value as a means of *tafsīr* in the *Muwaṭṭaʾ* is minimal. There are fifteen reports where overt reference is made to the *sabab al-nuzūl* of an *āya* (or *sūra*), but in the majority of these instances the information is of 'historical' rather than legal interest, merely indicating that a major change occurred within the *sharīʿa* or that a major new element was introduced into it, with little, if any, legal detail being given about the change. Thus, for instance, Mālik records the *ḥadīth* about when the 'verse of *tayammum*' (i.e. either Q 5: 6 or Q 4: 43)[28] was revealed, but it tells us little more than that this verse was revealed to allow an alternative means of purification (*ṭahāra*) before doing the prayer when there was no water available for the normal practice of *wuḍūʾ*,[29] and this much is apparent from the verse itself: the *ḥadīth* adds no details about how to do *tayammum*. The same applies to the change of *qibla* from Jerusalem to Makka;[30] the introduction of the procedure of *liʿān* in cases when a husband finds someone with his wife;[31] the limitation of divorce to a maximum of three times so as to prevent the husband causing indefinite harm to his wife by continually divorcing her and then taking her back before her *ʿidda* is over so that she is never free to remarry;[32] and the institution of the veil (*ḥijāb*) between those permitted to marry one another and the related practice of calling adopted sons by their real father's name so that there would be no confusion on this point.[33] There are also oblique references to the revelation of the verses which made the fast of Ramaḍān obligatory and superseded the fast of ʿĀshūrā' (which then became merely voluntary),[34] and to 'the *āya* which came down in the summer' about *kalāla*.[35] We are also given some information about the revelation of Sūrat ʿAbasa (Q 80) and Sūrat al-Fatḥ (Q 48).[36] In none of these instances, however, is there any explanation of the words involved or of the relevant legal details (except, perhaps, for the detail given at the end of the long report about *liʿān* that the man involved divorced his wife irrevocably 'before being told to do so by the Prophet', which, says Ibn Shihāb, became the *sunna* with regard to those doing *liʿān*).[37] What is provided rather is a historical context, which, as Rippin points out, may have the important theological (and polemical) function of confirming the historicity of the revelation itself, as well as having its own narrative value, but is not of much value for legal purposes.[38]

In only three instances in the *Muwaṭṭaʾ* can one find any indication of the direct derivation of a judgement from such *asbāb* material. The first is the instance we have already discussed about ʿUrwa's misunderstanding of the Qurʾanic statement that there is no harm in doing *saʿy* between Ṣafā and Marwa and how ʿĀʾisha had corrected his erroneous deduction that *saʿy* was only optional by pointing out that the verse had in fact been revealed to stay the misgivings of the Anṣār who, in the days before Islam, had always avoided doing *saʿy* of Ṣafā and Marwa.[39] The second instance is where Mālik notes that ʿUrwa said that the verse 'Do not say your prayer out loudly nor say it silently, but seek a way between the two (*lā tajhar bi-ṣalātika wa-lā tukhāfit bi-hā wa-btaghi bayna dhālika sabīlan*)' (Q 17: 110) refers to supplication (*duʿāʾ*).[40] The third is where Mālik gives his own opinion (although he also states that he has heard it from 'the people of knowledge', thus illustrating again how what he calls his own opinion may also be overtly attributed by him to others before him)[41] that the word *jidāl* ('argumentation') in Q 2: 197 refers to the disputes that the Quraysh used to have with the other tribes as to who was the most correct in their performance of *ḥajj*.[42]

The second of these examples – about *ṣalāt* meaning *duʿāʾ* – is typical of much of the material in the *Muwaṭṭaʾ*: it tells us one side of a controversy without mentioning the other, and Mālik does not tell us whether it is his own view or not.

The difference of opinion on Q 17: 110 centred around whether the word *ṣalāt* in this instance has its usual Qurʾanic meaning of 'ritual prayer' or its basic meaning of 'supplication' (*duʿāʾ*).[43] Ibn ʿAbbās is reported to have said that this verse came down during the difficult times in Makka: if the Prophet recited the Qurʾan out loudly it encouraged the idolaters to curse Allah, the Qurʾan and the Prophet, but if he simply recited it to himself his Companions were not able to hear him. Allah therefore sent down this verse telling him to steer a middle course between the two.[44] Another version of the story has it that the idolaters would move away if they heard the Prophet reciting the Qurʾan out loudly and this prevented those among them who were interested in hearing it from doing so; if, however, he recited it to himself, his Companions would not be able to hear him.[45] *Ṣalāt* in this instance is therefore interpreted as recitation (*qirāʾa*) in the prayer and thus, by extension, the prayer itself.

ʿĀʾisha, on the other hand (and Ibn ʿAbbās again according to certain authorities) is reported to have said that this verse came down about supplication (*duʿāʾ*) (as in the report in the *Muwaṭṭaʾ*), which is bolstered by the fact that the first part of the verse is overtly about *duʿāʾ*: *qulu dʿū llāha awu dʿū l-raḥmāna ayyan mā tadʿū fa-lahu l-asmāʾu l-ḥusnā* ('Say, call on Allah or call on the Raḥmān; whichever you use, He has the best names'). (Since al-Bukhārī and al-Ṭabarī relate this view of ʿĀʾisha's *via* ʿUrwa and his son Hishām,[46] and the ʿUrwa-ʿĀʾisha connection is well known, it would seem reasonable to assume that ʿĀʾisha was also the source of ʿUrwa's comment, related *via* Hishām, in the *Muwaṭṭaʾ*).

These two views were to some extent harmonised by the view that the verse did come down about making *duʿāʾ*, but *within* the prayer, or at least immediately after it. Thus there is a report (also from ʿĀʾisha) that the verse came down about the *tashahhud* at the end of the prayer,[47] and another (*via* ʿAbdallāh ibn Shaddād) that it came down about making *duʿāʾ* after the prayer.[48] There is also a report from Abu Hurayra that it refers to the Prophet raising his voice in *duʿāʾ* when doing the prayer near the Kaʿba,[49] and another, from Ibn Sīrīn, that the 'silent' recitation is that of Abū Bakr, and the 'loud' recitation that of ʿUmar.[50]

What, then, was Mālik's purpose in including the report from ʿUrwa and what was his own view on the matter?

This report is included in the section 'How *Duʿāʾ* is Made (*al-ʿamal fī l-duʿāʾ*)', and it would seem that Mālik's prime concern was not to resolve any controversy about the verse but to use the view mentioned to explain how *duʿāʾ* should be done. A loud voice should be avoided, but nor should the *duʿāʾ* be merely said silently in one's mind: it should be said out loud, but not in too loud a voice.

As for Mālik's own view on the meaning of the verse (rather than the judgement), we can only say that his inclusion of a view in the *Muwaṭṭaʾ* without any further comment suggests that this was also his own personal view but that this is not necessarily the case. Indeed, as regards this particular instance, it is related elsewhere that Mālik said, 'The best that I have heard about this is that it means, "Do not recite out loud during the prayers of the day, and do not recite silently during the prayers of the night or [the prayer of] *ṣubḥ*.'"[51] In other words, the verse is interpreted as meaning 'Do not recite out loud in [all of] your prayers, and do not recite silently in [all of] them, but seek a way between these two', i.e. reciting out loud in some and silently in others, as in the five daily prayers. Again, as with the *rafath* and *fusūq* instances mentioned above,[52] this is a typical '*fiqhī*' solution: the difference between the 'out-loud' and 'silent' prayers was well-known and naturally suggested itself in the context of the word *ṣalāt*. Al-Ṭabarī also allows that this meaning has much to commend it were it not for the strength of the other interpretations related from earlier authorities and the absence of this specific opinion among them,[53] which enables us to say that this report from Mālik may thus be an instance of later, independent, *tafsīr* that is not based on earlier opinions.

Consequently, the report from ʿUrwa in the *Muwaṭṭaʾ* may well not reflect Mālik's own view of the meaning of this particular phrase as it occurs in the Qurʾan, but rather an agreement on his part on the judgement implied in it, i.e. that one should not go to extremes in acts of worship involving the voice, especially *duʿāʾ*. Its inclusion in the *Muwaṭṭaʾ* would thus be because it illustrates how *duʿāʾ* should be made rather than because it illustrates the meaning of the Qurʾanic passage (even though it may be a perfectly acceptable *tafsīr* of it).

The third instance concerns the meaning of the word *jidāl* in Q 2: 197's *wa-lā jidāla fī l-ḥajj* ('and [let there be] no argument during the *ḥajj*'). Mālik tells us that in the days before Islam the Quraysh and other Arab tribes would argue amongst themselves during *ḥajj* as to who was the most correct in their performance of it. The Quraysh would stand by the Mashʿar al-Ḥarām at Qazaḥ in Muzdalifa, while the other tribes would stand on ʿArafa, with each claiming that they were right, whereupon Allah sent down the verse 'And for each of them We have appointed a rite which they follow, so do not let them dispute with you in the matter, but call to your Lord; surely you are on a straight path' (Q 22: 67). This, says Malik, is the *jidāl* that is being referred to in the above-mentioned verse, this being not only his opinion but also that of various 'people of knowledge' (*ahl al-ʿilm*).[54]

Again, the title-heading of the chapter in which this report is included – 'Standing (*al-wuqūf*) at ʿArafa and Muzdalifa' – gives us a clue to Malik's purpose in mentioning it. Firstly, he mentions two *ḥadīths*, one from the Prophet and the other from ʿAbdallāh ibn al-Zubayr, to the effect that all of ʿArafa is a standing-place (*mawqif*) except the hollow of ʿUrana, and that all of Muzdalifa is a standing-place except the hollow of Muḥassir, after which he mentions the report outlined above relating to Q 2: 197.[55] It is, therefore, reasonable to assume that it is included here because it relates to the question of where the standing should take place.

Various reasons were given as to why the Quraysh should have chosen a different *mawqif.* According to a report in al-Zurqānī from an unspecified 'Sufyān' (= Sufyān ibn ʿUyayna?), this was because the Quraysh felt that if they stood *outside* the limits of the *ḥaram* (and ʿArafa is outside the limits) they would no longer be respecting their own *ḥaram* and so other people would no longer respect it; the others, however, who stood on the plain of ʿArafa did so because they felt they were preserving the original Abrahamic practice.[56] According to a report from Ibn Zayd in al-Ṭabarī, their arguing was about which standing-place was actually that of Abraham.[57] Whatever the specific details, it was this arguing as to who was the more correct that is, according to Mālik, the *jidāl* that is being referred to.

This was, however, only one of a number of opinions on this word. Ibn ʿUmar and Ibn ʿAbbās held that it referred generally to arguing with one's fellow pilgrims while in *iḥrām* (with the addition in Ibn ʿAbbās' case of the meaning of 'until you make them angry').[58] Al-Qāsim ibn Muḥammad held that it referred to arguing about the actual day of the *ḥajj*,[59] while Mujāhid said that it meant arguing about which month the *ḥajj* should be in, since the practice of intercalation (*nasīʾ*) prevalent before Islam had resulted in the time of *ḥajj* moving gradually throughout the year, being in one month for two years, then the next month for two years, and so on; now, however, the time for *ḥajj* had been fixed in its proper month (i.e. by the Prophet), and there was no longer any argument about its time.[60] In this last instance, therefore, as in the case with arguing about the place of standing, there was no longer any cause for argument: both the time and the place of the rites had been decided and so now there was 'no argument about the *ḥajj* (*lā jidāla fī l-ḥajj*)'.

This interpretation contrasts the phrase *wa-lā jidāla fī l-ḥajj* grammatically with the two preceding negations, i.e. *lā rafatha* and *lā fusūqa,* in that whereas *lā rafatha* and *lā fusūqa* are understood to be negations implying prohibitions, *lā jidāla fī l-ḥajj* is understood rather to be a statement of fact. This difference is indicated in the reading of *fa-lā rafathun wa-lā fusūqun wa-la jidāla fī l-ḥajj,* adopted by the Basran and Makkan readers, where a contrast of meaning is explicitly maintained.[61] That the first two elements only should be considered prohibitions was further bolstered in this view by the *ḥadīth* 'Whoever does *ḥajj* of this House and neither commits lewdness (*lam yarfuth*) nor wrong action (*lam yafsuq*), returns [from *ḥajj*] as on the day his mother gave birth to him',[62] where *jidāl* is not mentioned precisely because it no longer applied.

However, the reading of *fa-lā rafatha wa-lā fusūqa wa-lā jidāla fī l-ḥajj,* which grammatically-speaking suggests a similar prohibitive quality to all three elements, was agreed upon by the readers of Madina,[63] Syria and Kufa, and this 'natural' reading of the grammar was presumably the reason for the view of Ibn ʿUmar, Ibn ʿAbbās and others who said that it referred in a general sense to people arguing while on *ḥajj* rather than specifically about the *ḥajj*. We have already noted above how Mālik opts for a restrictive interpretation of the words *rafath* and *fusūq* in the same verse despite his general tendency to go by the *ʿumūm*,[64] and with the word *jidāl* he does the same. It would therefore seem again that, as with the other two words in the verse (and also the instance of *ṣalāt* = *duʿā'* mentioned above), this is a '*fiqhī*' solution: to say that *jidāl* referred in general to any sort of argumentation might be to suggest that having an argument with somebody was as serious an offence as having intercourse while in *iḥrām*, or at least that it was a specific, recompensable, offence for someone in *iḥrām*, which was not the case, and therefore this meaning is not chosen. One thus finds that the interpretation of all three items in the verse, although backed up in each instance by sound arguments from the Qur'an and/or *ḥadīth*, seems to go against an ordinary, sraightforward understanding of the *āya*. When, however, we realise that each of these three interpretations is in fact firmly based on the known practices of *ḥajj*, we can see that once again it is effectively a case of *tafsīr* by *ʿamal*.

We must conclude, therefore, that although the *asbāb al-nuzūl* material in the *Muwaṭṭa'* helps to give a general understanding of the relevant Qur'anic passages and provides valuable pointers to the history of both the Islamic and pre-Islamic periods, it is of very limited significance from a legal point of view and rarely provides a direct source of *tafsīr* of Qur'anic words and phrases.[65] Indeed, given the existence of *ʿamal*, which itself answered all the questions of context and chronology that the *asbāb* material was later called upon to answer, the concept of *asbāb al-nuzūl* was, like that of *naskh*, almost irrelevant for Mālik as a technique for determining *fiqh*, and it was only later, with the development of *naskh* and *asbāb al-nuzūl* as textual sciences in their own right, that they were to assume the importance that they gained.

The Umayyad contribution

So far in the course of our investigations we have seen numerous judgements attributed to the Prophet, the first four caliphs, and other important Companions such as Ibn ʿUmar and ʿĀ'isha. We have also noted several judgements deriving from the activities of scholars among the Successors, particularly the 'Seven *Fuqahā'*'. One element that has not yet been discussed, however, is the contribution to the development of

Qurʾanic law, i.e. law derived from the Qurʾan, by the political rather than religious authorities of the Umayyad period, that is, the Umayyad caliphs and governors. The picture the *Muwaṭṭaʾ* gives us is of these governors and caliphs quite naturally participating in the process of developing the details of the law from its base in Qurʾan and *sunna* alongside the more specialised activities of the *fuqahāʾ*: they are in positions of authority and, as part of their task as upholders of justice and public order according to that law, are often called upon to give judgements in cases brought to their attention. They are not, however, working in a vacuum: when they themselves have insufficient knowledge we see them appealing to others with greater knowledge; at other times, though, they are confident of their own knowledge and make their own judgements independently. In many instances these judgements are accepted by the *fuqahāʾ*, but there are also instances where, firstly, their judgements are rejected, and, secondly, where the caliphs are brought to order, as it were, by the *fuqahāʾ* and called upon to change certain incorrect practices that have arisen in the areas under their jurisdiction. Thus, although the caliphs (and governors) have a large measure of independent authority with regard to the development of the details of the law, they are nevertheless subject to the *fuqahāʾ* in the sense that they also accept and indeed have to rely on the authority of the *fuqahāʾ* for many of these details.

We should note firstly that, despite the unfavourable light in which the religious qualifications of the Umayyads have often been seen by later historians (both Muslim and non-Muslim), many of the Umayyad caliphs were respected in their time as men of learning.[66] Muʿāwiya, of course, was a Companion (as well as having had the particular merit of having been one of the scribes of the Prophet),[67] and the *Muwaṭṭaʾ* includes three Prophetic *ḥadīths* related directly on his authority.[68] Both Marwān and ʿUmar ibn ʿAbd al-ʿAzīz are also cited as authorities for Prophetic *ḥadīths* in the *Muwaṭṭaʾ*.[69] On one occasion Marwān is referred to – alongside Ibn ʿUmar and ʿAbdallāh ibn al-Zubayr – as an *ʿālim*[70] and, on another, by implication, as a man of *waraʿ* ('scrupulousness').[71] As for ʿUmar ibn ʿAbd al-ʿAzīz, we have already noted his high standing in the eyes of Mālik,[72] and the man's quality is reflected in the generally accepted judgement of the Muslim community on his justice, learning and piety, so much so that he is known as the fifth Rightly-Guided Caliph.[73] Mention should also be made here of ʿAbd al-Malik ibn Marwān, who lived in Madina until the expulsion of the Umayyads in the year 63 AH and is often referred to as one of the *fuqahāʾ* of Madina.[74] Indeed, the many references in the *Muwaṭṭaʾ* to these and other caliphs keeping company with the *ʿulamāʾ* and/or referring to them for judgements, as well as to their own activities as the promulgators of independent judgements, are ample witness to their interest in, and concern for, the application of the *sharī'a.*[75] The following examples illustrate not only this interaction between the caliphs and the *fuqahā'*, but also highlight the caliphal contribution to the continuing process of Qur'anic interpretation as problems arose in the practical application of the Qur'an in the early Umayyad period. (Examples 1–4, 6 and 9 show caliphs and governors asking others for judgements; examples 3–7 and 9 show them giving judgements; examples 8 and 10–12 show their judgements being corrected or rejected).

1. The meaning of the word *qar'*

Mālik records that during Mu'āwiya's reign a man named al-Aḥwaṣ[76] divorced his wife but then died shortly afterwards just after his wife had begun her third menstrual period after beginning her *'idda.* Mu'āwiya (who according to al-Shaybānī's transmission had been asked to judge between the wife and the sons on the question of inheritance) was not clear whether she had the right to inherit in such circumstances or not (i.e. whether she was still his wife or not) and so wrote to Zayd ibn Thābit in Madina to ask him for his opinion on the matter. Zayd wrote back saying that once she had begun her third menstrual period she was no longer connected to him nor he to her, and so she would not inherit from him nor he from her.[77]

This problem arose from an ambiguity in the phrase *thalāthata qurū'* in Q 2: 228's *wa-l-muṭallaqātu yatarabbaṣna bi-anfusihinna thalāthata qurū'* ('And divorced women should wait for three courses'). Did the word *qurū'* refer to menstrual periods (*ḥiyaḍ*) or to the periods of purity (*aṭhār*) between menses, both of these meanings being acceptable from a linguistic point of view?[78] If it referred to the periods of bleeding, a divorced woman would still be considered married to her husband, and thus entitled to inherit from him, until the end of her third menstrual period, but if it referred to the periods of purity her *'idda* would be over at the end of the third period of purity, i.e. the beginning of the third menstrual period, at which point she would no longer be his wife and thus no longer entitled to inherit from him. This latter was the judgement that Zayd had given to Mu'āwiya.

In the chapter where this report occurs, Mālik notes that this latter judgement, as well as being that of Zayd, was also that of 'Ā'isha and Ibn 'Umar among the Companions, of al-Qāsim ibn Muḥammad, Sālim ibn 'Abdallāh ibn 'Umar, Abū Bakr ibn 'Abd al-Raḥmān and Sulaymān ibn Yasār among the older Successors, and Ibn Shihāb among the younger Successors, and that it was the generally accepted position in Madina (*wa-huwa l-amr 'indanā*); he also cites Abū Bakr ibn 'Abd al-Raḥmān's observation that all the Madinan *fuqahāʾ* he had met agreed with ʿĀʾisha's view that the word *qurūʾ* in Q 2: 228 referred to periods of purity.[79] Such consensus, however, had not always been the case in Madina. Not only does Mālik only claim that this is *al-amr ʿindanā* rather than *al-amr al-mujtamaʿ ʿalayhi ʿindanā*, which thus allows for at least some difference of opinion, but he records dissent from this albeit dominant view in the same chapter: certain (unspecified) people, he notes, had disagreed with ʿĀʾisha about her taking her niece Ḥafṣa into her house as soon as Ḥafṣa had begun her third menstrual period after starting her *ʿidda*, citing as their authority the *thalāthata qurūʾ* verse of Q 2: 228, to which ʿĀʾisha replied that that was exactly *her* argument also, only the word *qurūʾ* (she uses the plural *aqrāʾ*) referred to periods of purity.[80] It is not stated who these people were who held the view that ʿĀʾisha denied, but the view that the 'three *qurūʾ*' referred rather to menstrual periods was said to have been held by over ten prestigious Companions, including ʿUmar, ʿAlī and Ibn Masʿūd, and also, among the Madinan Successors, Saʿīd ibn al-Musayyab, and it later became that of the Iraqis.[81] Nevertheless, despite Saʿīd ibn al-Musayyab's contrary opinion (which would seem to limit the generality of Abū Bakr ibn ʿAbd al-Raḥmān's comment mentioned above), there would seem to have been a large measure of agreement in Madina by the turn of the century that the 'three *qurūʾ*' referred to three periods of purity rather than three menstrual periods.

Mālik himself, as so often in the *Muwaṭṭaʾ*, gives no clear explanation for the Madinan view beyond the fact that it is Madinan *ʿamal* (*wa-huwa l-amr ʿindanā*). However, he does include a Prophetic *ḥadīth* at the beginning of the same chapter which gives us a clue to the reasoning behind this *ʿamal*, namely, the *ḥadīth* referred to earlier about Ibn ʿUmar's incorrect divorce (he had divorced his wife while she was menstruating and was told by the Prophet to take her back as his wife, wait until she became pure again after her next menstrual period, and then divorce her if he wished at the beginning of that second period of purity, this being 'the *ʿidda* at which Allah has commanded that women be divorced').[82] This was seen as a clear statement that it was not correct for a man to divorce his wife while she was menstruating; rather, he should do so during a period of purity in which he has not had intercourse with her. (Indeed, divorce should preferably take place at the beginning of such a period of purity, this being the judgement contained in Ibn ʿUmar's reading of *fa-ṭalliqūhunna li-**qubuli** ʿiddatihinna*, i.e. at the beginning of the time when their *ʿidda* may correctly begin, and not just at any acceptable time.)[83] Since this showed that the *ʿidda* should begin during a period of purity, the conclusion was that the menstrual periods themselves were not what was 'counted' (as in

Q 65: 1's *wa-aḥṣū l-ʿidda* – 'and count the *ʿidda*') in order to determine when the *ʿidda* was over. Rather, it was the periods of purity that were important, and the 'three *qurūʾ*' were therefore taken to refer to three periods of purity, with no consideration being given to the menstrual periods.[84] This judgement is further emphasised by a report at the end of the chapter to the effect that the wife of one of the Anṣār had asked her husband for a divorce and he had told her to let him know firstly when her period began and then when it finished, at which point he divorced her, after which Mālik sums up the chapter by saying, 'This is the best that I have heard about this.'[85]

Al-Shāfiʿī, who agreed with Mālik on the Madinan view, adduces this same argument in his *Kitāb al-Umm*, but adds the linguistic argument that the original meaning of the root *qaraʾa* was 'to gather', as in the expressions *huwa yaqrī l-māʾ fī ḥawḍihi* ('He is gathering water in his watering-trough) and *huwa yaqrī l-ṭaʿām fī shidqihi* ('He is gathering food in his jaw'),[86] and that this meaning was much better suited to periods of purity, during which the blood 'gathered' in the womb, than to menstrual periods, when the blood was released.[87] (Later scholars were to mention two other linguistic arguments for this view, both of them of dubious merit. Firstly, it was said that the word *qarʾ* had two plurals (like the word *amr*), and that *qurūʾ* was the plural of *qarʾ* in the sense of *ṭuhr*, while *aqrāʾ* was the plural of the word in the sense of *ḥayḍa*.[88] This, however, is unconvincing in the light of ʿĀʾisha's use of the plural *aqrāʾ* to denote *aṭhār*. Even more unconvincing was the argument of some (including, according to al-Sarakhsī, al-Shāfiʿī) that the *tāʾ marbūṭa* at the end of *thalāthata* in the phrase *thalāthata qurūʾ* indicates that the singular of the word *qurūʾ* is a masculine noun, and since *ṭuhr* is masculine and *ḥayḍa* feminine it makes sense to consider the word *qarʾ* to mean *ṭuhr* rather than *ḥayḍa*, for this ignored the fact, as al-Sarakhsī points out, that it is not the meaning that carries the gender but the individual word).[89]

The Iraqis for their part had no objection *per se* to the *ḥadīth* mentioned above about Ibn ʿUmar's divorce with regard to the time when the *ʿidda* should begin,[90] but they favoured the idea that since the purpose of the *ʿidda* was to detect pregnancy and since it was menstruation that indicated absence of pregnancy it was the menstrual periods that were important.[91] This argument was backed up by various *ḥadīths* and verses from the Qurʾan, but, as al-Bājī points out, it really works both ways, since nobody denied the importance of the menstrual cycle in counting the *ʿidda*, and the beginning of a menstrual period was as good an indicator of the absence of pregnancy as was its end.[92] More importantly, they felt that taking the word *qurūʾ* to refer to menstrual periods allowed the word 'three' to be taken literally: since a woman could be divorced at any time during a period of purity, it could be, if the meaning of three menstrual periods was not assumed and the woman was divorced towards the end of a period of purity, that the *qurū'* in question would only amount to two and a bit rather than the specified three; taking the meaning as being three menstrual periods, however, allowed a literal interpretation of the word 'three'.[93] (Ibn al-ᶜArabī gives the counter-argument that a part of a thing is often counted as a whole, as in the example of Q 2: 197 – 'the *ḥajj* is [during] known months' – which referred to Shawwāl, Dhū l-Qaᶜda and only part of Dhū l-Ḥijja).[94] Furthermore, in addition to these arguments, there were also *ḥadīths* in which the word *qar'* was unambiguously used in the sense of 'menstrual period',[95] but these only went to show that both meanings were *a priori* possible, which was already accepted.[96]

This, then, was an instance of where a *mushtarak* word with two equally feasible meanings inevitably raised differences. What the sources suggest is that this was a case where a major divergence of opinion arose during the time of the Companions which was then later systematised into the 'Iraqi' and 'Madinan' views.

2. The inheritance of a grandfather

Muᶜāwiya similarly writes to Zayd about the inheritance rights of a grandfather alongside brothers and Zayd writes back to him saying that this is something for which there is no Prophetic precedent but only the judgement of the later caliphs (*lam yakun yaqḍī fī-hi illā l-umarā'*) but that ᶜUmar and ᶜUthmān (*al-khalīfatayni qablaka*, lit. 'the two caliphs before you') made the grandfather equal inheritor with one or two brothers and the recipient of a third, and never less than a third, in conjunction with more than two.[97] (This question has been discussed on pp. 109–11 above.)

3. *ᶜAmd versus khaṭa'* in cases of homicide

In two instances involving homicide, Muᶜāwiya, instead of being the one who asks, is the one who is asked. Marwān, who was governor of Madina under Muᶜāwiya, writes to Muᶜāwiya firstly about a madman (*majnūn*) who was brought to him for having killed someone, and secondly about a drunkard who was brought to him for a similar offence. With regard to the madman, Muᶜāwiya replies that retaliation (*qiṣāṣ*) should not be exacted but blood-money should be paid to the relatives (*awliyā'*) of the victim. As for the drunkard, however, he should be killed in return for having killed, even if he was drunk at the time.[98]

The question here was about what constituted intentional, or deliberate, killing (*ᶜamd*, i.e. murder) and what constituted unintentional, or accidental, killing (*khaṭaᶜ*). The Qur'an prescribes retaliation (*qiṣāṣ*) in cases of murder (although allowing blood-money as an option),[99] whereas the judgement for accidental killing is that blood-money should be paid and a *kaffāra* (of freeing a slave or fasting for two consecutive months) be done, or simply that a *kaffāra* be done, depending on circumstances.[100] In the above instance, the killing done by the madman was considered to come under the category of *khaṭaᶜ*, since he was not aware of what he was doing and was not responsible for his lack of awareness. The drunkard, on the other hand, although perhaps not fully aware of what he was doing, was, nevertheless, more aware than a madman, and, furthermore, was responsible for having made himself drunk, and so his drunkenness (in itself, of course, forbidden) could not be considered a valid excuse: his action therefore came under the category of *ᶜamd*, not *khaṭaᶜ*, and so retaliation could, and should, be exacted. This basic distinction, and the ensuing judgements, were universally accepted by the *fuqahā'*.[101]

In a later judgement related to the same problem of how to define the dividing line between *ᶜamd* and *khaṭaᶜ*, ᶜAbd al-Malik gave the *walī* of a man who had died as the result of being beaten by a stick the right to exact retaliation with a stick.[102] Mālik comments:

> The agreed-upon position about which there is no doubt here (*al-amr al-mujtamaᶜ ᶜalayhi lladhī lā khtilāfa fī-hi ᶜindanā*) is that if one man hits another with a stick or throws a stone at him or hits him deliberately (*ᶜamdan*) and the man dies as a result, that is *ᶜamd* and for it there is retaliation. Thus *ᶜamd* in our opinion (*ᶜindanā*) [includes] when a man deliberately goes (*yaᶜmid*) to another and hits him and the victim dies as a result.[103]

This constituted a point of difference between the Madinans on the one hand and the Iraqis (and later al-Shāfiᶜī) on the other, this latter group holding that this type of killing was in a third separate category – referred to as *shibh al-ᶜamd* – which should not warrant the death penalty since such 'murder' contained an element of doubt as to the original intention: sticks and the like were not normally used for killing and did not normally result in death, and so a man causing death in such a way should be given the benefit of the doubt and be spared the death penalty, especially since the general Prophetic dictum on this point was 'Do not apply the *ḥudūd* in cases of doubt (*idra'ū l-ḥudūd bi-l-shubuhāt*).'[104] The Madinan position, though, as we have seen, was that the action leading to the death was intentional, and therefore the consequences must be seen as the result of prior intention, i.e. *ᶜamd*.

4. The indemnity (*ᶜaql*) for molars

Just as such details needed to be worked out with regard to homicide, so too were there inevitable problems that arose with regard to injuries. As with homicide, there was a distinction between *ᶜamd*, for which there was *qiṣāṣ*, as in Q 5: 45's *al-ᶜayna bi-l-ᶜayni wa-l-anfa bi-l-anfi wa-l-udhna bi-l-udhni wa-l-sinna bi-l-sinni wa-l-jurūḥa qiṣāṣ* ('An eye for an eye, a nose for a nose, an ear for an ear, a tooth for a tooth, and for wounds [there is] retaliation'),[105] and *khaṭaᶜ*, for which, as with accidental killing, blood-money was to be paid (based, as we noted in the previous example, on the judgement in Q 4: 92). In his letter to ᶜAmr ibn Ḥazm, the Prophet had mentioned (among other judgements) that the blood-money for a life (i.e. the 'full' blood-money, or *diya*) was a hundred camels; for each finger, ten camels; and for a tooth, five camels.[106] This last point in particular was to become the subject of some considerable discussion during the Umayyad period, due to uncertainty as to whether back teeth (*aḍrās*, sing. *ḍirs*) should be considered the same as front teeth, presumably on the basis that the loss of back teeth was less serious and/or disfiguring than the loss of front teeth. Mālik records a report from Saᶜīd ibn al-Musayyab that ᶜUmar had judged the indemnity (*ᶜaql*) for a back tooth to be one camel (as he also judged it to be the indemnity for a collarbone or a rib)[107] but that Muᶜāwiya had judged it to be five camels, to which Saᶜīd adds the comment that 'the *diya* thus comes to less (*tanquṣ*) in ᶜUmar's judgement and more (*tazīd*) in Muᶜāwiya's. If it had been me I would have made it two camels for every molar, in which case the *diya* would come to the same as it is (*fa-tilka l-diya sawāʾ*); and every *mujtahid* is rewarded [for his *ijtihād*].'[108]

At first sight it is difficult to understand what is being said here, until we realise that the problem arises from the total number of teeth in the mouth, namely, twelve front teeth (incisors and canines) and twenty back teeth (molars). If an indemnity of five camels was allowed for every tooth (as in Muᶜāwiya's judgement, following the overt (*ẓāhir*) meaning of the Prophet's judgement, i.e. the *ᶜumūm* of the word 'tooth' in the phrase 'and for a tooth, five camels'), that would result in a theoretical maximum of 160 camels for all the teeth in the mouth, this being well over the full blood-money, or *diya*, of 100 camels. ᶜUmar's judgement, on the other hand, assumes a difference in importance, and therefore value, between front and back teeth: front teeth still bear the same indemnity value of five camels each, as in the directive of the Prophet (i.e. 60 camels for all twelve teeth), while the back teeth are given a value of one camel each (i.e. 20 camels for all twenty), thus giving a theoretical maximum of 80 camels for all the teeth in the mouth. This then is the meaning of Ibn al-Musayyab's statement that the *diya* comes to less in ᶜUmar's judgement (i.e. 80 camels) and more in Muᶜāwiya's (i.e. 160 camels) and why he himself said he would prefer it to be two camels for a molar, since that would result in a theoretical maximum of 40 camels for all twenty back teeth, together with the 60 camels for the front teeth (as in the Prophet's judgement), making a total of 100 camels, i.e. the same amount as the full blood-money (such as was due not only for the loss of a life, but also, for example, for the loss of a nose, or both lips, etc.).[109]

This consciousness of a potential difference between the indemnity value of front and back teeth is reflected in another report in the *Muwaṭṭaʾ* where Marwān sends a man to Ibn ᶜAbbās to ask about precisely this point, and, on hearing that Ibn ᶜAbbās said it was five camels, sends the man back to say, 'Do you consider front teeth (*muqaddam al-fam*) to be the same as molars?', to which Ibn ᶜAbbās replies, 'If only you were to consider the fingers: the blood-money for [each of] them is the same',[110] i.e. ten camels for each finger, regardless of its usefulness relative to the others, as specifically mentioned in the directive of the Prophet to ᶜAmr ibn Ḥazm mentioned above. This was thus still a point of discussion during Marwān's time (i.e. the middle of the first century). That it remained a matter of some uncertainty throughout the first century is further indicated by the fact that ᶜUmar ibn ᶜAbd al-ᶜAzīz (governor of Madina under al-Walīd from 86 to 96 and then caliph from 99 to 101) is said to have been impressed by Ibn al-Musayyab's judgement (although it is not stated whether he ever actually put it into practice).[111] Nevertheless, by Mālik's time the *ᶜamal* in Madina had clearly become established in favour of the judgement of Muᶜāwiya and Ibn ᶜAbbās, i.e. a general interpretation of the Prophet's directive, although we should note that, once again, Mālik's lack of claim of any consensus suggests the continued existence of other opinions even at his time. As Mālik says, stating not only the Madinan position, but also the reasoning behind it:

> The position here (*al-amr ᶜindanā*) is that front teeth (*muqaddam al-fam*), molars and canines all have the same blood-money, because the Prophet, may Allah bless him and grant him peace, said, 'for a tooth, five camels', and molars are teeth, and no teeth have any preference over any others.[112]

This was also the position of Abū Ḥanīfa and al-Shāfiᶜī, and for the same reasons.[113]

Here, then, we would seem to have another instance of where an earlier uncertainty was ironed out in the interests of consistency and simplicity. Whatever systematic considerations there may have been against a five-camel indemnity for every tooth in the mouth, obviously in practical terms such an eventuality was highly unlikely to occur, certainly less likely than, say, losing all the fingers of both hands (for which the full blood-money was payable). Accordingly, a general judgement of five camels per tooth – whatever the tooth – was seen in practice to be the most equitable interpretation of the Prophetic directive, despite earlier qualms.

5. *Īlāʾ*

Īlāʾ, or oath of abstinence from marital intercourse, was one of three types of 'divorce' prevalent in the Jāhiliyya (the other two being *ẓihār* and *ṭalāq*, or 'ordinary' divorce).[114] All of these were modified by the Qurʾan: the form and various *ʿidda* periods for ordinary divorce were specified, an obligatory *kaffāra* was instituted in cases of *ẓihār*, and a four month maximum for oaths of *īlāʾ* was stipulated. With regard to this latter, Q 2: 226–7 states: *li-lladhīna yuʾlūna min nisāʾihim tarabbuṣu arbaʿati ashhurin fa-in fāʾū fa-inna llāha ghafūrun raḥīm. Wa-in ʿazamū l-ṭalāqa fa-inna llāha samīʿun ʿalīm* ('Those who make an oath of abstinence from their wives may wait for four months. If they return [to their wives], Allah is Forgiving and Merciful; if they decide to divorce, Allah is All-Hearing and All-Knowing').

There was, however, an ambiguity here which remained the subject of some discussion throughout much of the Umayyad period. Mālik cites a report from ʿAlī to the effect that if a man makes such an oath and the four-month period passes without him 'returning' to his wife he should be asked whether he wishes to resume marital relations or to divorce. This judgement, which, says Mālik, is the general position in Madina (*al-amr ʿindanā*), is then supported by a similar report from Ibn ʿUmar.[115] However, he then cites a report from Ibn Shihāb that Saʿīd ibn al-Musayyab and Abū Bakr ibn ʿAbd al-Raḥmān (two of the 'Seven *Fuqahāʾ*') held that once the four months were up that automatically constituted a divorce, although the man could still take his wife back while she was observing her *ʿidda* (in other words, it was considered a *rajʿī*, or revocable, divorce). He also cites a report that Marwān used to pass judgement (*kāna yaqḍī*) according to this view, after which he adds that this was also the view of Ibn Shihāb.[116] There was thus considerable divergence of opinion on this point even in Madina.

The ambiguity concerned the phrase *fa-in fāʾū* ('And if they return ...'). Did it mean if they return during the four-month period or if they return after the four-month period is up? Abū Ḥanīfa and the Iraqis preferred the former interpretation, whereas Mālik and al-Shāfiʿī held the latter view.[117] The way in which *fa-in fāʾū* was interpreted then determined how *wa-in ᶜazamū l-ṭalāq* was interpreted: those who held the first view said that the *ᶜazīmat al-ṭalāq* referred merely to the four months expiring without the husband having decided to return to his wife, while the others held that it referred to his overt, verbal, expression of his desire to divorce rather than return to his wife *after* the four months were up.[118]

There was also a difference as to the type of divorce that was said to result if divorce was decided. According to the Iraqi view the divorce was *bā'in*, i.e. without the husband having the automatic right to take his wife back while she was still in her *ᶜidda* (which he would have if it were a *rajᶜī* divorce): if he wanted to marry her again, he was merely one suitor among others.[119] In other words, the four-month period was considered to be like the *ᶜidda* of a *rajᶜī* divorce, with the marriage fully dissolved when the period was up.[120] This *qiyās* was further supported by a variant reading from Ibn Masᶜūd of *fa-in fā'ū* ***fī-hinna***, i.e. within the period and not after, and this reading, as the reasoning goes, must have been based on something that Ibn Masᶜūd actually heard from the Prophet.[121] As for Mālik and those holding to his view, they held that *ṭalāq*, if chosen by the man after the four months, should, given the absence of any evidence to the contrary, be assumed to be the 'normal' form (*aṣl*) of *ṭalāq*, i.e. *ṭalāq rajᶜī*, with an *ᶜidda* and all the rights due to the husband (and wife) during that *ᶜidda*.[122] In other words, the disagreement here was, as so often, based on two conflicting analogies: the four-month period could be considered tantamount to an *ᶜidda* which, when over, left the couple completely divorced, or it could be simply the time allowed for a man to retract his oath (as suggested by the use of *li-* in *li-lladhīna yu'lūna min nisā'ihim*), with any subsequent divorce being treated as an ordinary divorce beginning at that time. Both were reasonable interpretations, given the ambiguity of *fa-in fā'ū* and the differing opinions of the Companions and those after them, and both remained current even in Madina, where Marwān's judgement and Ibn Shihāb's opinion against the 'Madinan' doctrine of the *Muwaṭṭa'* would suggest that there was some considerable flexibility on this point at least throughout the first century and that, as in the case of the 'three *qurū'*', it was possibly not until Mālik's time that what he describes as *al-amr ᶜindanā* finally became the dominant view.

6. 'Irrevocable' divorce (*al-batta*)

The Qur'an mentions that divorce can take place twice without creating any permanent bar between the couple but that after the third time the man may not marry his former wife until she has married someone else and that second marriage has ended (either by divorce or by the death of the husband).[123] However, there was dispute as to what constituted 'three times': if a man expressly mentioned that he was divorcing his wife irrevocably (*al-batta*), was that to be accepted as irrevocable, and thus equivalent to three divorces, or did it only count as one? Mālik tells us that Marwān gave the judgement (*kāna yaqḍī*) that an *al-batta* divorce counted as three divorces and was thus irrevocable.[124] He also records that ᶜUmar ibn ᶜAbd al-ᶜAzīz, on hearing that Abān ibn ᶜUthmān (a governor of Madina under ᶜAbd al-Malik) had considered *al-batta* divorce to count as only one divorce, gave his opinion that even if divorce were allowed a thousand times (i.e. rather than just three), the expression *al-batta* would use up all those thousand times. In other words, *al-batta* divorce was irrevocable, like three ordinary divorces. Mālik, acknowledging differences of opinion on this even in his own time, adds his own comment that this is the best that he has heard on the matter.[125]

In fact, although there was dispute on this point throughout the first century and later (as the references to Abān and ᶜUmar ibn ᶜAbd al-ᶜAzīz and Mālik's comment indicate), the middle of the second century saw a much more general acceptance of the view endorsed by Marwān and ᶜUmar ibn ᶜAbd al-ᶜAzīz – Mālik, Abū Ḥanīfa and al-Shāfiᶜī for instance all agreed on it – so that it was only a small minority (including, later, the Ẓāhirīs) who were to retain the other view.[126]

One practical application of the doctrine of the 'irrevocability' of *al-batta* divorce is referred to in a report involving al-Walīd ibn ᶜAbd al-Malik. When al-Walīd was in Madina,[127] he asked al-Qāsim ibn Muḥammad and ᶜUrwa about when a man who divorces one of four wives irrevocably (*al-batta*) may marry again and they told him that he could do so immediately without having to wait for the divorced wife's *ᶜidda* to expire.[128] In other words (as al-Zurqānī points out), it is only the woman and not the man who has to observe an *ᶜidda* before remarrying: once the man has forgone his right to take back his former wife by irrevocably divorcing her, he only has three wives and so is free to marry again.[129]

7. Triple divorce in *tamlīk*

Mālik records Marwān's judgement that a man who had given his wife the choice of divorce (i.e. *tamlīk*) and whose wife had then expressed her wish to be divorced from him three times although he did not accept her second and third pronouncements, should be made to swear on oath that he had only intended to allow her the choice of one divorce, not three, whereupon she would still be considered his wife. In other words, she could not be allowed to make it a triple divorce if that was not the man's intention.

Mālik notes that al-Qāsim ibn Muḥammad 'used to like this judgement and consider it the best he had heard on the matter', to which he adds his own comment that, as in the previous instance, this is the best that he also has heard on the matter.[130] This was also the view of Abū Ḥanīfa and al-Shāfiʿī, showing how, once again, although the contrary view, i.e. that the woman's decision be upheld, is recorded from some earlier authorities, by the end of the second century there was effectively complete agreement that divorce was the prerogative of the man and that in such cases it was the man's intention that counted.[131]

8. The rights due to a *mabtūta* divorcee

Another point arising out of the *al-batta* situation about which there was considerable discussion during the Umayyad period was that of the rights due to an irrevocably divorced woman (*mabtūta*) during her *ʿidda*. Q 65: 1 lays down that divorcees divorced in the 'ordinary' way (i.e. *rajʿī* divorce, in which the husband has the right to take back his wife and resume his marriage with her while she is still observing her *ʿidda*) should neither leave nor be made to leave their houses before their *ʿidda* period is up unless they are guilty of a 'clear abomination' (*fāḥisha mubayyina*).[132] Q 65: 6 further declares that divorcees should be given lodging in the marital home (*askinūhunna min ḥaythu sakantum*) and that if they are pregnant they should receive maintenance until they give birth (*wa-in kunna ulāti ḥamlin fa-anfiqū ʿalayhinna ḥattā yaḍaʿna ḥamlahunna*).

That Q 65: 1 related to *rajʿī* divorce in particular was understood from the reference at the end of the verse to Allah 'causing something to happen' (*laʿalla llāha yuḥdithu baʿda dhālika amran*), which was taken to refer to reconciliation and the husband's consequent retention of his wife and which would thus necessarily refer to *rajʿī* divorce, as well as the reference in Q 65: 2 to the options of retention or separation before the *ʿidda* was up, which would again necessarily refer to *rajʿī* divorce, as in Q 2: 229.[133] The reference in Q 65: 6, however, was not, as we shall see, considered quite so unambiguous.

It was agreed by all the *fuqahā'* that in cases of *rajʿī* divorce the wife was owed both lodging (*suknā*) and maintenance (*nafaqa*) by her husband while she was still in her *ʿidda*: not only did Q 65: 1 say that she should remain in her marital home until her *ʿidda* was over (and Q 65: 6 that she should be given lodging, if this applied to *rajʿī* divorcees), but lodging and maintenance were both rights that were due to a wife from her husband during marriage and, until her *ʿidda* was over, she was still his wife and so he was still responsible for her in that respect. What, however, was the judgement regarding an irrevocably divorced woman? All marriage ties were now severed and, as a result, he no longer had the option of taking her back as his wife during her *ʿidda*, nor would either of them inherit from the other if either of them were to die; but she still had to observe an *ʿidda* before she could remarry. Was she, then, entitled to lodging and/or maintenance from her former husband while she was still observing her *ʿidda*? It was agreed (because of Q 65: 6) that pregnant divorcees – whether divorced revocably or irrevocably – were entitled to both lodging and maintenance until they gave birth,[134] and so the question really came down to what were the rights during her *ʿidda* of a *mabtūta* divorcee who was not pregnant?

In the chapter entitled 'What Has Come Down About the Maintenance Rights (*nafaqa*) of Divorcees', Mālik relates a *ḥadīth* from Fāṭima bint Qays to the effect that, during the time of the Prophet, Fāṭima's husband, Abū ᶜAmr ibn Ḥafṣ, had divorced her irrevocably (*al-batta*) while he was away in Syria. His agent (*wakīl*) had sent her some barley but she was displeased with it (*sakhiṭathu*) and said so, whereupon the agent said, 'By Allah, we don't owe you anything (*wa-llāhi mā laki ʿalaynā min shayʾ*).' So she went to the Prophet and asked him about this and he confirmed that her former husband did not owe her any maintenance (*nafaqa*). The Prophet also told her to observe her *ʿidda* in the house of Umm Sharīk, but then, because of the number of people that Umm Sharīk had coming to her house (she was renowned for her generosity, especially towards those in need),[135] he told her to move to the house of ᶜAbdallāh ibn Umm Maktūm, who was blind, and in whose house she would thus find more freedom. The *ḥadīth* then goes on to mention the circumstances leading up to Fāṭima's marriage to Usāma ibn Zayd.[136]

From this *ḥadīth* the Madinans derived the judgement that an irrevocably divorced woman was not entitled to maintenance (*nafaqa*) (assuming, of course, that she was not pregnant): she was no longer the man's wife, and so he was no longer responsible for her upkeep.[137] However, contrary to the overt indication (*ẓāhir*) of the *ḥadīth*, which suggests that the woman should observe her *ʿidda* away from her former husband's home and that therefore it was not obligatory for him to provide her with lodging (*suknā*), the Madinans held (because of Q 65: 6, as we shall see) firstly that it *was* obligatory for him to provide lodging and secondly that she should not leave her house until her *ʿidda* was over.

Precisely because of the contra-indication of the Fāṭima bint Qays *ḥadīth*, this remained a point of contention well into the Umayyad period. Mālik records a report, from both al-Qāsim ibn Muḥammad and Sulaymān ibn Yasār, that Yaḥyā ibn Saᶜīd ibn al-ᶜĀṣ (i.e. son of the Saᶜīd who was a governor of Madina under Muʿāwiya) had irrevocably divorced the daughter of ʿAbd al-Raḥmān ibn al-Ḥakam (Marwān's brother), whereupon ʿAbd al-Raḥmān had taken his daughter away from Yaḥyā's house (presumably to his own). On hearing about this, ʿĀʾisha sent a message to Marwān, who was governor of Madina at the time, telling him to 'fear Allah and return the woman to her house'. According to Sulaymān, Marwān said that his brother had been too forceful for him to do anything about it (*ghalabanī*), while according to al-Qāsim, Marwān said, 'Haven't you heard about what happened to Fāṭima bint Qays?', to which ʿĀʾisha replied, 'It won't harm you if you don't mention the *ḥadīth* about Fāṭima', to which Marwān responded, 'If in your opinion that was because of evil (*in kāna bi-ki l-sharr*), then the evil between these two is enough for you (*fa-ḥasbuki mā bayna hādhayni min al-sharr*).'[138] In other words, ʿĀʾisha is saying that Fāṭima's case was an exception and that the judgement in Yaḥyā's case is not the same, while Marwān is saying that if that exception was due to the exceptional discord between the two, then the discord between the couple in question is likewise exceptional.

ʿĀʾisha's position, then, was that divorcees, regardless of the nature of their divorce, should remain in their former husband's home until their *ʿidda* was over, despite the second judgement of the Prophet in the Fāṭima bint Qays *ḥadīth* (whose authenticity she does not deny), i.e. that she should leave the marital home, and this, in conjunction with the first judgement of the Prophet in the Fāṭima bint Qays *ḥadīth*, i.e. that she was due no *nafaqa*, and the injunctions of, in particular, Q 65: 6, became the general Madinan view. As Mālik records Ibn Shihāb as saying: 'An irrevocably divorced woman should not leave her house until she is free to re-marry (i.e. until her *ʿidda* is over), nor does she have a right to maintenance (*nafaqa*) unless she is pregnant, in which case she has a right to maintenance until she gives birth', this, says Mālik, being the position in Madina (*al-amr ʿindanā*).[139] It also later became that of al-Shāfiʿī.[140]

This was not, however, the only view. Abū Ḥanīfa (and the Kufans generally) held that a *mabtūta* divorcee, like any other divorcee, was entitled to both lodging and maintenance until her *ʿidda* was over, while a third view (held later by Aḥmad ibn Ḥanbal and Dāwūd al-Ẓāhirī) was that *mabtūta* divorcees were owed neither lodging nor maintenance.[141]

Mālik's own argument for the Madinan position is given in detail in the *Mudawwana*:

> Allah's words 'Lodge them (*askinūhunna*) where you live, according to your means, and do not cause harm to them in order to straiten their circumstances' (Q 65: 6) refer to those women who have been

irrevocably divorced by their husbands – who thus have no right to take them back [as their wives] – and who are not pregnant: such a woman is entitled to lodging (*suknā*), but not to maintenance (*nafaqa*) or clothing, because she has been irrevocably divorced – neither of them inherits from the other, nor does he have the right to take her back. If [however] she is pregnant she is entitled to maintenance, clothing and lodging until her *ᶜidda* is over.

As for those who have not been irrevocably divorced, they are [still] their [husband's] wives, and would inherit as such: they should not leave [the marital home] while they are still in their *ᶜidda.* Their husbands have not been specifically commanded to provide them with lodging since that is already obligatory for them in addition to their duty to provide maintenance and clothing, regardless of whether [their wives] are pregnant or not. Allah has only [specifically] commanded lodging for those who have been irrevocably divorced.

[But] Allah says, 'And if they are pregnant, expend on them (*anfiqū ᶜalayhinna*) until they give birth', and so Allah has appointed both lodging and maintenance for [pregnant women] who have been irrevocably divorced [and not for those who are not]. Didn't the Messenger of Allah, may Allah bless him and grant him peace, tell the woman who had been irrevocably divorced and was not pregnant – Fāṭima bint Qays – that she was not entitled to any maintenance?[142]

Mālik's argument is thus that Q 65: 1 applies specifically to *rajᶜī* divorcees and Q 65: 6 applies specifically to *mabtūta* divorcees. Since Q 65: 6 refers to an obligation of lodging – *askinūhunna* – but then allows an exception in the case of pregnant women, who are to be provided with maintenance as well, the implication is that those referred to in the *askinūhunna* command are not initially entitled to maintenance. Since *rajᶜī* divorcees automatically have a right to lodging *and* maintenance, whether pregnant or not, this distinction between pregnant and non-pregnant in Q 65: 6 would not make sense if taken to refer to *rajᶜī* divorcees and so could only refer to *mabtūta* divorcees, hence Mālik's judgement that non-pregnant *mabtūta* divorcees are entitled to lodging but not maintenance. The only problem here was that although the Prophet had not allowed maintenance to Fāṭima bint Qays, he had seemingly not allowed her lodging either, but this was explained as an exceptional case (as suggested by ᶜĀʾisha's comment to Marwān), and in exceptional cases – such as if her house was in a remote place and she feared for her life or property, or if it was feared that she would be ill-spoken or otherwise badly behaved towards her in-laws – a divorced woman *was* allowed to observe her *ᶜidda* elsewhere.[143]

The second group (the 'Iraqis', represented by Abū Ḥanīfa) felt that there was no reason to posit a distinction between pregnant and non-pregnant *mabtūta* divorcees in Q 65: 6: the command to maintain pregnant divorcees until they gave birth was not in contrast to the *askinūhunna* command but merely emphasised the different *ᶜidda* (already mentioned in Q 65: 4) that they had to observe. Furthermore, the judgements about *rajᶜī* divorcees and pregnant divorcees receiving both lodging and maintenance were clear: so too then, by *qiyās*, should *mabtūta* divorcees receive the same. Moreover, this judgement had the backing of ᶜUmar ibn al-Khaṭṭāb and Ibn Masᶜūd (the latter's view also being recorded in the form of a variant reading from him of *wa-askinūhunna* ***wa-anfiqū ᶜalayhinna*** in Q 65: 6).[144] However, accepting this judgement meant denying the validity, or at least the serviceability, of the Fāṭima bint Qays *ḥadīth*, and indeed this was what the proponents of this view did, citing a statement attributed to ᶜUmar that 'We do not abandon the Book of Allah nor the *sunna* of our Prophet, may Allah bless him and grant him peace, for the word of a woman who may be right and may be wrong (*lā nadrī a-ṣadaqat am kadhabat*) and who may have remembered and may have forgotten'.[145]

The third group (represented later by the Ḥanbalīs and the Ẓāhirīs)[146] fully accepted the *ẓāhir* of the Fāṭima bint Qays *ḥadīth*. They, of course, did not deny the Qur᾿anic judgements, but, in order to make sense of the *ḥadīth*, they had to restrict the Q 65: 6 reference to *rajᶜī* divorcees, thus allowing the judgements for *mabtūta* divorcees to come entirely from the *ḥadīth*.[147]

What we thus have is three groups whose differences effectively centred around how to harmonise a *ḥadīth* with the Qur᾿an. For the Iraqis, a general interpretation of the Qur᾿an was given preference, backed up by the opinions of certain Companions, and the relevance of the *ḥadīth* was minimised. For the '*ẓāhirī*' group, the *ḥadīth* was given importance at the expense of a general interpretation of the Qur᾿an. For the Madinans, however, both the *ḥadīth* and the Qur᾿an were given due weight, but interpretational adjustments were necessary to both in order to harmonise the two. Here again, then, we have what is likely to be a late systematisation, but one that is firmly rooted in a Qur᾿an + *sunna* scenario.[148]

9. *Zakāt* on horses

Paying the *zakāt*, like doing the prayer, is a clear Qur᾿anic obligation although there is very little detail about it actually in the Qur᾿an.[149] That *zakāt* was collected in the time of the Prophet, and that there must therefore have been some at least minimally organised system for so doing, would seem clear not only from reports to that effect,[150] but also from the fact that the first war fought by Abū Bakr after the death of the Prophet was against the tribes who refused to pay *zakāt*: when ʿUmar questioned Abū Bakr about how he could fight Muslims when the Prophet had said that the life and property of anyone who said *lā ilāha illā llāh* were safe except where there was a right due on it (*illā bi-ḥaqqihi*), Abū Bakr said, 'By Allah, I will fight anyone who makes a separation (*farraqa*) between the prayer and *zakāt*. *Zakāt* is a right due on wealth (*ḥaqq al-māl*). By Allah, if they were to refuse to give me even a hobbling-cord that they used to give to the Messenger of Allah, may Allah bless him and grant him peace, I would fight them for it.'[151] The sources further indicate that certain basic judgements, such as the three categories on which *zakāt* is due, the minimum amount (*niṣāb*) that is necessary before it is due, and the amount actually due from each category, had been decided in the time of the Prophet,[152] but there were many other details that had to be worked out by succeeding generations.

One such detail concerned the *zakāt* on livestock. There was agreement about there being *zakāt* on camels, cattle, sheep and goats, but, despite a Prophetic directive that a Muslim does not have to pay *zakāt* on 'his horse' (*laysa . . . fī farasihi ṣadaqa*),[153] there was some disagreement on the details of this judgement during the first and early second centuries. According to a report in the *Muwaṭṭaʾ*, the Syrians in the time of ʿUmar ibn al-Khaṭṭāb had wanted their governor, Abū ʿUbayda ibn al-Jarrāḥ, to take *zakāt* from their horses (and slaves), but Abū ʿUbayda had refused, as too had ʿUmar when Abū ʿUbayda referred the matter to him. However, the people were not satisfied and spoke to Abū ʿUbayda again, who wrote to ʿUmar again, who this time told him to accept it from them if they so wished and then to distribute it amongst them again (meaning, Mālik says, amongst their poor).[154] Another report refers to ʿUmar ibn ʿAbd al-ʿAzīz informing Abū Bakr ibn ʿAmr ibn Ḥazm (a Madinan *qāḍī* during ʿUmar's governorship and, later, governor under both Sulaymān and ʿUmar) that he should not take *zakāt* from horses (or honey), thus indicating the continued existence of the contrary opinion throughout the first century.[155] (There is also a report of ʿUmar ibn ʿAbd al-ʿAzīz writing to his governor in Damascus to point out that *zakāt* should only be taken from three categories, namely, crops (*ḥarth*), gold and silver (*ʿayn*) and livestock (*māshiya*), the word *māshiya* normally referring only to camels, cattle, sheep and goats and thus implicitly excluding horses from this last category).[156]

The reason for this disagreement is not hard to understand. From one point of view horses were livestock like any other, and, if allowed to breed, would increase naturally like any other: should they not, then, be subject to *zakāt* like any other? Indeed, we find Abū Ḥanīfa holding the view that free-grazing (*sā'ima*) horses intended for breeding purposes should, like other free-grazing livestock, be subject to *zakāt*, thus restricting, by *qiyās*, the *'umūm* of the Prophetic directive mentioned above.[157] However, the initial response of Abū ʿUbayda and ʿUmar to the request of the Syrians mentioned above suggests that the norm at the time was that *zakāt* was not taken from horses, of whatever type, ʿUmar's eventual decision seemingly to the contrary being understood either as a concession in this particular instance to the opinion that free-grazing horses should be treated like any other free-grazing livestock, or (as is considered more likely by later commentators) as a kind of 'official' distribution of what was considered only voluntary *ṣadaqa* rather than actual *zakāt*, which thus satisfied both the people and the dictates of the *sharīʿa*.[158] Indeed, despite the continued existence of the contrary opinion, in an albeit attentuated form, until at least as late as Abū Ḥanīfa's time, the view that there was no *zakāt* on horses, based not only on the *'umūm* of the Prophetic directive mentioned above but also, and more importantly, on what was seen to be the original Prophetic practice in Madina, eventually won out, so that by the second half of the second century there was effectively complete agreement on this issue, with even Abū Yūsuf and al-Shaybānī rejecting Abū Ḥanīfa's opinion and holding to the majority view.[159]

This, then, was a judgement based on the Prophet's *tark* (i.e. his deliberate refraining from doing something). In this context we may note in passing a related and even clearer instance of a judgement based on the Prophet's *tark*, this being the Madinan judgement that there is no *zakāt* on fresh fruit and vegetables. As Mālik says: 'The *sunna* about which there is no disagreement among us, and that which I have heard from the people of knowledge, is that there is no *zakāt* on any sort of fruit (*fawākih*), . . . fodder (*qaḍb*) or vegetables (*buqūl*).'[160] Al-Shāfiʿī agreed with the Madinan judgement on this matter, namely, that *zakāt* was limited to those crops that were basic foodstuffs and could be dried and stored (*al-muqtāt al-muddakhar*), although for the seemingly similar but in fact very different reason that there was no '*sunna*', i.e. *ḥadīth*, about anything other than these,[161] but Abū Ḥanīfa disagreed, preferring a more general interpretation of the Prophetic directive to take a tenth from 'what is watered by the sky' and a twentieth from what needs to be irrigated and thus considering *zakāt* to be obligatory on all crops (except for grass, firewood and fodder, which were excepted by *ijmāʿ*).[162]

10. The prohibition against *ribā*

Ribā, like *zakāt*, was another situation where the general judgement in the Qurʾan was clear but the precise details problematic. The main prohibition against *ribā* comes in Q 2: 278–9 where we read that those who practise *ribā* should be aware that they have engaged in 'a war with Allah and His Messenger', from which the *ʿulamāʾ* derived the judgement that those who engage in *ribā* and refuse to repent are, if they have a power-base (*ʿaskar wa-shawka*), to be fought as rebels (*al-fiʾa al-bāghiya*) in the same way that Abū Bakr fought those who refused to pay *zakāt*.[163] *Ribā* and its definition was thus a very serious issue.[164]

Mālik overtly links the prohibition against *ribā* with the relevant Qurʾanic *āyas*:

> Some transactions may be allowed if the transaction has gone ahead and it is difficult to annul (*idhā tafāwata amruhu wa-tafāḥasha radduhu*) but *ribā* in a transaction automatically annuls it. Neither a little nor a lot of it is allowed, nor is there the same leeway with regard to it as there is for other types of transaction, because Allah, the Blessed and Exalted, says in His Book: 'And if you repent, you may have your capital back, without either wronging or being wronged.'[165]

However, the details of this prohibition were far from clear, and we have already noted ʿUmar's wish that the Prophet had given more details about *ribā* before he died.[166] One dispute on *ribā* that arose during ʿUmar's time (although in this instance ʿUmar was certain about the judgement) is that recorded by Mālik in the chapter 'Selling Gold for Silver in Unminted or Minted Form' where we are told that Muʿāwiya (who was presumably governor of Syria at the time) once sold a drinking-vessel (*siqāya*)[167] of gold or silver for more than its own weight of the same substance and, on hearing about this, Abū l-Dardāʾ told him that he had heard the Prophet forbid such transactions unless only the same amount (i.e. weight) of gold or silver was involved. Muʿāwiya said that he could not see any harm in it, to which Abū l-Dardāʾ replied, 'Who will excuse me with regard to Muʿāwiya (*man yaʿdhirunī min Muʿāwiya*)? I tell him what the Messenger of Allah, may Allah bless him and grant him peace, has said and he tells me what his own opinion is. I will not live in the same land as you!' Abū l-Dardāʾ then went to ʿUmar and mentioned this to him, whereupon ʿUmar wrote to Muʿāwiya telling him that the Prophet had indeed forbidden such transactions and that he could only exchange such items for their own kind and weight.[168]

This, then, was again a question of whether a general prohibition (in this case, of the Prophet, although based on the general prohbition of the

Qurʾan) should be interpreted generally or could be restricted by *qiyās*: Muʿāwiya presumably felt that the situation was an exception to the general rule (worked gold or silver not being the same as unworked), whereas Abū l-Dardāʾ (and ʿUmar) were certain that it came under the *ribā* prohibited by the Prophet.[169] Muʿāwiya's judgement was in fact rejected by all the *fuqahāʾ*, who derived from the Prophet's directives the principle that, where *ribawī* substances were concerned, no unequal transactions between the same substance were permitted.[170] Thus a fee could be charged for decorating gold, etc, but it would have to be paid in some other substance; what was used as money, i.e. as a means of exchange to express value, had to remain standard and could not be given one value at one time and then another at another, which is what *ribā* effectively entailed.

Mālik mentions another instance involving *ribā* that even better illustrates the interplay between the *fuqahāʾ* and the political authorities. He relates that during the time of Marwān (i.e. when he was governor of Madina under Muʿāwiya) chits (*ṣukūk*)[171] had been issued for the food at al-Jār (a port on the Red Sea coast not far from Madina) and these receipts had then been sold and re-sold before possession had been taken of the food in question. On learning about this, Zayd ibn Thābit and another (unspecified) Companion went to Marwān and said to him, 'Are you making *ribā ḥalāl*, Marwān?', to which Marwān replied, 'I seek refuge in Allah! How is that?' The two of them then explained that people had been selling their chits and that these were then being re-sold before the purchasers had actually taken possession of the food they had bought. Marwān therefore sent out officials (*ḥaras*) to collect up these receipts and return them to their rightful owners.[172]

Mālik includes this report in the same chapter as various *ḥadīths* about not selling food before taking possession of it, and this is clearly the import of its inclusion here. However, in the *ʿUtbiyya* he explains that there is no harm in someone selling food that he has not yet taken possession of if it has been acquired by way of a regular gift or stipend (*ʿaṭāʾ*) – such as the food at al-Jār – rather than as the result of an exchange for some item or services, since the prohibition of the Prophet was against re-selling food after having bought it and before taking possession of it, rather than against selling it after having acquired it as a gift. Thus, in the case of the Marwān episode related above, it was not the people selling their own receipts that was forbidden, even though they had not taken physical possession of the food, but rather the re-selling of these receipts by others before these others had taken possession of the food they had bought.[173]

11. The *ʿidda* of *umm walads*

Another instance of the outright rejection of a caliphal judgement by the *ʿulamāʾ* is the instance we have already noted where Yazīd ibn ʿAbd al-Malik gave a judgement that the *ʿidda* of an *umm walad* whose master has died should be the same as that of a free woman, and how this was categorically rejected by al-Qāsim ibn Muḥammad with the words, '*Subḥāna llāh!* Allah says in His Book, "Those among you who die and leave wives (*azwājan*) . . ." These are not wives!', although there were others who held the same opinion as Yazīd.[174]

12. The penalty for *qadhf*

Finally, we may note an instance where even a judgement of ʿUmar ibn ʿAbd al-ʿAzīz, despite his high reputation, was rejected by the *ʿulamāʾ*. Mālik records that ʿUmar, following the *ʿumūm* of Q 24: 4 – *wa-lladhīna yarmūna l-muḥṣanāti thumma lam yaʾtū bi-arbaʿati shuhadāʾa fa-jlidūhum thamānīna jalda* ('Those who accuse respectable women [of *zinā*] and then do not produce four witnesses, flog them eighty lashes') – had decided that the penalty for *qadhf* should be eighty lashes for all offenders, regardless of whether they were free men or slaves.[175] (We should bear in mind that the penalty for *qadhf* was universally understood as applying only to *qadhf* against free men or women – i.e. the '*muḥṣanāt*' of Q 24: 4[176] – and so it could be argued that since the right of the *maqdhūf* was involved and the *maqdhūf* was always by definition free, so too should the punishment be commensurate with the wrong done against the *maqdhūf* and thus remain the same for free men or slaves.) This, however, was never taken on by the majority of the *fuqahāʾ*, who considered that the penalty for slaves should be half that of free men, by *qiyās* with the half-punishment specified in Q 4: 25 for slave-girls guilty of *zinā* – *fa-ʿalayhinna nisfu mā ʿalā l-muḥṣanāti mina l-ʿadhāb* ('for them is half the punishment that there is for free women)' – and extended by *qiyās* to include male slaves.[177]

The above examples (and there are many more) show how the caliphs and governors were both interested and involved in the development of the law from its origins in the Qurʾan and *sunna*. However, although their judgements were often accepted (e.g. Muʿāwiya's judgements on a drunkard or a madman killing someone and on molars bearing the same indemnity as front teeth, and ʿAbd al-Malik's judgement on someone killing someone with a stick) and even praised by the Madinan *ʿulamā'* (e.g. Marwān's judgement on *tamlīk*), there were other occasions when they were either considered the weaker of two or more opinions (e.g. Marwān's decision on *īlā'*) or even rejected (e.g. Muʿāwiya's judgement on selling a gold item for more than its weight in gold, or, in a less categoric fashion, ʿUmar ibn ʿAbd al-ʿAzīz's penalty of eighty lashes for a slave guilty of *qadhf* and Yazīd's judgement on the *ʿidda* of *umm walads* whose masters had died).

It was Schacht's thesis that Islamic legal thought started at around the end of the first century AH from 'late Umaiyad administrative and popular practice' and that this was then gradually systematised and put into the form of *ḥadīths* from earlier and earlier authorities, culminating in the late second and early third centuries in their ascription primarily to the Prophet himself as his *sunna*.[178] As a result of these conclusions, Schacht felt it necessary to 'discard the opinion, often expressed as part of *a priori* ideas on the origins of Muhammadan jurisprudence, that the Medinese were stricter, more deeply inspired by the religious spirit of Islam, and more uncompromisingly opposed to the worldly spirit of the Umaiyads than the Iraqians', as he also felt it necessary to reject 'the historical fiction of early ʿAbbāsid times which made the Umaiyads convenient scapegoats.'[179] Working on a somewhat similar basis of debunking the traditional debunking of the Umayyads, Crone and Hinds, in their book *God's Caliph*, claim that not only all political but also all religious authority was concentrated in the caliphate at that time – at least conceptually if not in actuality – and that it was the caliph who was initially charged with the definition of Islamic law rather than the scholars, who then sought to undermine this authority by introducing the idea of *sunna* as meaning *sunna* of the Prophet and only the Prophet and of which they, as scholars, were the sole rightful interpreters.[180]

What the above examples show most clearly is that for Mālik and the Madinans the contribution of the Umayyad caliphs and governors was never in doubt and was part and parcel of the whole process of the development of the law. Indeed, that there should have been a significant caliphal contribution to the development of Islamic law is only to be expected, given the principle of continuous *ʿamal*, and the picture the *Muwaṭṭa'* gives us is that not only was this the case, but that it was positively accepted as such by the traditional scholars of Madina. However, the same picture also shows us this development as firmly rooted in an initial starting point of Qur'an and *sunna* (by which is meant the *sunna* of the Prophet). If we accept this picture as true, then the thesis of Schacht, Crone, Hinds *et al.* that it was 'Umayyad practice' (or 'caliphal *sunna*' in Crone/Hind's phrase) that came first and Prophetic *sunna* later would seem an over-reaction on their part to the anti-caliphal (i.e. anti-Umayyad) stance of later scholars referred to above, or, put another way, to the 'classical', i.e. post-Shāfiʿī, theory in which the Prophet is seen as the sole source of the normative practice of the Muslims, whereas this 'classical' position is in fact only that of al-Shāfiʿī and those of his inclination or under his influence, and certainly not that of the traditional Madinan scholars whom Mālik represents. By way of conclusion to this study, it is to a consideration of the position of Qurʾan and *sunna* in Islamic law in the time of Mālik, i.e. the pre-Shāfiʿī or pre-'classical' period, that we now turn.

PART THREE

Implications

CHAPTER EIGHT

Qur'an and *Sunna*

It is often said that Islam, and thus also Islamic law, is based on the two-fold source of Qur'an and *sunna* and this view we find expressed in the *ḥadīth* that Mālik records that the Prophet said, 'I have left among you two things, and as long as you hold fast to them you will not go astray: the Book of Allah and the *sunna* of His Prophet.'[1] However, although this view is accepted as an accurate representation of the 'classical' picture of Islam, considerable doubt has been expressed by many Western scholars as to its validity in the pre-'classical' or 'ancient' period. It is with the position of the Qur'an and the *sunna* in the 'ancient' schools, and particularly that of Madina as represented by Mālik in his *Muwaṭṭa'*, that this chapter deals.

The Qur'an in Islamic law

It will be evident from the examples in the preceding chapters that for Mālik, and indeed for his contemporaries, the Qur'an was the backbone of Islamic law, to be fleshed out firstly by the *sunna* and secondly by the *ijtihād* of later generations. This is amply demonstrated by the fact that the subject matter of Islamic law is overwhelmingly Qur'anic in its formulation, which in turn explains the remarkable uniformity in its infrastructure despite the diversity of positive doctrines: the discussions, and disagreements, are about the details rather than the basic ideas. Thus in all compendia of *fiqh*, from whatever period, we find the same basic discussions on the same basic subjects – the prayer, *zakāt*, *ḥajj*, inheritance, marriage, divorce, *ribā*, testimony, blood-money, etc – precisely because these were the issues raised by the legally relevant Qur'anic prescriptions. In other words, the prime motivation behind the inclusion of a subject in a book of *fiqh* is that that subject is mentioned in the Qur'an, however general that mention may be. Thus, out of 44 sections in the *Muwaṭṭa'* dealing with purely legal matters (i.e. excluding the more exhortatory material in the *Kitāb al-jāmi'* at the end of the book, although much of this, too, has Qur'anic antecedents), over two-thirds[2] can be shown to have direct Qur'anic antecedents, whilst all the remaining sections can be shown to relate back indirectly to some Qur'anic antecedent. In this latter third, for instance, there are a number of sections that deal with types of prayer that are not mentioned directly in the Qur'an, such as the *ʿīd* prayer, the eclipse prayer and the prayer for rain,[3] but all of these are subsumed under the general Qur'anic injunction to 'do the prayer'.[4] Similarly, although the various sections on business transactions include very little direct reference to the Qur'an, the overriding concern – as is evident from the vocabulary – is to avoid transactions that involve either *ribā* (usury) or *gharar* (uncertainty), both of which are prohibited by the Qur'an.[5] In other words, the impulse is Qur'anic. Even such sections as those dealing with the *ʿaqīqa* sacrifice, or *tadbīr*, or the oath of *qasāma*, which reflect pre-Islamic rather than Qur'anic norms, are effectively treated as extensions of the Qur'anic injunctions on sacrifices, setting free slaves and blood-money respectively, as is shown by their juxtaposition with these latter topics in the *Muwaṭṭaʾ*.[6]

The importance of the Qur'anic contribution to Islamic law has been doubted by certain Western scholars. Schacht in particular holds that the Qur'an is 'essentially ethical' and only 'incidentally legal' and denies that the Qur'an had any major importance in the earliest development of Islamic law. In his view

> Muhammadan law did not derive directly from the Koran but developed ... out of popular and administrative practice under the Umaiyads, and this practice often diverged from the intentions and even the explicit wording of the Koran. It is true that a number of legal rules, particularly in family law and inheritance, not to mention cult and ritual, were based on the Koran from the beginning. But [we] will show that apart from the most elementary rules, norms derived from the Koran were introduced into Muhammadan law almost invariably at a secondary stage. This applies not only to those branches of law which are not covered in detail by the Koranic legislation – if we may use this term of the essentially ethical and only incidentally legal body of maxims contained in the Koran – but to family law, the law of inheritance, and even cult and ritual.[7]

Since in his view the Qur'anic element was introduced 'at a secondary stage' (by which he presumably means in the post-Umayyad period at the earliest) he accordingly gives the subject a secondary place in his book, devoting no more than four pages to it in his *Origins*. Crone effectively takes the same position:

> Most legal doctrines are validated by a tradition. There are of course some which are based on the Qurʾan and others which rest on analogy (*qiyās*), mere preference (*istiḥsān*) and other modes of reasoning; but Ḥadīth is the real stuff of Islamic law.[8]

and Wansbrough overtly does so:

> Schacht's studies of the early development of legal doctrines within the community demonstrate that, with very few exceptions, Muslim jurisprudence was not derived from the contents of the Qurʾān.[9]

We should mention that it was of course Schacht's studies on early *ḥadīth*-literature and his conclusion that the vast majority of it was fabricated at a later date than claimed and then back-projected into the mouths of earlier and earlier authorities to give weight to the arguments of the fabricators that led him to doubt the importance of the Qurʾan as a source of law in the early period: if the *ḥadīths* speaking about the Qurʾan were later fabrications, then so too must the discussions giving rise to them have been historically later.

Schacht's conclusions, however, have been questioned by a number of scholars, notably Goitein, Coulson and Powers. Goitein felt that, from all the evidence available, it was 'abundantly clear' that many legal questions must have been brought before Muhammad and decided by him.[10] Coulson expanded somewhat on this position, saying that

> the Qurʾan itself posed problems which must have been of immediate concern to the Muslim community, and with which the Prophet himself, in his role of supreme political and legal authority in Medina, must have been forced to deal. When, therefore, the thesis of Schacht is systematically developed to the extent of holding that 'the evidence of legal traditions carries us back to about the year A.H. 100 [sc. A.D. 719] only', and when the authenticity of practically every alleged ruling of the Prophet is denied, a void is assumed, or rather created, in the picture of the development of law in early Muslim society. From a practical standpoint, and taking the attendant historical circumstances into account, the notion of such a vacuum is difficult to accept.[11]

Powers accepts this basic standpoint, adding his own view that

> anyone who wants to shed light on the origins of Islamic positive law ought to begin with the Qurʾanic legislation in the field of family law, inheritance, or ritual. Muslims living in the generations following

> Muhammad's death prayed on a daily basis, divorced, and divided up property, and it stands to reason, on *a priori* grounds, that the Qur'anic legislation on these matters would have provided them with guidance.[12]

We should add that it is not only the Qur'anic legislation that would have provided them with guidance, but also the *sunna*, which, as we shall see, did not have quite the meaning that either the Schachtians or the traditional, post-Shāfiʿī, Muslim scholars assume it to have.

This minimising of the Qur'anic element in Islamic law seems based on the assumption that religion is essentially a matter of morals and ethics and that therefore the Qur'an, as a religious text, is by definition, as we saw with Schacht's judgement, essentially moral and ethical in nature and only incidentally legal. Thus Coulson, although allowing greater scope for the Qur'an in early Islamic law than does Schacht, is nevertheless merely echoing Schacht when he says that not only is the legislation of the Qur'an 'predominantly ethical in quality', but also that its quantity 'is not great by any standards'.[13] There are, he says, only some six hundred verses (out of a total 6236 verses in most modern editions)[14] that deal with legal topics, and 'the vast majority of these are concerned with the religious duties and ritual practices of prayer, fasting and pilgrimage', with 'no more than approximately eighty verses [dealing] with legal topics in the strict sense of the word.'[15]

However, these figures, as Goitein has pointed out, are misleading and do not represent the true proportion of the legal matter in the Qur'an, for two reasons. Firstly, the legal verses are often considerably longer than other types of verse (Q 2: 282, the *āyat al-mudāyana* – which takes up at least a full page in most editions – being a particularly clear example). Secondly, although the Qur'an contains frequent repetitions, the legal verses are very rarely repeated and, when they are, there is usually some difference in content. In fact, says Goitein,

> If one condenses its subject matter to its mere content, under the five main headings of preaching, polemics, stories, allusions to the Prophet's life, and legislation, one will reach the conclusion that proportionately the Qur'ān does not contain less legal material than the Pentateuch, the Torah, which is known in world literature as 'The Law'.[16]

We should also note that this five-way division of content is usually reduced in the traditional sources to the three-way one of beliefs (*tawḥīd*, *ʿaqāʾid*), judgements (*aḥkām*) and stories (*qiṣaṣ*, *akhbār*), thus giving an even greater importance to the legal element,[17] although at the same time we should bear in mind that its importance is not of course dependent on the proportion of space devoted to it.

The importance of the Qur'an in the *Muwaṭṭa'*

Wansbrough argues that Mālik relies very little on the Qur'an as a source of judgements in the *Muwaṭṭa'*, noting how, for instance, in the whole section on *jihād* he cites the Qur'an on only four occasions (involving five verses) with only one citation serving a clearly juridical purpose. From this he concludes that the Qur'anic passages cited are little more than a 'superfluous embellishment', that '[no] serious appeal [is] made to the text of scripture', and that 'the role of scripture as witness to correct procedure was indeed minimal'.[18]

Such numerically-based assessments, are, as with the question of the legal import of the Qur'an discussed above, highly misleading. The foregoing chapters show clearly that not only is a large amount of the *Muwaṭṭa'* devoted entirely to discussions of details mentioned in the Qur'an, but, as a source of judgements in the book the Qur'an is everywhere implied and everywhere taken for granted. The very fact that *jihād* (to use Wansbrough's example) is given a whole section by itself is because it is a major theme in the Qur'an: the whole question of the division of spoils, for instance, which takes up over a third of the section in question,[19] is occasioned by the Qur'anic verses dealing with the subject.[20] The same is true for the rest of the section, and, indeed, for the rest of the *Muwaṭṭa'*, where, as we have mentioned, there is hardly a section that does not have some obvious Qur'anic antecedent.[21]

The *sunna*

We have seen how the importance that Mālik attached to the Qur'an is evident from his constant use of it in the *Muwaṭṭa'* as a point of reference, whether explicit or implied. It is also clear that he attached equal importance to the *sunna*. As he says, when speaking about objections to the Madinan practice of accepting the testimony of only one witness along with the oath of the plaintiff although the Qur'an specifies that there should be two witnesses:

> There are people who say that an oath with a single witness is not valid, taking as their argument the words of Allah, the Blessed and

> Exalted – and His word is the truth – 'And have two of your menfolk bear witness, or, if there are not two men, then one man and two women, from among those whom you are satisfied with as witnesses',[22] and saying that if someone does not produce a man and two women [i.e. as witnesses, if he does not have two men] he is entitled to nothing and cannot be allowed to take an oath along with only one witness.
>
> Part of the argument against people who say this is to ask them what their opinion would be if a man were to claim some property (*māl*) from another man [i.e. without there being any witnesses]? Would not the one against whom the claim is made [either] swear that the claim is false, in which case the claim would be dropped, or refuse to do so, in which case the claimant would be asked to swear an oath that his claim is true, and thus establish his claim against the other man as valid? This is something about which there is no disagreement among anybody, anywhere.[23] Why then do people accept this, and where in the Book of Allah does it occur? If people accept this, then let them accept an oath with one witness, even though it is not in the Book of Allah, the Mighty and Glorious, and that what has been established as *sunna* (*mā maḍā min al-sunna*) is enough. However, sometimes people like to know what the correct view is and where the proof lies, and in what we have said is a sufficient clarification of what is unclear in this matter, God willing.[24]

Mālik's argument clearly shows his respect for, and certainty about, the Qurʾan ('and His word is the truth') but equally clearly shows his conviction that not every judgement need necessarily derive from the Qurʾan and that exceptions to general Qurʾanic rules are valid. People accept, he says, the procedure for determining ownership when there are no witnesses available even though this is not mentioned in the Qurʾan; so too should they accept an oath with only one witness, even though it is not in the Qurʾan, since it is the *sunna*, and 'what has been established as *sunna* is enough'. Thus the *sunna* – and it is the *sunna* of the Prophet that is meant, as is made clear by the attribution of this judgement to him at the beginning of the chapter – is in effect the ultimate authority, or perhaps we should say the ultimate explication. The Qurʾan is not denied – Mālik describes it as 'the truth' – nor is the Qurʾanic judgement rejected – it is accepted for instance that two witnesses are always necessary in matters involving marriage, divorce, manumission, etc[25] – but as far as property is concerned this exception to the Qurʾan is accepted because it is the *sunna*, and 'what has been established as *sunna* is enough'.

There is thus an interplay between Qur'an and *sunna*. The *sunna* is, as it were, the living embodiment of the Qur'anic message. Indeed, given the nature of this message and its revelation over a period of twenty-three years, it is impossible to conceive of it without the concomitant creation of a *sunna* as the commands were progressively revealed and acted upon. Many of the fundamental obligations of the Qur'an, such as doing the prayer, paying *zakāt*, and going on *ḥajj*, could not possibly have been put into practice unless there were some practical demonstration of how to do so, and the obvious model for this was of course that of the one who first put these obligations into practice, i.e. the Prophet. The Qur'an could not, therefore, be divorced from its initial context, i.e. the life of the Prophet, and, although its supremacy as a text remained beyond question, it was always seen in the light of its first practical expression, namely, the *sunna* of the Prophet. This is evident not only from the above report but also, for instance, in ʿUmar's report about the stoning-verse where the point is that, whether or not people are prepared to give weight to a judgement which is no longer in the Qur'an, it is nevertheless the *sunna*.[26] Similarly, in response to a question about the travelling prayer[27] not being found in the Qur'an whereas the fear prayer and the ordinary prayer are mentioned in it, Ibn ʿUmar says: 'My nephew! Allah, the Noble and Majestic, sent us Muhammad, may Allah bless him and grant him peace, and we knew nothing. We simply do as we saw him doing.'[28]

The nature of this interplay between Qur'an and *sunna* is given clearer expression in the *ʿUtbiyya*, where Mālik says: 'All of the *ḥajj* is in the Book of Allah, whereas the prayer and *zakāt* are not given any explanation (*tafsīr*): the Messenger of Allah, may Allah bless him and grant him peace, clarified them (*bayyana dhālika*).'[29] Thus the Prophet's words and actions are understood by Mālik to clarify the general expressions in the Qur'an which would, as we have noted, have otherwise been impossible to act upon. Nor is the *ḥajj*, in one sense (despite Mālik's comment), any exception to this rule, since it is no more possible to put into practice the Qur'anic directives about *ḥajj* without further clarification than it is to put into practice the directives about the prayer or *zakāt*. This is the reason why Ibn Rushd (al-Jadd), in his commentary on this report, suggests that it should not be taken at face value but should be understood rather to mean: 'All of the *ḥajj* is in the Book of Allah, and the prayer and *zakāt*. None of them are given any explanation in the Book of Allah, but the Messenger of Allah clarified them.'[30] Despite Ibn Rushd's misgivings about the normal interpretation of Mālik's statement, however, it nevertheless remains true that the subject of *ḥajj* is given far more detailed treatment in the Qur'an than either the prayer or *zakāt*, and it must be this that Mālik meant.[31]

For Mālik, then, the Prophet is clearly a source of 'extra-Qur'anic' judgement but this 'extra-Qur'anic' element is considered to be within the general principles outlined by the Qur'an rather than a separate source.

The continuity of the *sunna*

Mālik frequently describes the general practice in Madina using *sunna* terms such as *maḍat al-sunna* ('The *sunna* has been established') and *al-sunna ʿindanā* ('The *sunna* here'),[32] and it is clear from both his letter to al-Layth ibn Saʿd[33] and his discussions with Abū Yūsuf about Madinan *ʿamal*[34] that Mālik considered the *sunna* as practiced by the Madinans to have a continuous link back to the time of its institutor, the Prophet, as an inheritance passed on from one generation to the next. We have also noted this link in the distinction investigated by Abd-Allah between Mālik's *sunna* and *amr* terms: the *sunna* terms invariably refer to practices seen as having their direct origin in the *sunna*, or practice, of the Prophet, rather than the *ʿamal* of later times,[35] thus presupposing not only the existence of a '*sunna* of the Prophet' for Mālik and his Madinan contemporaries but also the continuity of that *sunna* up to his own time.

This idea of continuity is particularly evident in Mālik's use of terms involving the word *maḍā*, such as *maḍat al-sunna* or *al-māḍī min al-sunna* ('The established *sunna*'),[36] which, as Bravmann has pointed out, indicate a continuous practice instituted in the past and still operative in the present rather than merely the idea of a past practice, as Schacht suggested.[37] It is even more evident in Mālik's use of terms such as *dhālika lladhī lam yazal ʿalayhi ahl al-ʿilm bi-baladinā* ('This is what the people of knowledge in our city have always held to') and *hādhā l-amr alladhī lam yazal ʿalayhi ahl al-ʿilm ʿindanā* ('This is the position that the people of knowledge have always held to here'),[38] which clearly indicate a continuity of opinion among the Madinan *ʿulamāʾ*. That this continuity was traced back to the Prophet is also openly stated, such as in the instance mentioned above about *iḥṣār* by an enemy,[39] or in Mālik's discussions with Abū Yūsuf about Madinan *ʿamal*,[40] or in the report where he records that there has never been either an *adhān* or an *iqāma* for either of the *ʿīd* prayers 'from the time of the Prophet ... up until today.'[41]

Sometimes it is evident that it is not merely the *ʿulamāʾ* who have preserved such *sunnas* but, rather, the whole community of the Muslims. Thus, for example, Mālik says that *ʿumra* is a *sunna*[42] and then adds that he does not know of 'anyone among the Muslims' who says that it is permissible not to do it.[43] In a similar vein, he mentions a report where Ibn

ʿUmar is asked whether the *witr* prayer is obligatory (*wājib*), to which he replies, 'The Prophet, may Allah bless him and grant him peace, did *witr*, and the Muslims have [always] done it.'[44]

One of the best examples in the *Muwaṭṭaʾ* of this idea is where Mālik, speaking about *iʿtikāf*, says that it is not permissible for someone to introduce any modifications into his *iʿtikāf* which would change the basic nature (*sunna*) of *iʿtikāf*. *Iʿtikāf*, he says, is an act of worship like the prayer, fasting, going on *ḥajj*, and other such acts, whether obligatory (*farīḍa*) or voluntary (*nāfila*). Once someone has begun doing any of them he should do them according to what has been established as *sunna* (*bi-mā maḍā min al-sunna*) and not introduce anything into them that has not been part of the practice of the Muslims (*mā maḍā ʿalayhi l-Muslimūn*). The Prophet, he says, did *iʿtikāf*, and from that time the Muslims have known what the *sunna* of *iʿtikāf* is (*wa-ʿarafa l-Muslimūna sunnat al-iʿtikāf*).[45]

These examples indicate that there was, in a sense, a '*sunna* of the Muslims', and, indeed, we find this expression explicitly used by Mālik in the *Muwaṭṭaʾ*. In the section on *qirāḍ*, Mālik says that it is 'the established *sunna* of the Muslims' (*mā maḍā min sunnat al-Muslimīn*) that someone providing money in a *qirāḍ* contract may not stipulate any guaranteed or fixed return but only a proportional one. Shortly afterwards he says that it is not permitted for an investor to make a *qirāḍ* contract with someone and stipulate that the man must buy only palms or animals so that he can keep them for a time and thus gain benefit from the date crop or the offspring of the animals while preventing sale of the original goods. This is so, he says, because 'it is not part of the *sunna* of the Muslims as regards *qirāḍ* (*sunnat al-Muslimīna fī l-qirāḍ*) unless he buys the goods and then sells them as any other goods are sold.'[46]

A further example of 'the people' being the authority for a practice occurs in the chapter on sharecropping (*musāqāt*). The normal position in Madina was that open land (*bayāḍ*) could be hired out but not sharecropped, and that land with a fixed crop on it, such as palms or vines, could be sharecropped but not hired out. Mālik makes an exception, however, to this general rule, saying that it is part of the practice of the people (*amr al-nās*) that where open land forms two-thirds or more of an area where there are also fixed crops it is permissible to hire it out but not to sharecrop it, and that where a fixed crop covers two-thirds or more of the land it is permissible to sharecrop it but not to hire it out, just as a Qurʾan or a sword embellished with gold that amounts to less than a third of the total value of the object may be sold for gold *dīnārs*, even though unequal amounts of gold may not normally be exchanged for each other. Such transactions, he says, have always been considered permissible by people (*lam tazal hādhihi l-buyūʿ jāʾiza yatabāyaʿuhā l-nās wa-yabtāʿūnahā*) and nothing has come down to suggest any specific limit beyond which such contracts become *ḥarām*. Rather, people have always accepted that such subsidiary elements are allowed in these transactions, and that 'subsidiary' is defined as what amounts to a third or less.[47]

We should, however, point out that although this particular practice is given the authority of 'the people', it would of course, like the other examples mentioned above, have had the sanction of the *ʿulamāʾ* behind it. This is implicit in that Mālik is mentioning the practice, and doing so favourably, and is thus sanctioning it with his own authority, but elsewhere it is stated overtly. Thus, referring to the acceptability of paying in advance for animals to be delivered at a later date (as long as the date is fixed, the animal clearly described and the amount paid in full), Mālik says, 'This has continued to be the practice of the people which is accepted by them and which the people of knowledge in our city have always held to.'[48] Similarly, although in the example about *iʿtikāf* mentioned above Mālik refers to 'the Muslims' knowing the *sunna* of *iʿtikāf*, he makes it clear that it is the *ʿulamāʾ* who are the true guardians of that *sunna* in its fullness, saying that he has never heard any of 'the people of knowledge' mentioning the possibility of allowing extra conditions in *iʿtikāf* that might alter its nature in any way.[49]

In this context two further points should be mentioned. Firstly, some authors have claimed that Mālik's concept of *sunna* was a parochial one.[50] It should now, however, be evident from the above – especially his comment to al-Layth ibn Saʿd that 'all people are subordinate to the people of Madina'[51] – that Mālik took the practice of the *sunna* in Madina to be not merely a local phenomenon to be preserved and practised in Madina but one that should ideally be practised by all the Muslims. That he did not seek to impose it on all the Muslims when, for example, he had the chance of doing so through the agency of Abū Jaʿfar al-Manṣūr, would seem to have been, as we mentioned earlier, not because he did not see it as universal, but rather that it was not something that could be imposed on people in this way, nor was it something that he could allow to be abused by the authorities in power.[52] Furthermore, we have seen above how Mālik was conscious of an agreed *sunna* of all the Muslims, as is evident in the examples about *ʿumra*, *witr*, *iʿtikāf*, *qirāḍ*, and the procedure for determining the ownership of goods in the event of neither litigant having any witnesses ('This is something about which there is no disagreement among anybody, anywhere'),[53] which again supports our contention that he accepted the ideal that all the *umma* should be agreed on something but that people had to accept it themselves rather than have it imposed upon them.

Secondly, it has been suggested that the 'practice' that Mālik is describing is in some way an 'ideal', rather than an actual, practice.[54] It should be equally clear from the above examples, especially those describing the 'practice of the people', that Mālik was describing an existing practice rather than an ideal one, however much individuals may or may not have chosen to abide by it. Furthermore, his frequent presentation of Madinan 'practice' as an option among options shows that it was not a theoretical and ideal construct but rather a practical response to actual situations, this practicality being reflected in the flexibility of his responses and his awareness of other possible positions: if it were an ideal construct, one would expect one view only, not options.

CHAPTER NINE

Sunna versus Ḥadīth

For Mālik the *sunna*, as we have seen, was the normative pattern of life established by the Prophet, put into practice by the Companions, and then inherited from them as *ʿamal* by the Successors and the Successors of the Successors down to his own time. This *ʿamal* could derive solely from the Prophet, in which case Mālik usually refers to it using the term '*sunna*', or it could contain additional elements from later authorities, in which case he usually refers to it using the term '*amr*'.[1] Furthermore, since *sunna* is part of *ʿamal*, what we observed about *ʿamal* in its relation to *ḥadīth* applies equally well to *sunna*: that although *sunna* and *ḥadīth* often overlap, *sunna* may or may not be recorded by *ḥadīth*, and *ḥadīth* may or may not record *sunna*.[2] Thus the two terms are quite distinct.

Today however (and indeed since the time of al-Shāfiʿī) this distinction has largely been ignored, and it is common to find the word *sunna* equated with *ḥadīth* both by Muslims and non-Muslims, although it is understood that the two words derive from quite different roots. Thus, while it is usual to find the Qurʾan and the *sunna* referred to as the two main sources of Islamic law, one frequently finds the word *ḥadīth* substituted for the word *sunna* or used interchangeably with it.[3] Thus Vesey-Fitzgerald speaks of 'traditions' (i.e. *ḥadīth*) as the second source of Islamic law,[4] while Robson entitles an article of his 'Tradition, the Second Foundation of Islam'.[5] Crone, as we have seen, even regards *ḥadīth* as the main source:

> Most legal doctrines are validated by a tradition ... Ḥadīth is the real stuff of Islamic law.[6]

Even when a distinction is noted between the two words, the outcome is often that they effectively mean the same. Thus Gibb says that 'hadīth is ... the vehicle of the *sunna*, and the whole corpus of the *sunna* recorded and transmitted in the form of hadīths is itself generally called "the hadīth"',[7] while Schacht observes that '[traditions] are not identical with the *sunna* but provide its documentation'.[8] Both these views thus reflect the post-

Shāfiʿī, 'classical', view that, although the two terms are not the same, the *ḥadīth* is nevertheless the total record of the *sunna* and thus the *sunna* can be reconstituted from *ḥadīth*.

This assumption is equally apparent in much modern Muslim scholarship. Thus Fyzee, although allowing that it is inaccurate to consider the two terms synonymous, nevertheless speaks of *fiqh* as being derived from the Qurʾan and *sunna* and then, in the very next sentence, speaks of the first two bases of Islamic law as being 'the Koran and the Traditions of the Prophet'.[9] More recently, Abdur Rahman Doi, in his book *Sharīʿah: The Islamic Law*, calls one chapter 'The Sunnah: Second Primary Source of Sharīʿah', and then devotes the entire chapter to a discussion on *ḥadīth*.[10] That he considers the two terms synonymous is evident from his statement that 'the primary sources of the Sharīʿah ... are the Qurʾan and the *Sunnah*',[11] while elsewhere he says that 'the primary sources of ... Islam are the Qurʾan and the Hadith',[12] and that 'the Ḥadīth ... is the second pillar after the Qurʾan'.[13] The same assumption is apparent in the work of other contemporary Muslim scholars: Suhaib Hasan, for example, has recently published a booklet entitled *An Introduction to the Sunnah* which he describes as an 'introductory booklet on Hadith',[14] while Azmi, in his otherwise valuable critique of Schacht's *Origins*, clearly assumes that 'the authority of the *sunna* of the Prophet'[15] is the same as what he calls 'the overriding authority of traditions from the Prophet'.[16] In the same vein, he translates the word *sunna* as 'traditions',[17] or 'a tradition',[18] and the word *ʿilm* ('knowledge') as *aḥādīth*, these *aḥādīth* being, he says, 'repositories for the *sunna* of the Prophet and the sole source of knowledge about it.'[19] Indeed, he equates the Qurʾanic commmand of obeying the Prophet with following the *ḥadīth* of the Prophet.[20] Thus Azmi (like the other scholars mentioned) fails to appreciate how the ancient schools, and particularly the Madinans, differentiated between *sunna* and *ḥadīth* and rejected certain 'irregular' (*shādhdh*) *ḥadīths* not, as he suggests, because they were considered spurious[21] (although this would of course be a reason for rejecting them), but because they did not reflect what was considered to be the normative *sunna* of the Prophet and thus of his Companions. Azmi's claim that all the scholars of the ancient schools 'were unanimous in their view of the overriding authority of the traditions from the Prophet'[22] must therefore be rejected as at least misleading, if not incorrect.

Goldziher came closer than many other Western scholars to recognising the distinction between the two terms, pointing out that *ḥadīth* means 'an oral communication derived from the Prophet', whereas *sunna* refers to 'a religious or legal point, without regard to whether or not there exists an oral tradition for it'.[23] He goes on to say:

> A norm contained in a ḥadīth is naturally regarded as a sunna; but it is not necessary that the sunna should have a corresponding ḥadīth which gives it sanction. It is quite possible that the contents of a ḥadīth may contradict the sunna.[24]

He then refers to the saying that we have mentioned above where al-Awzāʿī is referred to as an *imām* in the *sunna* but not in *ḥadīth*; Sufyān al-Thawrī as an *imām* in *ḥadīth* but not in the *sunna*; and Mālik as an *imām* in both.[25] Thus Goldziher recognises the normative element of *sunna* and the fact that (a) *ḥadīths* may or may not record the *sunna*, and (b) that the *sunna* may not necessarily be recorded in the form of *ḥadīths*.

Among contemporary Muslim scholars writing in English there are some who have noticed this distinction between *sunna* and *ḥadīth*. Ahmad Hasan notes that

> it is not necessary that *Sunnah* be always deduced and known from *Ḥadīth*, i.e. a report. Early texts on law show that the term *Sunnah* was used in the sense of the established practice of the Muslims claiming to have come down from the time of the Prophet. That is why *Sunnah* sometimes contradicts *Ḥadīth* and sometimes it is documented by *Ḥadīth*.[26]

Zafar Ishaq Ansari is also well aware of a difference between the two, particularly in relation to the Iraqi school,[27] and the same distinction is a key element in Abd-Allah's thesis on Mālik's concept of Madinan *ʿamal*, which we have had ample occasion to refer to above.[28]

This distinction is critical to an understanding of the development of Islamic law during its formative period in the second century. What we see taking place outside Madina is a general shift away from *ʿamal* – that is, taking the *dīn* directly from people's actions, on trust – to the need to support every doctrine with a valid textual authority, whether Qurʾan or *ḥadīth*. There was never any doubt amongst the ancient schools as to the authority of the *sunna*: what changed was the process whereby they arrived at establishing what that *sunna* was. Identifying the *sunna* with authentic *ḥadīths* from the Prophet began effectively with the Iraqis' rejection of *ʿamal* – i.e. the *ʿamal* of Madina – as a source of *sunna* in favour of well-attested and generally accepted reports from either the Prophet or one of his senior Companions, and culminated in al-Shāfiʿī's insistence that *sunna* could *only* be established by valid *ḥadīths* which went back to the Prophet and those alone.[29]

Schacht noted this shift of meaning in the word *sunna* and its redefinition by al-Shāfiʿī so that it meant simply the authentic *ḥadīths* of the Prophet. As Schacht says:

> For Shāfiʿī, the *sunna* is established only by traditions going back to the Prophet, not by practice or consensus. Apart from a few traces of the old idea of *sunna* in his earlier writings, Shāfiʿī recognises the '*sunna* of the Prophet' only in so far as it is expressed in traditions going back to him. This is the idea of *sunna* which we find in the classical theory of Muhammadan law, and Shāfiʿī must be considered as its originator there ...
>
> Shāfiʿī restricts the meaning of *sunna* so much to the contents of traditions from the Prophet, that he is inclined to identify both terms more or less completely.[30]

As a specific example of this, Schacht notes how al-Shāfiʿī accepts the testimony of a single witness along with the oath of the plaintiff because of a valid *ḥadīth* with a complete *isnād* rather than because of anyone's consensus (*ijmāʿ*) or practice (*ʿamal*), and that if it were a question of consensus or practice it would not be a valid argument in his view in face of what is in the Qurʾan and/or the *ḥadīth* (referred to as *sunna*).[31]

Mālik, for his part, as we have seen, accepts the same judgement, but not because of there being an authentic *ḥadīth* from the Prophet on the subject, although he knows and mentions one, and also mentions reports from ʿUmar ibn ʿAbd al-ʿAzīz, Abū Salama ibn ʿAbd al-Raḥmān and Sulaymān ibn Yasār confirming the continuity of the practice.[32] For Mālik it is enough that this practice is *sunna.* His concern is not with the authenticity of the *ḥadīth per se* (if it were not authentic he would not have recorded it) but with the authenticity of the *sunna.* In particular he is concerned to defend this part of the *sunna* against Iraqi objections that this practice went against the Qurʾan, which, as we noted above, specifies that there should be two witnesses.[33] But, he says, not everything occurs in the Qurʾan, and on the related question of the procedure for determining ownership of property (*māl*) in the event of neither litigant having any witnesses all are agreed on the basic procedure to be followed, even though it is not mentioned in the Qurʾan, so why should not a similar non-Qurʾanic judgement also be acceptable? 'If', he concludes, 'people accept this, then let them accept an oath with one witness, even though it is not in the Book of Allah, the Mighty and Glorious, and that what has been established as *sunna* (*mā maḍā min al-sunna*) is enough.'[34] Mālik's methodology is thus very different to that of al-Shāfiʿī, for whereas al-Shāfiʿī accepts the precept because of the *ḥadīth*, Mālik accepts it because of the *ʿamal* ('What has been established as *sunna* is enough'). The *ḥadīth* merely bolsters Mālik's argument, rather than being the mainstay of it as it is for al-Shāfiʿī.[35]

The Iraqis for their part distrusted both methodologies. They recognised the existence of this *ḥadīth* from the Prophet, but held that it was an isolated report that contravened the Qurʾanic injunction to provide two witnesses, and that it should not therefore be followed. Furthermore, it contradicted other reports indicating firstly that only the defendant, rather than the plaintiff, should be asked to take an oath, and secondly that this practice of accepting the evidence of only one witness along with the oath of the plaintiff was introduced as normative only in Umayyad times and was therefore not binding.[36] Thus, like al-Shāfiʿī, they rejected Madinan *ʿamal*, but, unlike him, they were not prepared to accept the normative status of the *ḥadīth* that he accepted, relying instead on other *ḥadīths* known to them, in addition to a broad interpretation of the Qurʾan.

Despite Schacht's correct identification of this shift in meaning of the word *sunna*, his reconstruction of its original meaning for the ancient schools is marred by a serious flaw. Schacht, following Margoliouth, holds that the original idea of *sunna* was 'the ideal or normative usage of the community' which 'only later acquired the restricted meaning of precedents set by the Prophet'.[37] Noting what he considers to be a 'constant' divergence between the 'living tradition' (i.e. the old idea of *sunna*) and traditions (i.e. Prophetic *ḥadīths*, or the new idea of *sunna*),[38] as well as a supposed 'hostility towards traditions' on the part of the early specialists on law,[39] Schacht assumes that these traditions were, generally speaking, later fabrications.[40] His argument is, briefly, that what were at first the anonymous and somewhat 'lax' practices[41] of individual, geographically defined, communities, then came under the influence of an initially small group of religious scholars who wanted to counteract and 'Islamise' these 'lax' practices, which they proceeded to do through the ruse of circulating false *ḥadīths* in the name of reputable authorities, firstly the Companions and the Successors, and then, increasingly, the Prophet himself. Once started, this process continued, with the local schools then providing their own *ḥadīths* to counteract the opposition to their original doctrines, and so on. This argument led Schacht to conclude that

> the traditions from the Prophet do not form, together with the Koran, the original basis of Muhammadan law, but an innovation begun at a time when some of its foundations already existed.[42]

Consequently,

> every legal tradition from the Prophet, until the contrary is proved, must be taken not as an authentic or essentially authentic, even if slightly obscured, statement valid for his time or the time of the

> Companions, but as the fictitious expression of a legal doctrine formulated at a later date.[43]

The *ḥadīths* that Mālik records in the *Muwaṭṭaʾ* are of course no exception to this rule:

> We shall find that the bulk of the legal traditions from the Prophet known to Mālik originated in the generation preceding him, that is in the second quarter of the second century A.H., and we shall not meet any legal tradition from the Prophet which can be considered authentic.[44]

However, in his rejection of *ḥadīth* as inauthentic, Schacht, despite seeming to understand the difference between *sunna* and *ḥadīth*, has in effect made the same mistake we outlined above of equating the two. For in noticing the 'rejection' of many *ḥadīths* by the ancient schools – especially, so the argument goes, Prophetic *ḥadīths* – he is led to deny the importance to them of *ḥadīths* in general, which then leads him to doubt the authenticity of these *ḥadīths*. This in turn leads him to deny the importance to the ancient schools of the *sunna* of the Prophet, and thus its authenticity, when this was never in question. Schacht thus builds his argument on evidence from the *ḥadīth* and assumes that it applies to the *sunna*, which, as we have seen, is a false equation with respect to the ancient schools, for whom the two terms were always distinct. What was at issue for them was not the *ḥadīth* but the *sunna*. The rejection of certain *ḥadīths* was in no way considered a rejection of the *sunna* of the Prophet: on the contrary, it was considered a clarification of it.

Schacht's assumption of fabrication makes little sense in the light of the early legal texts, such as the *Muwaṭṭaʾ*, that we possess. From everything we know of Mālik's exactitude and integrity in recording *ḥadīth* we may safely assume that he would not have recorded any *ḥadīth* in the *Muwaṭṭaʾ* about whose authenticity he had any doubt.[45] And although, as we have seen, there are many examples of where he chooses to reject the overt indications of a *ḥadīth*, he does so not because he has any doubt about its full authenticity, but, rather, in spite of his conviction of its authenticity.[46] Indeed, that he should record *ḥadīths* but nevertheless reject their import because they are not in accord with *ʿamal* is, if anything, a pointer to their authenticity, for despite their anomalous nature there is no attempt to deny them: it is only the normative force of their contents as a source of legal judgements that is denied.

It must be further remembered that records in general over-represent the unusual, and *ḥadīths* are no exception to this rule. What is usual – e.g.

the way of doing the *adhān*, or of standing for the prayer – will often be taken for granted and not merit any special mention, whereas what is unusual may well attract what seems undue attention. One must therefore approach the *ḥadīth*-literature with a certain amount of circumspection as to how accurately it represents the normative *sunna*, as well as bearing in mind that although the *fuqahā'* were concerned with recording the main norms, they were often more concerned with defining the finer details of the law and would thus be dealing with, and recording, a large proportion of exceptional cases. As a result, individual, 'one-off', events may appear from the literature to be as normal as something that happened very frequently, and, conversely, something that happened very frequently may not even be recorded.

The remarks made by the famous historian of the countryside, Oliver Rackham, albeit in a very different context, are pertinent here:

> Records are usually made for a specific purpose, not to tell a complete story. For example, the Forestry Commission's 'Censuses of Woodlands' are chiefly concerned with timber trees, and under-record non-timber species such as lime and hawthorn. Nevertheless, they have been accepted as definitive for other purposes, and *posterity may not realize that they tell a one-sided story* ...
>
> Most records were written by unobservant people. They noticed oak because it is easily identified, valuable, belongs to landowners, and has many uses for which other trees will not do; thorn because it hurts; birch because it is conspicuous; service because it is rare and curious. They did not often notice hornbeam, which is not distinctive and has no specific uses. One record of hornbeam must therefore be given the weight of many records of oak.
>
> People record sudden changes, especially those which advance civilization, more often than they record stability, gradual change, or decline. The felling of trees or their death through disease attracts attention; the growth of new trees from year to year is seldom recorded except by the camera. Grubbing out a wood to create a field is an event and an investment; an abandoned field turning into a wood is a symptom of decline and not noticed. *Many kinds of record over-represent the unusual; if something is not put on record, it may merely have been too commonplace to be worth mentioning.*[47]

It is therefore highly misleading to assume, as Schacht does, that the often contradictory material in the *ḥadīth* is an indication of later fabrication, especially as far as the *Muwaṭṭa'* is concerned, in which, as we have seen, Mālik is particularly conscious of *ḥadīths* which may well be authentic but which nevertheless do not record *ʿamal.* That fabrication occurred is of course not denied by anyone, Muslim or non-Muslim: what is disputed is its extent. As we have seen, one of Schacht's main arguments is the seemingly contradictory nature of the *ḥadīth*-material, in particular what he calls the 'constant' divergence between the 'living tradition' and 'traditions', i.e. between *ʿamal* and *ḥadīth.*[48] However, what seems a far more plausible explanation, as is indicated by the quotation from Ibn Qutayba in Chapter Three,[49] is that various Companions recorded various events from their own personal experience, often perhaps doing so without any clear indication of the normative value of the actions they recorded. Many people had kept company with the Prophet and heard and seen him doing different things at different times. They naturally preserved the specific details they knew, particularly if such details referred to them personally, and this gave a natural variety to their collective experience. Nevertheless, despite all this individual variation, there was a generally agreed core of experience which constituted the community's knowledge of what it meant to live as a Muslim. This knowledge was then passed down from generation to generation, in the form of both *ʿamal* and *ḥadīth* (with all the ensuing problems that transmission of both entailed), and it was the task of the *fuqahāʾ* to establish what amongst all this often contradictory material was the closest to the true *sunna* of the Prophet and the true spirit of his teachings, and thus the most worthy of being followed and/or used as a basis for future *ijtihād.* The concern of all the ancient schools was thus to know what represented the genuine, normative, *sunna* of the Prophet and his Companions, and in this respect the 'ancient' schools were all very similar.[50] The Iraqis referred to this *sunna* as '*al-sunna al-maʿrūfa*' ('the well-known *sunna*'), and it was this *sunna* that was accepted as normative by the majority of the *ʿulamāʾ*. As Abū Yūsuf says in his *Siyar al-Awzāʿī*:

> So make the Qurʾan and the well-known *sunna* (*al-sunna al-maʿrūfa*) your *imām* and guide. Follow that and judge on that basis whatever matters come to you that have not been clarified for you in the Qurʾan and the *sunna.*[51]

Elsewhere he says:

> So beware of irregular (*shādhdh*) *ḥadīth* and go by those *ḥadīth* which are accepted by the community and recognised by the *fuqahāʾ* [as valid], and which are in accordance with the Qurʾan and the *sunna.* Judge matters on that basis.[52]

Abū Yūsuf thus quite clearly distinguishes between irregular *ḥadīths* which do not represent the *sunna* and well-known *ḥadīths* which do.[53]

For Mālik, however, this knowledge of the *sunna* was arrived at not so much by well-accepted *ḥadīths* as opposed to irregular ones, as by *ʿamal*, regardless of whether this *ʿamal* was backed up by, or indeed was contradicted by, *ḥadīths*, and it was this lack of textual evidence for *ʿamal* that made the Iraqis, and later al-Shāfiʿī, so uncomfortable about accepting it. Thus both Abū Yūsuf and al-Shaybānī reject such unattributed (or insufficiently attributed) Madinan *ʿamal* because it may only derive from some market official or local governor and thus be in no way binding on other Muslims,[54] and al-Shāfiʿī follows them in using precisely the same argument.[55]

Mālik, then, preferred *ʿamal*, which was based ultimately on people's existential experience, as the true indicator of *sunna*, whereas the Iraqis, although holding a similar concept of a normative *sunna*, only felt comfortable when that *sunna* was backed up by formal reports which had a known direct link with either the Prophet or one of his senior Companions. Al-Shāfiʿī merely refined this tendency further in greatly increasing the authority of the Prophet in a formal sense, and, at the same time, proportionately minimising the authority of the Companions and Successors as guardians of the Prophetic *sunna*.

It is thus true, as Schacht says, that for the ancient schools the word *sunna* refers to 'the traditional usage of the community' that is 'verified by reference to ancient authorities', but this does not mean that it had no connection with the Prophet and that the idea of a '*sunna* of the Prophet' was a later idea which was somehow foisted upon people in order to counteract the supposedly 'lax' practices of earlier generations.[56] On the contrary, it is clear from all the early sources available and the *Muwaṭṭaʾ* in particular that the idea of *sunna* was always associated with those norms and practices that had been instituted by the Prophet and then been taken up and acted upon by succeeding generations. The difference, as we have seen, was in the degree to which the non-textual, experiential, *fact* of the *sunna* of the Prophet – his normative acts and instructions, etc – was actually reflected in, and thus could be reconstituted from, the textual and not infrequently ambiguous and/or unrepresentative records of the *ḥadīth*. To repeat: the function of the Prophet as a model to be followed was accepted by all: the only difference was in how this model was to be defined.

Schacht is also right in saying that the overwhelming emphasis on authentic traditions from the Prophet as the true indicators of the *sunna* of the Prophet resulted in a break with the 'living tradition' of the past, but he is wrong in assuming that this 'living tradition' had no connection with the Prophet. For Mālik in particular what he terms the *sunna* was very much a 'living tradition' rather than a set of *ḥadīths*, but it was by no means anonymous: on the contrary, it was the living tradition that had been either instituted or authorised by and then inherited from the Prophet. This is clear from Mālik's letter to al-Layth ibn Saʿd,[57] not to mention his use of the word *sunna* throughout the *Muwaṭṭaʾ* specifically to indicate a practice that had its origin in the *sunna* of the Prophet.[58] In other words, practices were maintained as '*sunna*' in Madina precisely because they were the *sunna* of the Prophet.

Conclusions

The main conclusions of this study can be summarised as follows:

1. There is a large and extensive body of Qur'anic material in the *Muwaṭṭa'*, much of which is stated overtly but most of which is implied and taken for granted.
2. The Qur'anic element is an integral part of early Islamic law as shown in the *Muwaṭṭa'* and not a later validation of it.
3. In terms of its application as law the Qur'an is not separable from the *sunna*; rather, the Qur'an is the impulse for the *sunna* and the *sunna* the demonstration of the Qur'an.
4. This *sunna* is known (for the Madinans) from *ʿamal* rather than *ḥadīth*; similarly, where there is textual interpretation of the Qur'an and the *ḥadīth*, it is against the background of *ʿamal* rather than simply from the texts.
5. The *ḥadīth* is thus illustrative rather than authoritative and the true understanding of 'Qur'an and *sunna*' as sources of law is achieved (for the Madinans) not so much by studying the texts of the Qur'an and the *ḥadīth* as by seeing what is done as *ʿamal*.
6. *ʿAmal* and *sunna* are not the same and cannot both be bracketed under the same translation of 'practice' or 'living tradition'. Rather, just as *sunna* consists of Qur'an in action with an additional element of *ijtihād* (in this instance of the Prophet), so too does *ʿamal* consist of Qur'an and *sunna* in action with an additional element of *ijtihād* (in this instance of later authorities, whether Companions or Successors, caliphs or scholars).
7. As a subsidiary conclusion, we may note that the development of Islamic law in the first and second centuries AH shows two opposing tendencies: a tendency to divergence engendered by the ambiguities of language and/or the different possibilities of interpretation, and a tendency to unity apparent in the increasing marginalisation of earlier

shādhdh views. That the *madhhabs* that have survived today are different, and yet in so many respects similar to each other, is the direct manifestation of these tendencies.

From the foregoing it can be seen that the growing insistence during the late 2nd and early 3rd centuries on the authority of Prophetic *ḥadīth* as opposed to *ḥadīths* from other authorities (which then became known by the distinguishing term *āthār*) was the result of a change of methodology rather than the creation of a new source to support already existing opinions. This is shown particularly clearly by al-Shaybānī's transmission of the *Muwaṭṭaʾ* and al-Shāfiʿī's *Umm*: both of them rely heavily on exactly the same material as in the other transmissions of Mālik's *Muwaṭṭaʾ* but the way they use it and thus the judgements they derive from it is very different. Both al-Shaybānī and al-Shāfiʿī consistently reject the authority of the *ʿamal* element in the *Muwaṭṭaʾ* and ignore it as a source for their judgements. But whereas al-Shaybānī still holds to the relatively broad 'ancient' Iraqi definition of *sunna* which includes the normative practice of the Companions as well as that of the Prophet and which can be established by *mursal* as well as *musnad ḥadīths*, al-Shāfiʿī restricts *sunna* to only those practices of the Prophet which can be established by authentic *ḥadīths* with full and authentic *isnāds*, thus effectively equating it with Prophetic *ḥadīth*.

Since systematically speaking this argument – pitching the well-documented, definitive, authority of the Prophet in authentic *ḥadīths* against the un-documented, possibly Prophetic authority of *ʿamal* and/or the documented, but again only possibly Prophetic authority of the opinions of later scholars – was hard to counter, the reliance on Prophetic *ḥadīth* rather than *ʿamal* took an upturn as a result of al-Shāfiʿī's work, thus leading to the importance given to the collections of *ḥadīth* that we see represented in the compilations of al-Bukhārī, Muslim, Abū Dāwūd and others from the first half of the third century onwards.

It was this change in methodology that led to the 'classical' formulation of Islamic law as being based on the four sources of the Qurʾan, the *sunna* (by which was meant *ḥadīth*), *ijmāʿ* and *qiyās*, with other techniques being subsumed under this fourth category. Most Western scholars, having noticed this relatively rapid change in the importance given to *ḥadīth*, which, as it were, suddenly began to appear out of nowhere (Goldziher's 'great flowering' of *ḥadīth* in the third and fourth centuries AH),[1] have assumed that this source was not an original one but one that reflected these later, theoretical, developments and that *sunna* therefore originally referred merely to the local traditions that held sway in the regional centres then dominant in the Islamic world, i.e. Madina (the Ḥijāz), Kufa (Iraq) and Damascus (Syria). What the *Muwaṭṭaʾ*, however, suggests is that this contrast between *sunna* as *ḥadīth* and *sunna* as 'living tradition' is not so much incorrect as misleading, as it does not distinguish between 'living tradition' that is seen as deriving from the Prophet, i.e. his normative *sunna* (Mālik's '*al-sunna ʿindanā*') and 'living tradition' that is the result of later *ijtihād* on an existent basis of Qurʾan and/or Prophetic *sunna* (Mālik's '*al-amr ʿindanā*'), both of which are referred to collectively as *ʿamal*. When these distinctions are understood, it can be seen that, for Mālik at least, and at least before the year 150 AH (when we know from ʿAlī ibn Ziyād's transmission that the *Muwaṭṭaʾ* was already in existence), Islamic law was quite definitely based on the two-fold source of Qurʾan and *sunna* (i.e. the *sunna* of the Prophet) and quite naturally included the additional element of later *ijtihād*, and that all three elements were subsumed under the umbrella term of *ʿamal*, which was nothing more nor less, in Mālik's view, than the expression of the Qurʾanic message in action.

Furthermore, if the Muwattan picture is historically true, or at least predominantly so – and Motzki's recent work on the broadly similar material in ʿAbd al-Razzāq's *Muṣannaf* suggests that this is highly likely[2] – then we can say that Madinan *ʿamal* as depicted in the *Muwaṭṭaʾ* represents a continuous development of the 'practice' of Islam from its initial origin in the Qurʾan, *via* the *sunna* of the Prophet as its first expositor and the efforts (*ijtihād*) of the Rightly-Guided Caliphs and the other Companions, right through the time of the early Umayyad caliphs and governors and other authorities among the Successors and the Successors of the Successors up to when Mālik, as a young man at the beginning of the second century, was collecting the material which he would later prune and present as the *Muwaṭṭaʾ*. Assuming this picture to be true, and there is no reason to think otherwise, then the practice of Islam, and hence the judgements of Islamic law (*fiqh*), has always been based on Qurʾan and *sunna*, as indicated by the *ḥadīth* 'I have left among you two things and if you hold to them both you will never go astray: the Book of Allah and the *sunna* of His Prophet.'

Notes

Introduction

1 For the basic conclusions of Goldziher and Schacht, see, for example, Goldziher, *Muslim Studies*, ii. 19 and Schacht, *Origins*, pp. 4–5, 149; also, for a convenient summary, Burton, *Introduction*, pp. ix-xxv. This position has since been broadly accepted by many Western scholars, e.g. Burton (ibid; also *Sources*, p. 13), Calder (*Studies*, p. vii), Coulson (*History*, p. 64), Crone (*Roman Law*, pp. 31, 34), Juynboll (*Muslim Tradition*, p. 10), and Powers (*Studies*, p. 6). One should note, however, the reservations – of differing degrees – expressed first by such as Guillaume (review of Schacht's *Origins*, p. 176), Gibb (*Mohammedanism*, p. 82), and Robson ('The *Isnād*', p. 20), later by such as Abbott (*SALP*, ii), Sezgin (*GAS*, i), Azmi (*Studies in Early* Ḥadīth; *On Schacht's Origins*), Ansari ('Early Development') and Bravmann (*Spiritual Background*, pp. 151ff), and, most recently, by Motzki ('The *Muṣannaf*'). For a simplified but convenient overview and comparison of the two approaches – the 'traditional' and the 'revisionist' – see Koren and Nevo, 'Approaches'.
2 For this last point, see, for example, Crone and Hinds, *God's Caliph*, pp. 59–68, esp. p. 66.
3 For Schacht's appreciation of these points, see below, pp. 170ff.
4 e.g. *Muw.* i. 201 and ii. 36.
5 See *Mad.* i. 96 (*al-khabar al-ḍaʿīf ʿindī khayr min al-qiyās* – 'weak *ḥadīths* are better in my opinion than analogy'). For a somewhat less severe judgement, see Suhaib Hasan, *Introduction to the Science of Hadith*, p. 16, where the author notes that 'weak' in this instance means 'not severely weak'.
6 See *Mad.* i. 96; Goldziher, *The Ẓāhirīs*, pp. 30, 35–6; *EI (2)*, ii. 182.
7 Brunschvig, 'Polémiques', p. 413.
8 *Siyar*, xviii. 103.
9 According to the most widely attested version, Mālik was beaten at the instigation of the governor of Madina, Jaʿfar ibn Sulaymān, in the year 146 or 147 AH, for insisting on relating the politically sensitive *ḥadīth* of Thābit ibn al-Aḥnaf about a forced divorce being invalid, the implication being that a forced oath of allegiance is also invalid (see *Mad.* i. 228–31; Ibn Khallikān, i. 556; and, for the *ḥadīth*, *Muw.* ii. 34–5).

Chapter One – Mālik and Madina

1 Although it is usually said that Mālik was born in Madina (e.g. *GAL*, i. 175; *GAS*, i. 457), some say that he was born in Dhū l-Marwa (see *Mad.* i. 115; Aḥmad ᶜAbd al-ᶜAzīz Āl Mubārak, *Mālik ibn Anas*, p. 11), which, according to al-Samhūdī, lies some 8 mail stages (*burud*), i.e. 96 miles, to the north of Madina in the Wādī l-Qurā region (see *Wafāʾ al-wafāʾ*, ii. 372, 182). Aḥmad ᶜAbd al-ᶜAzīz, however (*Mālik*, p. 11), mentions a distance of 192 km, i.e. 120 miles rather than 96.

2 This is the most usually accepted date for his birth. Other dates range between 90 and 97 (see, for example, *Intiqāʾ*, p. 10; *Mad.* i. 110–11; Ibn Khallikān, i. 555).

3 See Abd-Allah, 'Concept', p. 39.

4 See al-Fasawī, i. 683; *Intiqāʾ*, p. 12; *Mad.* i. 106.

5 See *Mad.* i. 107; *Dībāj*, i. 85; al-Zurqānī, i. 3. For doubts about his Companion status, see al-Dhahabī, *Tajrīd*, ii. 193. Such doubts are bolstered by his lack of mention in, for example, Ibn ᶜAbd al-Barr, *Istīᶜāb*, ii. 675f; Ibn al-Athīr, *Usd*, v. 238ff; and Ibn Ḥajar, *Iṣāba*, vii. 120f.

6 See Ibn Saᶜd, v. 45; Ibn Qutayba, *Maᶜārif*, p. 498; *Tahdhīb*, x. 19. A number of *ḥadīths* from Ibn Abī ᶜĀmir are recorded in the *Muwaṭṭaʾ*, e.g. *Muw.* i. 22, 71, 78, 96, 133, 145, 227, ii. 59, 210, 217, 257.

7 See *Mad.* i. 107; *Dībāj*, i. 85; al-Zurqānī, i. 3. For a *muṣḥaf* in Mālik's possession which his grandfather had copied out in the time of ᶜUthmān, see below, p. 56.

8 See *Mad.* i. 107; *Dībāj*, i. 85.

9 See *Tajrīd*, p. 184; *Mad.* i. 107; *Tahdhīb*, x. 409–10. For *ḥadīths* from Abū Suhayl in the *Muwaṭṭaʾ*, see, for example, *Muw.* i. 22, 71, 78, 133, 145, 227, ii. 210, 217, 257 (all *via* his father Mālik ibn Abī ᶜĀmir). Note also the report in *Muw.* ii. 208 [= *Muw. Abū Muṣᶜab*, ii. 70–1; *Muw. Suw.*, p. 535; cf. *Mud.* iii. 50; *Bayān*, xvi. 412; *Muw. Ibn Wahb*, Arabic text, pp. 25–6], where Abū Suhayl is asked for advice by ᶜUmar ibn ᶜAbd al-ᶜAzīz, which ᶜIyāḍ and Ibn Farḥūn (mistakenly?) assume to refer to Ibn Abī ᶜĀmir rather than Abū Suhayl (see *Mad.* i. 107–8; *Dībāj*, i. 86).

10 See Ibn Qutayba, *Maᶜārif*, p. 498; al-Samᶜānī, i. 282; *Siyar*, viii. 44.

11 See *Ḥilya*, vi. 340; *Siyar*, viii. 44; al-Zurqānī, i. 3.

12 See *Mad.* i. 115.

13 See *Aghānī*, iv. 39, ii. 78; and, for doubts about this report, Schacht, 'Mālik', p. 263.

14 See *Mad.* i. 119.

15 See *Siyar*, viii. 49.

16 For Mālik giving *fatwās* when he was twenty-eight, see Ibn Abī Ḥātim, pp. 26–7. For him having a circle of students a year after Nāfiᶜ's death, i.e. 118 AH, when he would have been about twenty-five, see al-Bukhārī, *Tārīkh*, iv/1. 310; al-Fasawī, i. 682; *Ḥilya*, vi. 319; *Tamhīd*, i. 73; *Intiqāʾ*, pp. 22–3; *Mad.* i. 126, 138; *Tadhkira*, i. 188; *Siyar*, viii. 66, 86, 114. For him having such a circle during Nāfiᶜ's life-time, see Ibn Abi Ḥātim, p. 26; *Tamhīd*, i. 64; *Intiqāʾ*, p. 22; *Mad.* i. 125–6; *Siyar*, viii. 66, 101. For him teaching when twenty-one, see *Siyar*, viii. 49. For reports that he even began teaching, with full authority from his elders, when he was only

seventeen, see *Mad.* i. 125, 126; and, for doubts about this in the conservative atmosphere of Madina at that time, Abd-Allah, 'Concept', p. 41 (citing Abū Zahra, *Mālik: ḥayātuhu wa-ʿasruhu, ārāʾuhu wa-fiqhuhu* [Cairo, 1963], p. 42).

17 See *Muw.* (ed. ʿAbd al-Bāqī), p. 20. This Ibn Hurmuz should not be confused with the well-known *muḥaddith* and Qurʾan-reciter ʿAbd al-Raḥmān ibn Hurmuz al-Aʿraj, as Abbott, despite her researches to the contrary (*SALP*, ii. 124, n. 31), and Abd-Allah ('Concept', pp. 62–3) have mistakenly done; neither is he the ʿAbdallāh ibn Muslim ibn Hurmuz with whom Schacht identifies him ('Abū Muṣʿab', p. 4, n. 23). For further references, see Biographical Notes.

18 See Ibn Saʿd, v. 209; al-Shīrāzī, p. 66; *Mad.* i. 158.

19 Mālik is said to have studied with Ibn Hurmuz for at least thirteen years (see al-Fasawī, i. 655; Ibn Abī Ḥātim, p. 28) and perhaps as much as thirty years, at least seven of which he spent with no other teacher (see *Mad.* i. 120; *Dībāj*, i. 99; cf. *Ḥilya*, vi. 320; *Siyar*, viii. 96).

20 See al-Fasawī, i. 655; *Mad.* i. 120; *Dībāj*, i. 99. Ibn Hurmuz is, however, mentioned elsewhere as an authority by Mālik, although not for *ḥadīth* (e.g. *Mud.* i. 222, vi. 105; *Bayān*, xvii. 41, 75, 337, 338–9, 484, 520, 626, xviii. 194, 195, 300; *Muw. Ibn Wahb*, Arabic text, p. 25; *Wāḍiḥa*, pp. 178–9, 190, 226). It is also said that the expressions *ʿalā hādhā adraktu ahl al-ʿilm bi-baladinā* ('This is what I found the people of knowledge in our city doing') and *al-amr ʿindanā* ('The position here') refer to Ibn Hurmuz along with Rabīʿa (see *Mad.* i. 195).

21 See Ibn Abī Ḥātim, p. 20; Ibn Khallikān, ii. 198.

22 See, for example, al-Nawawī, p. 531; Ibn Khallikān, ii. 198; *Siyar*, viii. 102; Ibn Kathīr, *Bidāya*, x. 174; *Tahdhīb*, x. 6; Ibn al-ʿImād, i. 133. Schacht's criticism of this *isnād* (*Origins*, pp. 176–9) has in turn been criticised by, among others, Robson and Azami (see Robson, 'The *Isnād*', pp. 22–3; Azmi, *Studies*, pp. 244–6; idem, *On Schacht*, p. 171). A recent article by Juynboll also casts doubt – to my mind unconvincingly – on the historicity of this *isnād* but, interestingly, finds fault with Schacht's criticism (see Juynboll, 'Nāfiʿ', esp. p. 217, n. 7).

23 For the 'Seven *Fuqahāʾ*', see, for example, *EI (2)*, Supplement, pp. 310ff; *Muw. Ibn Ziyād*, pp. 18ff. For the inclusion of Sālim instead of Abū Bakr ibn ʿAbd al-Raḥmān, see al-Fasawī, i. 471; Ibn ʿAsākir, vi. 51; *Tahdhīb*, iii. 437.

24 Abbott, for instance, mentions lists of between four and ten (see *SALP*, ii. 23, n. 180), to which we may add the following: *Bayān*, xviii. 455 (fourteen); al-Fasawī, i. 353, 714 [= *Tārīkh Baghdād*, x. 242–3] (nine + 'another'); al-Fasawī, i. 471 [= Ibn ʿAsākir, vi. 51] (seven); al-Ṭabarī, *Tārīkh*, ii. 1182–3 (ten); al-Shīrāzī, pp. 57–62 (twelve); *Mad.* i. 158 (eight); Ibn ʿAsākir, vi. 51 (twelve). Despite the variations in these lists, what is noticeable is the consistency of occurrence of the nine names mentioned at the end of the previous paragraph.

25 See al-Fasawī, i. 471; Ibn ʿAsākir, vi. 51; *Tahdhīb*, iii. 437.

26 See al-Ṭabarī, *Tārīkh*, ii. 1182–3; cf. Ibn Abī l-Zinād's report, below, p. 44.

27 See Abd-Allah, 'Concept', p. 69.

28 See *Tanwīr*, i. 8. The six exceptions al-Ghāfiqī mentions are: Abū l-Zubayr al-Makkī (Makka); Ḥumayd al-Ṭawīl (Basra); Ayyūb al-Sakhtiyānī (Basra); ʿAṭāʾ ibn ʿAbdallāh al-Khurāsānī (Khurāsān); ʿAbd al-Karīm al-Jazarī (Mesopotamia); and Ibrāhīm ibn Abī ʿUbla (Syria).

29 See the relevant entries in Ibn ʿAbd al-Barr's *Tajrīd*.

30 See *Tanwīr*, i. 7; al-Zurqānī, i. 8; Goldziher, *Muslim Studies*, ii. 202; Schacht, *Origins*, p. 22.

31 These figures are perhaps somewhat on the low side. In his *Tajrīd*, Ibn ʿAbd al-Barr mentions altogether 99 direct sources (rather than al-Ghāfiqī's 95) from whom Mālik transmits a total of 848 (rather than 822) *ḥadīths*. His biographical notes also suggest that al-Ghāfiqī's list of six non-Madinan transmitters could be expanded to include others, e.g. Ḥumayd ibn Qays al-Aʿraj al-Makkī (Makka); Zayd ibn Abī Unaysa al-Jazarī al-Ruhāwī (al-Ruhā = Edessa); Ziyād ibn Saʿīd al-Khurāsānī (Khurāsān); Ṣadaqa ibn Yasār al-Makkī (Makka); ʿAbdallāh ibn Abī Ḥusayn al-Makkī (Makka); ʿAbd al-Karīm ibn Abī l-Mukhāriq (Basra); and Abū ʿUbayd, the *mawlā* of Sulaymān ibn ʿAbd al-Malik (Syria), to whom we can add Ṭalḥa ibn ʿAbd al-Malik al-Aylī (Ayla), who, although not mentioned in the *Tajrīd* is mentioned in the same author's *Tamhīd* (iv. 89). These eight between them transmit a further fourteen *ḥadīths*, thus bringing the total number of non-Madinan transmitters to fourteen (rather than six), and the total number of *ḥadīths* they transmit to at least 38 (rather than 22). However, this is still less than five per cent of the total, and such small differences – which may be partly the result of differences between different transmissions – do not materially affect the argument.

32 For examples of such reports, see al-Fasawī, i. 444; *Tamhīd*, i. 80 (cf. Ibn Abī Ḥātim, *Ādāb*, p. 199); *Mad.* i. 150, 142; *Siyar*, viii. 61, 102.

33 See Abd-Allah, 'Concept', pp. 55–8; also, for Saʿīd ibn al-Musayyab, al-Fasawī, i. 468–9; *Jāmiʿ*, p. 146; and, for Ibn Shihāb, *SALP*, ii. 21ff.

34 Mālik transmits more *ḥadīths* from Ibn Shihāb in the *Muwaṭṭaʾ* than from any other source (132 Prophetic *ḥadīths* alone, compared with 80 from Nāfiʿ, the next best represented source; see *Tajrīd*, pp. 116, 170). For Mālik knowing many other *ḥadīths* from Ibn Shihāb, see below, p. 19.

35 See Ibn Taymiyya, *Ṣiḥḥat uṣūl*, p. 30.

36 Cf. Mālik's comment on this, below, p. 44.

37 *Mad.* i. 62; *Intiṣār*, p. 207.

38 See *Mad.* (Mo.) i. 78 [= *Mad.* i. 87], 160. For similar reports from Ibn Wahb mentioning either Ibn Abī Dhiʾb or ʿAbd al-ʿAzīz ibn al-Mājishūn in addition to Mālik, see al-Shīrāzī, p. 68; *Mad.* (Mo.) i. 160; Ibn Khallikān, i. 555; *Tadhkira*, i. 191; *Siyar*, viii. 97; al-Yāfiʿī, i. 375; *Tahdhīb*, vi. 344 (with the emendation of *lā yuftī l-nās illā Mālik* for *lā yuftaḥ al-bāb illā li-Mālik*).

39 See above, p. 12.

40 For this *ḥadīth* and its reference to Mālik, see, for example, al-Tirmidhī, ii. 113–4; *Tamhīd*, i. 84; *Intiqāʾ*, pp. 19–21, 22; *Mad.* i. 72–6; al-Nawawī, p. 531; *Tadhkira*, i. 187; Ibn Kathīr, *Bidāya*, x. 174–5; *Tahdhīb*, x. 8.

41 See *Mad.* i. 254–79.

42 See al-Fasawī, i. 683; *Mad.* i. 255, 162; *Siyar*, viii. 55; and, for this transmission in general, *Intiqāʾ*, pp. 11, 12, 31; al-Nawawī, p. 531; *Siyar*, viii. 47; Ibn Kathīr, *Bidāya*, x. 174; *Tahdhīb*, x. 5; also, for the particular example of the *ḥadīth* about *mutʿa* (= *Muw.* ii. 12) which Yaḥyā relates from Mālik, from Ibn Shihāb, see *Tamhīd*, x. 95; *Siyar*, viii. 105; al-Zurqānī, iii. 25.

43 See *Tamhīd*, xxi. 26 (but cf. *Intiqāʾ*, p. 12, where greater doubt is expressed); *Mad.* i. 143, 254–5; *Siyar*, viii. 103–4; al-Zurqānī, iii. 74; and, for the *ḥadīth* in question, *Muw.* ii. 36–7; also, for this transmission in general, al-Nawawī, p. 531; *Siyar*, viii. 47; Ibn Kathīr, *Bidāya*, x. 174; *Tahdhīb*, x. 5.

44 See *Mad.* i. 256; *GAS*, i. 99.
45 See *Intiqā'*, p. 12 (but note the editor's reservations in the footnote and Ibn ʿAbd al-Barr's own reservations in *Tamhīd*, xix. 74); *Siyar*, viii. 112; Ibn Ḥamdūn, i. 16.
46 See *Intiqā'*, p. 25; *Ḥilya*, vi. 330; *Siyar*, viii. 67; al-Shaybānī, *Ḥujja*, i. 1. For al-Shaybānī's transmission of the *Muwaṭṭa'*, see below, pp. 23, 24–5.
47 See *Mad.* i. 203.
48 See *Mad.* i. 202.
49 Aḥmad ibn Ḥanbal started his *ṭalab al-ʿilm* ('search for knowledge') in the year that Mālik died but did not travel to the Ḥijāz until later (see *EI (2)*, i. 272).
50 See *Tanwīr*, i. 9.
51 For a similar assessment, see *Ḥujjat Allāh*, i. 134.
52 See *Mad.* i. 133, 134; *Tanwīr*, i. 3.
53 See above, p. 12.
54 See *Mad.* i. 136, with the emendation of 'Abū Dāwūd' for 'Ibn Dāwūd', as in *Mad.* (Mo.) i. 164 and *Dībāj*, i. 105. Cf. Ibn al-ʿImād, i. 133.
55 *Tamhīd*, i. 63; *Intiqā'*, p. 32; *Mad.* (Mo.) i. 157; *Tahdhīb*, x. 9.
56 See *Tanwīr*, i. 5, where Ibn al-ʿArabī is cited as saying, 'The book of [al-Bukhārī] is the second source as regards this (i.e. authentic *ḥadīth*) while the *Muwaṭṭa'* is the first and the core. On these two all the others, such as Muslim and al-Tirmidhī, based their works'; and *Muw. Ibn Ziyād*, p. 63, where Ṣiddīq Khān is cited as saying, 'Everyone who compiled a "*Ṣaḥīḥ*" followed in his (i.e. Mālik's) path and used his method.'
57 *Mad.* i. 136.
58 *Mad.* i. 130, 150.
59 See *Mad.* i. 136; al-Suyūṭī, *Isʿāf*, pp. 2–4; also, for general praise on the same point, Ibn Ḥibbān, vii. 459 [= *Tahdhīb*, x. 9; al-Samʿānī, i. 282].

Mursal ḥadīths, together with '*balāghāt*' reports (i.e. *ḥadīths* introduced by the verb *balagha* – 'it has reached [me/him etc]' – rather than an *isnād*), are, according to the 'classical' theory of al-Shāfiʿī, considered weaker than *musnad ḥadīths* because their exact chain of authority is not stated, thus introducing doubt as to their authentic ascription to the authority stated (for al-Shāfiʿī's view on *mursal ḥadīths*, see, for example, *Umm*, vii. 293, 360 (margin); cf. Schacht, *Origins*, p. 39). However, for Mālik (and also the Iraqis) *mursal ḥadīths* were considered just as valid as *musnad ḥadīths*, provided that the authorities that transmitted them were themselves sufficiently reliable. In fact, if anything, *mursal ḥadīths* had a claim to being more trustworthy, since they represented received knowledge that was so well accounted for that there was no need to mention every single name in an *isnād*. Indeed, to have done so would, in many instances, have been unnecessarily cumbersome. In his *Tamhīd*, Ibn ʿAbd al-Barr mentions how Ibrāhīm al-Nakhaʿī was once asked why he would sometimes refer to Ibn Masʿūd without mentioning any intermediate source but at other times would do so, and Ibrāhīm replied, 'If I say that it is from ʿAbdallāh [ibn Masʿūd], then you know that a number of people have told me it. If I mention the person [from whom I heard the *ḥadīth*], then that person is the one who told me it.' 'This is why', Ibn ʿAbd al-Barr explains, 'a number of Mālikīs even claim that Mālik's *mursal ḥadīths* are preferable to those for which he gives *isnāds*, since this report indicates that Ibrāhīm al-Nakhaʿī's *mursal ḥadīths* are stronger than his *musnad* ones' (see *Tamhīd*, i. 37–8, also i. 3, 17;

Schacht, 'Manuscripts in Morocco', pp. 20–21. Cf. *Umm*, vii. 161 (l. 11); Schacht, *Origins*, p. 39, esp. n. 3). For the same Ibrāhīm preferring not to mention the Prophet when relating a *ḥadīth*, and the same attitude in al-Shaʿbī, see al-Dārimī, i. 82, 83; *Ḥujjat Allāh*, i. 144).

60 Ibn Abī Ḥātim, p. 14; idem, *Ādāb*, p. 196; *Ḥilya*, vi. 318; *Tamhīd*, i. 63, 64; *Intiqāʾ*, p. 23; *Mad.* i. 130; Ibn Kathīr, *Bidāya*, x. 174; *Tahdhīb*, x. 8. For this reliance of al-Shāfiʿī on Mālik, see also Brunschvig, 'Polémiques', p. 388.

61 *Muw.* (ed. ʿAbd al-Bāqī), p. 3; *Ḥilya*, vi. 329; *Tamhīd*, i. 76–7, 78–9.

62 In his *Ḥujja* (i. 222), for example, al-Shaybānī accuses Mālik and the Madinans of wantonly rejecting *ḥadīths* and acting instead according to what they personally feel is best (*bi-mā staḥsanū*). For a modern Muslim discussion of the same, see al-Mālikī, *Faḍl*, pp. 205–12.

63 See above, p. 16. It is interesting to note that the traditional judgement on Mālik's accuracy is confirmed by Zaman, whose intensive studies on *ḥadīth* have led to the conclusion that *ḥadīths* narrated through Mālik are not only highly consistent but 'outstanding in their uniformity' (see Zaman, 'The Science of *Rijāl*', pp. 3, 11, 18).

64 See al-Fasawī, i. 684; *Jāmiʿ*, pp. 147, 125; *Tamhīd*, i. 65–7; *Intiqāʾ*, pp. 15–17; *Mad.* i. 123; *Siyar*, viii. 61; Abd-Allah, 'Concept', pp. 73–4.

65 This phrase is recorded in particular from Ibn Sīrīn (see *Bayān*, xvii. 99, where Mālik mentions this origin; Muslim, i. 7; *Tamhīd*, i. 46), but also from other authorities (see *Tamhīd*, i. 45–7).

66 *Tamhīd*, i. 67; *Intiqāʾ*, p. 16; *Mad.* i. 123; al-Suyūṭī, *Isʿāf*, p. 3; Abd-Allah, 'Concept', p. 75; cf. al-Fasawī, iii. 32–3.

67 *Mad.* i. 123; Abd-Allah, 'Concept', p. 75.

68 Cf. al-Bukhārī, i. 59: 'The *ʿulamāʾ* are the inheritors of the prophets, whose legacy was knowledge (*warrathū l-ʿilm*).' Note also the warning in Q 2: 159 – 'Those who conceal the clear signs and the guidance that We have sent down after We have made it clear to people in the Book – such will be cursed by Allah, and cursed by those who curse' – which Mālik refers to overtly to describe those who acquire knowledge but do not then pass it on to others (see *Mad.* i. 190).

69 All instances of the verb *faquha* in the Qurʾan carry this meaning (for references, see *Muʿjam*, p. 525).

70 *Mad.* i. 132; *Siyar*, viii. 84.

71 *Ḥilya*, vi. 332; *Mad.* i. 132; Goldziher, *Muslim Studies*, ii. 25.

72 See *Jāmiʿ*, p. 119; cf. *Intiqāʾ*, p. 31.

73 See *Jāmiʿ*, p. 118.

74 See *Ḥilya*, vi. 322; *Mad.* i. 149; cf. Ibn Abī Ḥātim, *Ādāb*, p. 199.

75 *Mad.* i. 149.

76 See Ibn Abī Ḥātim, *Ādāb*, p. 199; *Ḥilya*, vi. 322; *Mad.* i. 148, 151; *Tadhkira*, i. 189; *Siyar*, viii. 56, 95.

77 See *Mad.* i. 90.

78 See *Mad.* i. 148–9. Cf. Abū Ḥanīfa's comment, when asked what all the books in a room of his were: 'These are *ḥadīths* which I have never taught, except for a few which would be useful [to people]' (see Abū Yūsuf, *Āthār*, p. iii).

79 See *Mad.* i. 193. As with the 'Seven *Fuqahāʾ*' (see above, p. 13), it is not, of course, necessary to consider these figures to be strictly accurate; they are, rather, in the nature of *topoi*.

80 See *Mad.* i. 193.
81 See *Mad.* i. 151.
82 See *Bayān*, xvi. 400, xviii. 504 (reading *taghrīr* rather than *taʿzīz*, as in the next reference); *Jāmiʿ*, p. 124. Cf. *Siyar*, viii. 92–3.
83 See *Ḥilya*, vi. 322; *Mad.* i. 148.
84 Cf. Ibn al-Mājishūn's comment to this effect, below, p. 44; and, for examples, pp. 45ff.
85 *Bayān*, xviii. 523; *Jāmiʿ*, p. 150.
86 See, for example, *Mad.* i. 185, 190; *Ḥujjat Allāh*, i. 141.
87 See, for example, *Mad.* i. 151; *Intiṣār*, p. 186; *Ḥujjat Allāh*, i. 141, 148; Abd-Allah, 'Concept', pp. 60, 86.
88 See *Mad.* i. 150–1.
89 *Mad.* i. 172.
90 *Mad.* i. 170.
91 This echoes the *innī ʿalā bayyinatin min rabbī* of Q 6: 57, etc (see *Muʿjam*, p. 142).
92 *Jāmiʿ*, p. 125; cf. *Ḥilya*, vi. 324; *Siyar*, viii. 88.
93 See, for example, *Jāmiʿ*, p. 150; *Ḥujjat Allāh*, i. 148.
94 See *Mad.* i. 145; cf. al-Fasawī, i. 546; *Jāmiʿ*, p. 148.
95 See *Tamhīd*, i. 73; *Intiqāʾ*, p. 38; *Mad.* i. 146; *Siyar*, viii. 69.
96 See *Mad.* i. 147; cf. *Ḥilya*, vi. 323; *Siyar*, viii. 97. For other reports about the same phrase either from or *via* Mālik, see al-Fasawī, i. 546, 652, 655; *Jāmiʿ*, pp. 150–1; *Intiqāʾ*, p. 37; *Mad.* i. 146–7; *Siyar*, viii. 69.

Chapter Two – The *Muwaṭṭaʾ*

1 Pride of place may possibly go to the *Majmūʿ al-fiqh* of Zayd ibn ʿAlī (d. 122) but there is doubt about its ascription to Zayd (see *GAS*, i. 552–6, 558; al-Khaṭīb, *Sunna*, pp. 370–1; Schacht, 'Mālik', p. 264; Abd-Allah, 'Concept', p. 97, n. 5; cf. *EI (2)*, vi. 278). It is, nevertheless, an early text.
2 Other collections made at around the same time, i.e. the first half of the second century, include those of Ibn Isḥāq, Ibn Abī Dhiʾb, Ibn Jurayj, Ibn ʿUyayna, Maʿmar, Ḥammād ibn Salama, Saʿīd ibn Abī ʿArūba, Abū ʿAwāna, Shuʿba ibn al-Ḥajjāj, al-Rabīʿ ibn Ṣabīḥ, Sufyān al-Thawrī, Hushaym, al-Awzāʿī, Ibn al-Mubārak and Jarīr ibn ʿAbd al-Ḥamīd (see Ibn al-Madīnī, *ʿIlal*, pp. 24–35; *Tanwīr*, i. 5; *Ḥujjat Allāh*, i. 145, 133; al-Khaṭīb, *Sunna*, pp. 337–8), some of which are at least partly extant and have been published, such as the collections of Ibn Jurayj and Maʿmar – in particular the latter's 'Jāmiʿ' – in ʿAbd al-Razzāq's *Muṣannaf* (see Bibliography; also, Motzki, 'The *Muṣannaf*', esp. pp. 5–6), Ibn al-Mubārak's *K. al-Zuhd wa-l-raqāʾiq* and *K. al-Jihād* (see Bibliography), and certain materials collected by al-Thawrī (see Raddatz, *Stellung*; Maḥmūd, *Sufyān al-Thawrī*). Earlier collections, such as ʿAbdallāh ibn ʿAmr ibn al-ʿĀṣ's (d. 65) 'al-Ṣaḥīfa al-ṣādiqa', the 'Ṣaḥīfa' of Jābir ibn ʿAbdallāh al-Anṣārī (d. 78) and Hammām ibn Munabbih's (d. *c.* 101) *al-Ṣaḥīfa al-ṣaḥīḥa*, are also known about and in some cases have been at least partially preserved, either separately or as parts of later works (see Hamidullah, *Sahifa Hammam*, pp. 22–3, 40ff; also, for these three works in general, al-Khaṭīb, *Sunna*, pp. 348–57), but do not concern us here since by their nature they are

arranged as *musnads*, i.e. reports from particular individuals, rather than *muṣannafs*, i.e. reports organised according to subject-matter and thus, potentially, formulations of law.

3 See Schacht, 'Mālik', p. 264; Azmi, *Studies*, pp. 298–9.

4 For the meaning of the word *muwaṭṭa*ʾ, see *Lisān*, i. 192–3; Abd-Allah, 'Concept', pp. 102–4; Schacht, 'Mālik', p. 264.

5 ʿAlī ibn Ziyād, who is credited with being the first to introduce the *Muwaṭṭa*ʾ into Ifrīqiyā (see *Mad.* i. 326), returned to Tunis in around the year 150 AH, which period his transmission must therefore predate (see Ibn ʿĀshūr, *Aʿlām*, p. 25; also Abdul-Qadir, 'Reception and Development', pp. 11, 14). This accords with the received picture that the the *Muwaṭṭa*ʾ was completed in or around 148 AH (see Gurāyā, 'Historical Background', p. 387, citing Ibn Qutayba's *al-Imāma wa-l-siyāsa* [Egypt, 1348 (1929)], p. 155; also al-Khaṭīb, *Sunna*, p. 371, where the author notes, without giving any sources, that Mālik had finished writing the *Muwaṭṭa*ʾ 'before the middle of the second Hijrī century'). For further details on the date of the *Muwaṭṭa*ʾ and its attribution to Mālik, see also below, pp. 26–7.

6 81 names are mentioned by al-Zurqānī, following Ibn Nāṣir al-Dīn (see al-Zurqānī, i. 6; cf. Muranyi, *Materialien*, pp. 127–30; *Muw.* [ed. ʿAbd al-Bāqī], p. 6). ʿIyāḍ mentions a further eight names (see *Mad.* i. 203; cf. *Tanwīr*, i. 9; *Muw.* [ed. ʿAbd al-Bāqī], p. 7), and al-Nayfar, following Ibn Ṭūlūn, mentions a further four (see *Muw. Ibn Ziyād*, pp. 80–2), making a possible total of 93 names altogether.

7 See *Mad.* i. 203.

8 See *Tanwīr*, i. 8.

9 e.g. *Muw.* (ed. ʿAbd al-Bāqī), pp. 9–15 (fourteen); *Muw. Sh.*, pp. 16–19 (sixteen); *Muw. Q.*, pp. 12–17 (fourteen); *Muw. Ibn Ziyād*, pp. 67–71 (sixteen); cf. Goldziher, *Muslim Studies*, ii. 205 (fifteen); Schacht, 'Mālik', p. 264 (fifteen).

10 See *Mad.* ii. 535.

11 See below, pp. 24–6.

12 For the latest edition, see Bibliography. For earlier editions, see Schacht, 'Mālik', p. 264.

13 For a discussion of this transmission in general and the attribution of the printed text to Ibn Bukayr, see Schacht, 'Deux éditions', pp. 483–92; idem, 'Manuscripts in Morocco', pp. 31–3.

14 See n. 5 above.

15 i.e. *Muw. Ibn Ziyād*. See also Schacht, 'Manuscripts in Kairouan', pp. 227f.

16 See *Tanwīr*, i. 7.

17 i.e. *Muw. Q.*

18 i.e. *Muw. Abū Muṣʿab*. Various portions of this transmission exist also in manuscript form in Tunis (see *Muw. Q.*, p. 15), Qayrawān (see Schacht, 'Manuscripts in Kairouan', pp. 242–4; idem, 'Abū Muṣʿab', p. 7), Damascus (see *GAS*, i. 460) and Dublin (i.e. Chester Beatty Ms. no. 5498 (3), entitled *al-Muntaqā min al-Muwaṭṭa*ʾ, which consists of *ḥadīths* from the *Muwaṭṭa*ʾ according to the *riwāya* of Abū Muṣʿab).

19 i.e. *Muw. Suw.* (for which, see also Schacht, 'Deux éditions', pp. 478ff). Most sections of the text are represented in this fragment except that there is no mention of penal law (*ḥudūd*) or war (*jihād*) (see ibid, p. 480).

20 See *Mad.* ii. 435, 436; *Muw. Ibn al-Qāsim*, p. 10.

21 See *Muw. Ibn Ziyād*, p. 69; *Muw. Ibn al-Qāsim*, p. 11; Schacht, 'Manuscripts in Kairouan', pp. 228–30.
22 i.e. *Muw. Ibn al-Qāsim*. See also Spies, 'Bibliotheken', p. 109; *GAS*, i. 460, 463; *Muw. Ibn Ziyād*, p. 77.
23 Schacht, 'Mālik', p. 264.
24 See Schacht, 'Manuscripts in Kairouan', pp. 230–1.
25 For reference to Ibn Wahb's own '*Muwaṭṭa*'', see, for example, *Jāmiʿ* (ed. Turkī), p. 323; *Mad.* iv. 468, ii. 433. See also *Muw. Ibn Wahb*, p. 43, where Muranyi, too, notes that the Qayrawān fragment represents an independent work, and not Ibn Wahb's transmission of Mālik's *Muwaṭṭa*'.
26 e.g. *Muw. Ibn Wahb*, Arabic text, pp. 47–8, fol. 18r. 15–21 [= *Muw.* ii. 188].
27 e.g. *Muw. Ibn Wahb*, Arabic text, pp. 49–50, fol. 6r. 24 – fol. 7r. 10 [= *Mud.* iii. 4], fol. 7r. 15 – 7v. 4 [= *Mud.* iii. 4–5], *et passim.*
28 e.g. *Muw. Ibn Wahb*, Arabic text, p. 15, fol. 6r. 22 – 6v. 9 [= *Bayān*, xvi. 373].
29 e.g. *Muw. Ibn Wahb*, Arabic text, p. 25, fol. 10r. 7–10 [= *Mud.* iii. 50; cf. *Muw.* ii. 208], and p. 51, fol. 19v. 7–11 [= *Mud.* xvi. 166; cf. *Muw.* ii. 188].
30 See n. 25 above.
31 See *SALP*, ii. 114–15; cf. *Muw.* ii. 257–8. This fragment, dated by Abbott to the second half of the second century AH (see below, p. 26), is to the best of my knowledge the oldest fragment of the *Muwaṭṭa*' known to exist.
32 See *Muw. Abū Muṣʿab*, ii. 173–6; *Muw. Suw.*, pp. 601–2.
33 From the similarity of the transmissions that we have to hand it would seem that the reports about Mālik's severe editing of his text from 'ten' or 'four' thousand *ḥadīths* until only some thousand or so remained (see above, p. 19) must refer to the editing of his original material for inclusion in the text rather than his editing of details once the main text was in place, which, as we have seen, was prior to the year 150 AH (see above, p. 22), i.e. some thirty years before his death. This is supported by the fact that the transmission which is said to be the latest (that of Abū Muṣʿab) is also said to be one of the longest (see *Tanwīr*, i. 7–8; *Muw. Sh.*, p. 18; *Muw. Ibn Ziyād*, pp. 64, 70; *Muw. Q.*, p. 15).
34 For a further comparison between the different transmissions currently available, see, in addition to the following paragraphs, Dutton, 'Juridical Practice'.
35 See *Muw.* i. 57–9, 80–82; *Muw. Q.*, pp. 68–74, 136–40; *Muw. Suw.*, pp. 91–3, 113–14; *Muw. Abū Muṣʿab*, i. 59–62, i. 94–7.
36 See *Muw. Sh.*, pp. 48–9, 59–63.
37 See *Muw. Sh.*, p. 199; *Muw.* ii. 23–5; *Muw. Abū Muṣʿab*, i. 622–6. (*Muw. Suw.* [p. 331] contains only the long *ḥadīth*.)
38 See *Muw.* i. 325–6, 328–9; *Muw. Ibn Ziyād*, pp. 189–97, 134–7; *Muw. Abū Muṣʿab*, ii. 197–8, 204–6; *Muw. Suw.*, pp. 384–5.
39 See *Muw. Sh.*, pp. 221, 225–6.
40 See *Muw.* i. 260–1; *Muw. Abū Muṣʿab*, i. 457–61; *Muw. Suw.*, pp. 487–9.
41 See *Muw. Sh.*, pp. 170–1. For a fuller discussion on *iḥṣār*, see below, pp. 92ff.
42 Cf. above, p. 16.
43 *Muslim Studies*, ii. 206.
44 Goldziher gained an 'unfavourable impression of the reliability of Islamic tradition in the second century' from the different versions of the *Muwaṭṭa*' and, as a consequence, criticised Mālik for looseness in his methods of transmission (*Muslim Studies*, ii. 204). However, Goldziher based his comments

on the two transmissions available to him, i.e. those of Yaḥyā and al-Shaybānī, which, as we have seen, hardly form a representative pair. If he had had access also to those of al-Qaᶜnabī, Abū Muṣᶜab, Suwayd and Ibn Ziyād, for instance, he would doubtless have arrived at different conclusions.

Schacht followed the same general line as Goldziher, saying that 'it is not Mālik who composed, in the modern sense of the word, his work, but [his] students who, each according to his own fashion, edited the "text" of their teacher' (Schacht, 'Deux éditions', p. 477). Elsewhere he also traces the differences between the transmissions to Mālik's students, claiming that 'in those days very little stress was laid on an accurate repetition of such texts and great liberty was taken by the transmitters' (Schacht, 'Mālik', p. 264). However, he also allows that Goldziher's implicit expectation of a 'fixed text' (see *Muslim Studies*, ii. 205) is inappropriate in the context of an orally-taught text, since 'Mālik did not always give exactly the same form to his orally-delivered teaching' (Schacht, 'Mālik', p. 264). Furthermore, although he states that 'the different *riwāyas* . . . differ in places very much' (ibid, p. 264), he also acknowledges that some of them, e.g. those of Ibn Wahb and Ibn al-Qāsim, closely resemble the *Muwaṭṭa'* of Yaḥyā ibn Yaḥyā (see ibid, p. 264; idem, 'Manuscripts in Kairouan', p. 230). Thus, as with Goldziher, his observation that the differences between the transmissions are due to the transmitters is obviously true in the case of al-Shaybānī but would seem not to apply (or to apply much less) to the transmissions of either ᶜAlī ibn Ziyād, whose chapter-headings are less detailed than Yaḥyā's but whose main text, even though considerably earlier, is remarkably similar, or al-Qaᶜnabī, Abū Muṣᶜab and Suwayd, whose chapter-headings and main text are all very close if not almost identical to Yaḥyā's) (see above, pp. 24–6).

45 See Calder, *Studies*, pp. 38, 146.

46 See above, p. 188, n. 5.

47 See above, p. 24.

48 See *SALP*, ii. 114, 121–8, esp. 127, where Abbott says: 'Thus the paleography, the scribal practices, the text, the order of the traditions and the *isnād* terminology of the papyrus show a remarkable degree of conformity with the scholarly practices of Mālik and his contemporaries. On the strength of this internal evidence the papyrus folio can be safely assigned to Mālik's own day.' The slight variations in the 'order of the traditions', however (for which, see also ibid, pp. 119 and 121), would seem to be most easily explained by assuming a different transmission of the text.

49 See above, p. 23.

50 Perhaps Ḥasan ibn Aḥmad ibn Muᶜtab (see *Muw. Ibn Ziyād*, pp. 99–101).

51 See *Muw. Ibn Ziyād*, pp. 44–5.

52 See above, p. 188, n. 5.

53 See *Muw. Ibn Ziyād*, pp. 44, 104.

54 See above, p. 23.

55 See Calder, *Studies*, p. 21.

56 See above, pp. 24–5.

57 For references, see above, p. 188, n. 6.

58 For this expression, see, for example, *Umm*, vii. 214, l. 21.

59 See the section entitled '*Kitāb Ikhtilāf Mālik wa-l-Shāfiᶜī*' in *Umm*, vii. 177–249.

60 See *Muw. Ibn Ziyād*, p. 50.

61 See *GAS*, i. 459.
62 See *EI (2)*, ix. 392–3.
63 Al-Qaᶜnabī settled in Basra and died either there or, according to some reports, in or on the way to Makka (see *Mad.* i. 397–9; *Tahdhīb*, vi. 31–3).
64 See *Tahdhīb*, iv. 275.
65 See *GAS*, i. 471.
66 See *Tahdhīb*, xi. 237–8 (Ibn Bukayr); *EI (2)*, iii. 817 (Ibn al-Qāsim); *EI (2)*, iii. 963 (Ibn Wahb); *EI (2)*, ix. 183 (al-Shāfiᶜī).
67 See above, p. 22.
68 An early parchment fragment of Ibn Wahb's *Tafsīr gharīb al-Muwaṭṭaʾ* (assuming this refers to a commentary on Mālik's *Muwaṭṭaʾ* rather than on his own), dated 293 AH and transmitted from Yaḥyā ibn ᶜAwn (d. 298) from ᶜAwn ibn Yūsuf (d. 239), from Ibn Wahb, exists in Qayrawān (see *Muw. Ibn Wahb*, pp. 54–5; also *Mad.* i. 200, ii. 433, where ᶜIyāḍ mentions a *tafsīr* of the *Muwaṭṭaʾ* by Ibn Wahb).
69 A fragment of al-Akhfash's *Tafsīr gharīb al-Muwaṭṭaʾ* exists in Qayrawān (see Schacht, 'Manuscripts in Kairouan', 244–5; *GAS* i. 460; also *Mad.* i. 200).
70 Extensive fragments of Ibn Muzayn's *Tafsīr al-Muwaṭṭaʾ* compiled from these four authorities exist in Qayrawān (see Schacht, 'Manuscripts in Kairouan', 235–7; *GAS*, i. 460, 473). For Ibn Muzayn's *Tafsīr*, see also *Mad.* iii. 133, and, for those of the four authorities, *Mad.* i. 200.
71 Among other early commentators, ᶜIyāḍ mentions Ibn Nāfiᶜ (d. 186) (*Mad.* i. 200, 357), Ibn Ḥabīb (d. 238) (*Mad.* i. 200, iii. 35; also *Wāḍiḥa*, pp. 38–9), Ḥarmala ibn Yaḥyā (d. 243) (*Mad.* i. 200, iii. 77) and Muḥammad ibn Saḥnūn (d. 256) (*Mad.* i. 200, iii. 106).
72 For a more extensive critique of Calder's thesis, the reader is referred to my review of his *Studies* (see Bibliography).
73 See below, pp. 33–4.
74 The technique of indicating points of *fiqh* in the chapter-headings is one that Mālik seems to have developed progressively during his life, as is apparent from a comparison of the different stages of the text as represented by earlier and later transmissions (see *Muw. Ibn Ziyād*, pp. 85–93). This technique was then further developed by the main third century compilers such as al-Bukhārī, about whom it is said that 'his *fiqh* is in his chapter-headings' (see ibid, p. 90; Goldziher, *Muslim Studies*, ii. 217).
75 See, for example, the chapters entitled '*Al-nawm ᶜan al-ṣalāt*' (*Muw.* i. 26), '*Mā jāʾa fī bawl al-ṣabī*' (i. 63), '*Qadr al-suḥūr min al-nidāʾ*' (i. 72), '*Ṣalāt al-nabī fī l-witr*' (i. 107), '*Faḍl ṣalāt al-qāʾim ᶜalā ṣalāt al-qāᶜid*' (i. 119), etc.
76 Statements of *ᶜamal* alone are particularly evident in the section on business transactions (*Kitāb al-buyūᶜ*), e.g. the chapters entitled '*Bayᶜ al-fākiha*' (*Muw.* ii. 57), '*Bayᶜ al-laḥm bi-l-laḥm*' (ii. 71), '*Bayᶜ al-nuḥās wa-l-ḥadīd wa-mā ashbahahumā mimmā yūzan*' (ii. 73), and '*Al-bayᶜ ᶜalā l-barnāmaj*' (ii. 78).
77 Occasionally one comes across exceptions to this rule, such as in *Muw.* i. 77, where a Prophetic *ḥadīth* is mentioned after two Companion *ḥadīths*, and i. 82, where a Prophetic *ḥadīth* comes after a Companion *ḥadīth* and a statement of *ᶜamal*.
78 See *Muw.* i. 225.
79 See *Muw.* i. 291.
80 i.e. '*Jāmiᶜ mā jāʾa fī l-ᶜumra*' (*Muw.* i. 252), '*Jāmiᶜ al-ṭawāf*' (i. 266), '*Jāmiᶜ al-saᶜy*' (i. 267), '*Jāmiᶜ al-hady*' (i. 274), and '*Jāmiᶜ al-fidya*' (i. 290).

81 According to al-Qarāfī, this technique is specific to the literature of the Mālikī *madhhab* (see *Jāmi*ʿ, p. 81).

82 See *Muw. Sh.*, p. 330; al-Fasawī, i. 442, 443, 644–5; Ibn Abī Ḥātim, p. 21; *Tamhīd*, i. 80–81; al-Khaṭīb al-Baghdādī, *Taqyīd*, pp. 105–6; *Mad.* i. 62; *Tanwīr*, i. 4; *SALP*, ii. 23, 25–32.

83 See Ibn ʿAbd al-Barr, *Bayān*, pp. 98, 94; *Tanwīr*, i. 4. I take this '*tadwīn*' of Ibn Shihāb's to refer to his wide-ranging collection of *ḥadīth* made in the time of Hishām (see *SALP*, ii. 33) rather than the more specific collection of '*sunnas*' undertaken for ʿUmar ibn ʿAbd al-ʿAzīz (for this distinction, see *SALP*, ii. 30–31, 32). Other collections of *ḥadīth* are known about before this time, e.g. the '*ṣaḥīfas*' of the first century (see above, p. 187, n. 2), but they are all of a limited, *musnad*, nature in contrast to the broad-based compilation of *ḥadīth* that Ibn Shihāb was engaged in.

84 Ibn Shihāb's first project for ʿUmar ibn ʿAbd al-ʿAzīz is said to have resulted in written *daftars* ('registers') which were then sent to the various provinces under ʿUmar's control (see Ibn ʿAbd al-Barr, *Bayān*, p. 98; *SALP*, ii. 31) but these *daftars* would seem to have been more in the nature of administrative instructions, for which ʿUmar was famous (see, for example, al-Fasawī, i. 590; *SALP*, ii. 24, 32), rather than a book such as Mālik's *Muwaṭṭa*ʾ or the other early second-century collections (for which, see above, p. 187, n. 2).

85 It would seem that writing down *ḥadīths* was still disapproved of, or at least still not the norm, at the beginning of the second century AH. Mālik, who would have been a student at that time, said that he had never written on 'these boards' (*hādhihī l-alwāḥ*) and on asking Ibn Shihāb once whether he used to write down knowledge Ibn Shihāb had replied 'No' (al-Fasawī, i. 622; *Jāmi*ʿ, p. 152). For fuller discussions on the written compilation of *ḥadīth* and the changeover from oral to written methods of transmission, see, for example, al-Khaṭīb al-Baghdādī, *Taqyīd*, pp. 29–113; Ibn ʿAbd al-Barr, *Bayān*, pp. 79–100; Hamidullah, *Sahifa Hammam*, pp. 14–41, 62–7; al-Khaṭīb, *Sunna*, esp. pp. 292–342; *SALP*, ii. 33ff.

86 See Ibn Saʿd (*qism mutammim*), p. 440; al-Ṭabarī, *Tārīkh*, iii. 2519; Ibn Abī Ḥātim, pp. 12, 29; *Intiqā*ʾ, pp. 41, 40, n. 1; *Mad.* i. 192–3; *Tadhkira*, i. 189; *Siyar*, viii. 55–6, 70; *Ḥujjat Allāh*, i. 145; *SALP*, ii. 123; Abd-Allah, 'Concept', pp. 99–100, 385–6. For similar reports mentioning al-Mahdī (r. 158–169), see al-Ṭabarī, *Tārīkh*, iii. 2519; *Intiqā*ʾ, p. 40; *Siyar*, viii. 70; *SALP*, ii. 124. For mention of Hārūn al-Rashīd (r. 170–193), see *Ḥilya*, vi. 332; Ibn Taymiyya, *Ṣiḥḥat uṣūl*, p. 28 (cf. Wakīʿ, i. 143, n. 1, citing Ibn Taymiyya's student Ibn al-Qayyim); *Siyar*, viii. 87 (where al-Dhahabī comments on the unlikeliness of this); Ibn al-ʿImād, i. 290; *Ḥujjat Allāh*, i. 145; *SALP*, ii. 124. Even al-Maʾmūn (r. 198–218) is mentioned in this context (see *Ḥilya*, vi. 331), but since he was caliph long after Mālik's death this is either a mistake or refers to long before he was caliph.

87 See below, pp. 37ff.

88 See al-Murabit, *Root Islamic Education*, pp. 139–40, where the author cites and endorses this view of Shaykh al-Nayfar.

89 See *Tamhīd*, i. 86; *Mad.* i. 195; *Tanwīr*, i. 6. The fragment of a work by this same Ibn al-Mājishūn recently edited and published by Muranyi may possibly be from this '*muwaṭṭa*ʾ' (see Muranyi, *Fragment*, esp. pp. 34–5, but note that Muranyi refers to this ʿAbd al-ʿAzīz as 'al-Mājishūn', whereas this is generally

understood to be the name of either ᶜAbd al-ᶜAzīz's grandfather, Abū Salama, or his uncle, Yaᶜqūb ibn Abī Salama [see *Mad.* i. 360; *Mad.* (Mo.), iii. 136; Ibn Khallikān, ii. 302–3]). It is also said that Ibn Abī Dhiʾb, another famous Madinan contemporary, wrote a '*muwaṭṭa*ʾ' at about the same time as Mālik (see *Ḥujjat Allāh*, i. 133, 145; al-Khaṭīb, *Sunna*, p. 337).

90 Al-Ṭabarī says that al-Manṣūr went on *ḥajj* in 147 and 152 (see *Tārīkh*, iii. 353, 369), while Ibn Abī Ḥātim (p. 30) and al-Dhahabī (*Siyar*, viii. 100) mention the year 150. Abbott (*SALP*, ii. 123) gives a useful summary of the options.

91 See Ibn Saᶜd (*qism mutammim*), p. 440; also al-Ṭabarī, *Tārīkh*, iii. 2519; *Intiqā*ʾ, p. 41; *Siyar*, viii. 70.

92 See al-Fasawī, i. 683.

93 See al-Ṭabarī, *Tārīkh*, iii. 200.

94 See above, p. 188, n. 5.

95 See above, p. 19.

96 See above, p. 20.

97 Random examples include: al-Bukhārī, vi. 81 ('*Sūrat «waylun li-l-muṭaffifīn»*'); Muslim, i. 67 ('*Bāb ithbāt al-shafāᶜa*'), i. 295–6 ('*Bāb tark istiᶜmāl āl al-nabī ᶜalā l-ṣadaqa*'); al-Fasawī, i. 279–80, 517; and various *ḥadīths* in *Ḥilya*, vi. 332–55. For other sources of non-Muwattan *ḥadīths* from Mālik, see *GAS*, i. 464; *Mad.* i. 199–200; *Siyar*, viii. 77.

98 See above, p. 27.

99 Ibn Rushd's *Bayān*, which is a commentary on the *ᶜUtbiyya*, contains a full edition of the text. See also *GAS*, i. 472; Schacht, 'Manuscrits à Fès', pp. 275, 279–80; idem, 'Manuscripts in Kairouan', p. 245; idem, 'Manuscripts in Morocco', pp. 25–30; Muranyi, *Materialien*, pp. 50–65.

100 See *Wāḍiḥa* (which includes an edition of the chapters on purity [*abwāb al-ṭahāra*] from this book); *GAS*, i. 362, 468; Schacht, 'Manuscrits à Fès', pp. 272–3; idem, 'Manuscripts in Kairouan', pp. 241–2; Muranyi, *Materialien*, pp. 14–29, 72–6; Fierro, '*Ḥadīth*', p. 75.

101 See *GAS*, i. 474; Schacht, 'Manuscripts in Kairouan', p. 247; Muranyi, *Materialien*, pp. 70–2.

102 See *GAS*, i. 467–8; Schacht, 'Manuscripts in Kairouan', pp. 239–40; Muranyi, *Materialien*, pp. 7–13.

103 See *GAS*, i. 472; Schacht, 'Manuscrits à Fès', pp. 273–4; idem, 'Abū Muṣᶜab', pp. 1–14.

104 See *GAS*, i. 470, 481; Schacht, 'Manuscrits à Fès', pp. 274–5; idem, 'Manuscripts in Morocco', pp. 11–13; Muranyi, *Materialien*, pp. 30–112.

105 See below, pp. 37–8. For Mālik's other writings, see *GAS*, i. 464; Schacht, 'Mālik', pp. 264, 265; idem, 'Manuscripts in Kairouan', p. 227; *Mad.* i. 204–7; *Siyar*, viii. 79–80.

Chapter Three – The *ᶜAmal* of the People of Madina

1 See Gannūn, '*Mālik*', p. 3. Sulaymān was described by Mālik as the most learned man in Madina after the death of Saᶜīd ibn al-Musayyab (see *Bayān*, xvii. 11; *Jāmiᶜ*, p. 150).

2 See, for example, Gannūn, '*Mālik*'; Ahmed Bekir, *Histoire*, p. 42; *Muw. Ibn Ziyād*, p. 94; al-Nayfar, '*ʿAmal ahl al-Madīna*', p. 7. Cf. Schacht, 'Manuscripts in Morocco', p. 49; idem, *Origins*, p. 25.
3 See Ibn Taymiyya, *Ṣiḥḥat uṣūl*, p. 29.
4 Out of approximately 250 references to ʿUmar in the *Muwaṭṭaʾ* some 180, i.e. nearly three-quarters, can be construed as judgements.
5 Of the forty or so references to Abū Bakr in the *Muwaṭṭaʾ*, only about a half can be construed as judgements presumably dating from his caliphate.
6 Numerous reports from Mālik speak of ʿUmar's justice and sense of responsibility as a ruler; see, for example, *Bayān*, xvii. 211, 385, 424, 509, 547, 568, xviii. 301, 398, 406; *Mad.* i. 208, 216–17.
7 See *Mad.* i. 115.
8 See above, p. 13.
9 See *Bayān*, xviii. 246; Ibn Saʿd, v. 145; al-Fasawī, i. 556; *Tahdhīb*, iii. 437.
10 See Ibn Abī Ḥātim, p. 30; *Mad.* i. 212; *Siyar*, viii. 100.
11 See *Muw. Ibn Ziyād*, pp. 94–5.
12 For references, see n. 9 above.
13 See above, p. 12; also p. 184, n. 34.
14 For Nāfiʿ and his transmission from Ibn ʿUmar, see above, p. 12. For Sālim as one of the 'Seven *Fuqahāʾ*', see above, p. 183, n. 23.
15 See above, p. 32.
16 See above, p. 193, n. 1.
17 See Ibn Saʿd, v. 89; al-Fasawī, i. 470–1, 475, 622, 468. Cf. *Bayān*, xvii. 24 [= al-Fasawī, i. 468].
18 See below, p. 219, n. 75.
19 See *Bayān*, xviii. 555; also xvii. 24.
20 See *Jāmiʿ*, p. 117; *Mad.* i. 172. Cf. *Bayān*, xviii. 374; *Ḥilya*, vi. 324; *Siyar*, viii. 88.
21 See *Origins*, p. 311; cf. Abd-Allah, 'Concept', pp. 302–3.
22 See above, p. 27.
23 Bekir's edition (*Mad.* i. 194) has *raʾyun*, but *raʾyī*, as in the Moroccan (Mohammedia) edition (ii. 74) and as later in the same sentence and also later in the same paragraph, makes better sense.
24 *Mad.* i. 194.
25 *Mad.* i. 194; cf. ibid, i. 192 (*lam akhruj ʿanhum*), and i. 193 (*lam akhruj ʿan jumlatihim ilā ghayrihim*).
26 Abd-Allah notes that all these concepts occur in one form or another in the other Sunnī *madhhabs* (see 'Concept', pp. 125–6). For a detailed discussion of these concepts, see ibid, pp. 209–79.
27 Cf. Abd-Allah, 'Concept', p. 304.
28 Cf. Schacht, *Origins*, p. 113.
29 See below, pp. 37–8.
30 See *Mad.* i. 68ff [= 'Polémiques', pp. 420ff; *Intiṣār*, pp. 215ff]; Ibn Taymiyya, *Ṣiḥḥat uṣūl*, pp. 23ff.
31 For this and the following paragraph, see *Mad.* i. 68–9 [= 'Polémiques', pp. 420–1; *Intiṣār*, pp. 215–18].
32 For this judgement, see *Muw.* i. 210.
33 For this judgement, see *Muw.* i. 69–70; *Mud.* i. 57–8.
34 For this judgement, see *Muw.* i. 78; *Mud.* i. 62.
35 For this judgement, see *Mud.* xv. 100.

36 For this judgement, see *Muw.* ii. 48.
37 For this judgement, see *Muw.* i. 206; also below, p. 148.
38 See below, pp. 42–3.
39 *Mad.* i. 69. Cf. al-Bājī, *Iḥkām*, p. 484. In *Mad.* i. 224, Mālik's interlocutor is specified as being Abū Yūsuf (see below, pp. 42–3).
40 See *Ṣiḥḥat uṣūl*, p. 25. For Abū Yūsuf and the Madinan *ṣāᶜ*, see below, pp. 42–3. For the two judgements on *zakāt*, see *Mab.* iii. 2–3 (where they are justified by *ḥadīths* rather than Madinan practice). For Abū Yūsuf accepting the judgement on endowments, see *Mab.* xii. 28; Ibn Abī Ḥātim, *Ādāb*, pp. 197–9; al-Bājī, *Iḥkām*, p. 483; Ibn al-ᶜArabī, ii. 697–8; *Siyar*, viii. 98.
41 For the differences on these points, see, for example, *Mab.* i. 128–9, 15–16; Ibn Rushd, i. 82–3, 97–8.
42 The fourth caliph, ᶜAlī (r. 35–40), should also be included in the first thirty years of the post-Prophetic caliphate since his reign is also included in the thirty years after the death of the Prophet. Ibn Taymiyya, however, chooses to overlook this, since he is concerned with the time of the specifically Madinan caliphate, whereas during the time of ᶜAlī the centre of the caliphate moved to Kufa, from which time people could more justifiably claim that Kufa had an equal right as a religious and intellectual centre, as indeed they did (see *Ṣiḥḥat uṣūl*, p. 30; cf. above, pp. 14–15).
43 See *Ṣiḥḥat uṣūl*, p. 27.
44 See *Mad.* i. 69–70 [= 'Polémiques', pp. 421–2; *Intiṣār*, pp. 218–19].
45 *Mad.* i. 64–5 [= 'Polémiques', pp. 417 (Arabic text), 381–2 (French translation); al-Fasawī, i. 695–7; al-Mālikī, *Faḍl*, pp. 66–7]. See also Abd-Allah, 'Concept', pp. 311–21; al-Murabit, *Root Islamic Education*, pp. 62–4. Both Brunschvig and Schacht have expressed doubts about the formal authenticity of this letter but both acknowledge that this question is of little practical importance since the attitude expressed in it is so obviously that of the 'ancient' Madinans and thus also that of Mālik (see Brunschvig, 'Polémiques', pp. 380–1; Schacht, 'Abū Muṣᶜab', p. 10, n. 47).
46 Cf. above, p. 29, for Mālik's response to al-Manṣūr's suggestion that the *Muwaṭṭaʾ* should become the standard law code for all the Muslims in his empire.
47 See *Bayān*, xvii. 134–7, 332; al-Fasawī, i. 438–41 (where a second similar situation is also mentioned); *Mad.* i. 62; Ibn Taymiyya, *Ṣiḥḥat uṣūl*, p. 28; cf. *Muw.* ii. 7. The point in question concerned the interpretation of Q 4: 23 – *wa-ummahātu nisāʾikum wa-rabāʾibukumu llātī fī ḥujūrikum min nisāʾikumu llātī dakhaltum bi-hinna fa-in lam takūnū dakhaltum bi-hinna fa-lā junāḥa ʿalaykum* ('And [prohibited for you are] the mothers of your wives, and your step-daughters who are in your care [who are the daughters] of wives of yours with whom you have consummated your marriage; but if you have not consummated your marriage with them there is no harm in you marrying them') – and whether it was permissible for a man to marry his wife's mother if he had separated from his wife before consummating his marriage with her. Ibn Masᶜūd had initially allowed this (as ᶜAlī, another authority often cited in Kufa, is also said to have done; see Ibn Juzayy, *Tafsīr*, p. 115), on the basis that the phrase 'if you have not consummated your marriage with them' refers back to 'the mothers of your wives' as well as 'your step-daughters who are in your care', whereas the Madinan *ʿulamāʾ* prohibited it, saying that the phrase 'of wives of yours with

whom you have consummated your marriage' refers back only to the 'step-daughters' and not to 'the mothers of your wives', which remains unqualified (*mubhama*): therefore marriage is permissible only with step-daughters of wives and never their mothers 'if you have not consummated your marriage with them'. In other words, a man is forbidden from ever marrying his wife's mother as soon as the contract of marriage has been made with no account being taken of whether or not the marriage has been consummated, whereas he is only forbidden from marrying a step-daughter if he has consummated his marriage with her mother (see *Muw.* ii. 7).

48 For the full version see al-Fasawī, i. 687–95; *Iʿlām*, iii. 72–7; al-Mālikī, *Faḍl*, pp. 177–84. For ʿIyāḍ's abridgement, see *Mad.* i. 65 [= Brunschvig, 'Polémiques', pp. 417–8]. See also Abd-Allah, 'Concept', pp. 321–31; al-Murabit, *Root Islamic Education*, p. 65. Despite the doubts mentioned above about the formal authenticity of Mālik's letter to al-Layth (see above, p. 195, n. 45), al-Layth's reply is considered highly likely to be authentic (see Brunschvig, 'Polémiques', p. 380; Schacht, 'Abū Muṣʿab', p. 10, n. 47).

49 Al-Fasawī, i. 688; *Iʿlām*, iii. 72 (where *akdah* should be emended to *akrah*); al-Mālikī, *Faḍl*, p. 178. (Italics added.)

50 For references, see n. 48 above. Among the examples which al-Layth cites that are pertinent to our theme are the differences regarding the testimony of only one witness in addition to the oath of the plaintiff (see below, pp. 161–2, 171–2), and the interpretation of the *īlāʾ* verse in the Qurʾan (see below, pp. 139ff).

51 See above, p. 38.

52 See above, p. 35.

53 Goldziher and Schacht, for example, mention Mālik's terms but do not discuss them, while Ahmad Hasan and Ansari assume them to be interchangeable, or nearly so (see Goldziher, *Muslim Studies*, ii. 199; Schacht, *Origins*, pp. 58, 62; Ahmad Hasan, *Early Development*, pp. 100–1; Ansari, 'Terminology', pp. 276–7; also Abd-Allah, 'Concept', pp. 308–9).

54 See Abd-Allah, 'Concept', pp. 25–7, 300–1, 309, 419–33 (esp. 423–4).

55 See above, p. 35.

56 See Abd-Allah, 'Concept', pp. 28–9, 425–7; cf. al-Bājī, *Iḥkām*, p. 485. It should be noted that the qualification *al-mujtamaʿ ʿalayhi ʿindanā* does not occur with the *sunna* terms.

57 See Abd-Allah, 'Concept', pp. 28, 301, 428–9; cf. al-Bājī, *Iḥkām*, p. 485.

58 Cf. Abd-Allah, 'Concept', pp. 382–391 (esp. 386–7). Note also Mālik's frequent use of the expression 'the best I have heard ...', which indicates various possible options (for examples, see below, pp. 86, 88, 100, 102, 103, 115, 117, 141, 142, also 60).

59 See Abd-Allah, 'Concept', pp. 28, 430–1, 652–6. Cf. *Muw.* i. 44–7.

60 See *Mud.* i. 41; *Muw. Sh.* p. 44; cf. Schacht, *Origins*, pp. 263f.

61 See above, p. 29.

62 A third category, *mashhūr ḥadīths*, where there are only one or a very few Companions who originally transmit a *ḥadīth* but many transmitters taking it from this one or few, is distinguished by the Ḥanafīs and considered by them to be tantamount to *mutawātir ḥadīths*. In the other schools, *mashhūr ḥadīths* are considered a sub-category of *akhbār al-āḥād* (see, for example, Abū Zahra, p. 108; Zaydān, pp. 170–1).

63 See *Mad.* i. 73.

64 See above, pp. 36–7. For this and the following paragraph, see *Mad.* i. 70–1 [= Brunschvig, 'Polémiques', pp. 422–3; *Intiṣār*, pp. 220–1].
65 See al-Shāṭibī, *Muwāfaqāt*, iii. 64–76, esp. 73; also Abd-Allah, 'Concept', pp. 509–12.
66 See al-Shāṭibī, *Muwāfaqāt*, iii. 66–7; also Abd-Allah, 'Concept', pp. 186–7, 513. For the report itself, see *Bayān*, i. 392; and, for Mālik's dislike of *sajdat al-shukr*, *Mud.* i. 108.
67 i.e. saying the two *shahādas* quietly after the initial *takbīr* of the *adhān* before repeating them again loudly (cf. *Mud.* i. 57).
68 *Mad.* i. 224–5. For their discussion about the *adhān*, see also above, p. 36. For their discussion about the *ṣāᶜ*, see also above, pp. 35, 36; al-Bājī, *Iḥkām*, pp. 483–4; *Mab.* iii. 90, xii. 28. It should be noted that although Abū Yūsuf accepted Mālik's opinion about the *ṣāᶜ* and the *mudd*, and also endowments, the Madinan way of doing the *adhān* was never accepted by the Iraqis (see above, p. 35).
69 It could be argued that this is ᶜIyāḍ's view which he is then attributing to Mālik. However, since there is no reason to doubt ᶜIyāḍ's accuracy and honesty, and since many of the reports he cites are known from earlier sources such as the *ᶜUtbiyya* and Ibn Abī Zayd's *Kitāb al-Jāmiᶜ*, there seems little reason to doubt the general authenticity of the reports in this passage. Furthermore, as Brunschvig and Schacht noted with regard to Mālik's letter to al-Layth ibn Saᶜd (see above, p. 195, n. 45), the argument is so obviously that of the ancient Madinan school that concerns of complete authenticity are hardly relevant.
70 Bekir (*Mad.* i. 66) and Brunschvig ('Polémiques', pp. 418) both have *al-akthar* ('the majority') rather than *al-athar* as in *Mad.* (Mo.) i. 44 and *Intiṣār*, p. 200.
71 For comments by Mālik to this effect, see (i) *Jāmiᶜ*, p. 117; (ii) Mālik's reply to Abū Yūsuf (see above, pp. 42–3); and (iii) the second following report concerning Muḥammad ibn Abī Bakr ibn Ḥazm.
72 For the same report, see *Bayān*, xvii. 604 (also in Schacht, 'Manuscripts in Morocco', p. 29); *Jāmiᶜ*, p. 118.
73 For the same report, with slight variations, see *Bayān*, xvii. 331; al-Ṭabarī, *Tārīkh*, iii. 2505 (mentioned in Schacht, *Origins*, p. 64); Wakīᶜ, i. 176; *Jāmiᶜ*, p. 118. For variants in the *Madārik* report itself, see *Mad.* (Mo.) i. 45.
74 For similar reports from Mālik and Ibn Abī l-Zinād, see *Intiṣār*, p. 225; Wakīᶜ, iii. 188–9.
75 For the same report, see *Jāmiᶜ*, p. 118; *Tamhīd*, i. 79, 81.
76 This report is incompletely cited by Brunschvig ('Polémiques', p. 419) and Bekir (*Mad.* i. 66). For the complete version, and variants, see *Mad.* (Mo.) i. 45; *Intiṣār*, p. 202.
77 For ᶜUmar gathering the *fuqahāʾ*, see above, p. 13.
78 *Mad.* i. 66–7 [= Brunschvig, 'Polémiques', pp. 418–19; *Intiṣār*, pp. 201–6, where all but the very last report occur]. See also al-Murabit, *Root Islamic Education*, pp. 72–4.
79 For this idea, see also the quotation from Ibn Qutayba below, pp. 50–1.
80 See above, p. 41.
81 See above, p. 41.
82 It may be noted that the *ḥadīth* recording the Madinan way of doing the *adhān* in *Mud.* i. 57 has a Makkan *isnād*, the *ḥadīth* about beginning the prayer without the *basmala* (*Muw.* i. 78; *Mud.* i. 67) has a Basran *isnād*, while there are

no Prophetic *ḥadīths* specifically on *irsāl al-yadayn*, but only on *qabḍ* (see example (i) below). In other words, there were no *ḥadīths* on these matters in Madina because there was no need for them.

83 See above, p. 19.

84 See above, pp. 43–4.

85 See *Muw.* i. 133.

86 *Mud.* i. 74; cf. *Bayān*, i. 394–5, xviii. 71–2.

87 See Khalīl, *Mukhtaṣar*, p. 29: '*wa-sadlu yadayhi*'.

88 See ᶜAbd al-Razzāq, ii. 276; Ibn Abī Shayba, i. 391–2; *Tamhīd*, xx. 74–6.

89 Zaydīs: Ibn al-Murtaḍā, i. 241. Ithnā ᶜAsharī Shīᶜa: al-Ṭūsī, p. 69; al-ᶜĀmilī, ii/2. 710. Ismāᶜīlīs: *Daᶜāim*, i. 159. Ibāḍīs: al-Muṣᶜabī, i. 57.

90 For a more detailed study of this question, see Dutton, '*ᶜAmal* v. *Ḥadīth*'.

91 See *Muw.* i. 74, 75 [= *Muw. Abū Muṣᶜab*, i. 79–80, 81]. Cf. *Muw. Sh.*, p. 57 [= *Muw. Suw.*, p. 103; *Muw. Ibn al-Qāsim*, p. 113], where the Sālim *ḥadīth* includes mention of raising the hands before *rukūᶜ* as well as after.

92 See *Mud.* i. 68.

93 See *Muw. Sh.*, pp. 58–9; *Umm*, vii. 215 (margin). Cf. *Mud.* i. 69, where the same Kufan authorities are also cited in support of Mālik's position.

94 See *Umm*, vii. 233. Cf. ibid, vii. 211ff (margin), especially p. 217, where al-Shāfiᶜī recognises – but rejects – the Madinans' *ᶜamal* argument on this point, saying effectively, 'Who are these people because of whose *ᶜamal* these *ḥadīths* are not acted upon?'; also Dutton, '*ᶜAmal* v. *Ḥadīth*', p. 39.

95 See Ibn Rushd, i. 104–5. This particular instance was later to become a major point of dispute in al-Andalus between the traditional Mālikīs and the increasingly influential *ahl al-ḥadīth*, as discussed in recent articles by Fierro (e.g. 'Polémique'; '*Ḥadīth*', esp. pp. 83–4, 90; 'Derecho Mālikí', esp. pp. 130–1). Fierro, however, along with many classical Muslim scholars, accepts the designation of *ahl al-raʾy* for these opponents of the *ahl al-ḥadīth* position ('Polémique', p. 90; '*Ḥadīth*', p. 90; 'Derecho Mālikí', pp. 127ff) whereas in fact one would prefer to see them as *ahl al-ᶜamal* – having an *ᶜamal*-based, rather than a *raʾy*- or *ḥadīth*-based, *fiqh* – which is a very different proposition.

96 See *Muw.* i. 260.

97 See al-Bājī, ii. 269.

98 See al-Bājī, ii. 271; *Bayān*, iii. 419; al-Zurqānī, ii. 199; cf. Ibn Rushd, i. 257.

99 See *Bayān*, iii. 419 (also 444–5, 454), iv. 47–8, 52–4.

100 See al-Zurqānī, ii. 199.

101 See *Umm*, vii. 196; cf. ibid, ii. 98.

102 This is the view of Abū Ḥanīfa as suggested by al-Shaybānī (*Muw. Sh.*, p. 163), al-Sarakhsī (*Mab.* iv. 153, 161) and Ibn Rushd (i. 258). Al-Sarakhsī, however, does record an opinion *via* al-Ḥasan al-Luʾluʾī that Abū Ḥanīfa held it to be obligatory (see *Mab.* iv. 153), which might explain the suggestion in al-Jaṣṣāṣ (ii. 25) and the statement in al-Bājī (ii. 269) that this was the case.

103 See *Umm*, ii. 104; al-Bajī, ii. 269; Ibn Rushd, i. 258.

104 See above, p. 12.

105 *Bayᶜ al-khiyār* refers to sales where an option period for withdrawal – variously defined for different types of goods by the *fuqahāʾ* – is allowed. See Ibn Rushd, ii. 174ff; Ibn Juzayy, *Qawānīn*, pp. 269–70.

106 *Muw.* ii. 79–80.

107 e.g. Q 2: 177, 3: 76, 5: 1, 17: 34.

108 See Ibn Rushd, i. 141–3; Ibn Juzayy, *Qawānīn*, p. 270; *Muw. Sh.*, p. 277; *Umm*, vii. 204. For discussions on the ambiguities of this *ḥadīth* – particularly whether the phrase *mā lam yatafarraqā* referred to physically parting company or to merely verbal separation, i.e. reaching agreement on a contract – and on the ambiguities of Mālik's comment, which could be taken to refer to either the *mā lam yatafarraqā* phrase or to the mention of *bayʿ al-khiyār*, see *Mad.* i. 72 [= Brunschvig, 'Polémiques', pp. 423–4]; *Intiṣār*, pp. 222–5; Abd-Allah, 'Concept', pp. 640–9, esp. p. 642.

109 See *Muw.* ii. 45; *Muw. Sh.*, pp. 211; *Umm*, vii. 208.

110 See *Muw.* ii. 43; *Muw. Sh.*, p. 212; Ibn Rushd, ii. 29–30.

111 See al-Bājī, iv. 156; Abd-Allah, 'Concept', p. 637.

112 See al-Bājī, iv. 156–7. For this instance, see also below, pp. 57, 60, 122–3.

113 All printed texts vocalise this as *maṭras*, which is obviously a corruption of the Persian *ma-tars* ('Don't be afraid'), with the negative prefix *ma-* rather than the more usual *na-* (for which, see Lambton, *Persian Grammar*, p. 28). The Chester Beatty manuscript, however, vocalises it as *maṭṭaras*, with a marginal gloss to the effect that it also said to be pronounced *maṭras* (see Ch. B. MS. 3001, f. 25r).

114 See *Muw.* i. 298; al-Zurqānī, ii. 296; cf. Abd-Allah, 'Concept', pp. 632–6.

115 *Mud.* iv. 28f; also Abd-Allah, 'Concept', pp. 179–81. For the *ḥadīth* in question, see *Muw.* ii. 18; and, for the judgement in the last paragraph, *Muw.* ii. 3. Schacht takes this passage as clear evidence that the 'practice' existed first and traditions from the Prophet and from Companions later (see *Origins*, p. 63). What the passage in fact shows is not a contrast between *ḥadīths* on the one hand and practice, unconnected to *ḥadīths*, on the other, but rather a contrast between two types of *ḥadīth*, namely, those that were accompanied by *ʿamal* and those that were not (cf. Azmi, *On Schacht*, pp. 57f).

116 See Abd-Allah, 'Concept', p. 380.

117 See ibid, p. 399.

118 See ibid, p. 300.

119 Ibn Qutayba, *Mukhtalif al-ḥadīth*, pp. 331–2. The same passage is (incompletely) cited in Goldziher, *Muslim Studies*, ii. 88.

120 See *Bayān*, xvii. 604 (also 331–2). The same passage is (incompletely) cited in Schacht, 'Manuscripts in Morocco', p. 30). For this ancient Madinan attitude to *ʿamal versus ḥadīth*, see also Schacht, 'Manuscrits à Fès', p. 274; idem, 'Abū Muṣʿab', pp. 9–10.

Chapter Four – Textual Considerations

1 Of the 'Seven' commonly acknowledged *mutawātir* readings (as, for example, in Ibn Mujāhid's *Kitāb al-Sabʿa fī l-qirāʾāt*), Nāfiʿ's reading is the only Madinan one. Another Madinan reading, that of Abū Jaʿfar Yazīd ibn al-Qaʿqāʿ (the main Qurʾan-reader in Madina until his death in 130 AH when his place was taken by Nāfiʿ), is included in the 'Ten' readings accepted by, for example, Ibn al-Jazarī in his *Nashr*. For an introductory comparison between these two readings, which, as one might expect, exhibit a great deal of similarity, see Qamḥāwī, *Tarājim*, pp. 77–81, 89–91.

2 See *Mad.* i. 143, 255; al-Qāḍī, *Naẓm*, p. 6; cf. *Siyar*, viii. 99.

3 Qamḥāwī, *Tarājim*, p. 10. Cf. *Ghāya*, ii. 333; al-Dhahabi, *Maʿrifa*, p. 108.

4 See Ibn Mujāhid, p. 62; al-Dhahabī, *Maʿrifa*, i. 108; *Ghāya*, ii. 331; *Nashr*, i. 112. The normative nature of Nāfiʿ's reading is evident from a report cited by Ibn Mujāhid (pp. 61–2) in which Nāfiʿ explains that he would accept variants (*ḥurūf*) that at least two of his teachers were agreed upon but would reject those that only one of his teachers had taught him, and that his reading was composed only of such well attested variants.

5 For a comparison of the reading of Ḥafṣ with that of Nāfiʿ (i.e. Warsh and Qālūn), see al-Qāḍī, *Naẓm*; also Brockett, 'Ḥafṣ and Warsh'.

6 Examples include:

i) the Kufan *fa-jazāʾun mithlu mā qatala … aw kaffāratun ṭaʿāmu masākīn* (Q 5: 95) in *Muw.* i. 258, 274 [= *Muw.* (ed. ʿAbd al-Bāqī), pp. 233–4, 251; *Muw.* (ed. ʿAmrūsh), pp. 244, 266; *Tanwīr* (1984), i. 326, 346; *Muw. Abū Muṣʿab*, i. 455, 477] instead of the Madinan *fa-jazāʾu mithli mā qatala … aw kaffāratu ṭaʿāmi masākīn* (clearly vocalised as such in Chester Beatty MS. no. 3001, f. 10v).

ii) the Kufan *wa-in kānat wāḥidatan* (Q 4: 11) in *Muw.* i. 330 [= *Muw.* (ed. ʿAbd al-Bāqī), pp. 313; *Muw.* (ed. ʿAmrūsh), pp. 339; *Tanwīr* (1984), ii. 47; *Muw. Abū Muṣʿab*, ii. 522] instead of the Madinan *wa-in kānat wāḥidatun.* (These words are not vocalised in the Chester Beatty manuscript (f. 43v)).

iii) the Kufan *arbaʿu shahādātin … anna laʿnata llāhi … wa-l-khāmisata anna ghaḍaba llāhi* (Q 24: 6–9) in *Muw.* ii. 24 [= *Muw.* (ed. ʿAbd al-Bāqī), p. 351; *Muw.* (ed. ʿAmrūsh), p. 387; *Tanwīr* (1984), ii. 90; *Muw. Abū Muṣʿab*, i. 624] instead of the Madinan *arbaʿa shahādātin … an laʿnatu llāhi … wa-l-khāmisatu an ghaḍiba llāhu* (clearly vocalised as such in Chester Beatty MS. 3001, f. 84v).

(For these and the other variants mentioned in this chapter, see the relevant entries in *qirāʾāt* books such as Ibn Mujāhid's *K. al-Sabʿa*, Ibn Mihrān's *Mabsūṭ*, Makkī's *Kashf* and Ibn al-Jazarī's *Nashr*.)

7 Examples of the survival of such Madinan variants include:

i) *maliki yawmi l-dīn* (Q 1: 3) in *Muw.* i. 81 [= *Muw.* (ed. ʿAmrūsh), p. 66; *Tanwīr* (1984), i. 107; al-Zurqānī, i. 160] rather than the Kufan *māliki yawmi l-dīn* as in *Muw.* (ed. ʿAbd al-Bāqī), p. 74; al-Bājī, i. 156; *Muw. Abū Muṣʿab*, i. 194; *Muw. Ibn al-Qāsim*, p. 194; *Muw. Q.*, p. 139; *Muw. Sh.*, p. 60; *Muw. Sh.*, Bodleian Library MS. Bodl. Or. 641, f. 12v.

ii) *yaẓẓahharūna* (Q 58: 2, 3) in *Muw.* i. 316, ii. 21 [= *Tanwīr* (1984), ii. 29, 85; Chester Beatty MS. no. 3001, f. 41r (vocalised), f. 82r (unvocalised, but without an *alif*); *Muw.*, Bodleian Library MS. Arab. e. 181, f. 19r] rather than the *yuẓāhirūna* of ʿĀṣim as in *Muw.* (ed. ʿAbd al-Bāqī), pp. 294, 346; *Muw.* (ed. ʿAmrūsh), pp. 317, 382; al-Bājī, iii. 241, iv. 49; al-Zurqānī, ii. 335, iii. 42; *Muw. Abū Muṣʿab*, ii. 216, i. 614; *Muw. Sh.*, p. 264; *Muw. Sh.*, Bodleian Library MS. Bodl. Or. 641, f. 12v.

iii) *dhurriyyātihim* (Q 7: 172) in al-Bājī, vii. 201 and al-Zurqānī, iv. 85 rather than the Kufan *dhurriyyatahum* as in *Muw.* ii. 207; *Muw.* (ed. ʿAbd al-Bāqī), p. 560; *Muw.* (ed. ʿAmrūsh), p. 648; *Tanwīr* (1984), iii. 92; *Muw. Abū Muṣʿab*, ii. 69; *Muw. Suw.*, p. 534 (unvocalised, but without an *alif*).

8 See *Bayān*, xvii. 33–4, xviii. 275. Cf. *Muqniʿ* (ed. Qamḥāwī), p. 116 [= Pretzl, p. 120]; *Jāmiʿ*, p. 166. For Mālik's grandfather, see above, p. 11.

9 The reading *allāh* in no. 7 is specifically Basran, rather than Iraqi; *aw an* in no. 9 is the Kufan reading but not that of all Basrans; and *mā tashtahī* in no. 11, although in general the reading of the Iraqis, is not that of Ḥafṣ.

10 See *Muqniʿ* (ed. Qamḥāwī), p. 116 [= Pretzl, p. 120]. For these variants in particular, and the differences in general between the *muṣḥafs* that were copied out under ʿUthmān's orders, see al-Bāqillānī, *Nukat*, pp. 389–92; *Muqniʿ* (ed. Qamḥāwī), pp. 106ff, esp. 112–14 [= Pretzl, pp. 108ff, esp. 116–17]; *GdQ*, iii. 11–14.

11 We may note here that according to a report in al-Nīsābūrī's *Gharāʾib al-Qurʾān* (i. 21), Mālik was of the opinion that the variants referred to in the famous *ḥadīth* about how the Qurʾan was revealed according to 'seven *aḥruf*' (*Muw.* i. 159–60), i.e. seven types of variant (?), referred to differences such as:

(i) singular/plural variation, as in *kalimatu/kalimātu rabbika* (Q 6: 115; 10: 33, 96; 40: 6)
(ii) masculine/feminine variation, as in *lā yuqbalu/tuqbalu* (Q 2: 48)
(iii) variations in the case-endings of nouns, as in *hal min khāliqin ghayru-llāhi/ghayri-llāhi* (Q 35: 3)
(iv) variations in the inherent vowels of verbs, as in *yaʿrishūna/yaʿrushūna* (Q 7: 137; 16: 68)
(v) variations in particles (*adawāt*), as in *wa-lākinna l-shayāṭīna/wa-lākini l-shayāṭīnu* (Q 2: 102)
(vi) variations in individual letters (*ḥurūf*), such as the *tāʾ* and *yāʾ* in *taʿlamūna/yaʿlamūna* (Q 2: 74, etc), and the *rāʾ* and the *zāy* in *nunshiruhā* (var. *nanshuruhā*) /*nunshizuhā*) (Q 2: 259)
(vii) variations in pronunciation, such as the velarisation or otherwise of *lām* and *rāʾ*, the pronunciation of *alif* with *imāla*, the different possible lengths of long vowels, whether *hamzas* are pronounced or not, and whether certain consonants are assimilated or not, etc.

This report, however, assuming its accuracy, represents a very limited view of the possible variants. It does not include, for example, instances where the readings differ not just in the vocalisation or pointing of a single consonantal text, but in the inclusion or exclusion of extra letters, although such variants were clearly recognised and accepted by Mālik as is evident from the report about his grandfather's *muṣḥaf* mentioned above (see above, p. 56). Nor does it include the possibility of synonyms or change of word-order, although this, being the province of the *shādhdh* readings, is less surprising. One must therefore assume that, if it *is* a statement of Malik, it is nevertheless not a complete statement of his view.

12 See *Muw.* i. 97. Cf. Jeffery, *Materials*, p. 221 (also pp. 101, 170, 191, 206, 229, 265); Ibn Khālawayh, p. 156.

13 See *Muw.* i. 120. Cf. Jeffery, pp. 232, 214 (also pp. 122, 196, 235, 237).

14 See *Muw.* i. 223. Cf. Jeffery, p. 129 (also pp. 40, 198, 289).

15 See *Muw.* ii. 35. Cf. Jeffery, p. 206 (also pp. 102, 171, 283, 308, 337); Ibn Khālawayh, p. 158; Ibn Juzayy, *Tafsīr*, p. 771.

16 See *Muw.* ii. 45.

17 See *Muw.* ii. 168. For possible indirect reference in the *Muwaṭṭaʾ* to other *shādhdh* variants, see the discussions below on *kalāla* (p. 108), *īlāʾ* (p. 140) and *nafaqat al-muṭallaqa* (p. 146).

18 See *Mud.* i. 84 and *Bayān*, ix. 374, where Mālik indicates that the prayer behind someone using Ibn Masᶜūd's reading is invalid.
19 See al-Zurqānī, i. 197; al-Bājī, i. 194.
20 See *Muw.* i. 67.
21 See *Muw.* i. 226–8; also i. 263, where *yasᶜā* is used as a synonym for *yarmulu*, 'to go at a light run'.
22 See below, p. 97.
23 See *Muw.* ii. 153; also below, p. 96.
24 See *Bayān*, i. 220, also 312; and, for Ibn ᶜUmar increasing his pace, *Muw.* i. 71. Cf. al-Shaybānī's comment that a man may speed up his pace when going to the prayer 'as long as he does not overly exert himself (*mā lam yujhid nafsahu*)' (*Muw. Sh.*, p. 55).
25 See *Muw.* i. 217–18.
26 There is also the consideration in this instance of *ḥaml al-muṭlaq ᶜalā l-muqayyad*, for which see below, pp. 104ff.
27 *Muw.* i. 223. Cf. *Mud.* i. 212–13, iii. 122.
28 See *Muw.* i. 222; al-Bājī, ii. 66; al-Zurqānī, ii. 112–13.
29 Abū Ḥanīfa and the Iraqis went by the judgement of this reading, saying that the three days had to be done consecutively, whereas, as we have seen, Mālik (and also al-Shāfiᶜī), although preferring this, did not make it obligatory (see al-Jaṣṣāṣ, ii. 461; Ibn Rushd, i. 339).
30 See *Muw.* ii. 29; cf. *Mud.* v. 102.
31 See *Umm*, v. 191; Ibn Juzayy, *Tafsīr*, p. 771; cf. Ibn Khālawayh, p. 158.
32 For this meaning of *qubul*, see Jalālayn, p. 579; *Lisān*, xiv. 53; cf. al-Bājī, iv. 124; Ibn Juzayy, *Tafṣir*, p. 771; al-Zurqānī, iii. 70.
33 See *Bayān*, xviii. 120.
34 See *Muw.* i. 121. ᶜAlī is also said to have changed his mind and held later that *al-ṣalāt al-wusṭā* was in fact *ᶜaṣr* (see al-Bājī, i. 247; al-Zurqānī, i. 156).
35 See *Bayān*, xviii. 120; al-Bājī, i. 245.
36 See al-Bājī, i. 245; al-Zurqānī, i. 256; also *Bayān*, xviii. 120.
37 See *Bayān*, xviii. 120; al-Bājī, i. 245–6; al-Zurqānī, i. 255–7. For reports indicating the superiority of the *ṣubḥ* prayer over the other prayers, see also *Muw.* i. 115–16.
38 *Muw.* i. 121.
39 See *Muw.* ii. 45; also, above, pp. 48–9; below, pp. 122–3.
40 See *Muw.* ii. 168; also below, pp. 123–4.
41 See above, pp. 57–8.

Chapter Five – The Qurʾan as a Source of Judgements in the *Muwaṭṭaʾ*

1 See *Muw.* i. 157–8.
2 See *Muw.* i. 159.
3 See *Muw.* i. 162–3.
4 See *Muw.* i. 77–8, 80–2.
5 See *Muw.* i. 75–7, 79, 102, 105, 147, 266.
6 See *Muw.* i. 160–1. See also the section on *asbāb al-nuzūl* below, pp. 125ff.

7 See *Muw.* i. 79–80, 163–4.
8 See *Muw.* i. 159–60; also above, p. 201, n. 11.
9 For examples of such personal and/or hortatory use of the Qur'an, see *Muw.* i. 76, 107, 154, 267, 296, ii. 227, 257–8.
10 See *Muw.* ii. 33 and 29, echoing Q 4: 35 and Q 2: 228 respectively; also below, pp. 117 and 132ff.
11 See *Muw.* i. 23 and 274, echoing Q 17: 28 and Q 2: 196 respectively.
12 For inheritance, see *Muw.* i. 329–41, reflecting Q 4: 11, 12, 176, etc; also below, pp. 71ff, 106ff. For the *ʿidda*, see *Muw.* ii. 28–33, 35–8, reflecting Q 2: 228, 234; 33: 49; 65: 4; also below, pp. 80–1, 91, 106, 132ff. For usury, see *Muw.* ii. 46–97, reflecting Q 2: 275–9, 3: 130, etc; also below, pp. 149ff.
13 See Q 2: 43, etc. For *zakāt*, see also below, pp. 146ff.
14 See Q 2: 275–9; also below, p. 149.
15 *Gharar* is implicitly forbidden by extension from the prohibition of *maysir* (i.e. gambling) in Q 2: 219 and 5: 90–1. It is, of course, explicitly forbidden in the *ḥadīth* literature (e.g. *Muw.* ii. 75).
16 Q 26: 195 (cf. also Q 16: 103).
17 Q 16: 89.
18 This is the term used by later Mālikī scholars such as Rāshid ibn Abī Rāshid (d. 675), quoting his teacher Abū Muḥammad Ṣāliḥ (d. *c.* 653) (see al-Wansharīsī, *Īḍāḥ*, Introduction, p. 116), and Ibn Ḥamdūn (d. *c.* 1273) (see Ibn Ḥamdūn, i. 16). For this term, see also, for example, al-Qarāfī, *Tanqīḥ*, p. 18 [= *Dhakhīra*, p. 55]; Abū Zahra, p. 119; Wuld Abbāh, p. 58; al-Bājaqnī, pp. 40–1). The Ḥanafīs had a somewhat different definition of the term *naṣṣ*, for which see, for example, Khallāf, pp. 161ff; Abū Zahra, pp. 119ff; Zaydān, p. 340.
19 *Mafhūm al-muwāfaqa* ('what is understood by similarity') and *al-mafhūm bi-l-awlā* ('what is understood as being [even] more appropriate') refer to the technique of *a fortiori* deduction (see further below, pp. 114–15). Weiss (*God's Law*, p. 485) suggests the term 'congruent implication' for this concept.
20 *Mafhūm al-mukhālafa* ('what is understood by contrast') and *dalīl al-khiṭāb* (lit. 'the implications of what is said') refer to the technique of 'argument *a contrario*', to use Brunschvig's term ('Averroès Juriste', p. 51), or 'counter-implication', to use Weiss's term (*God's Law*, p. 485), meaning that if you say X about Y, it only applies to Y and not to anything other than Y (see further below, pp. 115ff).
21 *Ẓihār* is a form of oath whereby a man declares that his wife is 'like his mother's back (*ẓahr*)', i.e. is *ḥarām* for him.
22 See *Muw.* ii. 20.
23 *Liʿān*, or 'mutual invocation of curses', is the procedure whereby a man who accuses his wife of adultery without sufficient witnesses may avoid the penalty for *qadhf* (accusations of illicit sexual intercourse), and she the penalty for adultery, by their both swearing that they are telling the truth on pain of bringing the curse of Allah on themselves if they are lying (see Q 24: 6–9).
24 See *Muw.* ii. 24.
25 Q 58: 3–4, cited in *Muw.* ii. 20.
26 See *Umm*, v. 262; *Mab.* vi. 223.
27 See *Muw.* ii. 20. Cf. *Mud.* vi. 49; *Bayān*, v. 171.
28 See *Mud.* vi. 49. Cf. al-Bājī, iv. 38.

29 See *Mab.* vi. 227, 228; *Umm*, iv. 119–20 (margin), v. 263; Ibn Rushd, ii. 87; *Qawānīn*, pp. 240–1.
30 For *īlā'*, see below, pp. 139ff.
31 See *Muw.* ii. 21; *Mud.* vi. 51; Ibn Rushd, ii. 89.
32 See *Mab.* vi. 227–8; *Umm*, v. 262; Ibn Rushd, ii. 89.
33 See *Muw.* ii. 20, 21. Cf. *Mud.* vi. 55–56.
34 This phrase, cited as a legal maxim in *Muw.* ii. 128, is found elsewhere as a Prophetic *ḥadīth* (e.g. al-Bukhārī, iii. 262; al-Tirmidhī, i. 253; Abū Dāwūd, iii. 221). For the principle itself, note also Q 5: 1 – *awfū bi-l-ʿuqūd* ('Fulfil your contracts').
35 See Ibn Rushd, ii. 89–90; *Mab.* vi. 230.
36 See *Muw.* ii. 21; Ibn Rushd, ii. 91.
37 See *Umm*, v. 265; Ibn Rushd, ii. 91.
38 See *Mab.* vi. 232–3; cf. Ibn Rushd, ii. 91.
39 See Ibn Rushd, ii. 91.
40 See *Mab.* vi. 224; Ibn Rushd, ii. 88; *Qawānīn*, p. 241.
41 See *Muw.* ii. 20–1.
42 See Ibn Rushd, ii. 87; cf. *Mab.* vi. 226.
43 See *Umm*, v. 265; Ibn Rushd, ii. 88; *Mab.* vi. 224–5.
44 See *Muw.* ii. 20.
45 See *Umm*, v. 264; *Mab.* vi. 226; Ibn Rushd, ii. 94.
46 See *Umm*, v. 264; *Mab.* vi. 226; Ibn Rushd, vi. 94.
47 See *Muw.* ii. 20; *Mud.* vi. 54–5; al-Bājī, iv. 47.
48 See *Umm*, v. 264; *Mab.* vi. 226; Ibn Rushd, ii. 94.
49 See *Muw.* ii. 20. Cf. *Mud.* vi. 63–4; al-Bājī, iv. 47.
50 See Ibn Rushd, ii. 94–5.
51 See *Muw.* ii. 20; also *Bayān*, v. 202; al-Bājī, iv. 48.
52 See Ibn Rushd, ii. 90; *Mab.* vi. 227.
53 See Ibn Rushd, ii. 91.
54 See *Muw.* ii. 21; also Ibn Rushd, ii. 91. Cf. *Mud.* vi. 61.
55 Cf. *Muw.* ii. 190: '*al-ʿabd silʿa min al-silaʿ*'.
56 See *Mud.* vi. 64; al-Bājī, iv. 51–2; *Mab.* vi. 234; al-Zurqānī, iii. 43.
57 See *Mud.* vi. 65; al-Bājī, iv. 52–3; *Mab.* vi. 234; al-Zurqānī, iii. 43.
58 For *muḥṣanāt* as 'free women', see below, pp. 98–9.
59 See *Muw.* ii. 21; al-Bājī, iv. 53. For *īlā'* in the case of slaves, see *Muw.* ii. 20; al-Zurqānī, iii. 41.
60 See Ibn Rushd, ii. 92; also, for al-Shāfiʿī's view, *Umm*, iv. 127 (margin), v. 266. For the principle of *ḥaml al-muṭlaq ʿalā l-muqayyad*, see below, pp. 104ff. Al-Qarāfī says that Mālik goes by this principle 'in the case of *ẓihār* and elsewhere' (*Tanqīḥ*, pp. 117–18), but also states that most Mālikīs do not accept it in situations where the judgement is similar but the reason for it different, as with the *kaffāra* for *ẓihār* and the *kaffāra* for accidental killing (see *Tanqīḥ*, p. 117 [= *Dhakhīra*, pp. 97–8]).
61 See *Muw.* ii. 141; *Mud.* ii. 60, iii. 120–1.
62 See *Umm*, iv. 127 (margin), v. 266.
63 See *Mab.* vii. 2–4.
64 For Mālik's view, see the immediately preceding example; for al-Shāfiʿī's, see *Umm*, iv. 127–8 (margin), 138 (margin). For *zakāt* being only for Muslims, see also *Umm*, ii. 52; al-Jaṣṣāṣ, iii. 135; *Mab.* ii. 202–3; *Qawānīn*, p. 108. An

exception to this was the disputed category of *al-muʾallafati qulūbuhum* (Q 9: 60) which could include non-Muslims (see, for example, al-Ṭabarī, x. 98–100; Ibn al-ʿArabī, ii. 950–4; Ibn Rushd, i. 251).

65 See *Mab.* vii. 18, also ii. 202–3, iii. 111. The Qurʾanic reference is to Q 60: 8–9.

66 i.e. Hishām ibn Ismāʿīl al-Makhzūmī, governor of Madina under ʿAbd al-Malik and al-Walīd (see al-Zurqānī, ii. 82).

67 See *Muw.* i. 210; *Mud.* vi. 69; al-Bājī, iv. 45; Ibn Rushd, ii. 94.

68 See al-Bājī, iv. 45.

69 See *Mud.* iii. 119, vi. 69.

70 See *Umm,* v. 272; *Mab.* vii. 16; Ibn Rushd, ii. 94.

71 See Ibn Rushd, i. 338.

72 See Ibn Rushd, i. 338.

73 See *Mud.* vi. 60–1; *Bayān,* v. 176–7; Ibn Rushd, ii. 90.

74 See *Mud.* vi. 70, 83, iii. 120; *Umm,* v. 272; *Mab.* vii. 17.

75 See Ibn Rushd, ii. 95; *Umm,* v. 272 (al-Shāfiʿī). Al-Sarakhsī, presumably mistakenly, attributes the same view as Ibn Ḥazm's to Mālik (see *Mab.* vi. 225), while Abū Zahra (p. 172) suggests that it was only the Ḥanafīs who held that the *kaffāra,* whatever its type, must be finished before the man resumed sexual relations with his wife. In fact, this latter judgement is overtly attributed to Mālik in the *Mudawwana* (vi. 78), where he says that someone who makes an oath of *ẓihār* against his wife and then has intercourse with her before having finished all his fasting or providing of food should begin his fasting or providing of food anew (see also *Mud.* vi. 60ff and *Bayān,* v. 176f, where the judgements regarding a man having intercourse with his wife before finishing the *kaffāra* obviously relate to all three types of *kaffāra*).

76 See *Muw.* i. 329–32.

77 *Muw.* i. 329.

78 For the decision of the Prophet on which this judgement is based, see below, p. 214, n. 202.

79 See the next following paragraph.

80 See Ibn Rushd, ii. 284; *Qawānīn,* p. 382. Cf. *Muw.* i. 338.

81 See Ibn Rushd, ii. 284.

82 Interestingly, Mālik uses the same *āya* in *Muw.* i. 338 to justify the Madinan point of view on the order of preference for agnatic inheritance!

83 See Ibn Rushd, ii. 284–5; *Qawānīn,* p. 383. Cf. Mālik's comment in *Muw.* i. 341: '*wa-kāna mā baqiya li-l-muslimīn*'.

84 See Ibn Rushd, ii. 285–6. Cf. al-Bukhārī, viii. 477, 479–80; and al-Zurqānī, ii. 364. The Shīʿa also held that a grand-daughter may not inherit alongside a daughter (see Ibn Rushd, ii. 286).

85 See Ibn Rushd, ii. 285.

86 For the interpretation of this notoriously difficult phrase, see below, pp. 106ff.

87 See al-Zurqānī, ii. 364–5; also Ibn Rushd, ii. 285; Jalālayn, p. 78. Ibn ʿAbbās, however, is also said to have held the view of the majority (see Ibn Rushd, ii. 285). This judgement of Ibn ʿAbbās is an example of going by *mafhūm al-mukhālafa* (see Ibn Rushd, ii. 285; and, for this principle, below, pp. 114, 115ff).

88 See Ibn Rushd, ii. 287; also al-Bājī, vi. 229 (with the emendment of *laysa* for *a-laysa*).

89 See *Muw.* i. 331 (cf. *Bayān*, xviii. 431). In his *Iḥkām*, al-Bājī mentions a report to the effect that this was the *ᶜamal* from before the time of ᶜUthmān (see *Iḥkām*, pp. 251–2; cf. al-Bājī, vi. 229).
90 See al-Qarāfī, *Dhakhīra*, p. 91 [= *Tanqīḥ*, p. 103].
91 See *Qawānīn*, p. 384; Pearl, *Muslim Law*, pp. 126–7.
92 A *mudabbar* is a slave who has been granted freedom on his master's death.
93 See *Muw.* ii. 162.
94 See *Muw.* ii. 162.
95 See *Muw.* ii. 163; and, for the restriction of bequests to a third, *Muw.* ii. 131–2, 138–9; Ibn Rushd, ii. 281.
96 The printed text has *yūṣā bi-hā* ('that is made'), which is the Ḥafṣ vocalisation of this phrase in Q 4: 12. If, however, we assume the Madinan reading of *yūṣī bi-hā* (as in Chester Beatty MS. 3001, f. 69v), this phrase could be part of either Q 4: 11 or 12.
97 *Muw.* ii. 164.
98 See *Muw.* ii. 161, also 131.

Chapter Six – Techniques of Qurʾanic Interpretation in the *Muwaṭṭaʾ*

1 e.g. Ibn Ḥamdūn, i. 16; al-Wansharīsī, *Īḍāḥ*, Introduction, p. 116 (citing Rāshid ibn Abī Rāshid on the authority of his teacher Abū Muḥammad Ṣāliḥ); cf. Abū Zahra, pp. 119, 167.
2 Q 2: 187.
3 *Muw.* i. 230–1.
4 See *Umm*, ii. 90; *Mab.* iii. 115, 117–8. Al-Bājī notes that although the predominant view from Mālik is that leaving *iᶜtikāf* to go to the Jumuᶜa breaks *iᶜtikāf*, it is also recorded from him that doing so does not break *iᶜtikāf*, although he still disliked the practice (see al-Bājī, ii. 79).
5 See *Mab.* iii. 115; Ibn Rushd, i. 220; *Qawānīn*, p. 122.
6 Q 24: 6.
7 *Muw.* ii. 25.
8 See *Muw.* ii. 25.
9 See *Mud.* vi. 105–6; cf. *Bayān*, vi. 410.
10 See Ibn Rushd, ii. 98; *Mab.* vii. 40.
11 See Ibn Rushd, ii. 98; *Mab.* vii. 39–40; Ibn Juzayy, *Tafsīr*, p. 465.
12 See Ibn Rushd, ii. 98.
13 An *umm walad* is a slave-girl who is the mother of a child by her master. Such a slave-girl was automatically free on her master's death.
14 Q 2: 234. The complete phrase is: 'Those among you who die and leave wives should observe an *ᶜidda* of four months and ten days.'
15 *Muw.* ii. 37–8.
16 See Ibn Rushd, ii. 80; al-Bājī, iv. 140.
17 See above, pp. 13, 33.
18 See al-Bājī, iv. 140. Ibn Rushd connects this view back to a *ḥadīth*, considered weak by Ibn Ḥanbal, to the same effect from ᶜAmr ibn al-ᶜĀṣ (see Ibn Rushd, ii. 80). However, a more generalised version of the same *ḥadīth* is related by

al-Shaybānī, from Mālik, as support for the Iraqi view, which merely says that an *umm walad's ʿidda* is that of a free woman (see *Muw. Sh.*, p. 203).

19 See *Muw. Sh.*, p. 203; Ibn Rushd, ii. 80; al-Bājī, iv. 140.

20 This view is attributed to Ṭāwūs and Qatāda (see al-Bājī, iv. 140; also Ibn Rushd, ii. 80. Cf. *Muw.* ii. 38).

21 See *Muw.* ii. 38.

22 See above, p. 40.

23 See above, pp. 65–6.

24 See *Muw.* ii. 7. Cf. above, p. 195, n. 47.

25 See *Muw.* ii. 7.

26 *Muw.* ii. 8.

27 See Ibn Rushd, ii. 29; al-Zurqānī, iii. 16. Al-Bājaqnī (p. 64) refers to the 'marriage' meaning of *nikāḥ* as its *ḥaqīqa sharʿiyya* ('literal meaning in the *sharīʿa*') and its more general meaning as *majāz sharʿī* ('metaphorical meaning in the *sharīʿa*'). For the meaning of *nikāḥ* as '[contract of] marriage' see, for example, Ibn Juzayy, *Tafsīr*, p. 113; and, for this being its usual Qurʾanic meaning and thus its *ḥaqīqa sharʿiyya*, *Lisān*, iii. 465.

28 *Muw.* ii. 8, citing Q 4: 22.

29 See *Muw.* ii. 11. It is also clear from this chapter that the idea of *nikāḥ* in Q 4: 22, although restricted by the Madinans to the meaning of lawful, as opposed to unlawful, intercourse, was also extended by them to include any kind of sexual enjoyment (*istimtāʿ*), including even looking with sexual pleasure (*al-naẓar bi-ladhdha*) (for which, see also al-Bājī, iii. 326–7; *Bayān*, xviii. 489; Ibn al-ʿArabī, i. 371, 378–9).

30 Cf. al-Bājī, iii. 307: '[Mālik] means that the word *nisāʾ* is customarily (*fī l-ʿurf wa-l-ʿāda*) taken to refer to wives and not women with whom someone has had intercourse by way of *zinā*.' Al-Bājī goes on to give three reasons why this should be so: (i) in the phrase 'and the mothers of your women' (*wa-ummahātu nisāʾikum*), 'mothers' are also women and so 'your women' must refer to a subset of women rather than all women; (ii) if the meaning intended was 'mothers of your women' in a general sense, every woman with a daughter would be *ḥarām*, which is a universally rejected interpretation; (iii) the general usage is that if someone refers to 'so-and-so's woman (*imraʾat fulān*)' he means his wife, as, for example, in Q 33: 32 – 'O women (*nisāʾ*) of the Prophet! You are not like any other women' – where the intended meaning is the wives of the Prophet.

31 See *Muw.* ii. 10; al-Bājī, iii. 325. Cf. *Mab.* iv. 201; *Umm*, v. 2, where the same judgement is endorsed by Abū Ḥanīfa and al-Shāfiʿī.

32 Q 5: 95.

33 *Muw.* i. 258. These judgements were universally acknowledged, although there were differences of detail with regards to who, if anybody, could eat the resulting meat (see Ibn al-ʿArabī, ii. 659; *Qawānīn*, p. 135).

34 See *Muw.* i. 324.

35 This judgement about the *miʿrāḍ* was shared by all the main *madhhabs* (see Ibn Rushd, i. 369; *Qawānīn*, p. 175).

36 Q 16: 8.

37 Q 8: 60.

38 *Muw.* i. 303. For this comment of Saʿīd's, see also *Muw.* i. 206.

39 See al-Zurqānī, ii. 307–8.

40 *Muw.* i. 295–6, citing Q 99: 7–8.
41 For a similar assessment, see al-Zurqānī, ii. 291.
42 See *Muw.* ii. 193, citing Q 5: 45.
43 See *Muw.* ii. 193.
44 For the blood-money for a woman, see *Muw.* ii. 183; *Qawānīn*, p. 341.
45 See Ibn Rushd, ii. 335; *Qawānīn*, p. 340; *Umm*, vi. 18; al-Jaṣṣāṣ, i. 138–40.
46 See *Bayān*, iv. 260–2; al-Bājī, *Iḥkām*, pp. 394ff; al-Qarāfī, *Dhakhīra*, pp. 103ff [= *Tanqīḥ*, pp. 129ff]; al-Zurqānī, iv. 50; also Abū Zahra, pp. 305ff; Zaydān, pp. 263ff.
47 For the first judgement, see *Bayān*, iv. 260–2; al-Bājī, *Iḥkām*, p. 395; cf. *Muw.* ii. 3; Ibn Rushd, ii. 4–5. For the second judgement, see Ibn Rushd, ii. 17; al-Qarāfī, *Tanqīḥ*, p. 131. The father of the two girls is said to have been the prophet Shuᶜayb (see Ibn Juzayy, *Tafsīr*, p. 517; Jalālayn, p. 397).

In this context, mention may also be made of the Prophet's use of the Qurᵓanic command *aqimi l-ṣalāta li-dhikrī* in Q 20: 14, addressed there to Moses, to support the judgement that someone who sleeps through the proper time for the prayer, or forgets to do it at that time, should do it as soon as he wakes up or remembers, thus illustrating the application of an earlier command to the present (as well as indicating that the meaning of the phrase is 'Establish the prayer when you remember Me' rather than the more immediately obvious 'in order to remember Me') (see *Muw.* i. 27; *Bayān*, iv. 261; al-Bājī, *Iḥkām*, p. 396).

48 See *Muw. Ibn Ziyād*, p. 156.
49 See *Mud.* iii. 67.
50 Q 2: 178.
51 *Muw.* ii. 193.
52 See Ibn Rushd, ii. 333–4. For this *ḥadīth*, see also Abū Dāwūd, iv. 144; al-Nasāᵓī, ii. 242; Ibn Mājah, ii. 78f; and, for the same idea, the 'Constitution of Madina' (*Tahdhīb Sīrat Ibn Hishām*, pp. 175–8).
53 See Ibn Rushd, ii. 333–4; *Qawānīn*, p. 340. (For the equality of slaves and free men with respect to *qiṣāṣ* in the Ḥanafī *madhhab*, see also, for example, *Mab.* xxvii. 30, 35).
54 See Ibn Rushd, ii. 334; *Qawānīn*, p. 340.
55 *Muw.* ii. 173.
56 *Muw.* ii. 173.
57 See al-Zurqānī, iv. 19; *Muw. Sh.*, p. 240, n. 690; *Mab.* ix. 140; cf. ᶜAbd al-Razzāq, x. 242–3.
58 See Ibn al-ᶜArabī, ii. 617; also al-Nasāᵓī, ii. 262, for the 'journey' *ḥadīth*, and al-Tirmidhī, i. 274, for the '*jihād*' *ḥadīth*, contrary to Ibn al-ᶜArabī's attributions of the same.
59 See Ibn Rushd, ii. 373.
60 See Ibn Rushd, ii. 373.
61 Q 2: 187. For this interpretation of *mina l-fajr*, see, for example, al-Ṭabarī, ii. 96–7, 99; Jalālayn, p. 30; Ibn Juzayy, *Tafsīr*, p. 47.
62 *Muw.* i. 224.
63 *Muw.* i. 224.
64 See al-Jaṣṣāṣ, i. 234; al-Bājī, ii. 68; al-Zurqānī, ii. 114.
65 See al-Jaṣṣāṣ, i. 234; al-Zurqānī, ii. 114; Ibn Rushd, i. 298.
66 See al-Bājī, *Iḥkām*, p. 190.

67 This was the view of Mālik and the majority of his followers, as it was also the view of the majority of the *fuqahā*ʾ; other views were that, rather than obligation (*wujūb*), commands initially indicated recommendation (*nadb*), or either of these two, or permissibility (*ibāḥa*), or any of these three (see al-Bājī, *Iḥkām*, pp. 195, 198; al-Qarāfī, *Dhakhīra*, p. 74 [= *Tanqīḥ*, p. 58]; al-Bājaqnī, p. 25; Wuld Abbāh, p. 46; Abū Zahra, pp. 176, 177; Zaydān, pp. 293–4).

68 Q 24: 33. The word *khayr* ('good') was understood by Mālik to mean 'the ability to pay [the instalments] (*al-quwwa ʿalā l-adā*ʾ)', i.e., effectively, 'money' (see *Bayān*, xviii. 185; also, Ibn Juzayy, *Tafsīr*, p. 473).

69 *Muw.* ii. 146.

70 See al-Jaṣṣāṣ, iii. 321; al-Bājī, vii. 5; Ibn al-ʿArabī, iii. 1370; Ibn Rushd, ii. 313; Ibn Juzayy, *Tafsīr*, p. 473. Note al-Bājī's harmonising interpretation of ʿUmar's action and his comment that Mālik had the best knowledge of ʿUmar's judgements and those of the other *imāms* of Madina, whom he had never heard condone such a judgement, and that even ʿAṭāʾ did not claim to have taken his view from anyone else (see al-Bājī, vii. 5. Cf. *Umm*, vii. 362).

71 See *Bayān*, xviii. 185; al-Jaṣṣāṣ, iii. 322; *Umm*, vii. 364; al-Bājī, vii. 7.

72 See *Muw.* ii. 146; also, *Mud.* vii. 82.

73 See al-Bājī, vii. 7–8. Cf. al-Ṭabarī, xviii. 90–2; al-Jaṣṣāṣ, iii. 322; *Bayān*, xviii. 185–6, also xv. 215. Ibn al-ʿArabī's claim (iii. 1372) that this was also Mālik's view would seem to be an error.

74 See Abd-Allah, 'Concept', p. 625. For further discussion on this point, see also ibid, pp. 623ff; Ibn Rushd, ii. 315; Schacht, *Origins*, pp. 279f.

75 See, for example, Abū Zahra, p. 158; Zaydān, p. 318.

76 See al-Bājaqnī, p. 65; and above, pp. 81–2.

77 See above, p. 86.

78 See below, pp. 96ff, 104ff.

79 See above, pp. 68–9.

80 See *Muw.* ii. 140–1, citing Q 47: 4. Al-Bājī points out that there is a certain licence in this interpretation, since, according to the Mālikīs, the *imām* has five choices with regard to prisoners, i.e. killing them, ransoming them, setting them free for nothing (*mann*), taking them as slaves, or accepting them as *dhimmīs*, thus indicating that 'setting them free' is an option that would apply before they are actually made slaves (see al-Bājī, vi. 277). Ibn al-ʿArabī also feels that Mālik's interpretation is not strictly speaking accurate (see Ibn al-ʿArabī, iv. 1689).

81 *Muw.* i. 254, 257, relating to the prohibition against hunting while in *iḥrām* in Q 5: 95 in particular (see above, pp. 83–4) and whether, if such a prohibited act takes place, the resulting meat is *ḥalāl* or not.

82 *Muw.* i. 317, relating to the *kaffārat al-aymān* verse (Q 5: 89).

83 *Muw.* ii. 172, 176, relating to the prohibition against stealing in Q 5: 38.

84 See *Muw.* ii. 7. For this prohibition, see also below, pp. 105–6.

85 See *Muw.* ii. 8; also above, pp. 81–2.

86 See *Muw.* ii. 35, 37, 38; also, for the first two of these, p. 106 below and pp. 80–1 above respectively.

87 See also below, p. 106.

88 For *muḥṣanāt* as 'free women', see below, pp. 98–9. For Q 4: 25's 'half' penalty, see above, p. 68.

89 *Muw.* ii. 38.

90 See *Muw.* i. 260, 261.
91 See *Muw. Sh.*, pp. 170–1; al-Jaṣṣāṣ, i. 268.
92 See *Umm*, ii. 135ff; al-Bājī, ii. 273, 274.
93 *Tamattuʿ* refers to doing an *ʿumra* in the months of *ḥajj* and then staying in Makka out of *iḥrām* until the time of the *ḥajj* itself.
94 See al-Suyūṭī, *Lubāb*, p. 38; al-Wāḥidī, *Asbāb*, p. 40; also, for the incident itself, *Muw.* i. 289.
95 See *Umm*, ii. 135, 139; cf. al-Jaṣṣāṣ, i. 269.
96 Ibn Rushd mentions three other arguments for al-Shāfiʿī's view, namely: (a) the mention of safety (*fa-idhā amintum*) later in the *āya*, which suggests a contrast with an initial state of fear; (b) the fact that the specific mention of sickness after mention of *iḥṣār* (*fa-man kāna minkum marīḍan*) suggests that they are two different situations; and also (c) the fact that although normally the form *aḥṣara* is used for obstruction by sickness and *ḥaṣara* for obstruction by an enemy, nevertheless *aḥṣara* can be used for both meanings (see Ibn Rushd, i. 286). I have not come across these arguments in al-Shāfiʿī's writings, but all three are referred to by al-Jaṣṣāṣ (i. 270, 268), although not attributed directly to al-Shāfiʿī, while al-Sarakhsī (*Mab.* iv. 107–8) overtly attributes argument (a) to him, as well as referring in general terms to argument (c).
97 See *Umm*, ii. 135.
98 See *Umm*, ii. 135.
99 See *Umm*, ii. 139: 'So I hold that the verse is general (*ʿāmma*) and refers to anyone doing *ḥajj* or *ʿumra*.'
100 See *Umm*, ii. 139.
101 See al-Jaṣṣāṣ, i. 268; *Mab.* iv. 107, 108.
102 See *Mab.* iv. 106, 107.
103 See *Mab.* iv. 106, 107. Al-Shāfiʿī attributes this view to ʿAṭāʾ (see *Umm*, ii. 135).
104 See *Mab.* iv. 107; cf. above, pp. 87–8.
105 See *Muw.* i. 273, 261.
106 See above, pp. 87–8.
107 *Muw.* i. 260.
108 See *Muw.* i. 260; *Mud.* i. 429, 366.
109 See *Muw.* i. 279.
110 Cf. ʿUmar's comment in *Muw.* i. 265 that Q 22: 33 means that the all the rites of the *ḥajj* should end in Makka, and thus that the *ḥajj* itself should end with a 'farewell' *ṭawāf* around the Kaʿba. See also below, p. 105.
111 See below, p. 105.
112 *Muw.* i. 275, citing Q 5: 95. For this judgement, see also below, pp. 104–5.
113 i.e. the *fitna* between the Umayyads and the Zubayrids during ʿAbd al-Malik's caliphate. Ibn al-Athīr (iv. 350) tells us that Ibn ʿUmar went on *ḥajj* in the year 72 while ʿAbd al-Malik's general, al-Ḥajjāj ibn Yūsuf, was besieging ʿAbdallāh ibn al-Zubayr in Makka. For Ibn ʿUmar meeting al-Ḥajjāj on *ḥajj* in the year 73, shortly before his death, see *Istīʿāb*, i. 369; also *Muw.* i. 280.
114 See *Muw.* i. 260.
115 See above, p. 57.
116 For references, see above, p. 58, and the notes thereto. Note also the echo of the Qurʾanic *fa-lammā balagha maʿahu l-saʿy* (Q 37: 102).

117 See above, p. 58.
118 Q 2: 205.
119 Q 80: 8–9.
120 Q 79: 22.
121 Q 92: 4.
122 *Muw.* i. 97.
123 See above, p. 58.
124 The apparent disagreement referred to by Ibn Rushd is not about the basic judgement but rather about what constitutes the degree of 'running' (*saʿy*) that is forbidden (see Ibn Rushd, i. 117; also above, p. 58).
125 Q 2: 187.
126 Q 6: 145, cited in *Muw.* i. 276.
127 See, for example, al-Ṭabarī, ii. 148ff.
128 See, for example, al-Ṭabarī, ii. 151ff.
129 See above, p. 78.
130 See al-Bājī, iii. 18.
131 Al-Ṭabarī, for instance, prefers the general sense of *rafath* (see al-Ṭabarī, ii. 150), although opting for the meaning that *fusūq* means acts that break *iḥrām*, since that is specific to *ḥajj* (ibid, ii. 152); al-Jaṣṣāṣ goes for the most general meaning in both cases (see al-Jaṣṣāṣ, i. 307–8); al-Bājī, although explaining Mālik's view, nevertheless feels inclined towards a more general interpretation (see al-Bājī, iii. 18); Ibn Juzayy and al-Suyūṭī, although preferring the more restrictive meaning of 'sexual intercourse' for *rafath*, nevertheless gloss *fusūq* as *maʿāṣī* ('wrong actions') (see Ibn Juzayy, *Tafsīr*, p. 50; Jalālayn, p. 32).
132 Q 4: 25.
133 *Muw.* ii. 9.
134 See, for instance, al-Ṭabarī, v. 11; al-Jaṣṣāṣ, ii. 157; Jalālayn, p. 81; Ibn Juzayy, *Tafsīr*, p. 116.
135 Q 5: 5.
136 Q 4: 25.
137 *Muw.* ii. 11. For the same report (with slight differences) and the same argument, see also *Mud.* iv. 156.
138 For this being an example of *mafhūm al-mukhālafa*, see below, pp. 115–16. The interpretation of *ṭawl* as wealth (cf. *Mud.* iv. 55) was a point of difference between Mālik and Abū Ḥanīfa, who, although agreeing that a free Muslim could only marry a slave-girl under the two conditions mentioned in Q 4: 25, held that *ṭawl* referred to a man's already having a free wife (see Ibn Rushd, ii. 36; also al-Jaṣṣāṣ, ii. 158; *Mab.* v. 108ff).
139 See *Muw.* ii. 11.
140 See al-Zurqānī, iii. 22; also *Mud.* iv. 157, where this view is recorded from Mālik and also attributed to ʿAmmār ibn Yāsir.
141 For the judgement of Ibn ʿUmar, who held that Jews and Christians should be considered as much idolaters as any others and that their women should thus be prohibited for marriage by Q 2: 221 – *wa-lā tankiḥū l-mushrikāti ḥattā yuʾminna* ('Do not marry idolatrous women until they believe') – see al-Jaṣṣāṣ, ii. 163, 324–5; cf. Ibn Rushd, ii. 36–7.
142 See al-Jaṣṣāṣ, ii. 162, 324.
143 See al-Jaṣṣāṣ, ii. 163; Ibn Rushd, ii. 37. Cf. al-Ṭabarī, vi. 60 and al-Jaṣṣāṣ, ii. 162–3, where there is also the argument that *muḥṣanāt* in Q 5: 5 means

'respectable women' (*ʿafāʾif*) – as in Q 24: 4 – rather than 'free women' (*ḥarāʾir*), thus allowing Q 5: 5 to be interpreted as referring to *kitābiyyāt* in general, whether free or slave. This interpretation, however, conflicts with the understanding that *muḥṣanāt* in Q 24: 4 refers specifically to Muslim women, as reflected in the universally agreed judgement that the punishment for *qadhf* only applies if the *maqdhūf* is a Muslim (for which see, for example, al-Ṭabarī, xviii. 53; al-Jaṣṣāṣ, iii. 267; *Mab.* ix. 40; Ibn Rushd, ii. 368; also above, p. 80).

144 For Abū Ḥanīfa's rejection of *mafhūm al-mukhālafa*, see al-Bājaqnī, p. 77; al-Qarāfī, *Dhakhīra*, p. 98 [= *Tanqīḥ*, p. 119]; Abū Zahra, pp. 148–50; Zaydān, pp. 371–2; cf. al-Jaṣṣāṣ, ii. 157. For the principle in general, see below, pp. 114, 115ff.

145 See Ibn Rushd, ii. 37.

146 Q 11: 71.

147 This is the meaning given in Jalālayn (p. 175), where *ṣāliḥ* is glossed as *sawī* ('well-formed', 'healthy').

148 Q 7: 189.

149 Q 2: 233.

150 Q 46: 15.

151 *Muw.* ii. 133.

152 For the restrictions operative on gifts, see, for example, Ibn Rushd, ii. 274ff; also *Muw.* ii. 125–6, 137. For the restriction of bequests to a third, see above, p. 75.

153 Q 46: 15.

154 Q 2: 233.

155 *Muw.* ii. 168–9.

156 See above, pp. 33–4; and, for another example, below, pp. 126, 172.

157 See al-Bājī, vii. 141; al-Jaṣṣāṣ, i. 412.

158 See al-Bājī, vi. 175.

159 See above, pp. 84–5.

160 Q 16: 8.

161 'Camels' is a loose translation of the word *anʿām*, which refers more normally to camels, cattle, sheep and goats. However, of these, only camels are normally ridden, which is the point of the quotation here.

162 Q 40: 79.

163 The first part of this quotation is from Q 22: 34 and the second from Q 22: 36, as it is also in *Muw. Abū Musʿab*, ii. 200, and *Muw. Suw.*, p. 381. The same report also occurs in *Muw. Ibn Ziyād* (p. 181) but with the second part of the quotation from Q 22: 28 (*fa-kulū minhā wa-aṭʿimū l-bāʾisa l-faqīr*) rather than Q 22: 36 (*fa-kulū minhā wa-aṭʿimū l-qāniʿa wa-l-muʿtarr*). However, Mālik's glosses on the words *qāniʿ*, *muʿtarr*, *bāʾis* and *faqīr*, which occur in all three transmissions, necessarily relate to both Q 22: 28 and 36.

164 *Muw.* i. 326–7. Cf. *Muw. Ibn Ziyād*, pp. 179–81; *Muw. Suw.*, p. 381.

165 *Muw. Ibn Ziyād*, p. 181. Cf. *Muw. Suw.*, p. 381 (*wa-dhālika l-amr ʿindanā*).

166 See al-Jaṣṣāṣ, iii. 183–4; al-Bājī, iii. 133; Ibn Rushd, i. 381; *Qawānīn*, p. 172; al-Ramlī, viii. 143.

167 Q 56: 79.

168 Q 80: 11–16, cited in *Muw.* i. 158.

169 See, for example, al-Jaṣṣāṣ, iii. 415–16; al-Bājī, i. 344; Ibn Rushd, i. 32; al-Ramlī, i. 109.

170 See Ibn Hishām (ed. Wüstenfeld), p. 226; also, al-Jaṣṣāṣ, iii. 415; Ibn al-ᶜArabī, iv. 1726.
171 See al-Bājī, i. 344.
172 See Ibn Rushd, i. 32; al-Jaṣṣāṣ, iii. 416; al-Ramlī, i. 109.
173 For *taqyīd al-muṭlaq*, see, for instance, al-Qarāfī, *Dhakhīra*, pp. 97–8 [= *Tanqīḥ*, pp. 117–19]; al-Bājaqnī, pp. 55–6, 68–70; Wuld Abbāh, p. 45; Abū Zahra, pp. 170–4; Zaydān, pp. 284–91.
174 See above, pp. 68–9.
175 See above, p. 71.
176 *Muw.* i. 275, citing Q 5: 95.
177 For Q 2: 196, see above, pp. 92–3.
178 See al-Jaṣṣāṣ, i. 272, 282, iii. 243; Ibn Rushd, i. 305.
179 See above, p. 96.
180 See *Muw.* i. 290; Ibn Rushd, i. 305.
181 See Ibn al-ᶜArabī, i. 125; al-Zurqānī, ii. 272.
182 See *Umm*, ii. 136–7, 185.
183 See *Umm*, ii. 157; al-Jaṣṣāṣ, i. 282.
184 See *Umm*, ii. 183; Ibn Rushd, i. 305.
185 See *Bayān*, iv. 16; Ibn Rushd, i. 305. Cf. *Muw.* i. 278, where a slightly different version of the same *ḥadīth* is given.
186 See, for example, *Umm*, ii. 183 (*lā hadya illā fī l-ḥaram*) compared with ibid, ii. 184 (*lā yakūnu … l-hady illā bi-Makka wa-Minā*); al-Jaṣṣāṣ, i. 273 (*lā tajūzu l-hadāyā illā fī l-ḥaram*) compared with ibid, iii. 244 (*fa-lammā lam tajuz al-hady illā bi-Makka …*).
187 See *Muw.* ii. 10;
188 See al-Bājī, iii. 325–6; al-Zurqānī, iii. 21; Ibn Rushd, ii. 34; also above, p. 83.
189 See *Muw.* ii. 35–6; *Umm*, v. 205; al-Jaṣṣāṣ, i. 415; al-Bājī, iv. 132; Ibn Rushd, ii. 79.
190 See *Muw.* ii. 36. This was also said to have been the view of ᶜAlī (see al-Bājī, iv. 132).
191 *Muw.* ii. 36.
192 For this interpretation of the grammar of the phrase, see below, pp. 107–8.
193 For this restrictive interpretation of *walad*, see below, pp. 108–9.
194 See *Muw.* i. 336.
195 See al-Ṭabarī, iv. 177.
196 See al-Ṭabarī, iv. 177, vi. 25–6. (The other two points were the inheritance due to a grandfather and various aspects of *ribā*).
197 This view is attributed to Ibn ᶜAbbās and ᶜUmar, although both are also said to have held the dominant view referred to above, and ᶜUmar is also said to have held that *kalāla* meant 'those who died without children', thus illustrating (assuming the accuracy of these reports) some of his confusion about the term (see al-Ṭabarī, iv. 177–8).
198 See al-Zurqānī, ii. 371; also al-Ṭabarī, iv. 178.
199 See al-Zurqānī, ii. 371.
200 See al-Ṭabarī, xiv. 178; Ibn Juzayy, *Tafsīr*, p. 111; al-Zurqānī, ii. 371; *Lisān*, xiv. 111–4.
201 For *ukhtun* ***min ummin*** (Saᶜd, Ibn Masᶜūd), see al-Zurqānī, ii. 271; al-Zamakhsharī, p. 276. For ***mina l-ummi*** (Ubayy), see al-Zamakhsharī, p. 276; Jeffery, *Materials*, p. 126.

202 The actual decision was that the daughter received her full Qurʾanic share of one half, the son's daughter the remaining sixth of the two-thirds that would be due to two daughters, and the sister, as residuary, the remaining third of the estate (see al-Bukhārī, viii. 480; Ibn Rushd, ii. 288–9; Coulson, *Succession*, pp. 54–5, 66).
203 See Coulson, *Succession*, p. 66. Elsewhere in the verses on inheritance, e.g. Q 4: 11, the word *walad* is given the broader, and more usual, interpretation of 'child'.
204 See al-Ramlī, vi. 20; Coulson, *Succession*, p. 73. This case is also known as *al-Mushtaraka* (see Ibn Rushd, ii. 289; Coulson, *Succession*, p. 74).
205 See *Muw.* i. 332; Ibn Rushd, ii. 289–90; Coulson, *Succession*, pp. 74–5. This situation would only apply when there were two or more uterines who would thus theoretically be due the remaining third of the estate and thereby exclude the germanes; if there was only one uterine collateral, it was agreed that he or she would take a sixth, while any agnatic collaterals, however many there were, would share the remaining sixth between them (see Ibn Rushd, ii. 290).
206 See al-Ramlī, vi. 23, 24; also, Coulson, *Succession*, p. 79.
207 See al-Ṭabarī, vi. 26, and above, p. 107.
208 See *Muw. Sh.*, p. 252; *Mab.* xxix. 180; Ibn Rushd, ii. 290.
209 See *Muw.* i. 333–4; *Umm*, iv. 11.
210 For these arguments, see *Umm*, iv. 11; Ibn Rushd, ii. 290.
211 For these judgements, see *Muw.* i. 333–4; Ibn Rushd, ii. 291.
212 This assumes the presence of a male amongst the germanes: consanguines are not excluded by a single germane sister (see *Muw.* i. 333; Coulson, *Succession*, p. 67).
213 For these judgements, see *Muw.* i. 334–5; Coulson, *Succession*, pp. 85–6.
214 See Ibn Rushd, ii. 292–3; Coulson, *Succession*, pp. 79ff (where other solutions, including two different ones by Ibn Masʿūd, are mentioned).
215 See above, p. 74, for the interpretation of *ikhwa* as 'more than one collateral'.
216 See above, p. 109.
217 See *Muw.* i. 337; Coulson, *Succession*, p. 87.
218 See Coulson, *Succession*, pp. 87–8.
219 See *Muw.* i. 334.
220 See Ibn Rushd, ii. 298.
221 See *Muw.* i. 331–2, 336–7.
222 See *Muw.* i. 336–7.
223 The same point is made by Ziadeh in his review of Powers' *Studies*: 'The often-quoted *ḥadīth* about ʿUmar not knowing what *kalāla* was ... refers to uncertainty about collaterals and their shares, not to what the word itself means' (see Ziadeh, review of Powers' *Studies*, pp. 488).
224 See above, p. 64.
225 For this principle and the example mentioned, see, for example, al-Qarāfī, *Dhakhīra*, p. 59 [= *Tanqīḥ*, p. 25]; al-Bājaqnī, p. 75–7; Wuld Abbāh, pp. 50–1; Abū Zahra, pp. 141–3; Zaydān, pp. 361–3; for the alternative name see, for example, Ibn Ḥamdūn, i. 16.
226 This is a loose translation. The original reads *wa-mā llāhu aʿlamu bi-ʿudhri dhālika mina l-ʿabd* in *Muw.* i. 221, *Muw.* (ed. ʿAbd al-Bāqī), p. 201, and al-Zurqānī, ii.

110 [cf. *Muw. Abū Muṣʿab*, i. 315: '*mā llāhu aʿlamu bi-ʿudhri dhālika min ʿabdihi*'], and *wa-llāhu aʿlamu bi-qadri dhālika mina l-ʿabd* in al-Bājī, ii. 161.

227 Q 2: 184.

228 *Muw.* i. 221.

229 See al-Ṭabarī, ii. 84–5 and *Qawānīn*, p. 119 (where such a view is attributed to Ibn Sīrīn); ʿAbd ar-Razzāq, iv. 219 and Ibn al-ʿArabī, i. 77 (where such a view is attributed to ʿAṭāʾ).

230 See al-Bājī, ii. 62.

231 See above, p. 97.

232 See above, p. 98.

233 For the different types of *mafhūm al-mukhālafa*, see al-Qarāfī, *Dhakhīra*, p. 59 [= *Tanqīḥ*, pp. 25f]; also: Abū Zahra, pp. 152ff; Zaydān, pp. 366ff; al-Bājaqnī, pp. 79ff; Wuld Abbāh, p. 51.

234 See above, p. 100.

235 See above, pp. 102–3.

236 See above, p. 82.

237 See above, pp. 82–3.

238 See above, p. 83.

239 See al-Zurqānī, ii. 273; *Qawānīn*, p. 136; cf. Ibn Rushd, i. 290.

240 *Muw.* i. 290.

241 See *Qawānīn*, p. 136.

242 See al-Bājī, ii. 253, iii. 73. Cf. Ibn Rushd, i. 289, 290.

243 *Muw.* ii. 33.

244 This represents the usual interpretation (e.g. Jalālayn, p. 83; Ibn Juzayy, *Tafsīr*, p. 119). The pronouns in both 'if they desire' and 'agreement between them' are also said by some to refer to the two arbiters, and, by others, to the husband and wife (see Ibn Juzayy, *Tafsīr*, p. 119).

245 See *Muw.* ii. 33.

246 See al-Bājī, iv. 114; al-Jaṣṣāṣ, ii. 189ff (esp. 191); Ibn Rushd, ii. 81; Ibn Juzayy, *Tafsīr*, p. 119.

247 See Ibn Rushd, ii. 82, 84.

248 See *Muw.* i. 267; and, for a slightly different version, Ibn al-ʿArabī, i. 46–7.

249 See al-Ṭabarī, ii. 29; al-Bājī, ii. 301; al-Zurqānī, ii. 218. The reading *an* ***lā*** *yaṭṭawwafa bi-himā* is attributed in particular to Ibn Masʿūd, Ibn ʿAbbās, Anas, ʿAlī and Ubayy (see al-Ṭabarī, ii. 29; Ibn Khālawayh, p. 11; Jeffery, *Materials*, pp. 28, 120, 185, 195, 216).

250 See al-Jaṣṣāṣ, i. 96; Ibn Rushd, i. 278; *Qawānīn*, pp. 128–9.

251 See *Muw.* i. 258.

252 See above, pp. 85–6.

253 For these exceptions to *mafhūm al-mukhālafa*, see al-Qarāfī, *Dhakhīra*, p. 99 [= *Tanqīḥ*, pp. 119–20]; al-Bājaqnī, pp. 77–9; Abū Zahra, pp. 151–2; Zaydān, p. 370.

Chapter Seven – Chronological Considerations

1 See *Jāmiʿ*, p. 211. Cf. al-Ṭabarī, xviii. 112; Ibn al-ʿArabī, iii. 1384–5; Ibn Juzayy, *Tafsīr*, p. 478.

2 Another example of how the *sharīʿa* was adapted to local circumstances is that whereas Mālik had ruled that there was *zakāt* on raisins but not on figs, the judgement of the Mālikī *ʿulamāʾ* in al-Andalus was that in al-Andalus *zakāt* applied to figs as well as raisins, since figs there were a common food that was dried and stored and thus came under the *zakāt*-able category of *qūt* ('staples'), whereas in Madina they were never found in any great quantity and were usually eaten as a fresh fruit (see al-Bājī, ii. 171; Ibn al-ʿArabī, ii. 753; cf. *Muw.* i. 206).
3 See above, p. 40.
4 *Muw.* i. 215–6. (The example in question relates to being allowed not to fast when travelling).
5 For Muslim views on *naskh*, including that of the Muʿtazila, see, for example: al-Qarāfī, *Dhakhīra*, pp. 104–8 [= *Tanqīḥ*, pp. 132–40]; al-Bājaqnī, pp. 85–91; Abū Zahra, pp. 184–97; Zaydān, pp. 388–92; Ahmad Hasan, '*Naskh*', pp. 181–200, esp. pp. 184–8; Powers, *Studies*, pp. 143–4; Burton, *Sources*, pp. 30–1.
6 See *Muw.* ii. 133.
7 See Abū ʿUbayd (Arabic text), p. 81; Ibn Rushd, ii. 280, 281. For bequests, see also above, p. 75.
8 See Abū ʿUbayd (Arabic text), p. 82; Ibn Rushd, ii. 280. For the *ḥadīth* in question, see *Muw.* ii. 138–9.
9 See above, pp. 48–9, also 57, 60.
10 *Muw.* ii. 45.
11 See *Umm*, v. 23, vii. 208; Abd-Allah, 'Concept', p. 639; cf. Burton, *Collection*, pp. 88, 89.
12 e.g. al-Layth ibn Saʿd (see al-Zurqānī, iii. 94).
13 See *Muw.* ii. 42–3, 45; *Muw. Sh.*, p. 212.
14 See Ibn Rushd, ii. 29–30; *Hidāya*, i. 223; al-Zurqānī, iii. 94; cf. *Muw.* ii. 45.
15 See *Muw.* ii. 45.
16 See *Muw.* ii. 44; Ibn Rushd, ii. 30.
17 See al-Bājī, iv. 156; al-Zurqānī, iii. 93; and above, pp. 41, 60.
18 See above, p. 49.
19 *Muw.* ii. 168.
20 Burton mentions that Mālik gives 'three possible sources' for the stoning penalty and that he 'was not . . . too concerned about the actual source of the stoning penalty' ('Exegesis of Q 2: 106', p. 466, n. 45) and 'made no attempt to resolve his materials' (*Collection*, p. 94; see also *Sources*, pp. 127–36). This argument, however, presupposes that not all three options can be 'right' at the same time and that only one (if any) is the true source, whereas in fact they are not necessarily mutually contradictory or irreconcilable (and certainly were not in Mālik's eyes). Burton himself denies the historical validity of all three of these 'sources', inclining rather to the view that the penalty is a later borrowing from Judaism brought in initially for exegetical purposes and only later acquiring a legal reality (see *Collection*, pp. 70–1; 'Origin', pp. 25–6; 'Law and Exegesis', p. 269).
21 In a related context, Burton notes, in my opinion correctly, that '[Mālik's] doctrine that slaves do not acquire *iḥṣān* had not resulted from his knowledge of the Qurʾān but from his knowledge of the Fiqh, i.e. from his observation that slaves are not in practice stoned' ('Iḥṣān', p. 54); and, again: 'One

perceives that, throughout, the really significant factor is the practice, that is, the Fiqh' (*Collection*, p. 33).

22 See Ibn Ḥajar, *Fatḥ*, xii. 118; Burton, 'Iḥṣān', p. 47; idem, *Collection*, pp. 91, 93. For Mālik's strong criticism of the Khawārij and other sectarian groups, see, for example, *Mud.* i. 83–4, 182; *Jāmiᶜ*, p. 125.

23 This word is also interpreted as meaning 'suitable [for marriage]' (see al-Zamakhsharī, p. 950; al-Bayḍāwī, iv. 79; Ibn Juzayy, *Tafsīr*, p. 472).

24 See *Muw. Sh.*, pp. 344–5.

25 See Ibn al-ᶜArabī, iii. 1316–20 (where Ibn al-ᶜArabī says that this is in fact a case of an exception to a general rule (*takhṣīṣ al-ᶜumūm*) rather than *naskh*); Ibn Rushd, ii. 33–4; *Muw. Sh.*, p. 345; Abū ᶜUbayd, pp. 33–8 (Arabic text).

26 See, for example, 'Origin', p. 22; 'Exegesis of Q 2: 106', p. 469; 'Introductory essay' to Abū ᶜUbayd, p. 34; *Sources*, pp. 3–4; cf. also 'Cranes', p. 259, where Burton speaks of the 'invention' of the stoning and suckling verses. For the related views of Wansbrough and Powers, see Wansbrough, *Quranic Studies*, p. 197; Powers, *Studies*, p. 145, also 52, 188.

27 See al-Suyūṭī, *Itqān*, i. 84; al-Wāḥidī, p. 3; cf. Burton, *Collection*, p. 16.

28 For the uncertainty about which verse is the 'verse of *tayammum*', see Ibn al-ᶜArabī, i. 441–2; *Tanwīr*, i. 57.

29 See *Muw.* i. 57.

30 See *Muw.* i. 155, referring to Q 2: 144, 149–50.

31 See *Muw.* ii. 23–4, referring to Q 24: 6–9.

32 See *Muw.* ii. 35 (twice), referring to Q 2: 229 and 231.

33 See *Muw.* ii. 42, 44, referring to Q 33: 59 (this being the *āyat al-ḥijāb* according to *Jāmiᶜ*, p. 210, n. 3; but cf. also Q 33: 53 and 24: 31) and Q 33: 5 respectively.

34 See *Muw.* i. 219, referring to Q 2: 183–7.

35 See *Muw.* i. 336, referring to Q 4: 176 (see also above, p. 107).

36 *Muw.* i. 161, 160.

37 See *Muw.* ii. 24.

38 See Rippin, 'Al-Zarkashī and al-Suyūṭī', p. 258; idem, '*Asbāb al-Nuzūl*', p. 2; also below, p. 218, n. 65.

39 See above, pp. 117–18.

40 See *Muw.* i. 170.

41 See above, p. 102; also, pp. 33–4.

42 See *Muw.* i. 276.

43 For these meanings, see *Lisān*, xix. 198–9; *Tāj*, x. 213.

44 See al-Bukhārī, vi. 208; al-Ṭabarī, xv. 114–15.

45 See al-Ṭabarī, xv. 115; Ibn al-ᶜArabī, iii. 1214–15.

46 See al-Bukhārī, vi. 208; al-Ṭabarī, xv. 113.

47 See al-Ṭabarī, xv. 115; al-Wāḥidī, p. 224; al-Suyūṭī, *Lubāb*, p. 142.

48 See al-Ṭabarī, xv. 114 (where 'ᶜAbdallāh ibn Rāshid' is presumably an editorial or scribal error); al-Wāḥidī, p. 224; al-Zurqānī, i. 392.

49 See al-Suyūṭī, *Lubāb*, p. 142; al-Zurqānī, i. 391.

50 See al-Ṭabarī, xv. 115; al-Jaṣṣāṣ, iii. 211–12; Ibn al-ᶜArabī, iii. 1215.

51 See al-Zurqānī, i. 392, citing the *Istidhkār* of Ibn ᶜAbd al-Barr. This view is also mentioned by al-Bājī as being that of Ziyād ibn ᶜAbd al-Raḥmān (the Andalusian transmitter of the *Muwaṭṭa'* from whom Yaḥyā ibn Yaḥyā al-Laythī first learnt it), and by al-Jaṣṣāṣ and Ibn al-ᶜArabī as that of certain

unspecified authorities (see al-Bājī, i. 360–1; al-Jaṣṣāṣ, iii. 211; Ibn al-ᶜArabī, iii. 1215).

52 See above, pp. 97–8.
53 See al-Ṭabarī, xv. 116.
54 See *Muw.* i. 276. Al-Bājī (iii. 18) specifies that this was the opinion of Mālik's teacher Rabīᶜa.
55 See *Muw.* i. 275–6. For the part of this report referring to the words *rafath* and *fusūq* in the same verse, see above, p. 97.
56 See al-Zurqānī, ii. 233.
57 See al-Ṭabarī, ii. 154.
58 See al-Ṭabarī, ii. 152–3.
59 See al-Ṭabarī, ii. 154; al-Bājī, iii. 18.
60 See al-Ṭabarī, ii. 154; Mujāhid, *Tafsīr*, p. 102.
61 See Ibn Mujāhid, p. 180; *Nashr*, ii. 204, i. 285; al-Fārisī, ii. 286–92.
62 See al-Bukhārī, ii. 347–8; al-Ṭabarī, ii. 155.
63 In fact, the Madinan Abū Jaᶜfar read all three nouns with *tanwīn* (see *Nashr*, ii. 204), but this is effectively the same as reading them all with *lā li-nafy al-jins* in that no contrast is made between any of the terms.
64 See above, p. 98.
65 See above, p. 126. This is in agreement with Rippin, who concludes, against Wansbrough's view that the essential function of the *asbāb* material is to provide a chronology of revelation (see Wansbrough, *Quranic Studies*, pp. 38, 141, 177), that 'the primary (i.e., predominant) function of the *sabab* in exegetical texts is not halakhic' and that 'the essential role of the material is found in haggadic exegesis; that is, the *sabab* functions to provide an interpretation of a verse within a basic narrative framework' (see '*Asbāb al-Nuzūl*', p. 19).
66 Goldziher, for example, refers to the Umayyads as 'godless' (*Muslim Studies*, ii. 40, 101, 107) and 'completely opposed to religion' (p. 89), and to their rule as 'entirely secular' (pp. 40, 60), 'showing little concern with religious law' (p. 40), echoing what he sees as the traditional Muslim view of the Umayyads' 'godlessness and opposition to religion' (p. 62) and their being 'the enemies of Islam' (p. 345). Among more recent scholars, Crone and Hinds, although not holding the view themselves, also speak of a traditional Islamicist and Muslim view that the Umayyads had little, if any, religious authority (*God's Caliph*, p. 1) and that their concept of the caliphate was 'an un-Islamic deviation' (p. 58). For acknowledgement, though not necessarily acceptance, of the same anti-Umayyad prejudice, see, for instance, *EI (1)*, iv. 999; Schacht, *Origins*, p. 213 (cited below, p. 152); Hawting, *Dynasty*, pp. 11–18, 123–8; *SALP*, ii. 18; Bosworth, *Dynasties*, p. 4. In this context, it is refreshing to note Burton's disagreement with Goldziher on this point, and his acknowledgement of 'the lively interest believed to have been taken in the details of religious affairs by several representatives of the ruling house, and by numbers of their high officials and functionaries' (see Burton, *Introduction*, p. xiii).
67 See *Istīᶜāb*, i. 253; *Usd*, iv. 385; *Iṣāba*, vi. 113; *EI (2)*, vii. 264; *SALP*, ii. 19.
68 See *Muw.* i. 219–20, ii. 208–9, 231–2.
69 See *Muw.* i. 49 (Marwān) and ii. 83, 204 (ᶜUmar ibn ᶜAbd al-ᶜAzīz).
70 See *Muw.* i. 261.

71 See *Muw.* ii. 11.
72 See above, p. 33.
73 See Ibn al-Jawzī, *Manāqib*, pp. 72–3; Ibn Kathīr, *ʿUmar ibn ʿAbd al-ʿAzīz*, p. 70.
74 See Ibn Ḥibbān, v. 119; al-Shīrāzī, p. 62; *Tahdhīb*, vi. 423; *SALP*, ii. 20; cf. Dixon, *Caliphate*, pp. 20–1.
75 The main references are to the following six caliphs (although in many instances relating to when they were governors rather than caliphs):
   i) Muʿāwiya ibn Abī Sufyān (*Muw.* i. 189, 219–10, 241, 250, 284, 333, ii. 29, 31, 59, 117, 182, 187, 193, 208, 231–2)
   ii) Marwān ibn al-Ḥakam (*Muw.* i. 49, 213, 261, 326, ii. 11, 16, 18, 19, 30, 63, 112, 154, 176, 177, 182, 187, 188, 193, 221)
   iii) ʿAbd al-Malik ibn Marwān (*Muw.* i. 244, 280, ii. 11, 116, 146, 193, 250).
   iv) al-Walīd ibn ʿAbd al-Malik (*Muw.* i. 241, ii. 15).
   v) ʿUmar ibn ʿAbd al-ʿAzīz (*Muw.* i. 11, 118, 188, 193, 194, 201–2, 206, 207, 248, 270, 298, 303, 339, ii. 4, 16, 52, 83, 108, 111, 163, 170, 171, 173, 174–5, 188, 203, 204, 208, 255).
   vi) Yazīd ibn ʿAbd al-Malik (*Muw.* ii. 37).

   There are also several references to other Madinan governors during the Umayyad period, such as Saʿīd ibn al-ʿĀṣ (*Muw.* ii. 173), Jābir ibn al-Aswad (*Muw.* ii. 35), Ṭāriq ibn ʿAmr (*Muw.* i. 177), al-Ḥajjāj ibn Yūsuf (*Muw.* i. 280), Abān ibn ʿUthmān (*Muw.* i. 37, 244, 253–4, ii. 16, 48, 71, 139, 145) and Hishām ibn Ismāʿīl (*Muw.* ii. 48, 71). Ṭalḥa ibn ʿAbdallāh ibn ʿAwf, who was a *qāḍī* and, later, governor of Madina, is referred to in *Muw.* ii. 26, while Abū Bakr ibn Ḥazm, also a *qāḍī* and, later, governor, is referred to in *Muw.* i. 206, ii. 16, 64, 107, 131, 145, 177, 181, 195, 240, 260. Certain other governors from this period are also referred to, e.g. ʿAbdallāh ibn al-Zubayr, referred to as the 'governor' (*amīr*) of Makka in *Muw.* ii. 34, Zurayq ibn Ḥakīm, who was ʿUmar ibn ʿAbd al-ʿAzīz's governor of Ayla (*Muw.* ii. 171, 173), and ʿAbd al-Ḥamīd ibn ʿAbd al-Raḥmān ibn Zayd ibn al-Khaṭṭāb, who was his governor of Kufa (*Muw.* ii. 108).
76 This man is identified by al-Zurqāni, following Ibn Ḥajar, as al-Aḥwaṣ ibn ʿAbd (*sic*) ibn Umayya ibn ʿAbd Shams, a former governor of Baḥrayn under Muʿāwiya (see al-Zurqāni, iii. 60; *Iṣāba*, i. 20–1), but given as al-Aḥwaṣ ibn ʿAbd Umayya (*sic*) ibn ʿAbd Shams by Ibn al-Kalbī (i. 58; Caskel, ii. 146), al-Zubayrī (pp. 151–2) and Ibn Ḥazm (p. 69). Al-Shāfiʿī, however, identifies him as al-Aḥwaṣ ibn Ḥakīm (Ḥukaym?), a Syrian narrator of *ḥadīth* (see *Umm*, v. 192; *Tahdhīb*, i. 192–3).
77 See *Muw.* ii. 29–30; *Muw. Sh.*, p. 205.
78 See *Lisān*, i. 125–6.
79 See *Muw.* ii. 29–30.
80 See *Muw.* ii. 29.
81 See *Muw. Sh.*, p. 206 ('thirteen Companions'); also *Mab.* vi. 13 ('more than ten', including also Abū Bakr, Abū l-Dardāʾ, ʿUbāda ibn al-Ṣāmit and ʿAbdallāh ibn Qays); Ibn Rushd, ii. 74 ('eleven or twelve', including also Abū Mūsā al-Ashʿarī).
82 See above, p. 59.
83 See above, p. 59.
84 See al-Bājī, iv. 95; Ibn al-ʿArabī, i. 184; Ibn Rushd, ii. 74–5.
85 See *Muw.* ii. 30.

86 Although al-Shāfiʿī's two examples contain a third radical *yāʾ* rather than *hamza*, the form *qaraʾa* is also attested for the same meaning in the expression *mā qaraʾat (hādhihī) l-nāqa salan qaṭṭ* ('(This) camel['s womb] has never enclosed a foetus') (see *Mab.* vi. 13; al-Bājī, iv. 94; Ibn Rushd, ii. 74; *Lisān*, i. 123; cf. al-Bukhārī, vii. 184).

87 See *Umm*, v. 191; cf. Ibn Rushd, ii. 74; *Lisān*, i. 126.

88 See Ibn Rushd, ii. 74; al-Bājaqnī, pp. 42–3, 46.

89 See *Mab.* vi. 13; Ibn al-ʿArabī, i. 185; Ibn Rushd, ii. 74; al-Bājaqnī, p. 46.

90 See *Muw. Sh.*, p. 186.

91 See *Mab.* vi. 14–15; Ibn Rushd, ii. 75.

92 See al-Bājī, iv. 95.

93 See *Mab.* vi. 14; Ibn Rushd, ii. 74.

94 See Ibn al-ʿArabī, i. 185.

95 See *Mab.* vi. 14; *Lisān*, i. 125–6.

96 See, for example, al-Bājī, iv. 94–5.

97 See *Muw.* i. 333–4.

98 See *Muw.* ii. 182, 193. (The judgement on drunkards is also mentioned in *Muw.* ii. 35).

99 See Q 2: 178: *kutiba ʿalaykumu l-qiṣāṣu fī l-qatlā ... fa-man ʿufiya lahu min akhīhi shayʾun fa-ttibāʿun bi-l-maʿrūfi wa-adāʾun ilayhi bi-iḥsān* ('Retaliation has been prescribed for you in cases of murder ... but if anyone [i.e. the victim or his relatives] is given anything [i.e. blood-money] by his brother [i.e. the perpetrator], it should be sought from him [i.e. by the victim's relatives] in an acceptable fashion and paid to him [i.e. the victim's relatives] in a correct manner'). (This translation represents one of two interpretations and follows Mālik's *tafsīr* of the verse as given in *Muw.* ii. 189; see al-Bājī, vii. 103; Ibn al-ʿArabī, i. 66; Ibn Juzayy, *Tafsīr*, p. 45; cf. *Lisān*, xix. 304). For details about these options (including the third option of pardon), see, in addition to the above references, Ibn Rushd, ii. 336; *Qawānīn*, p. 340.

100 See Q 4: 92.

101 See al-Bājī, iv. 125 (also vii. 71, 120); *Umm*, v. 235. Cf. *Bayān*, v. 361–2, xvi. 97, 144–6, where the judgement concerning madmen is further discussed.

102 See *Muw.* ii. 193. Cf. *Bayān*, xv. 461.

103 *Muw.* ii. 193.

104 See al-Shaybānī, *Ḥujja*, iv. 389ff; *Mab.* xxvi. 124; *Umm*, vi. 4–6, vii. 299–300; Ibn Rushd, ii. 332–3. For the *ḥadīth*, see Ibn Rushd, ii. 322; cf. al-Tirmidhī, i. 267; Ibn Mājah, ii. 58.

105 For this being an instance of *sharʿ man qablanā*, see above, p. 85.

106 See *Muw.* ii. 181.

107 See *Muw.* ii. 187.

108 *Muw.* ii. 187.

109 See *Muw.* ii. 185. For the mathematics of the judgement about molars, see al-Bājī, vii. 93.

110 *Muw.* ii. 187.

111 See al-Bājī, vii. 93.

112 *Muw.* ii. 187.

113 See *Muw. Sh.*, p. 229; *Umm*, vii. 287.

114 See *Umm*, v. 262; *Mab.* vii. 19.

115 See *Muw.* ii. 18–19.

116 *Muw.* ii. 19; cf. *Muw. Sh.*, p. 195.
117 See *Muw.* ii. 19; *Umm*, v. 247–8, 256; *Muw. Sh.*, p. 195; *Mab.* vii. 20; Ibn Rushd, ii. 83.
118 See Ibn Rushd, ii. 83; Ibn al-ᶜArabī, i. 180; *Muw. Sh.*, p. 195.
119 See *Muw. Sh.*, p. 195.
120 See *Mab.* vii. 21; Ibn Rushd, ii. 83.
121 See *Mab.* vii. 20; and, for the reading itself, Jeffery, pp. 30, 121. This reading does not otherwise seem to appear in the arguments of either group, a fact which may indicate either a lack of importance given to it (it only represented the *ijtihād* of an individual Companion), or possibly a late origin (for this last possibility with regard to another reading mentioned by al-Sarakhsī but not obviously referred to before his time, see Hawting, 'Role', pp. 432–3; and below, p. 222, n. 144). Cf. al-Ṭabarī, ii. 241ff, where the reading is not mentioned, although the view of Ibn Masᶜūd reflected in the reading is.
122 See Ibn Rushd, ii. 84. Cf. *Muw.* ii. 19 and *Umm*, v. 257, where this judgement is clearly assumed.
123 See Q 2: 229–30: 'Divorce is twice; then either retention in an acceptable manner or dismissal (*tasrīḥ*) with kindness ... If he divorces her, he may not remarry her [lit. 'she is not *ḥalāl* for him'] afterwards until she has married a husband other than him ...'
124 See *Muw.* ii. 16.
125 See *Muw.* ii. 16.
126 See Ibn Rushd, ii. 50; *Qawānīn*, p. 228.
127 This was presumably in the year 91 AH, when al-Walīd, as caliph, led the pilgrimage and also visited Madina; he may also have led the pilgrimage in 78 (see Caetani, pp. 1111, 928).
128 See *Muw.* ii. 15.
129 See al-Zurqānī, iii. 34.
130 See *Muw.* ii. 18.
131 See *Muw. Sh.*, pp. 191–2; al-Ramlī, vi. 430; Ibn Rushd, ii. 59.
132 This was variously interpreted as referring to either the woman's committing *zinā*, or her leaving the marital home before the *ᶜidda* was up, or wrong actions in general, or her being ill-spoken towards her in-laws, or her disobedience (*nushūz*) to her husband before divorce, these last two being reflected in the *shādhdh* variant *illā an* ***yafḥushna ᶜalaykum*** attributed to Ubayy and Ibn Masᶜūd (see Ibn Juzayy, *Tafsīr*, p. 772; ᶜAbd al-Razzāq, vi. 322–3; al-Ṭabarī, xxviii. 78–80; and, for the variant reading, Jeffery, pp. 102, 171, 206, 265, 274, 308). For a probable origin of these interpretations, see below, p. 222, n. 143.
133 See al-Ṭabarī, xxviii. 80 (cf. Abū Dāwūd, ii. 244); al-Jaṣṣāṣ, iii. 455 (also i. 380); Ibn al-ᶜArabī, iv. 1817–21; Ibn Juzayy, *Tafsīr*, p. 772; Jalālayn, p. 579.
134 See, for example, Ibn al-ᶜArabī, iv. 1827; Ibn Rushd, ii. 78.
135 See al-Zurqānī, iii. 63; also *Istīᶜāb*, ii. 782; *Iṣāba*, viii. 247ff.
136 See *Muw.* ii. 31.
137 See *Mud.* v. 20 (cited below, pp. 144–5), 153; cf. *Muw.* ii. 31–2.
138 *Muw.* ii. 30; *Muw. Sh.*, p. 201.
139 *Muw.* i. 31–2.
140 See *Umm*, v. 209.
141 See Ibn Rushd, ii. 78; Ibn Juzayy, *Tafsīr*, p. 774; Hawting, 'Role', p. 433.

142 *Mud.* v. 20; cf. ibid, v. 153. Note that Hawting's overlooking of *Mud.* v. 20 leads him to wrongly conclude that 'Mālik's denial of *nafaqa* for the woman who is irrevocably divorced and who is not pregnant is justified solely by reference to the report (*athar*) of Fāṭima bint Qays' and not to the Qur'an (see Hawting, 'Role', p. 435; also n. 148 below.

143 These were the three reasons given for Fāṭima being told to observe her *ʿidda* elsewhere (see al-Bukhārī, vii. 186; Abū Dāwūd, ii. 244–6; al-Bājī, iv. 102; al-Zurqānī, iii. 62) and are presumably the reasons that led to the various interpretations of Q 65: 1's *fāḥisha mubayyina* (see above, p. 221, n. 132).

144 For ʿUmar's judgement, see *Umm*, vii. 146, and the references in n. 145 below. For Ibn Masʿūd's reading, see Jeffery, p. 102; for its relative lack of importance in the arguments on this point, despite Schacht's opposite view, see Hawting, 'Role', pp. 430–3, and, for a similar instance, above, p. 221, n. 121.

145 For these arguments, see *Mab.* v. 202; Ibn Rushd, ii. 79. For ʿUmar's *ḥadīth*, see also Abū Dāwūd, ii. 244; al-Nasāʾī, ii. 116.

146 See Ibn Rushd, ii. 78; Hawting, 'Role', p. 434.

147 See Hawting, 'Role', p. 436.

148 Hawting comes to the conclusion that the references to the Qur'an in this debate 'are likely to be secondary' ('Role', p. 444). He argues that 'it is relatively easy to understand how the debate about the position of the divorced woman during her *ʿidda* would have arisen in early Islam as it strove to adopt the *ʿidda* and the attenuated divorce process into a system of marriage which previously knew neither. To that extent, therefore, we do not need to postulate either the Sunna or the Qurʾān as starting points for the debate ... However, it seems that the *ḥadīth* of Fāṭima bint Qays is likely to have been the earliest ingredient', from which he concludes that this debate about the rights of *mabtūta* divorcees 'seems to provide evidence of the use of a prophetic tradition in support of a legal argument at a stage prior to the use of companion traditions or the Qurʾān' (p. 445). We should, however, remember that observing the *ʿidda* is itself a practice introduced by the Qur'an and that the whole debate is therefore essentially Qur'anic in its origin (for the Qur'anic origin of the *ʿidda*, see, for example, Abū Dāwūd, ii. 241; and, for the different types of *ʿidda* mentioned in the Qur'an, above, p. 203, n. 12). Indeed, that the Qur'anic commands *askinū* and *anfiqū* should refer to the rights of divorcees during their *ʿidda* is only natural: this is, after all, the context, which is emphasised even more clearly by the judgement later in the same verse that a divorcee has the right to receive a fee for nursing her and her (former) husband's child. Furthermore, that this was so for Mālik at least is shown by his overt reference to the Qur'an in his discussions on this point, despite Hawting's statement to the contrary (see n. 142 above).

149 Q 9: 60, which details the eight categories of people entitled to receive *zakāt*, is the main exception. Mālik, contrary to some authorities, also considered Q 6: 141 – *wa-ātū ḥaqqahu yawma ḥiṣādihi* ('And give its due on the day of its harvest') – to refer specifically to the *zakāt* on crops (see *Muw.* i. 204). The numerous other references to *zakāt* in the Qur'an are all of a general nature.

150 Such reports include: (i) the Prophet's instructions to Muʿādh to collect *zakāt* from the people of Yemen (see al-Bukhārī, ii. 271), reflected in a report in the *Muwaṭṭaʾ* (i. 196) where Muʿādh is reported to have taken *zakāt* on forty and

thirty cows but not from less than that because he had not received instructions from the Prophet on less than that; (ii) his instructions to ʿAmr ibn Ḥazm, again for the people of Yemen, regarding (amongst other things) *zakāt* and blood-money (see *Tanwīr*, ii. 181; *SALP*, ii. 24; also above, p. 137); and (iii) the 'book' (*kitāb*) about *zakāt* on livestock which ʿUmar is said to have inherited from Abū Bakr, who in turn got it from the Prophet (see *Tanwīr*, i. 195; and, for the 'book' itself, *Muw.* i. 195).

151 See Muslim, i. 22–3; al-Bukhārī, ix. 286–7. For the same report, but with the word *ʿanāq* ('she-kid') rather than *ʿiqāl* ('hobbling-cord'), see al-Bukhārī, ii. 274, ix. 46–7 (also ix. 340–1). Cf. *Muw.* i. 201, where Mālik says that he has heard (*balaghahu*) that Abū Bakr said, 'If they were to withhold even a hobbling-cord from me (*law manaʿūnī ʿiqālan*), I would fight them for it.'

152 See above, p. 222, n. 150; also, for example, *Muw.* i. 188, where there are Prophetic *ḥadīths* detailing the *niṣāb* for camels, silver and dates.

153 See *Muw.* i. 206; *Muw. Sh.*, p. 118.

154 See *Muw.* i. 206; *Muw. Sh.*, p. 118.

155 See *Muw.* i. 206.

156 See *Muw.* i. 188. For the meaning of *māshiya*, see *Lisān*, xx. 150.

157 See *Muw. Sh.*, p. 118; Ibn Rushd, i. 231.

158 See *Umm*, vii. 220; al-Bājī, ii. 172; al-Zurqānī, ii. 72.

159 See Ibn Rushd, i. 231; also *Muw.* i. 206, 303; *Muw. Sh.*, p. 118; *Umm*, ii. 22, vii. 220. For the question of the original practice in Madina, see al-Bājī, ii. 171–2; also *Umm*, ii. 22.

160 *Muw.* i. 206.

161 See *Umm*, ii. II: 29; Ibn Rushd, i. 232.

162 See *Muw. Sh.*, p. 115 [= *Muw.* i. 202]; *Mab.* iii. 2–3; al-Bājī, ii. 171; Ibn Rushd, i. 232 (reading *qaḍb* for the printed *qaṣb*, as in al-Bājī [ii. 71] and as specified by al-Zurqānī [ii. 71]).

163 See al-Nīsābūrī, iii. 88. Since Abū Bakr's opponents were referred to as apostates, this judgement suggests that the refusal to abandon *ribā* could, in certain circumstances, also be considered tantamount to apostasy (*ridda*).

164 Note also the severe warnings in the *ḥadīth*-literature against *ribā*, the least form of which is described as being equivalent to a man having intercourse with his mother (see Ibn Mājah, ii. 22).

165 *Muw.* ii. 89, citing Q 2: 279. Notice also the 'inclusive' interpretation of *ribā* implied in the phrase 'neither a little nor a lot of it is allowed.'

166 See above, p. 213, n. 196.

167 For this meaning, see al-Zurqānī, iii. 112; *Lisān*, xix. 115.

168 See *Muw.* ii. 59; *Muw. Sh.*, p. 290. For similar reports mentioning ʿUbāda ibn al-Ṣāmit and/or Abū Saʿīd (al-Khudrī?) rather than Abū l-Dardāʾ, see Ibn Mājah, i. 7; al-Zurqānī, iii. 112; Ibn Rushd, ii. 164.

169 Cf. *Muw.* ii. 58, where in a *ḥadīth* from the Prophet a similar transaction is specifically referred to as *ribā.*

170 See al-Zurqānī, iii. 112 (citing Ibn ʿAbd al-Barr); Ibn Rushd, ii. 163, 164; also *Muw.* ii. 58–61. *Ribawī* substances were differently defined by the different schools of law, but all included the six categories of gold, silver, wheat, barley, dates and salt (see Ibn Rushd, ii. 107).

171 The word *ṣukūk* refers to written orders issued for the payment of a stipend, pension or allowance by the government (see Lane, *Lexicon*, p. 1707).

172 See *Muw.* ii. 63; cf. *Bayān*, vii. 355–7.
173 See *Bayān*, vii. 355–6; al-Bājī, iv. 285.
174 See above, pp. 80–1.
175 See *Muw.* ii. 170.
176 See above, p. 211, n. 143.
177 See al-Bājī, vii. 146–7; Ibn Rushd, ii. 369; al-Zurqānī, iv. 15. Cf. Wakīᶜ, i. 139, where we are told that Abū Bakr ibn Ḥazm endorsed the penalty of eighty lashes against a slave who had slandered a free man or woman; also ibid, i. 139, n. 1, where the same opinion is recorded from al-Awzāᶜī and Ibn Masᶜūd in addition to ᶜUmar ibn ᶜAbd al-ᶜAzīz.
178 See *Origins*, pp. 5, 190ff.
179 *Origins*, p. 213.
180 See *God's Caliph*, pp. 1, 43ff, especially pp. 58–9.

Chapter Eight – Qurᵓan and *Sunna*

1 *Muw.* ii. 208.
2 i.e. 31 out of 44, these being sections 1–3, 5, 7, 8, 11, 14–25, 27–31, 36–39, 41–43 in the English translation (Norwich, 1982).
3 i.e. sections 4, 6, 9, 10, 12 and 13 in the English translation.
4 e.g. Q 2: 43, *et passim.*
5 The words *ribā* and/or *gharar* are overtly mentioned in eighteen out of forty-six chapters in the *Kitāb al-buyūᶜ* (*Muw.* ii. 46–87), quite apart from their being implied in many others. For the Qurᵓanic prohibition against *ribā*, see above, p. 149, also p. 203, n. 12. *Gharar* is implicitly forbidden by extension from the prohibition of *maysir*, i.e. gambling, in Q 2: 219 and 5: 90–91 (for the equation of *gharar* with gambling (*qimār*), see *Muw.* ii. 55; and, for the mention of *maysir* in this context, *Muw.* ii. 70), as well as being explicitly forbidden in the *ḥadīth* (e.g. *Muw.* ii. 75).
6 See sections 26 (*ᶜaqīqa*); 40 (*tadbīr*); and 44 (*qasāma*).
7 *Origins*, pp. 224–5.
8 *Roman Law*, p. 23.
9 *Quranic Studies*, p. 44.
10 See Goitein, 'Birth-Hour', p. 24.
11 *History*, pp. 64–5; cf. ibid, p. 22.
12 *Studies*, p. 7.
13 See Coulson, *History*, p. 12.
14 This is the Kufan numbering, usual in printed editions of Ḥafṣ and also some modern editions of Warsh (e.g. Algiers, *ca.* 1399/1979). The traditional Madinan numbering results in a total of 6213 verses (e.g. *riwāyat* Qālūn, Beirut/Tunis, 1974; *riwāyat* Warsh, Bodleian Library MS. Arab. d. 141) or 6208 (e.g. *riwāyat* Warsh, Beirut, *ca.* 1392/1972).
15 See *History*, p. 12. Before him, Count Ostrorog had given the more traditional figure of five hundred rather than six hundred legal verses – which goes back at least to Muqātil (d. 150), whose *tafsīr* on these verses is entitled *Tafsīr al-khamsmiᵓat āya* ('The *Tafsīr* of the Five Hundred Verses') – although at the same time giving a rather surprising total of 'seven thousand

and sundry' verses in all, these figures deriving, he says, from 'original Oriental sources' (see Count Ostrorog, *The Angora Reform*, pp. 19 and 7). We should note also that certain modern Muslim authors, notably Khallāf and, following him, Zaydān, state that there are some seventy verses on family law, seventy on business and civil law, thirty on criminal law, thirteen on juridical procedure, ten on constitutional law, twenty-five on international law, and ten on taxation and social welfare, making a total of 228 altogether (see Khallāf, pp. 32–3; Zaydān, pp. 156–7).

16 'Birth-Hour', p. 24.

17 See, for example, al-Bayḍāwī, vi. 200; Ibn Juzayy, *Tafsīr*, p. 863; al-Zurqānī, i. 373.

18 See *Quranic Studies*, pp. 171–2.

19 See *Muw.* i. 299–305.

20 i.e. Q 8: 1, 41; 33: 50; 59: 6, 7; also 3: 161.

21 See above, pp. 157–8.

22 Q 2: 282. Cf. Q 5: 106 – 'Witnessing between you ... [should be done by] two men of integrity from among you (*shahādatu baynikum ... ithnāni dhawā ʿadlin minkum*)'; and Q 65: 2 – 'And have two men of integrity from among you bear witness (*wa-ashhidū dhaway ʿadlin minkum*)'.

23 In fact, the Kufans held that if the defendant refused to take an oath the property was automatically considered to belong to the plaintiff without the latter being required to take an oath himself. However, the point here, as Ibn ʿAbd al-Barr points out, is that the basic procedure is accepted by all and the oath of the defendant, or his refusal to take one, is considered valid evidence, even though this is not mentioned in the Qurʾan but derives, rather, from the *sunna* (see al-Zurqānī, iii. 184; Schacht, *Origins*, pp. 311–12, 314; also Ibn Rushd, ii. 391).

24 *Muw.* ii. 110.

25 See *Muw.* ii. 108.

26 See above, pp. 123–4.

27 i.e. shortening the prayer while travelling.

28 *Muw.* i. 124.

29 *Bayān* iii. 406, xvii. 148.

30 See *Bayān*, iii. 406, xvii. 148.

31 Two long sections of the Qurʾan (Q 2: 196–203 and Q 22: 27–37) deal specifically with the topic of *ḥajj*, whereas there is practically no mention of any details about the prayer, except for the fear prayer in Q 4: 101–3 and a disputed reference to *duʿāʾ* in Q 17: 110 (see above, pp. 126ff); nor are there any details about *zakāt*, except for Q 9: 60, and a possible reference in Q 6: 141 (see above, p. 222, n. 149). It is true, however, that the names and times of some of the prayers are referred to in Q 2: 238, 11: 114, 17: 78, 24: 58, 62: 9–10; cf. also 4: 103.

32 Abd-Allah notes forty instances of such *sunna*-terms (see 'Concept', pp. 549, 778–9).

33 See above, pp. 37–8.

34 See above, pp. 42–3.

35 See above, p. 40.

36 For examples, see above, pp. 74, 162; below, 164.

37 See Bravmann, *Spiritual Background*, pp. 139ff, 148, 159ff, where this concept is discussed in some detail; Schacht, *Origins*, pp. 62, 70; also Ansari,

'Terminology', p. 274, esp. n. 7. Guillaume, in his review of Schacht's *Origins* (p. 177), also noted that '*sunna māḍiya* is not, as Dr. Schacht translates, a "past *sunna*", but an established practice of the *present* going back to the past.' In this connection, it should be noted that in the Fourth Impression (1967) of Schacht's *Origins* the expression 'past *sunna*' on p. 70 has been changed to 'valid *sunna*', although the translation '*sunna* in the past' on p. 62 has been (inadvertently?) retained.

38 e.g. *Muw.* i. 70 (the *iqāma* is not doubled), 247 (when to stop the *talbiya*), 263 (how to do the *ṭawāf al-qudūm*), ii. 36 (the *ʿidda* for a pregnant widow is like that of a pregnant divorcee), 179 (different types of dates or dried fruits should not be steeped together). See also Abd-Allah, 'Concept', pp. 585–99, 780.

39 See above, p. 96.

40 See above, pp. 42–3.

41 *Muw.* i. 146.

42 We should point out that *sunna* here, in its undefined form, is not quite the same as the defined form *al-sunna* in Mālik's *sunna* terms. Here it has the rather more specific sense of a particular practice not being obligatory but nevertheless being recommended (because the Prophet did it), as opposed to its being the correct way of doing something (because that was how the Prophet did it). Cf. *Muw.* i. 322, where sacrificing an animal for the *ʿīd* is described as being a *sunna* rather than an obligatory practice.

43 See *Muw.* i. 252.

44 *Muw.* i. 111.

45 See *Muw.* i. 231.

46 *Muw.* ii. 91. Cf. Mālik's use of the expressions 'the *qirāḍ* of the Muslims' (*Muw.* ii. 90) and 'the *sunna* of *qirāḍ*' (*Muw.* ii. 97), and his comment that a certain practice 'is not one of the transactions of the Muslims' (*Muw.* ii. 60). The expression '*sunna* of the Muslims' also occurs three times in the section on *kitāba* (see *Muw.* ii. 148, 156 [twice]).

47 See *Muw.* ii. 101, and, for the same judgement, *Muw.* ii. 60. Cf. Abd-Allah, 'Concept', pp. 618ff.

48 See *Muw.* ii. 70; cf. Abd-Allah, 'Concept', pp. 615ff.

49 See *Muw.* i. 231.

50 See Gibb, *Mohammedanism*, p. 82; Schacht, 'Pre-Islamic Background', p. 42; Coulson, *History*, pp. 39, 56; Imtiaz Ahmad, '*Sunna* and *Ḥadīth*', pp. 44, 46.

51 See above, p. 37.

52 See above, p. 29.

53 See above, pp. 164–5, 161–2.

54 See Schacht, *Origins*, p. 68; idem, 'Pre-Islamic Background', p. 42; Burton, *Sources*, pp. 15, 213.

Chapter Nine – *Sunna versus Ḥadīth*

1 See above, p. 40.

2 Cf. above, p. 45.

3 The confusion between the two words has, in my view, been further exacerbated by translation of the word *ḥadīth* ('verbal report') as 'tradition',

thus giving it a meaning very much closer to the idea of *sunna* in the sense of 'general practice' or 'custom', which is clearly not the same as 'verbal report'. For the same general point, see Hodgson, *Venture*, i. 63–6.

4 See Vesey-Fitzgerald, *Muhammadan Law*, p. 3.

5 See Robson, 'Tradition'.

6 See above, p. 159.

7 Gibb, *Mohammedanism*, pp. 74–5. Ahmad Hasan also states that '*Ḥadīth* is the "carrier" and "vehicle" of the *Sunnah. Sunnah* is contained in *Ḥadīth*' (*Early Development*, pp. 86–7); elsewhere, though, he is aware of a different distinction (see below, p. 170).

8 *Origins*, p. 3; cf. ibid, p. 77. Schacht, however, although generally recognising a difference in meaning between the two terms, nevertheless makes the same mistake of equating the two as, for instance, when he says that 'the particular reputation of Medina as the "true home of the *sunna*" ... [is] incompatible with Shāfiʿī's terse statement: "We follow this [tradition from the Prophet], and so do all scholars in all countries except Medina"' (*Origins*, p. 8), which does not make sense unless one understands *sunna* to mean *ḥadīth*, which it obviously did not for the Madinans, as Schacht is at pains to point out later on (ibid, pp. 58ff; see also below, pp. 170–1, 172).

9 See Fyzee, *Outlines*, p. 18.

10 See Doi, *Sharīʿah*, pp. 45–63.

11 Ibid, p. 64.

12 Ibid, p. 48.

13 Ibid, p. 49.

14 See Suhaib Hasan, *Introduction to the Sunnah*, p. 23.

15 See Azmi, *On Schacht*, p. 91.

16 Ibid, pp. 80, 90; also 85.

17 Ibid, p. 102.

18 Ibid, p. 103.

19 Ibid, p. 109.

20 See ibid, p. 79.

21 See ibid, p. 86; also p. 81.

22 Ibid, p. 90.

23 *Muslim Studies*, ii. 24.

24 Ibid, ii. 24. Note that Aghnides, in his *Mohammedan Theories of Finance* (p. 36), follows Goldziher in saying that 'a *sunnah* may be embodied in a *ḥadīth* but is not itself a *ḥadīth*' and that 'it is ... possible for a *ḥadīth* to contradict the *sunnah*', but nevertheless misses Goldziher's second, and more important, point that not every *sunna* need necessarily be recorded in a *ḥadīth*.

25 See *Muslim Studies*, ii. 25; and above, pp. 18–19.

26 Ahmad Hasan, *Early Development*, p. 87.

27 See Ansari, 'Terminology', pp. 273–4. Note, however, how Ansari, like Ahmad Hasan, assumes that the terms *sunna* and *amr* mean the same, or nearly so, for Mālik (see above, p. 196, n. 53).

28 See 'Concept', *passim*, esp, pp. 79–80, 282–3. Interestingly, Abd-Allah's discussion of 'The *Sunnah*' in his section on Mālikī legal theory (pp. 155ff) concentrates mainly on the various types of *ḥadīth*.

29 Al-Sarakhsī, for example, comments that what is meant by *sunna* for the Iraqis is both the *sunna* of the Prophet and the *sunna* of the Companions,

whereas for al-Shāfiʿī it means only the *sunna* of the Prophet (see al-Sarakhsī, *Uṣūl*, i. 113–14, also i. 318).

For the shift away from Madinan *ʿamal* to 'classical' *ḥadīth*, via Iraq, see Ansari, 'Early Development', *passim*, esp. pp. 14, 23–4, 176, 212, 234, 243, 250, 370, 377, 381; cf. *Origins*, pp. 73, 76, 77, 80, 223, where Schacht argues that Islamic jurisprudence (i.e. the formalisation of *ʿamal*) began in Iraq.

30 *Origins*, p. 77; see also ibid, pp. 4, 59 and 44, n. 2.

31 See *Origins*, p. 77, referring to *Umm*, vii. 249.

32 See *Muw.* ii. 108; also above, pp. 161–2. Cf. Wakīʿ, i. 113, 118, where the practice is recorded from Madinan *qāḍīs* during the caliphate of Muʿāwiya; ibid, i. 140, where it is recorded from Abū Bakr ibn Ḥazm, i.e. during the caliphate of Sulaymān or ʿUmar ibn ʿAbd al-ʿAzīz; and al-Fasawī, i. 691 [= *Iʿlām*, iii. 74], where al-Layth acknowledges in his letter to Mālik that this practice was the continuous *ʿamal* in Madina but was never imposed anywhere else.

33 See above, pp. 161–2.

34 See above, p. 162.

35 See *Umm*, vii. 182–3, 248–9, 352ff (margin); Schacht, *Origins*, pp. 62, 311–12, 314; Abd-Allah, 'Concept', pp. 141–2, 571–6.

36 See *Muw. Sh.*, p. 301; *Umm*, vii. 182–3; Ibn Rushd, ii. 390–1; al-Zurqānī, iii. 181; Abd-Allah, 'Concept', pp. 141–2, 571–6.

37 See *Origins*, p. 58; Margoliouth, *Early Development*, p. 69f, 75 (esp. ll. 2–5); cf. above, p. 227, n. 8.

38 *Origins*, p. 80.

39 Ibid, p. 40.

40 See ibid, p. 80. Cf. p. 63, where Schacht expresses the same idea but, in so doing, completely misrepresents the statement of Ibn al-Qāsim about *ʿamal* mentioned above (see above, p. 199, n. 115).

41 See *Origins*, p. 75. This idea of an initially lax attitude towards 'religious' matters, followed by an increased strictness and 'Islamisation' of the law, is characteristic of Goldziher's analysis of the early period of Islam, particularly the rule of the Umayyads, whom, as we have noted earlier, he brands as 'godless' and 'completely opposed to religion' (see above, p. 218, n. 66). It is, however, a highly suspect premise, given the obvious concern, however motivated, of many of the Umayyad rulers for matters of religious law (see above, pp. 130ff; also *SALP*, ii. 18–25).

42 *Origins*, p. 40.

43 Ibid, p. 149 (cf. pp. 4–5). See also Schacht, 'Pre-Islamic Background', p. 46; idem, *Introduction*, p. 34.

44 *Origins*, p. 149.

45 For Mālik's care and accuracy with regard to *ḥadīth*, see above, pp. 16ff.

46 See above, pp. 45ff.

47 Rackham, *History of the Countryside*, p. 24. (Italics added.)

48 See above, p. 172.

49 See above, pp. 50–1.

50 Schacht recognises the similarity in attitude between the ancient schools but, for reasons that we have explained, he does not accept a connection between their idea of *sunna* and the idea of the *sunna* of the Prophet (see *Origins*, pp. 21, 27, 34, 75, 80; idem, 'Pre-Islamic Background', p. 42; above, p. 173).

51 Recorded in *Umm*, vii. 308.
52 Recorded in *Umm*, vii. 308. For this and the immediately preceding quotation, see also Schacht, *Origins*, pp. 28, 74–5; Ahmad Hasan, *Early Development*, pp. 105–6; Ansari, 'Terminology', pp. 273–4; Abd-Allah, 'Concept', pp. 174–5, 455.
53 For al-Shaybānī's similar use of the phrase *al-sunna al-maʿrūfa*, see Ahmad Hasan, *Early Development*, p. 107.
54 See *Umm*, vii. 303, 311, 302; cf. Schacht, *Origins*, pp. 74, 68.
55 See *Umm*, vii. 297; cf. Schacht, *Origins*, p. 63.
56 See above, p. 172.
57 See above, pp. 37–8.
58 See above, p. 40.

Conclusions

1 See *Muslim Studies*, ii. 13 (also 18 and 210).
2 See, for example, Motzki, 'The *Muṣannaf*'.

Glossary

adhān	the call to prayer
ʿadl	(as an adjective) just, of high moral integrity
aḥādīth	pl. of *ḥadīth* (q.v.)
ahl al-ḥadīth	'the people of the *ḥadīth*'
ahl al-raʾy	'the people of opinion'
aḥruf	modes, or ways, of reciting the Qurʾan
akhbār al-āḥād	pl. of *khabar al-wāḥid* (q.v.)
alif	the Arabic letter that may (a) carry the *hamza* (q.v.) or (b) represent the long 'a' vowel in Arabic
ʿālim	scholar, man of knowledge, especially of the sciences of Islam
Allāhu akbar	'God is greater'; an expression used, amongst other things, to begin the obligatory prayer
ʿamal	action, practice, especially that based on the established legal principles and precepts of the Madinan community
asbāb al-nuzūl	the occasions, or circumstances, of revelation [of specific Qurʾanic verses]
ʿaṣr	the mid-afternoon prayer
āya	a verse of the Qurʾan
bayt al-māl	lit. 'the house of wealth'; the treasury of the Muslims
Companion	one who saw the Prophet and believed in him; one of the Muslims living at the time of the Prophet
dīn	'religion', but with the broader sense of 'life-transaction' (etymologically, the word refers to the credit/debit situation between a man and his Creator)
duʿāʾ	prayer, in the sense of supplication
faqīh	one versed in *fiqh* (q.v.)
Fātiḥa	the opening *sūra* of the Qurʾan
fatwā	an authoritative legal opinion issued by a *faqīh*

fiqh — lit. 'understanding', i.e. understanding how to derive and apply the Divine law from a knowledge of its sources; jurisprudence; the judgements of Islamic law

fuqahāʾ — pl. of *faqīh*

gharar — uncertainty, especially in business transactions

ghusl — the 'major' ablution, or act of purification, necessary after sexual intercourse, menstruation, etc, before doing the prayer

ḥadd — prescribed penalty for a crime as laid down in the Qurʾan

ḥadīth — a saying or report, especially of the Prophet and/or his Companions; also used collectively to indicate the body of such sayings and reports preserved in the *ḥadīth* literature

hady — sacrificial animal

ḥajj — the pilgrimage to Makka, performed at a specific time of the year; the Fifth Pillar of Islam

ḥalāl — lawful, permitted, allowed

ḥaml al-muṭlaq ʿalā l-muqayyad — the assumption that an expression that is unqualified (*muṭlaq*) in one place will be qualified by the same qualification that it has in another, provided the context is similar

hamza — the glottal stop, and the sign that represents it in the Arabic script

ḥaram — the area around Makka which should not normally be entered by anyone who is not in *iḥrām* (q.v.)

ḥarām — unlawful, prohibited, forbidden

ḥudūd — pl. of *ḥadd* (q.v.)

ʿīd — festival; one of the two festival days in Islam

ʿidda — period of waiting after divorce before a woman may re-marry

iḥrām — the special state involving certain restrictions of clothing and general behaviour that a person doing *ḥajj* or *ʿumra* must be in

iḥṣār — being prevented from doing *ḥajj* or *ʿumra*

ijmāʿ — consensus

ijmāl — the phenomenon of words and phrases being *mujmal* (q.v.)

ijtihād — independent reasoning, especially as used to arrive at new judgements in the absence of any clear precedent

īlā'	oath of abstinence from marital intercourse
imāla	the phenomenon of fronting an 'a' vowel so that it sounds like an 'e'
imām	leader (of the prayer, and also of the community in a political sense); man of knowledge, expert
iqāma	the version of the *adhān* which is said immediately before the prayer is begun
'ishā'	the later evening prayer
ishtirāk	the phenomenon of words and phrases being *mushtarak* (q.v.)
isnād	chain of authority, especially of a *ḥadīth*
i'tikāf	retreat, especially in a mosque while fasting during the last few days of the month of Ramaḍān
Jāhiliyya	the 'Period of Ignorance' before Islam
jihād	struggle, especially fighting for the sake of Allah to establish Islam
jizya	'poll-tax'; a protection tax levied annually on the adult males of non-Muslim communities living under Muslim rule
kaffāra	[act of] expiation
kalāla	inheritance in the absence of parents and/or children
khabar al-wāḥid	an 'isolated' *ḥadīth*, a *ḥadīth* transmitted from one or very few Companions
kitāba	an arrangement whereby a slave will be free once he has earned a certain amount of money for his master, usually paid in instalments
kitābiyyāt	Jewish and/or Christian women
lām	the Arabic letter that represents the 'l' sound
li'ān	'mutual invocation of curses'; the procedure whereby a man who accuses his wife of adultery without sufficient witnesses may avoid the penalty for *qadhf* (q.v.), and she the penalty for adultery, by their both swearing that they are telling the truth on pain of bringing the curse of Allah on themselves if they are lying
madhhab	school of law and/or jurisprudence
mafhūm al-mukhālafa	lit. 'what is understood by contrast'; the technique of 'argument *e* [or *a*] *contrario*', or 'counter-implication', meaning that if you say X about Y, it only applies to Y and not to anything other than Y (see above, p. 64)
mafhūm al-muwāfaqa	lit. 'what is understood by similarity'; the technique of *a fortiori* deduction (see above, p. 64)

maghrib	the sunset prayer
mansūkh	abrogated
maqdhūf	one who has been subject to *qadhf* (q.v.)
mashhūr	(of a *ḥadīth*) 'well-known', i.e. with many transmitters relating from one or very few Companions
mawlā	freed slave
maysir	game of chance involving divining arrows played in Arabia in the pre-Islamic period
mudabbar	a slave who, by his master's decision, will be free when his master has died
mudd	a measure, roughly equivalent to a double-handful of grain
mufassir	one who practices *tafsīr* (q.v.)
muḥaddith	a scholar or transmitter of *ḥadīth*
muḥṣar	someone subject to *iḥṣār* (q.v.)
mujmal	(of a word or phrase) stated in general terms
mujtahid	one who is qualified to exercise *ijtihād* (q.v.)
mukātab	a slave who has agreed to a *kitāba* (q.v.) arrangement with his master
mursal	(of a *ḥadīth*) with an incomplete *isnād* (q.v.) back to the Prophet, especially when the Companion link is missing
muṣḥaf	an individual copy of the Qurʾan
mushtarak	(of a word or phrase) having more than one meaning
musnad	(of a *ḥadīth*) with a complete *isnād* (q.v.) going back to the Prophet
mutawātir	(of a *ḥadīth*) with so many transmitters among the Companions that it cannot be supposed that any forgery has taken place
nāsikh	abrogating
naskh	abrogation
naṣṣ	lit. 'text', i.e. a clearly-worded, unambiguous, text
niṣāb	the minimum amount of wealth necessary before *zakāt* is due
qadhf	accusations of illicit sexual intercourse
qaḍāʾ	making up a missed act of worship
qāḍī	judge
qāriʾ	Qurʾan reciter, especially one with specialist knowledge of a reading (*qirāʾa*) or readings of the Qurʾan
qirāḍ	business partnership in which one party puts up money for another to trade with, the profits being divided between them

qiyās	[reasoning by] analogy
rāʾ	the Arabic letter that represents the 'r' sound
rajʿī	(of divorce) revocable
rajm	the stoning penalty for adultery
rakʿa	one cycle of the prayer, involving standing, bowing and prostrating
raṭl	a weight (variously defined; the Baghdādī *raṭl* is roughly equivalent to 400 gm.)
raʾy	opinion; a legal decision based on the use of independent reasoning and personal opinion
rāwī	transmitter, especially of *ḥadīth*
ribā	usury
rukūʿ	the bowing position in the prayer
ṣāʿ	a measure of four *mudds* (q.v.)
sabab al-nuzūl	sing. of *asbāb al-nuzūl* (q.v.)
ṣadaqa	alms-giving, charity
saʿy	the rite of going between Ṣafā and Marwa (near the Kaʿba in Makka) as part of either *ḥajj* or *ʿumra*
sadd al-dharāʾiʿ	lit. 'blocking the means', i.e. preventing the use of lawful means to achieve unlawful ends
ṣaḥīḥ	(of a *ḥadīth*) sound, authentic
shādhdh	irregular, non-canonical
shahāda	testimony; specifically, the declaration that there is no god but God and that Muḥammad is His Messenger, which is also the First Pillar of Islam
sharīʿa	the divinely revealed law (lit. 'pathway') of the Muslims
ṣubḥ	the early morning prayer
subḥāna llāh	'God be glorified!'; an expression of surprise or wonderment at something unexpected, whether of a positive or negative nature
Successor	a Muslim who saw one of the Companions; one of the generation following the Companions
sunna	normative practice or custom, especially of the Prophet
sūra	a chapter of the Qurʾan
tadbīr	the process of making a slave *mudabbar* (q.v.)
tafsīr	commentary, interpretation, exegesis, especially of the Qurʾan
takbīr	saying '*Allāhu akbar*' ('God is greater'), as at the beginning of the ritual prayer
takhṣīṣ	making an exception

takhṣīṣ al-ʿumūm	making an exception to, or restricting, an otherwise general interpretation
ṭalāq	'ordinary' divorce
talbiya	saying '*Labbayka, allāhumma labbayka* ... etc' ('Here I am, O Lord, here I am ...') while on *ḥajj*
tamattuʿ	a way of doing *ḥajj* whereby a person does an *ʿumra* in the months of *ḥajj* and then comes out of *iḥrām* and stays in Makka until the actual time of the *ḥajj*
taslīm	saying '*al-salāmu ʿalaykum*' ('Peace be upon you') at the end of the prayer
ṭawāf	circumambulation of the Kaʿba in Makka
ṭawāf al-qudūm	the *ṭawāf* of arrival in Makka
tawātur	the phenomenon of a *ḥadīth* being *mutawātir* (q.v.)
tayammum	'dry' ablution, i.e. using dust or earth instead of water as a replacement for *wuḍūʾ* or *ghusl*
ʿulamāʾ	pl. of *ʿālim* (q.v.)
umm walad	a slave-girl who is the mother of a child by her master, and who automatically becomes free on her master's death
umma	community, especially the Muslim community
ʿumra	the 'little' pilgrimage, or visit, to Makka, performed at any time of the year
ʿumūm	general or inclusive sense of a word or phrase
uṣūl al-fiqh	the 'roots of jurisprudence', the sources of Islamic law
uṣūlī	one versed in the science of *uṣūl al-fiqh* (q.v.)
walāʾ	the affiliation of a slave after he has been set free
waṣiyya	bequest
wasq	a measure equal to 60 *ṣāʿs* (q.v.)
witr	'odd' in number; the prayer which involves an odd number of *rakʿas* (usually three) which is done after the *ʿishāʾ* prayer
wuḍūʾ	the 'minor' ablution, or act of purification, necessary after urination, etc, before doing the prayer
ẓāhir	apparent, overt, obvious or literal meaning of a word or phrase
zakāt	the obligatory alms-tax which forms the Third Pillar of Islam
ẓihār	a form of oath whereby a man declares that his wife is 'like his mother's back (*ẓahr*)', i.e. *ḥarām* for him
zinā	illicit sexual intercourse
ẓuhr	the mid-day prayer

Biographical Notes

I have aimed to minimise references by citing those that in turn cite the main references (especially, where appropriate, the *Encyclopaedia of Islam* and the works of Brockelmann and Sezgin), although this procedure has been not been followed in all cases. Many other sources are of course available. The descriptions given are similarly brief and apply in particular to this study: further details may be gained from the references cited.

Abān ibn ᶜUthmān ibn ᶜAffān (d. before 105/724): *rāwī*; governor of Madina (76–*c.* 83/695–*c.* 702) under ᶜAbd al-Malik. See *EI (2)*, i. 2–3; *GAS*, i. 277–8.

ᶜAbd al-ᶜAzīz [ibn ᶜAbdallāh] ibn Abī Salama al-Mājishūn (d. 164/780): Madinan *faqīh*. See Muranyi, *Materialien*, p. 88; idem, *Fragment*, pp. 30–2 (but see above, p. 192, n. 89).

ᶜAbd al-ᶜAzīz ibn al-Mājishūn, *see* ᶜAbd al-ᶜAzīz [ibn ᶜAbdallāh] ibn Abī Salama al-Mājishūn

ᶜAbd al-Ḥamīd ibn ᶜAbd al-Raḥmān ibn Zayd ibn al-Khaṭṭāb (d. between 105/724 and 125/743): governor of Kufa (99–101/717–720) under ᶜUmar ibn ᶜAbd al-ᶜAzīz. See *Tahdhīb*, vi. 119.

ᶜAbd al-Karīm al-Jazarī (d. 127/744): *rāwī*. See *Tahdhīb*, vi. 373–5.

ᶜAbd al-Karīm ibn Abī l-Mukhāriq (d. 126/743): *rāwī*. See *Tahdhīb*, vi. 376–9.

ᶜAbd al-Malik ibn ᶜAbd al-ᶜAzīz ibn al-Mājishūn (d. 212/827): Madinan *faqīh*, son of the Madinan *faqīh*. See Muranyi, *Materialien*, pp. 87–8.

ᶜAbd al-Malik ibn Marwān (d. 86/705): Umayyad caliph, 65–86/685–705. See *EI (2)*, i. 76–7; *Tahdhīb*, vi. 422–3.

ᶜAbd al-Raḥmān ibn Abī l-Zinād ᶜAbdallāh ibn Dhakwān (d. 174/790): *rāwī*; son of the Madinan *faqīh*. See *Tahdhīb*, vi. 170–3.

ᶜAbd al-Raḥmān ibn al-Ḥakam (d. ?): poet; brother of the caliph Marwān. See Caskel, ii. 129.

ᶜAbd al-Raḥmān ibn Hurmuz al-Aᶜraj (d. 117/735): *rāwī*. See *Tahdhīb*, vi. 290–1.

ᶜAbd al-Raḥmān ibn Zayd ibn Aslam (d. 182/798): *mufassir*. See *GAS*, i. 38.

ᶜAbd al-Razzāq al-Ṣanᶜānī (d. 211/827): compiler of *ḥadīth*. See *GAS*, i. 99.

ᶜAbd al-Wahhāb, al-Qāḍī, *see* al-Qāḍī ᶜAbd al-Wahhāb

ᶜAbdallāh ibn ᶜAbbās (d. 68/687): Companion. See *EI (2)*, i. 40–1.

ᶜAbdallāh ibn Abī Bakr [ibn Muḥammad] ibn ᶜAmr ibn Ḥazm. (d. 130/747 or 135/752): *rāwī*; son of the Madinan *qāḍī* and governor. See *GAS*, i. 284.

ᶜAbdallāh ibn Abī Ḥusayn al-Makkī (d. ?): *rāwī.* See *Tahdhīb*, v. 293.
ᶜAbdallāh ibn ᶜAmr ibn al-ᶜĀṣ (d. 65/684): Companion. See *GAS*, i. 84.
ᶜAbdallāh ibn Masᶜūd (d. 32/652): Companion. See *EI (2)*, iii. 873–5.
ᶜAbdallāh ibn Muslim ibn Hurmuz (d. ?): *rāwī.* See *Tahdhīb*, vi. 29–30.
ᶜAbdallāh ibn Shaddād (d. *c.* 82/701): *rāwī.* See *Tahdhīb*, v. 251–2.
ᶜAbdallāh ibn ᶜUmar (d. 73/692): Companion. See *EI (2)*, i. 53–4.
ᶜAbdallāh ibn Umm Maktūm (d. ?): Companion. See *Iṣāba*, iv. 284–5.
ᶜAbdallāh ibn Wahb (d. 197/812): transmitter of *Muw.* See *EI (2)*, iii. 963; *GAS*, i. 466; *Muw. Ibn Wahb*, pp. 17–42.
ᶜAbdallāh ibn Yazīd ibn Hurmuz (d. 148/765): Madinan *faqīh.* See Ibn Saᶜd (*qism mutammim*), pp. 327–8; al-Fasawī, i. 651–5; *Siyar*, vi. 379.
ᶜAbdallāh ibn al-Zubayr (d. 73/692): Companion; 'anti-caliph', 64–73/683–692. See *EI (2)*, i. 54–5.
Abū ᶜĀmir (d. ?): Mālik's great-grandfather, possibly Companion. See above, p. 182, n. 5.
Abū ᶜAmr ibn Ḥafṣ (d. ?): Companion. See *Tahdhīb*, xii. 177–8.
Abū ᶜAwāna al-Wāsiṭī (d. 176/792): compiler of *ḥadīth.* See *Tahdhīb*, xi. 116–20.
Abū Ayyūb al-Anṣārī (d. *c.* 52/672): Companion. See *EI (2)*, i. 108–9.
Abū Bakr al-Ṣiddīq (d. 13/634): Companion; first caliph, 11-13/632–634. See *EI (2)*, i. 109–11.
Abū Bakr ibn ᶜAbd al-Raḥmān ibn al-Ḥārith ibn Hishām (d. *c.* 94/713): one of the 'Seven *Fuqahā*ʾ' of Madina. See *EI (2)*, Supplement, p. 311.
Abū Bakr ibn Ḥazm, *see* Abū Bakr [ibn Muḥammad] ibn ᶜAmr ibn Ḥazm
Abū Bakr [ibn Muḥammad] ibn ᶜAmr ibn Ḥazm (d. *c.* 120/727): governor of Madina (96–101/715–720) during the caliphates of Sulaymān and ᶜUmar ibn ᶜAbd al-ᶜAzīz; formerly *qāḍī* See Wakīᶜ, i. 135–46; *Tahdhīb*, xii. 38–40.
Abū l-Dardāʾ (d. 32/652): Companion. See *EI (2)*, i. 113–14.
Abū Dāwūd (d. 275/888): compiler of *ḥadīth.* See *EI (2)*, i. 114; *GAS*, i. 149–52.
Abū Ḥanīfa (d. 150/767): Kufan *faqīh*; 'founder' of the Ḥanafī *madhhab.* See *EI (2)*, i. 123–4; *GAS*, i. 409–19.
Abū Hurayra (d. *c.* 58/678): Companion. See *EI (2)*, i. 129.
Abū l-Ḥusayn ibn Abī ᶜUmar (d. 328/939): *uṣūlī*, etc. See *Mad.* iii. 278–81; Ibn al-ᶜImād, ii. 313; al-Ziriklī, v. 221.
Abū Isḥāq al-Isfarāyīnī (d. 418/1027); *uṣūlī*, etc. See *GAL*, Supplement, i. 667; al-Ziriklī, i. 59.
Abū Jaᶜfar al-Manṣūr (d. 158/775): ᶜAbbāsid caliph, 136–158/754–775. See *EI (2)*, vi. 427–8.
Abū Jaᶜfar Yazīd ibn al-Qaᶜqāᶜ (d. *c.* 130/747): Madinan *qāriʾ*. See *Ghāya*, ii. 382–4.
Abū Muḥammad Ṣāliḥ al-Haskūrī (d. *c.* 653/1255): Fāsī scholar. See *Salwa*, ii. 42–3; Makhlūf, i. 185; *GAL*, i. 178.
Abū Mūsā al-Ashᶜarī (d. *c.* 42/662): Companion. See *EI (2)*, i. 695–6.
Abū Muṣᶜab al-Zuhrī (d. 242/856): transmitter of *Muw.* See *GAS*, i. 471; Schacht, 'Abū Muṣᶜab'.
Abū Qilāba (d. *c.* 104/722): Basran *faqīh.* See *Tahdhīb*, v. 224–6.
Abū Saᶜīd al-Khudrī (d. *c.* 74/693): Companion. See *Tahdhīb*, iii. 479–81.
Abū Salama ibn ᶜAbd al-Raḥmān ibn ᶜAwf (d. 94/713 or 104/722): Madinan *qāḍī* and *faqīh*, sometimes included as one of the 'Seven *Fuqahā*ʾ'. See *Tahdhīb*, xii. 115–18; Wakīᶜ, i. 116–18.

Abū Suhayl Nāfiʿ ibn Mālik ibn Abī ʿĀmir (d. between 132/750 and 136/754): *rāwī*; Mālik's uncle. See *Tahdhīb*, x. 409–10.
Abū Thawr (d. 240/854): Iraqi *faqīh*. See *EI (2)*, i. 155; *GAS*, i. 491.
Abū ʿUbayd, the *mawlā* of Sulaymān ibn ʿAbd al-Malik (d. ?): *rāwī*. See *Tahdhīb*, xii. 158.
Abū ʿUbayda ibn al-Jarrāḥ (d. 18/639): Companion; governor of Syria under ʿUmar. See *EI (2)*, i. 158–9.
Abū Yūsuf (d. 182/798): Kufan *faqīh*. See *EI (2)*, i. 164–5; *GAS*, i. 419–21.
Abū l-Zinād ʿAbdallāh ibn Dhakwān (d. 131/748): Madinan *faqīh*. See *GAS*, i. 405.
Abū l-Zubayr al-Makkī (d. 126/743): *rāwī*. See *GAS*, i. 86–7.
Aḥmad ibn Ḥanbal (d. 241/855): compiler of *ḥadīth*; 'founder' of the Ḥanbalī *madhhab*. See *EI (2)*, i. 272–7; *GAS*, i. 502–9.
ʿĀʾisha bint Abī Bakr al-Ṣiddīq (d. 58/678): Companion. See *EI (2)*, i. 307–8.
al-Akhfash, Aḥmad ibn ʿImrān (d. before 250/864): commentator on *Muw.* See *GAS*, i. 460; Schacht, 'Manuscripts in Kairouan', p. 244.
ʿAlī ibn Abī Ṭālib (d. 40/660): Companion; fourth caliph, 35–40/656–61. See *EI (2)*, i. 381–6.
ʿAlī ibn al-Madīnī (d. 234/849): *ḥadīth*-scholar. See *GAS*, i. 108.
ʿAlī ibn Ziyād al-Tūnisī (d. 183/799): transmitter of *Muw.* See *GAS*, i. 465; Abū l-ʿArab, i. 251–3, ii. 345–7; *Riyāḍ*, i. 234–7; *Mad.* i. 326–9; *Muw. Ibn Ziyād*, pp. 29–50.
ʿAmmār ibn Yāsir (d. 37/657): Companion. See *EI (2)*, i. 448.
ʿAmr ibn al-ʿĀṣ (d. *c.* 43/663): Companion. See *EI (2)*, i. 451.
ʿAmr ibn Ḥazm (d. *c.* 51/671): Companion. See *Tahdhīb*, viii. 20–1.
Anas ibn Mālik al-Anṣārī (d. *c.* 93/711): Companion. See *EI (2)*, i. 482.
al-Aʿraj, *see* ʿAbd al-Raḥmān ibn Hurmuz al-Aʿraj
Aṣbagh ibn al-Faraj (d. 225/840): commentator on *Muw.* See *Mad.* ii. 561–5; Schacht, 'Manuscripts in Kairouan', p. 235.
ʿĀṣim (d. 127/745): Kufan *qāriʾ*. See *EI (2)*, i. 706–7; *GAS*, i. 7.
ʿAṭāʾ ibn ʿAbdallāh al-Khurāsānī (d. 135/752): *rāwī*. See *GAS*, i. 33.
ʿAṭāʾ ibn Abī Rabāḥ (d. 114/732): Makkan *faqīh*. See *EI (2)*, i. 730; *GAS*, i. 31.
ʿAwn ibn Yūsuf (d. 239/853): *rāwī* from Ibn Wahb. See *Muw. Ibn Wahb*, p. 54; Schacht, 'Manuscripts in Kairouan', p. 250.
al-Awzāʿī (d. 157/774): Syrian *faqīh*. See *EI (2)*, i. 772–3; *GAS*, i. 516.
Ayyūb al-Sakhtiyānī (d. 131/748): *rāwī*. See *GAS*, i. 87–8; *Tajrīd*, p. 21.
al-Bājī (d. 474/1081): Andalusian scholar; commentator on *Muw.* See *EI (2)*, i. 864–5.
al-Bukhārī (d. 256/870): compiler of *ḥadīth*. See *EI (2)*, i. 1296–7; *GAS*, i. 115–34.
al-Dānī (d. 444/1053): scholar of Qurʾanic readings. See *EI (2)*, ii. 109–10.
Dāwūd al-Ẓāhirī (d. 270/884): 'founder' of the Ẓāhirī *madhhab*. See *EI (2)*, ii. 182–3; *GAS*, i. 521.
al-Dhahabī (d. 748/1348): biographer. See *GAL*, Supplement, ii. 45–7.
al-Fasawī (d. 277/890): historian. See *GAS*, i. 319.
Fāṭima bint Qays (d. ?): Companion. See *Tahdhīb*, xii. 443–4.
al-Furayʿa bint Mālik (d. after 23/644): Companion. See *Tahdhīb*, xii. 445.
al-Ghāfiqī, Abū l-Qāsim al-Jawharī (d. 381/991 or 385/995): Mālikī *faqīh*; author of *Musnad al-Muwaṭṭaʾ*. See *Mad.* (Mo.), vi. 204 [= *Mad.* iv. 482–3]; *ʿIbar*, i. 341; *Dībāj*, i. 470–1.

Habbār ibn al-Aswad (d. ?): Companion. See *Iṣāba*, vi. 279–81.
Ḥafṣ (d. 180/812): Kufan *qāriʾ*. See *EI (2)*, iii. 63; *GAS*, i. 10.
Ḥafṣa bint ʿAbd al-Raḥmān ibn Abī Bakr al-Ṣiddīq (d. ?): niece of ʿĀʾisha and wife of al-Mundhir ibn al-Zubayr. See *Tahdhīb*, xii. 410.
Ḥafṣa bint ʿUmar ibn al-Khaṭṭāb (d. *c.* 41/661): Companion. See *EI (2)*, iii. 63–5.
al-Ḥajjāj ibn Yūsuf (d. 95/714): general, and also governor of Madina (74–75/693–694), under ʿAbd al-Malik. See *EI (2)*, iii. 39–43.
Ḥammād ibn Salama (d. 167/783): compiler of *ḥadīth*. See *GAS*, i. 807; *Tahdhīb*, iii. 11–16.
Ḥammād ibn Zayd (d. 179/795): Basran *faqīh*. See *Tahdhīb*, iii. 9–11.
Hammām ibn Munabbih (d. *c.* 101/719): compiler of *al-Ṣaḥīfa al-ṣaḥīḥa*. See *GAS*, i. 86; Hamidullah, *Sahifa Hammam*, pp. 41–3.
Ḥarmala ibn Yaḥyā (d. 243/857): *faqīh*, commentator on *Muw*. See *Mad.* iii. 76–7.
Hārūn al-Rashīd (d. 193/809): ʿAbbāsid caliph, 170–193/786–809. See *EI (2)*, iii. 232–4. Ḥarmala ibn Yaḥyā (d. 243) (*Mad.* i. 200, iii. 77)
al-Ḥasan al-Baṣrī (d. 110/728): Basran scholar and *faqīh*. See *EI (2)*, iii. 247–8; *GAS*, i. 591–4.
al-Ḥasan al-Luʾluʾī (d. 204/819): Kufan *faqīh*. See *GAS*, i. 433.
Hishām ibn ʿAbd al-Malik (d. 125/743): Umayyad caliph, 105–125/724–743. See *EI (2)*, iii. 493–5.
Hishām ibn Ismāʿīl al-Makhzūmī (d. ?): governor of Madina (*c.* 82–86/*c.* 701–705) under ʿAbd al-Malik and al-Walīd. See Caskel, ii. 284.
Hishām ibn ʿUrwa (d. 146/763): Madinan *faqīh*, son of the *faqīh*. See *GAS*, i. 88–9.
Ḥumayd ibn Qays al-Aʿraj al-Makkī (d. *c.* 130/747): *rāwī*. See *Tahdhīb*, iii. 46–7.
Ḥumayd al-Ṭawīl (d. *c.* 142/759): *rāwī*. See *GAS*, i. 89.
Hushaym al-Wāsiṭī (d. 183/799): compiler of *ḥadīth*. See *GAS*, i. 38.
Ibn ʿAbbās, *see* ʿAbdallāh ibn ʿAbbās
Ibn ʿAbd al-Barr (d. 463/1071): Andalusian scholar. See *EI (2)*, iii. 674.
Ibn ʿAbd al-Ḥakam, ʿAbdallāh (d. 214/829): Mālikī *faqīh*. See *EI (2)*, iii. 674–5; Muranyi, *Materialien*, pp. 7, 81.
Ibn Abī ʿĀmir, *see* Mālik ibn Abī ʿĀmir
Ibn Abī Dhiʾb, Muḥammad ibn ʿAbd al-Raḥmān ibn al-Mughīra (d. 159/776): Madinan *faqīh* and *ḥadīth*-scholar. See *Tahdhīb*, ix. 303–7.
Ibn Abī Ḥātim (d. 327/938): *ḥadīth*-scholar and biographer. See *GAS*, i. 178–9.
Ibn Abī Ḥāzim Salama ibn Dīnār, ʿAbd al-ʿAzīz (d. *c.* 184/800). Madinan *faqīh*. See *Tahdhīb*, vi. 333–4.
Ibn Abī Zayd al-Qayrawānī (d. 386/996): Mālikī *faqīh*. See *EI (2)*, iii. 695; *GAS*, i. 478–81.
Ibn Abī l-Zinād, *see* ʿAbd al-Raḥmān ibn Abī l-Zinād
Ibn al-ʿArabī, Abū Bakr (d. 543/1148): Andalusian scholar and *qāḍī*. See *EI (2)*, iii. 707.
Ibn Bukayr, Yaḥyā ibn ʿAbdallāh (d. 231/845): transmitter of *Muw*. See *GAS*, i. 460.
Ibn Farḥūn (d. 799/1397): Mālikī biographer and *faqīh*. See *EI (2)*, iii. 763.
Ibn Ḥabīb, ʿAbd al-Malik (d. 238/852): author of the *Wāḍiḥa*. See Muranyi, *Materialien*, pp. 14, 72; *Wāḍiḥa*, pp. 11–23.
Ibn Ḥajar (d. 852/1449): biographer, etc. See *EI (2)*, iii. 776–8.
Ibn Ḥamdūn, al-Ṭālib ibn al-Ḥājj (d. *c.* 1273/1857): Fāsī scholar. See al-Ziriklī, vii. 40–1.
Ibn Ḥanbal, *see* Aḥmad ibn Ḥanbal

Ibn Ḥazm (d. 456/1064): Andalusian Ẓāhirī scholar. See *EI (2)*, iii. 790–9; *GAL*, Supplement, i. 692.
Ibn Hurmuz, *see* ʿAbdallāh ibn Yazīd ibn Hurmuz
Ibn Isḥāq (d. *c.* 150/767): historian. See *EI (2)*, iii. 810–11; *GAS*, i. 288.
Ibn al-Jazarī (d. 833/1429): scholar of Qurʾanic readings. See *EI (2)*, iii. 753.
Ibn Jurayj (d. 150/767): compiler of *ḥadīth*. See *GAS*, i. 91
Ibn Juzayy al-Kalbī, Muḥammad ibn Aḥmad (d. 741/1340): Andalusian scholar. See *EI (2)*, iii. 756.
Ibn al-Madīnī, *see* ʿAlī ibn al-Madīnī
Ibn Mahdī, ʿAbd al-Raḥmān (d. 198/813): *ḥadīth*-scholar. See *Tahdhīb*, vi. 279–81.
Ibn Mājah (d. 273/886): compiler of *ḥadīth*. See *EI (2)*, iii. 856; *GAS*, i. 147–8.
Ibn al-Mājishūn, *see* ʿAbd al-ʿAzīz ibn al-Mājishūn *and* ʿAbd al-Malik ibn ʿAbd al-ʿAzīz ibn al-Mājishūn
Ibn Masʿūd, *see* ʿAbdallāh ibn Masʿūd
Ibn al-Mawwāz, Muḥammad (d. 269/882): author of 'al-Mawwāziyya'. See Muranyi, *Materialien*, p. 70.
Ibn al-Muʿadhdhal, Aḥmad (d. 240/854): Mālikī *faqīh*. See *Mad.* ii. 550–8; *ʿIbar*, i. 341; *Dībāj*, i. 6, 141–3.
Ibn al-Mubārak, ʿAbdallāh (d. 181/797): compiler of *ḥadīth*. See *EI (2)*, iii. 879; *GAS*, i. 95.
Ibn Mujāhid (d. 324/936): scholar of Qurʾanic readings. See *EI (2)*, iii. 880.
Ibn al-Mundhir (d. 318/930): *faqīh* and *mujtahid*. See *GAS*, i. 495–6.
Ibn Muzayn, Yaḥyā ibn Zakariyyā ibn Ibrāhīm (d. 259/783 or 260/784): commentator on *Muw*. See *Mad.* iii. 132–4; Schacht, 'Manuscripts in Kairouan', p. 235; *GAS*, i. 460, 473.
Ibn Nāfiʿ al-Ṣāʾigh, ʿAbdallāh (d. 186/802): *rāwī* from Mālik, commentator on *Muw*. See *Mad.* i. 356–8.
Ibn Nāṣir al-Dīn, Muḥammad ibn ʿAbdallāh al-Qaysī (d. 842/1438): Syrian scholar. See Muranyi, *Materialien*, p. 113.
Ibn al-Qāsim (d. 191/806): transmitter of *Muw*., and of Mālik's opinions in the *Mudawwana*. See *EI (2)*, iii. 817; *GAS*, i. 465, 460.
Ibn Qayyim al-Jawziyya (d. 751/1350): Syrian scholar. See *EI (2)*, iii. 821–2.
Ibn Qutayba (d. 276/889): Iraqi scholar. See *EI (2)*, iii. 844–7.
Ibn Rushd (al-Ḥafīd) (d. 595/1198): Andalusian *qāḍī*, *faqīh* and philosopher. See *EI (2)*, iii. 909–20.
Ibn Rushd (al-Jadd) (d. 520/1126): Andalusian *qāḍī* and *faqīh*. See *GAL*, i. 384, Supplement, i. 662; *GAS*, i. 469, 472.
Ibn Saʿd (d. 230/845): biographer. See *EI (2)*, iii. 922–3; *GAS*, i. 300–1.
Ibn Shihāb al-Zuhrī (d. 124/742): Madinan *faqīh* and *ḥadīth*-scholar. See *GAS*, i. 280–3; Azmi, *Studies*, pp. 278–92.
Ibn Sīrīn (d. 110/728): Basran *faqīh*. See *EI (2)*, iii. 947–8; *GAS*, i. 633–4.
Ibn Taymiyya (d. 728/1328) see *EI (2)*, iii. 951–5.
Ibn Ṭūlūn (d. 953/1546): Syrian scholar. See *EI (2)*, iii. 957–8.
Ibn ʿUmar, *see* ʿAbdallāh ibn ʿUmar
Ibn ʿUyayna, *see* Sufyān ibn ʿUyayna
Ibn Wahb, *see* ʿAbdallāh ibn Wahb
Ibn Zayd, *see* ʿAbd al-Raḥmān ibn Zayd ibn Aslam
Ibn Ziyād, *see* ʿAlī ibn Ziyād

Ibrāhīm al-Ḥarbī (d. 285/898): *ḥadīth*-scholar. See *GAL*, Supplement, i. 188.
Ibrāhīm al-Nakhaʿī (d. 96/715): Kufan *faqīh*. See *GAS*, i. 403–4.
Ibrāhīm ibn Abī ʿUbla (d. *c.* 152/769): *rāwī*. See *Tahdhīb*, i. 142–3.
ʿĪsā ibn Dīnār (d. 212/827): *faqīh*, commentator on *Muw.* See *Mad.* iii. 16–20; Schacht, 'Manuscripts in Kairouan', p. 235.
ʿIyāḍ ibn Mūsā al-Yaḥṣubī, al-Qāḍī (d. 544/1149): Andalusian scholar and *qāḍī.* See *EI (2)*, iv. 289–90.
Jabala ibn Ḥammūd (d. 299/911): *rāwī* of *Muw.* See *Mad.* iii. 247–54; *Muw. Ibn Ziyād*, pp. 101–3.
Jābir ibn ʿAbdallāh al-Anṣārī (d. 78/697): Companion. See *GAS*, i. 85.
Jābir ibn al-Aswad (d. ?): twice governor of Madina (*c.* 64/683, *c.* 68–*c.* 70/*c.* 687–*c.* 689) under ʿAbdallāh ibn al-Zubayr. See al-Zubayrī, p. 273.
Jaʿfar ibn Sulaymān (d. 177/793): ʿAbbāsid governor of Madina (146–150/763–767) under al-Manṣūr. See Zambaur, p. 24.
Jarīr ibn ʿAbd al-Ḥamīd (d. 188/804): compiler of *ḥadīth*. See *Tahdhīb*, ii. 75–7.
al-Jaṣṣāṣ (d. 370/981): Ḥanafī scholar. See *EI (2)*, ii. 486; *GAS*, i. 444.
Kaʿb ibn ʿUjra (d. *c.* 52/672): Companion. See *Tahdhīb*, viii. 435.
Khalīl ibn Isḥāq (d. *c.* 776/1374): Mālikī *faqīh*. See *GAL*, Supplement, ii. 96–9.
Khārija ibn Zayd ibn Thābit (d. *c.* 99/717): one of the 'Seven *Fuqahā'*' of Madina. See *EI (2)*, Supplement, p. 311.
al-Layth ibn Saʿd (d. 175/791): Egyptian *faqīh*. See *EI (2)*, v. 711–12.
al-Mahdī (d. 169/785): ʿAbbāsid caliph, 158–169/775–785. See *EI (2)*, v. 1238–9.
Mālik ibn Abī ʿĀmir (d. 74/693?): *rāwī*; Mālik's grandfather. See *Tahdhīb*, x. 19.
Mālik ibn Anas al-Aṣbaḥī (d. 179/795): Madinan *faqīh* and *ḥadīth*-scholar; 'founder' of the Mālikī *madhhab*. See *EI (2)*, vi. 262–5; *GAS*, i. 457–64; *GAL*, Supplement, i. 297–9; also: Ibn Saʿd (*qism mutammim*), pp. 433–44; al-Fasawī, i. 682–7 and Index; Ibn Abī Ḥātim, pp. 11–32; Ibn Ḥazm, pp. 408–9; *Tamhīd*, i. 61–92; *Mad.* i. 102–253; *Siyar*, viii. 43–121.
Maʿmar ibn Rāshid (d. 154/770): compiler of *ḥadīth*. See *GAS*, i. 290.
al-Maʾmūn (d. 218/833): ʿAbbāsid caliph, 198–218/813–833. See *EI (2)*, vi. 331–9.
al-Manṣūr, *see* Abū Jaʿfar al-Manṣūr
Marwān ibn al-Ḥakam (d. 65/685): Umayyad caliph, 64–65/684–685; formerly twice governor of Madina (*c.* 41–*c.* 49/*c.* 661–*c.* 669 and *c.* 54–*c.* 57/*c.* 674–*c.* 677) under Muʿāwiya. See *EI (2)*, vi. 621–3.
Muʿādh ibn Jabal (d. *c.* 17/638): Companion. See *Tahdhīb*, x. 186–8.
Muʿāwiya ibn Abī Sufyān (d. 60/680): Companion; Umayyad caliph, 41–60/661–680; formerly governor of Syria under ʿUmar and ʿUthmān. See *EI (2)*, vii. 263–8.
Muḥammad ibn ʿAbdallāh ('al-Nafs al-Zakiyya') (d. 145/762): ʿAlid rebel against the ʿAbbāsid caliph Manṣūr. See *EI (2)*, vii. 388–9.
Muḥammad ibn Abī Bakr [ibn Muḥammad] ibn ʿAmr ibn Ḥazm (d. 132/750): Madinan *qāḍī*, son of the Madinan *qāḍī* and governor. See Wakīʿ, i. 175–6; *Tahdhīb*, ix. 80.
Muḥammad ibn ʿĪsā ibn ʿAbd al-Wāḥid al-Aʿshā (d. 218/833 or 221/836 or 222/837): commentator on *Muw.* See *Mad.* iii. 23–5; Schacht, 'Manuscripts in Kairouan', p. 235.
Muḥammad ibn Saḥnūn (d. 256/879): *faqīh*, commentator on *Muw.* See *Mad.* iii. 104–18; *GAS*, i. 472–3; Schacht, 'Manuscripts in Kairouan', p. 248.

Muḥammad al-ᶜUtbī (d. 255/869): author of the *ᶜUtbiyya*. See *GAS*, i. 472; Muranyi, *Materialien*, p. 50.
Mujāhid (d. 104/722): *mufassir*. See *EI (2)*, vii. 293; *GAS*, i. 29.
al-Mundhir ibn al-Zubayr (d. 64/683 or 73/692): brother of ᶜAbdallāh ibn al-Zubayr and nephew of ᶜĀ'isha. See Caskel, ii. 430; al-Ṭabarī, *History*, xx. 114, n. 455.
Muqātil ibn Sulaymān (d. 150/767): *mufassir*. See *EI (2)*, vii. 508–9; *GAS*, i. 36–7.
Muslim (d. 261/875): compiler of *ḥadīth*. See *EI (2)*, vii. 691–2; *GAS*, i. 136–43.
Nāfiᶜ, the *mawlā* of Ibn ᶜUmar (d. 117/735): Madinan *rāwī* and *faqīh*. See *Tahdhīb*, x. 412–15; Ibn Saᶜd (*qism mutammim*), pp. 142–5.
Nāfiᶜ ibn ᶜAbd al-Raḥmān ibn Abī Nuᶜaym (d. 169/785): Madinan *qāri'*. See *GAS*, i. 9; Ibn Saᶜd (*qism mutammim*), p. 451.
al-Nasā'ī (d. 303/915): compiler of *ḥadīth*. See *GAS*, i. 167–9.
al-Qābisī (d. 403/1012): Qayrawānī *faqīh*. See *GAS*, i. 482–3.
al-Qāḍī ᶜAbd al-Wahhāb (d. 422/1031): Mālikī *faqīh*. See *GAL*, Supplement, i. 660; al-Ziriklī, iv. 335.
Qālūn (d. 220/835): Madinan *qāri'*. See *GAS*, i. 12.
al-Qaᶜnabī, ᶜAbdallāh ibn Maslama ibn Qaᶜnab al-Ḥārithī (d. 221/836): transmitter of *Muw.* See *Tahdhīb*, vi. 31–3.
al-Qarāfī (d. 684/1285): Mālikī *uṣūlī* and *faqīh*. See *GAL*, Supplement, i. 665–6.
al-Qāsim ibn Muḥammad ibn Abī Bakr (d. *c.* 106/724): one of the 'Seven *Fuqahā'*' of Madina. See *EI (2)*, Supplement, p. 311–2; *GAS*, i. 279.
Qatāda (d. 118/736): *mufassir*. See *EI (2)*, iv. 748; *GAS*, i. 31–2.
al-Rabīᶜ ibn Mālik (d. 160/776): *rāwī*; Mālik's uncle. See al-Samᶜānī, i. 282–3.
al-Rabīᶜ ibn Ṣabīḥ (d. 160/776): compiler of *ḥadīth*. *Tahdhīb*, iii. 247–8.
Rabīᶜa ibn Abī ᶜAbd al-Raḥmān ('Rabīᶜat al-ra'y') (d. 136/753): Madinan *faqīh*. See *GAS*, i. 406–7.
Rāshid ibn Abī Rāshid al-Walīdī (d. 675/1276): Fāsī scholar. See *Nayl*, p. 101; *Jadhwa*, p. 123; Makhlūf, i. 201.
Saᶜd ibn Abī Waqqāṣ (d. *c.* 51/671): Companion. See *EI (2)*, viii. 696–7.
Ṣadaqa ibn Yasār al-Makkī (d. after 132/749): *rāwī*. See *Tahdhīb*, iv. 419.
Sahla bint Suhayl (d. ?): Companion. See al-Zurqānī, iii. 90.
Saḥnūn (d. 240/854): compiler of the *Mudawwana*. See *GAS*, i. 468–71.
Saᶜīd ibn Abī ᶜArūba (d. *c.* 157/774): compiler of *ḥadīth*. See *GAS*, i. 91–2.
Saᶜīd ibn al-ᶜĀṣ (d. *c.* 58/678): governor of Madina (*c.* 49–*c.* 54/*c.* 669–*c.* 674) under Muᶜāwiya. See *EI (2)*, viii. 853; *Tahdhīb*, iv. 48–50.
Saᶜīd ibn Jubayr (d. 95/714): Kufan scholar and *faqīh*. See *GAS*, i. 28–9.
Saᶜīd ibn al-Musayyab (d. *c.* 94/713): one of the 'Seven *Fuqahā'*' of Madina. See *EI (2)*, Supplement, p. 311; *GAS*, i. 276.
Sālim ibn ᶜAbdallāh ibn ᶜUmar (d. *c.* 106/724): Madinan *faqīh*, sometimes included as one of the 'Seven *Fuqahā'*'. See *Tahdhīb*, iii. 436–8.
al-Samhūdī (d. 911/1506): historian. See *GAL*, Supplement, ii. 223–4.
al-Sarakhsī (d. *c.* 483/1090): Ḥanafī *uṣūlī* and *faqīh*. See *GAL*, Supplement, i. 638.
al-Shaᶜbī (d. 103/721): Kufan *faqīh*. See *EI (2)*, ix. 162–3; *GAS*, i. 277.
al-Shāfiᶜī (d. 204/820): *uṣūlī* and *faqīh*; 'founder' of the Shāfiᶜī *madhhab*. See *EI (2)*, ix. 181–5; *GAS*, i. 484–90.
al-Shāṭibī (d. 790/1388): Andalusian *uṣūlī*. See *GAL*, Supplement, i. 374.
al-Shaybānī, Muḥammad ibn al-Ḥasan (d. 189/805): Kufan *faqīh*. See *EI (2)*, ix. 392–4; *GAS*, i. 421–33.

Shuʿba ibn al-Ḥajjāj (d. 160/776): compiler of *ḥadīth*. See *GAS*, i. 92.
Ṣiddīq Khān (d. 1307/1889): Indian scholar. See *GAL*, Supplement, ii. 859–60.
Subayʿa al-Aslamiyya (d. ?): Companion. See *Tahdhīb*, xii. 424.
Sufyān al-Thawrī (d. 161/778): compiler of *ḥadīth*. See *EI (1)*, iv. 500–2; *GAS*, i. 518–19.
Sufyān ibn ʿUyayna (d. 198/813): *faqīh* and *ḥadīth*-scholar. See *GAS*, i. 96 (where the death-date 196 seems to be an error).
Sulaymān ibn ʿAbd al-Malik (d. 99/717): Umayyad caliph, 96–99/715–717. See *EI (1)*, iv. 518–19.
Sulaymān ibn Yasār (d. *c*. 100/718): one of the 'Seven *Fuqahā*ʾ' of Madina. See *EI (2)*, Supplement, p. 311.
Suwayd al-Ḥadathānī, Abū Saʿīd (d. 240/854): transmitter of *Muw*. See *GAS*, i. 460.
al-Suyūṭī (d. 911/1505): Egyptian scholar; commentator on *Muw*. See *EI (1)*, iv. 573–5; *GAL*, Supplement, ii. 178.
al-Ṭabarī (d. 310/923): *mufassir* and historian. See *EI (1)*, iv. 578–9; *GAS*, i. 323–8.
Ṭalḥa ibn ʿAbd al-Malik al-Aylī (d. ?): *rāwī*. See *Tahdhīb*, v. 19–20.
Ṭalḥa ibn ʿAbdallāh ibn ʿAwf (d. *c*. 97/715): governor of Madina (*c*. 70–*c*. 72/*c*. 689–*c*. 691) under ʿAbdallāh ibn al-Zubayr; formerly *qāḍī* See Caskel, ii. 555; Wakīʿ, i. 120; *Tahdhīb*, v. 19.
Ṭāriq ibn ʿAmr (d. ?): governor of Madina (*c*. 72–*c*. 73/*c*. 691–*c*. 693) under ʿAbd al-Malik. See *Tahdhīb*, v. 5–7.
Ṭāwūs (d. *c*. 110/728): Yemeni *faqīh*. See *Tahdhīb*, v. 8–10
Thābit ibn al-Aḥnaf (d. ?): Successor, *rāwī*. See *Tahdhīb*, ii. 11.
al-Thawrī, *see* Sufyān al-Thawrī
al-Tirmidhī (d. *c*. 279/892): compiler of *ḥadīth*. See *EI (1)*, iv. 796–7; *GAS*, i. 154–9.
ʿUbāda ibn al-Ṣāmit (d. *c*. 34/654): Companion. See *Tahdhīb*, v. 111–12.
ʿUbaydallāh ibn ʿAbd al-Karīm (Abū Zurʿa al-Rāzī) (d. 264/877): *ḥadīth*-scholar. See *GAS*, i. 145.
ʿUbaydallāh ibn ʿAbdallāh ibn ʿUtba ibn Masʿūd (d. *c*. 98/716): one of the 'Seven *Fuqahā*ʾ' of Madina. See *EI (2)*, Supplement, p. 311.
Ubayy ibn Kaʿb (d. *c*. 32/652): Companion. See *Tahdhīb*, i. 187–8
ʿUmar ibn ʿAbd al-ʿAzīz (d. 101/720): Umayyad caliph, 99–101/717–720; formerly governor of Madina (*c*. 87–*c*. 93/*c*. 706–*c*. 712) under al-Walīd ibn ʿAbd al-Malik. See *EI (1)*, iii. 977–9.
ʿUmar ibn al-Khaṭṭāb (d. 23/644); Companion; second caliph, 13–23/634–644. See *EI (1)*, iii. 982–4.
Umm Sharīk (d. ?): Companion. See *Tahdhīb*, xii. 472.
ʿUrwa ibn al-Zubayr (d. *c*. 94/713): one of the 'Seven *Fuqahā*ʾ' of Madina. See *EI (2)*, Supplement, p. 311; *GAS*, i. 278–9.
Usāma ibn Zayd (d. 54/673): Companion. See *Tahdhīb*, i. 208–10.
al-ʿUtbī, *see* Muḥammad al-ʿUtbī
ʿUthmān ibn ʿAffān (d. 35/655): Companion; third caliph, 24–35/644–656. See *EI (1)*, iii. 1008–11.
al-Wāḥidī (d. 468/1075): scholar of the Qurʾan. See *GAL*, Supplement, i. 730–1.
al-Walīd ibn ʿAbd al-Malik (d. 96/715): Umayyad caliph, 86–96/705–715. See *EI (1)*, iv. 1111.
Warsh (d. 197/812): Egyptian *qāri*ʾ. See *GAS*, i. 11.
Yaḥyā ibn ʿAwn (d. 298/910): *rāwī* from his father, ʿAwn ibn Yūsuf, from Ibn Wahb. See *Muw. Ibn Wahb*, p. 54; Schacht, 'Manuscripts in Kairouan', p. 249.

Yaḥyā ibn Saʿīd al-Anṣārī (d. 143/760): Madinan *qāḍī* and *faqīh*. See *GAS*, i. 407.
Yaḥyā ibn Saʿīd ibn al-ʿĀṣ (d. ?): *rāwī*; son of the Madinan governor. See *Tahdhīb*, xi. 215–16.
Yaḥyā ibn Saʿīd al-Qaṭṭān (d. 198/813): *ḥadīth*-scholar. See *Tahdhīb*, xi. 216–20.
Yaḥyā ibn Yaḥyā al-Laythī (d. 234/848): transmitter of *Muw.* See *GAS*, i. 459; *Mad.* ii. 534–47; *Dībāj*, ii. 352–3.
Yazīd ibn ʿAbd al-Malik (d. 105/724): Umayyad caliph, 101–105/720–724. See *EI (1)*, iv. 1162.
Zayd ibn Abī Unaysa al-Jazarī al-Ruhāwī (*or* al-Rahāwī) (d. *c.* 125/743): *rāwī.* See *Tahdhīb*, iii. 397–8.
Zayd ibn ʿAlī (d. 122/740): eponymous 'founder' of the Zaydi sect and presumed author of the *Majmūʿ al-fiqh.* See *EI (1)*, iv. 1193–4; *GAS*, i. 556–60.
Zayd ibn Aslam (d. 136/753): Madinan *faqīh.* See *GAS*, i. 405–6.
Zayd ibn Thābit (d. *c.* 45/666): Companion. See *GAS*, i. 401–2.
Ziyād ibn ʿAbd al-Raḥmān (Shabṭūn) (d. *c.* 193/808): Andalusian transmitter of *Muw.* to Yaḥyā ibn Yaḥyā al-Laythī. See Muranyi, *Materialien*, pp. 99–100.
Ziyād ibn Saʿīd al-Khurāsānī (d. ?): *rāwī.* See *Tahdhīb*, iii. 369–70.
al-Zuhrī, *see* Ibn Shihāb al-Zuhrī
Zurayq ibn Ḥakīm (*or* Ruzayq ibn Ḥukaym) (d. ?): *rāwī*; governor of Ayla (presumably 99–101/717–720) under ʿUmar ibn ʿAbd al-ʿAzīz. See al-Bukhārī, *Tārīkh*, ii/1. 318; Ibn Ḥibbān, vi. 347; Ibn Mākūlā, iv. 47, 48, n. 3, ii. 489; *Tahdhīb*, iii. 273.
al-Zurqānī (d. 1122/1710): Egyptian scholar; commentator on *Muw.* See *GAL*, Supplement, ii. 439.

Bibliography and Bibliographical Abbreviations

Arabic

ʿAbd al-Razzāq al-Ṣanʿānī (d. 211/827), *al-Muṣannaf*, 11 vols., ed. Ḥabīb al-Raḥmān al-Aʿẓamī, Beirut, 1390–2 (1970–2)

Abū l-ʿArab Muḥammad ibn Aḥmad ibn Tamīm (d. 333/945), *Ṭabaqāt ʿulamāʾ Ifrīqīya*, ed. Mohammed Ben Cheneb, Paris, 1915–20

Abū Dāwūd (d. 275/888), *Sunan* (on the margin of al-Zurqānī's *Sharḥ*, q.v.), 4 vols., Cairo, 1399/1979

Abū Nuʿaym (d. 430/1038), *Ḥilyat al-awliyāʾ*, 10 vols., Cairo, 1351–7/1932–8

Abū ʿUbayd (d. 224/838), *Kitāb al-Nāsikh wa-l-mansūkh*, in J. Burton, *Abū ʿUbaid al-Qāsim b. Sallām's* K. al-nāsikh wa-l-mansūkh, Cambridge, 1987

Abū Yūsuf (d. 182/789), *Kitāb al-Āthār*, ed. Abū l-Wafā, Cairo, 1355 (1936)

Abū Zahra, Muḥammad, *Uṣūl al-fiqh*, Cairo, n.d.

Aḥmad Bābā al-Tinbuktī (d. *c.* 1032/1624), *Nayl al-ibtihāj bi-taṭrīz al-Dībāj*, Fez, 1317 (1900)

Āl Mubārak, Aḥmad ʿAbd al-ʿAzīz, *Mālik ibn Anas*, Abu Dhabi, 1406/1986

al-ʿĀmilī, Muḥammad ibn al-Ḥasan al-Ḥurr (d. 1104/1692), *Wasāʾil al-Shīʿa*, 20 vols., 4th edn., Beirut, 1391/1971

al-Bājī (d. 474/1081), *Iḥkām al-fuṣūl fī aḥkām al-uṣūl*, ed. ʿAbd al-Majīd Turkī, Beirut, 1409/1986

—— *al-Muntaqā, sharḥ Muwaṭṭaʾ al-Imām Mālik*, 7 vols., Beirut, n.d. (originally Cairo, 1331–2 [1913–14]) (cited as al-Bājī)

al-Bājaqnī (?), Muḥammad ʿAbd al-Ghanī, *al-Madkhal ilā uṣūl al-fiqh al-Mālikī*, Beirut, n.d.

al-Bāqillānī, Abū Bakr (d. 403/1013), *Nukat al-intiṣār li-naql al-Qurʾān*, ed. Muḥammad Zaghlūl Sallām, Alexandria, 1971

Bayān, see Ibn Rushd (al-Jadd), *al-Bayān wa-l-taḥṣīl*

al-Bayḍāwī, ʿAbdallāh ibn ʿUmar (d. 685/1286), *Anwār al-tanzīl wa-asrār al-taʾwīl*, Cairo, 1330/1912

al-Bukhari (d. 256/870), *Ṣaḥīḥ al-Bukhārī*, in Arabic and English, translated by Muhammad Muhsin Khan, 9 vols., Lahore, 1979

—— *al-Tārīkh al-kabīr*, 8 parts in 4 vols., Hyderabad, 1st and 2nd edn., 1360–82/1941–63

Daʿāim, see al-Nuʿmān ibn Muḥammad

al-Dānī (d. 444/1053), *al-Muḥkam fī naqṭ al-maṣāḥif*, ed. ʿIzzat Ḥasan, Damascus, 1379/1960

—— *al-Muqniʿ fī rasm maṣāḥif al-amṣār maʿa Kitāb al-Naqṭ*, ed. Muḥammad al-Ṣādiq Qamḥāwī, Cairo, n.d.

—— *al-Muqniʿ*, ed. O. Pretzl, in *Orthographie und Punktierung des Koran*, Leipzig/ Istanbul, 1932

al-Dārimī (d. 255/869), *Sunan*, 2 vols., Damascus, 1349 (1930)

al-Dhahabī (d. 748/1348), *al-ʿIbar fī khabar man ghabar*, 4 vols., Beirut, 1405/1985

—— *Maʿrifat al-qurrāʾ al-kibār ʿalā l-ṭabaqāt wa-l-aʿṣār*, 2 vols., Beirut, 1404/1984

—— *Siyar aʿlām al-nubalāʾ*, 25 vols., Beirut, 1401–9/1981–8

—— *Tadhkirat al-ḥuffāẓ*, 4 vols. in two, Hyderabad, 1315 (1897)

—— *Tajrīd asmāʾ al-ṣaḥāba*, 2 vols. in one, Hyderabad, 1315 (1897)

Dībāj, *see* Ibn Farḥūn, *al-Dībāj*

al-Dihlawī, Shāh Walī Allāh (d. *c.* 1176/1762), *Ḥujjat Allāh al-bāligha*, 2 vols. in one, Cairo, 1352 (1933)

al-Fārisī, Abū ʿAlī al-Ḥasan ibn ʿAbd al-Ghaffār (d. 377/987), *al-Ḥujja li-l-qurrāʾ al-sabʿa*, 2 vols., Beirut, 1984/1404

al-Fasawī, Abū Yūsuf Yaʿqūb ibn Sufyān (d. 277/890), *Kitāb al-Maʿrifa wa-l-tārīkh*, ed. Akram Ḍiyāʾ al-ʿUmarī, 3 vols., Beirut, 1401/1981

Gannūn, ʿAbdallāh, '*Mālik: ḥayātuhu wa-fiqhuhu wa-Muwaṭṭaʾuhu*', paper delivered at the First Conference of Mālikī *Fiqh*, Norwich, England, 1982 (unpublished transcript)

Ghāya, *see* Ibn al-Jazarī, *Ghāyat al-nihāya fī ṭabaqāt al-qurrāʾ*

Hidāya, *see* al-Marghīnānī, *al-Hidāya*

Ḥilya, see Abū Nuʿaym, *Ḥilyat al-awliyāʾ*

Ḥujjat Allāh, *see* al-Dihlawī, *Ḥujjat Allāh*

ʿIbar, *see* al-Dhahabī, *al-ʿIbar*

Ibn ʿAbd al-Barr (d. 463/1071), *al-Intiqāʾ fī faḍāʾil al-aʾimma al-thalātha al-fuqahāʾ*, Cairo, 1350/1931

—— *Jāmiʿ bayān al-ʿilm wa-faḍlihi*, ed. ʿAbd al-Raḥmān Ḥasan Maḥmūd, Cairo, 1975/1395

—— *Tajrīd al-tamhīd*, Beirut, n.d.

—— *al-Tamhīd li-mā fī l-Muwaṭṭaʾ min al-maʿānī wa-l-asānīd*, 24 vols., Mohammedia, 1397–1411/1977–1991

—— *al-Istīʿāb fī maʿrifat al-aṣḥāb*, 2 vols., Hyderabad, 1336 (1917)

Ibn Abī Ḥātim (d. 327/938), *Taqdimat al-maʿrifa li-Kitāb al-Jarḥ wa-l-taʿdīl*, Hyderabad, 1271/1952 (cited as Ibn Abī Ḥātim)

—— *Ādāb al-Shāfiʿī wa-manāqibuhu*, ed. ʿAbd al-Ghanī ʿAbd al-Khāliq, Ḥalab, 1372/ 1953

Ibn Abī Shayba (d. 235/849), *Muṣannaf Ibn Abī Shayba fī l-aḥādīth*, vol. i., Hyderabad, 1386/1966

Ibn Abī Zayd al-Qayrawānī (d. 386/996), *Kitāb al-Jāmiʿ*, Beirut/Tunis, 1402/1982 (cited as *Jāmiʿ*)

—— *Kitāb al-Jāmiʿ*, ed. ʿAbd al-Majīd Turkī, 2nd ed., Beirut, 1990

Ibn al-ʿArabī (d. 543/1148), *Aḥkām al-Qurʾān*, 4 vols., Cairo?, 1376/1957

Ibn ʿAsākir (d. 571/1176), *Tārīkh Dimashq*, 7 vols., Damascus, 1329–32 (1911–14)

Ibn ʿĀshūr, Muḥammad al-Fāḍ il, *Aʿlām al-fikr al-islāmī fī tārīkh al-Maghrib al-ʿArabī*, Maktabat al-Najāḥ, Tunis, n.d.

Ibn al-Athīr (d. 630/1233), *al-Kāmil fī l-tārīkh*, 13 vols., Beirut, 1385–7/1965–7 (cited as Ibn al-Athīr)

—— *Usd al-ghāba fī maʿrifat al-ṣaḥāba*, 5 vols., Cairo 1280 (1863)

Ibn Farḥūn (d. 799/1397), *al-Dībāj al-mudhhab*, 2 vols., ed. Muḥammad al-Aḥmadī Abū l-Nūr, Cairo, 1972?

Ibn Ḥabīb, ʿAbd al-Malik (d. 238/852), *al-Wāḍiḥa (Abwāb al-ṭahāra)*, in B. Ossendorf-Conrad, *Das 'Kitāb al-Wāḍiḥa' des ʿAbd al-Malik b. Ḥabīb. Edition and Kommentar zu Ms. Qarawiyyīn 809/40 (Abwāb al-ṭahāra)*, Beirut/Stuttgart, 1994

Ibn Ḥajar (d. 852/1449), *Fatḥ al-bārī bi-sharḥ Ṣaḥīḥ al-Bukhārī*, ed. ʿAbd al-ʿAzīz ibn ʿAbdallāh ibn Bāz *et al.*, 14 vols., Beirut, 1959–70

—— *al-Iṣāba fī tamyīz al-ṣaḥāba*, 8 vols. in four, Cairo, 1323–5 (1905–7)

—— *Tahdhīb al-Tahdhīb*, 12 vols. in six, Hyderabad, 1325–7 (1907–9)

Ibn Ḥamdūn (d. *c.* 1273/1857), *Ḥāshiyat Ibn Ḥamdūn ʿalā sharḥ Mayyāra li-manẓūmat al-Murshid al-muʿīn li-ʿAbd al-Wāḥid ibn ʿĀshir*, 2 vols. in one, Beirut, 1392/1972

Ibn Ḥazm (d. 456/1064), *Jamharat ansāb al-ʿArab*, ed. E. Lévi-Provençal, Cairo, 1948

Ibn Ḥibbān (d. 354/965), *Kitāb al-Thiqāt*, 9 vols., Hyderabad, 1393–1403/1973–83 (cited as Ibn Ḥibbān)

—— *Mashāhīr ʿulamāʾ al-amṣār*, ed. M. Fleischhammer, Cairo, 1379/1959

Ibn Hishām (d. *c.* 218/834), *Sīrat Ibn Hishām*, ed. F. Wüstenfeld, Göttingen, 1860

—— *al-Sīra al-nabawiyya*, ed. Ṭāhā ʿAbd al-Raʾūf Saʿd, 4 vols. in two, Cairo, 1397/1978

—— *Tahdhīb Sīrat Ibn Hishām*, ed. ʿAbd al-Salām Hārūn, Cairo, 1374/1955

Ibn al-ʿImād (d. 1089/1679), *Shadharāt al-dhahab*, 8 vols., Cairo, 1350–1 (1931–2)

Ibn al-Jawzī (d. 597/1200), *Manāqib ʿUmar ibn ʿAbd al-ʿAzīz*, ed. Naʿīm Zarzūr, Beirut, 1404/1984

Ibn al-Jazarī (d. 833/1429), *Ghāyat al-nihāya fī ṭabaqāt al-qurrāʾ*, ed. G. Bergstraesser, 2 vols. in one, Cairo, 1351–2/1932–3

—— *al-Nashr fī l-qirāʾāt al-ʿashr*, ed. Muḥammad Aḥmad Dahmān, 2 vols., Damascus, 1345 (1926)

Ibn Juzayy (d. 741/1340), *al-Qawānīn al-fiqhiyya*, Beirut, 1404/1984

—— *Tafsīr*, Beirut, 1403/1983

Ibn al-Kalbī (d. *c.* 204/819), *Jamharat al-nasab*, ed. Maḥmūd Firdaws al-ʿAẓm, 3 vols., Damascus, 1406/1986

Ibn Kathīr (d. 774/1373), *al-Bidāya wa-l-nihāya*, 16 vols., Cairo and Beirut, 1351/1932–

—— *ʿUmar ibn ʿAbd al-ʿAzīz*, ed. Aḥmad al-Sharbāṣī, 2nd ed., Cairo?, n.d.

Ibn Khālawayh (d. 370/980), *Mukhtaṣar fī shawādhdh al-Qurʾān min Kitāb al-Badīʿ*, in *Ibn Khālawaih's Sammlung Nichtkanonischer Koranlesarten*, ed. G. Bergsträsser, Cairo/Leipzig, 1934

Ibn Khallikān (d. 681/1282), *Wafayāt al-aʿyān*, 2 vols., Būlāq, 1299 (1882)

Ibn al-Madīnī (d. 234/849), *ʿIlal al-ḥadīth wa-maʿrifat al-rijāl*, ed. ʿAbd al-Muʿṭī Amīn Qalʿajī, Halab, 1400/1980

Ibn Mājah (d. 273/886), *Sunan*, 2 vols. in one, Cairo, 1313 (1895)

Ibn Mākūlā (d. 475/1095), *al-Ikmāl*, 6 vols., Hyderabad, 1st and 2nd edn., 1381–92/1961–72

Ibn Manẓūr (d. 711/1311), *Lisān al-ʿArab*, 20 vols., Būlāq, 1300–7/1882–9

Ibn Mihrān al-Iṣbahānī (d. 381/991), *al-Mabsūṭ fī l-qirāʾāt al-ʿashr*, ed. Subayʿ Ḥamza Ḥākimī, Damascus, *c.* 1401/1981

Ibn al-Mubārak (d. 181/797), *Kitāb al-Zuhd wa-l-raqāʾiq*, ed. Ḥabīb al-Raḥmān al-Aʿẓamī, Malegaon, 1385/1966

—— *Kitāb al-Jihād*, ed. Nazīh Ḥammād, Beirut, 1391/1971

Ibn Mujāhid (d. 324/936), *Kitāb al-Sabʿa fī l-qirāʾāt*, ed. Shawqī Ḍayf, 2nd edn., Cairo, n.d.

Ibn al-Murtaḍā, Aḥmad ibn Yaḥyā (d. 840/1437), *al-Baḥr al-zakhkhār al-jāmiᶜ li-madhāhib al-amṣār*, 5 vols., Cairo, 1366–8/1947–9

Ibn al-Qāḍī (d. 1025/1616), *Jadhwat al-iqtibās fī man ḥalla min al-aᶜlām madīnat Fās*, Fez, 1309 (1893)

Ibn Qayyim al-Jawziyya (d. 751/1350), *Iᶜlām al-muwaqqiᶜīn*, Idārat al-Ṭibāᶜa al-Munīriyya, Cairo, n.d.

Ibn Qutayba (d. 276/889), *Kitāb al-Maᶜārif*, ed. Saroite Okacha (Tharwat ᶜUkāsha), Cairo, 1960

—— *Kitāb Taʾwīl mukhtalif al-ḥadīth*, Cairo, 1326 (1908)

Ibn Rushd al-Qurṭubī (al-Ḥafīd) (d. 595/1198), *Bidāyat al-mujtahid*, 2 vols. in one, Cairo, 1329 (1911) (cited as Ibn Rushd)

Ibn Rushd al-Qurṭubī (al-Jadd), Abū l-Walīd (d. 520/1126), *al-Bayān wa-l-taḥṣīl wa-l-sharḥ wa-l-tawjīh wa-l-taᶜlīl fī masāʾil al-Mustakhraja*, ed. Muḥammad Ḥajjī, 20 vols., Beirut, 1404–7/1984–7

Ibn Saᶜd (d. 230/845), *al-Ṭabaqāt al-kubrā*, ed. E. Sachau, 10 vols., Leiden, 1940

—— *al-Ṭabaqāt al-kubrā, al-qism al-mutammim li-tābiᶜī ahl al-Madīna wa-man baᶜdahum*, ed. Ziyād Muḥammad Manṣūr, Madina, 1408/1987

Ibn Taymiyya (d. 728/1328), *Ṣiḥḥat uṣūl madhhab ahl al-Madīna*, ed. Zakariyyā ᶜAlī Yūsuf, Cairo, n.d.

Ibn Wahb, ᶜAbdallāh (d. 197/812), *Al-Muwaṭṭaʾ: Kitāb al-muḥāraba*, in M. Muranyi, *ᶜAbd Allāh b. Wahb, Leben und Werk. Al-Muwaṭṭaʾ: Kitāb al-muḥāraba*, Wiesbaden, 1992

Iᶜlām, *see* Ibn Qayyim al-Jawziyya

Intiqāʾ, *see* Ibn ᶜAbd al-Barr, *al-Intiqāʾ*

Intiṣār, *see* al-Rāᶜī

Iṣāba, *see* Ibn Ḥajar, *al-Iṣāba*

Istīᶜāb, *see* Ibn ᶜAbd al-Barr, *al-Istīᶜāb*

ᶜIyāḍ ibn Mūsā al-Yaḥṣubī, al-Qāḍī (d. 544/1149), *Tartīb al-madārik wa-taqrīb al-masālik li-maᶜrifat aᶜlām madhhab Mālik*, ed. Aḥmad Bakīr Maḥmūd, 5 vols. in three, Beirut/Tripoli, 1387/1967

—— *Tartīb al-madārik*, ed. Muḥammad Tāwīt al-Ṭanjī *et al.*, 8 vols., 2nd edn., Mohammedia, 1402–3/1982–3

Jadhwa, *see* Ibn al-Qāḍī

Jalālayn, *see* al-Maḥallī and al-Suyūṭī, *Tafsīr al-Jalālayn*

Jāmiᶜ, *see* Ibn Abī Zayd al-Qayrawānī

al-Jaṣṣāṣ (d. 370/981), *Aḥkām al-Qurʾān*, 3 vols. in two, Constantinople, 1335–8 (1916–19)

Kashf, *see* Makkī ibn Abī Ṭālib

al-Kattānī, Muḥammad ibn Jaᶜfar (d. 1345/1927), *Salwat al-anfās wa-muḥādathat al-akyās bi-man uqbira min al-ᶜulamāʾ wa-l-ṣulaḥāʾ bi-Fās*, 3 vols., Fez, 1316 (1898)

Khalīl ibn Isḥāq (d. *c.* 776/1374), *Mukhtaṣar Khalīl*, ed. al-Ṭāhir Aḥmad al-Zāwī, Cairo, n.d.

Khallāf, ᶜAbd al-Wahhāb, *ᶜIlm uṣūl al-fiqh*, 11th edn., Cairo, 1397/1977

al-Khaṭīb, Muḥammad ᶜAjjāj, *al-Sunna qabl al-tadwīn*, Baghdad, 1383/1963

al-Khaṭīb al-Baghdādī (d. 463/1071), *Taqyīd al-ᶜilm*, ed. Yūsuf al-ᶜIshsh, 2nd edn., 1395/1975

—— *Tārīkh Baghdād*, 14 vols., Cairo, 1349/1931

al-Khirshī (d. 1101/1689), *Sharḥ al-Khirshī ᶜalā Mukhtaṣar Khalīl*, 5 vols., Cairo, 1307–8 (1889–90) al-Khushanī, Muḥammad ibn al-Ḥārith ibn Asad, *see* Abū l-ᶜArab

Lisān, *see* Ibn Manẓūr

Mab., *see* al-Sarakhsī, *al-Mabsūṭ*

Mad., *see* ᶜIyāḍ, *Tartīb al-madārik* (ed. Aḥmad Bakīr Maḥmūd)

Mad. (Mo.), *see* ᶜIyāḍ, *Tartīb al-madārik* (Mohammedia edition)

al-Maḥallī, Jalāl ad-Dīn (d. 864/1459) and al-Suyūṭī, Jalāl ad-Dīn (d. 911/1505), *Tafsīr al-Jalālayn*, n. pl., n. d.

Maḥmūd, ᶜAbd al-Ḥalīm, *Sufyān al-Thawrī: amīr al-muʾminīna fī l-ḥadīth*, Cairo, 1970

Makhlūf, *Shajarat al-nūr al-zakiyya fī ṭabaqāt al-Mālikiyya*, two parts in one, Beirut, 1974 (offset from 1349 [1930] edition)

Makkī ibn Abī Ṭālib (d. 437/1045), *al-Kashf ᶜan wujūh al-qirāʾāt al-sabᶜ wa-ᶜilalihā wa-ḥujajihā*, ed. Muḥyī l-Dīn Ramaḍān, 2 vols., Beirut, 1401/1981

Mālik ibn Anas (d. 179/795), *al-Muwaṭṭaʾ* (*riwāya* of Yaḥyā ibn Yaḥyā al-Laythī, printed with al-Suyūṭī's *Tanwīr al-ḥawālik*), 2 vols., Cairo, 1349 (1930)

—— *al-Muwaṭṭaʾ* (*riwāya* of Yaḥyā ibn Yaḥyā al-Laythī), ed. Aḥmad Rātib ᶜAmrūsh, 8th edn., Beirut, 1404/1984

—— *al-Muwaṭṭaʾ* (*riwāya* of Yaḥyā ibn Yaḥyā al-Laythī), ed. Muḥammad Fuʾād ᶜAbd al-Bāqī, Cairo, *c.* 1371/1951

—— *al-Muwaṭṭaʾ* (= the middle third of the *riwāya* of Yaḥyā ibn Yaḥyā), Chester Beatty MS. no. 3001 (dated 277 AH).

—— *al-Muwaṭṭaʾ* (= fragments of the *riwāya* of Yaḥyā ibn Yaḥyā al-Laythī), Bodleian Library MS. Arab. e. 181

—— *al-Muwaṭṭaʾ* (*riwāya* of Abū Muṣᶜab al-Zuhrī), ed. Bashshār ᶜAwwād Maᶜrūf and Maḥmūd Muḥammad, 2 vols., Beirut, 2nd ed., 1413/1993

—— *al-Muntaqā min al-Muwaṭṭaʾ* (= selections from the *riwāya* of Abū Muṣᶜab al-Zuhrī), Chester Beatty MS. no. 5498 (3)

—— *Muwaṭṭaʾ al-Imām Mālik ibn Anas, riwāyat Ibn al-Qāsim wa-talkhīṣ al-Qābisī*, ed. Muḥammad ibn ᶜAlawī ibn ᶜAbbās al-Mālikī, 2nd edn., Jeddah, 1408/1988

—— *Muwaṭṭaʾ al-Imām Mālik, qiṭᶜa minhu bi-riwāyat Ibn Ziyād* (*see* al-Nayfar, *Muw. Ibn Ziyād*)

—— *al-Muwaṭṭaʾ* (parts of the *riwāya* of al-Qaᶜnabī), ed. ᶜAbd al-Ḥafīẓ Manṣūr, Kuwait, n.d.

—— *al-Muwaṭṭaʾ* (*riwāya* of al-Shaybānī), ed. ᶜAbd al-Wahhāb ᶜAbd al-Laṭīf, Beirut, n.d.

—— *al-Muwaṭṭaʾ* (*riwāya* of al-Shaybānī), Bodleian Library MS. Bodl. Or. 641

—— *al-Muwaṭṭaʾ* (parts of the *riwāya* of Suwayd al-Ḥādathānī), al-Manāma, 1415/1994

al-Mālikī, Abū Bakr ᶜAbdallāh ibn Muḥammad (d. after 464/1071), *Riyāḍ al-nufūs*, 3 vols., Beirut, 1403/1983

al-Mālikī al-Ḥasanī, Muḥammad ibn ᶜAlawī ibn ᶜAbbās, *Faḍl al-Muwaṭṭaʾ*, Cairo, 1398/1978

al-Marghīnānī (d. 593/1197), *al-Hidāya, sharḥ Bidāyat al-mubtadī*, 4 vols. in two, Cairo, 1384/1965

Mud., = *al-Mudawwana al-kubrā* (opinions of Mālik, Ibn al-Qāsim and others, compiled by Saḥnūn), 16 vols. in five, Cairo, 1323–4 (1905–6)

Mujāhid (d. 104/722), *Tafsīr Mujāhid*, ed. ᶜAbd al-Raḥmān al-Ṭāhir al-Sūratī, Doha, 1396/1976

Muᶜjam = *al-Muᶜjam al-mufahras li-alfāẓ al-Qurʾān al-Karīm*, ed. Muḥammad Fuʾād ᶜAbd al-Bāqī, Cairo, 1378/1958

*Muqni*ᶜ, *see* al-Dānī, *al-Muqni*ᶜ
al-Muṣᶜabī, ᶜAbd al-ᶜAzīz ibn Ibrāhīm (d. 1223/1808), *Kitāb al-Nīl wa-shifāʾ al-ᶜalīl*, 2 vols. in one, Cairo, 1305 (1888)
Muslim (d. 261/875), *al-Jāmiᶜ al-ṣaḥīḥ*, 2 vols. in one, Būlāq, 1290 (1873)
Muw., *see* Mālik ibn Anas, *Muwaṭṭaʾ al-Imām Mālik* (Cairo, 1370/1951)
Muw. Abū Muṣᶜab, *see* Mālik ibn Anas, *al-Muwaṭṭaʾ* (*riwāya* of Abū Muṣᶜab al-Zuhrī)
Muw. Ibn Wahb, *see* Ibn Wahb
Muw. Ibn Ziyād, *see* al-Nayfar, *Muwaṭṭaʾ al-Imām Mālik, qiṭᶜa minhu bi-riwāyat Ibn Ziyād*
Muw. Q., *see* Mālik ibn Anas, *al-Muwaṭṭaʾ* (parts of the *riwāya* of al-Qaᶜnabī)
Muw. Sh., *see* Mālik ibn Anas, *al-Muwaṭṭaʾ* (*riwāya* of al-Shaybānī), ed. ᶜAbd al-Wahhāb ᶜAbd al-Laṭīf
Muw. Suw., *see* Mālik ibn Anas, *al-Muwaṭṭaʾ* (parts of the *riwāya* of Suwayd al-Ḥādathānī)
al-Nasāʾī (d. 303/915), *Sunan*, 2 vols., Cairo, 1312 (1894)
Nashr, *see* Ibn al-Jazarī, *al-Nashr*
al-Nawawī (d. 676/1277), *Tahdhīb al-asmāʾ*, ed. F. Wüstenfeld, Göttingen, 1842–7
al-Nayfar, Muḥammad al-Shādhilī, *Muwaṭṭaʾ al-Imām Mālik, qiṭᶜa minhu bi-riwāyat Ibn Ziyād*, Beirut, 1400/1980 (cited as *Muw. Ibn Ziyād*)
—— '*ᶜAmal ahl al-Madīna: maᶜnāhu wa-ḥujjiyyatuhu*', paper delivered at 4th Conference of Mālikī *Fiqh*, Abu Dhabi, 1406/1986 (unpublished transcript)
al-Nīsābūrī, Niẓām al-Dīn al-Ḥasan ibn Muḥammad ibn Ḥusayn (d. 8th/14th or 9th/15th century?), *Gharāʾib al-Qurʾān* (on the margin of al-Ṭabarī's *Tafsīr*, q.v.)
al-Nuᶜmān ibn Muḥammad (d. 363/974), *Daᶜāim al-Islām*, ed. A.A.A. Fyzee, 2 vols., Cairo, 1383/1963
Q = the Qurʾan
al-Qāḍī, ᶜAbd al-Fattāḥ, *Sharḥ al-Naẓm al-jāmiᶜ li-qirāʾat al-Imām Nāfiᶜ*, Tanta, 1961
Qamḥāwī, Muḥammad al-Ṣādiq, *al-Baḥth wa-l-istiqrāʾ fī tarājim al-qurrāʾ*, Cairo, 1401/1981
al-Qarāfī (d. 684/1285), *al-Dhakhīra*, ed. ᶜAbd al-Wahhāb ᶜAbd al-Laṭīf and ᶜAbd al-Samīᶜ Aḥmad Imām, Kuwait, 1402/1982
—— *Sharḥ Tanqīḥ al-fuṣūl fī l-uṣūl*, Cairo, 1306 (1888)
Qawānīn, *see* Ibn Juzayy, *al-Qawānīn al-fiqhiyya*
Qurʾan, *riwāyat* Qālūn *ᶜan* Nāfiᶜ, Beirut/Tunis, 1974
—— *riwāyat* Warsh *ᶜan* Nāfiᶜ, Beirut, *c.* 1392 (1972)
—— *riwāyat* Warsh *ᶜan* Nāfiᶜ, Algiers, *c.* 1399 (1979)
—— *riwāyat* Warsh *ᶜan* Nāfiᶜ (19th century, from Nigeria), Bodleian Library MS. Arab. d. 141
al-Rāᶜī al-Andalusī, Muḥammad (d. 853/1450), *Intiṣār al-faqīr al-sālik li-tarjīḥ madhhab al-Imām Mālik*, ed. Muḥammad Abū l-Ajfān, Beirut, 1981
al-Ramlī (d. 1004/1595), *Nihāyat al-muḥtāj ilā sharḥ al-Minhāj*, 8 vols., Cairo, 1357/1938
Riyāḍ, *see* al-Mālikī, Abū Bakr
Salwa, *see* al-Kattānī, Muḥammad ibn Jaᶜfar, *Salwat al-anfās*
al-Samᶜānī (d. 562/1167), *al-Ansāb*, 13 vols., Hyderabad, 1382–1402/1962–1982
al-Samhūdī (d. 911/1506), *Wafāʾ al-wafāʾ bi-akhbār dār al-Muṣṭafā*, 2 vols. in one, Cairo, 1326 (1908)
al-Ṣanᶜānī, *see* ᶜAbd al-Razzāq al-Ṣanᶜānī
al-Sarakhsī (d. *c.* 483/1090), *al-Mabsūṭ*, 30 vols. in thirteen, Cairo, 1324–31 (1906–12)

—— *Uṣūl al-Sarakhsī*, ed. Abū l-Wafā al-Afghānī, 2 vols., Cairo, 1372/1952
al-Shāfiʿī (d. 204/820), *Kitāb al-Umm*, 7 vols., Cairo, 1321–6 (1903–8)
al-Shāṭibī (d. 790/1388), *al-Muwāfaqāt fī uṣūl al-sharīʿa*, 4 vols., Cairo, n.d.
al-Shaybānī (d. 189/805), *Kitāb al-Ḥujja ʿalā ahl al-Madīna*, ed. Mahdī Ḥasan al-Kīlānī al-Qādirī, 4 vols., Beirut, n.d. (originally Hyderabad, 1385/1965)
al-Shīrāzī, Abū Isḥāq (d. 476/1083), *Ṭabaqāt al-fuqahāʾ*, ed. Iḥsān ʿAbbās, Beirut, 1970
Siyar, see al-Dhahabī, *Siyar*
al-Suyūṭī, Jalāl al-Dīn (d. 911/1505), *Isʿāf al-mubaṭṭaʾ bi-rijāl al-Muwaṭṭaʾ* (at the end of his *Tanwīr*, q.v.)
—— *al-Itqān fī ʿulūm al-Qurʾān*, ed. Muḥammad Sharīf Sukkar, 2 vols., Beirut, 1407/1987
—— *Lubāb al-nuqūl fī asbāb al-nuzūl*, Beirut, 1978
—— *Tafsīr al-Jalālayn* (*see* al-Maḥallī)
—— *Tanwīr al-ḥawālik*, 2 vols., Cairo, 1370/1951 (printed with *Muw.*)
—— *Tanwīr al-ḥawālik*, 3 vols. in one, Cairo, 1984 (printed with *Muw.*)
al-Ṭabarī (d. 310/923), *Kitāb Ikhtilāf al-fuqahāʾ*, ed. J. Schacht, Leiden, 1933
—— *Tafsīr*, 30 vols. in ten, Cairo, 1321 (1903) (cited as al-Ṭabarī)
—— *Tārīkh al-rusul wa-l-mulūk*, ed. de Goeje and others, 3 vols. in fifteen, Leiden, 1879–1901
Tadhkira, see al-Dhahabī, *Tadhkirat al-ḥuffāẓ*
Tahdhīb, see Ibn Ḥajar, *Tahdhīb al-tahdhīb*
Tajrīd, see Ibn ʿAbd al-Barr, *Tajrīd al-tamhīd*
Tamhīd, see Ibn ʿAbd al-Barr, *al-Tamhīd*
Tanwīr, see al-Suyūṭī, *Tanwīr al-ḥawālik*
Tārīkh Baghdād, see al-Khaṭīb al-Baghdādī
al-Tirmidhī (d. *c.* 279/892), *Ṣaḥīḥ al-Tirmidhī*, Būlāq, 1292 (1875)
al-Ṭūsī (d. *c.* 459/1067), *al-Nihāya fī mujarrad al-fiqh wa-l-fatāwā*, Beirut, 1390/1970
Usd, see Ibn al-Athīr, *Usd al-ghāba*
Wāḍiḥa, see Ibn Ḥabīb
al-Wāḥidī (d. 468/1075), *Asbāb al-nuzūl*, Beirut, n.d.
Wakīʿ (d. 306/918), *Akhbār al-quḍāt*, ed. ʿAbd al-ʿAzīz Muṣṭafā al-Marāghī, 3 vols., Cairo, 1366/1947
al-Wansharīsī (d. 914/1508), *Īḍāḥ al-masālik ilā qawāʿid al-Imām Mālik*, ed. Aḥmad Bū Ṭāhir al-Khaṭṭābī, Mohammedia, 1400/1980
Wuld Abbāh (?), Muḥammad al-Mukhtār, *Madkhal ilā uṣūl al-fiqh al-Mālikī*, Tripoli/Tunis, 1987
al-Yāfiʿī (d. 768/1367), *Mirʾāt al-janān wa-ʿibrat al-yaqẓān*, 4 vols. in two, Hyderabad, 1337–9 (1918–20)
al-Zabīdī (d. 1145/1732), *Tāj al-ʿarūs*, 10 vols., Būlāq, 1306–7 (1888–9)
al-Zamakhsharī (d. 538/1144), *al-Kashshāf ʿan ḥaqāʾiq al-tanzīl*, Calcutta, 1856
Zayd ibn ʿAlī (d. 122/740), *Majmūʿ al-fiqh* (= *'Corpus Iuris' di Zaid ibn ʿAlī*), ed. E. Griffini, Milan, 1919
Zaydān, ʿAbd al-Karīm, *al-Wajīz fī uṣūl al-fiqh*, Beirut, 1405/1985
al-Ziriklī, *al-Aʿlām*, 10 vols, n. pl., n. d.
al-Zubayrī, Muṣʿab ibn ʿAbdallāh (d. 236/851), *Kitāb Nasab Quraysh*, ed. E. Lévi-Provençal, Cairo, 1953
al-Zurqānī (d. 1122/1710), *Sharḥ al-Muwaṭṭaʾ*, 4 vols., Cairo, 1399/1979

European

Abbott, N., *Studies in Arabic Literary Papyri*, ii. *Qur'anic Commentary and Tradition*, Chicago, 1967

Abd-Allah, Umar Faruq, 'Mālik's Concept of *ʿAmal* in the Light of Mālikī Legal Theory', Ph.D. thesis, University of Chicago, 1978

Abdul-Qadir, Muhammad Al-Aroosi, 'The Reception and Development of Malikite Legal Doctrine in the Western Islamic World', unpublished Ph.D. thesis, Edinburgh University, 1973

Aghnides, N.P., *Mohammedan Theories of Finance with an Introduction to Mohammedan Law*, New York, 1916

Ahmad, Imtiaz, 'The Significance of *Sunna* and *Ḥadīth* and Their Early Documentation', unpublished Ph.D. thesis, Edinburgh, 1974

Ansari, Z.I., 'The Early Development of Islamic Fiqh in Kūfa, with Special Reference to the Works of Abū Yūsuf and Shaybānī', unpublished Ph.D. thesis, McGill University, 1968

—— 'Islamic Juristic Terminology Before Shāfiʿī: A Semantic Analysis with Special Reference to Kūfa', *Arabica*, xix (1972), pp. 255–300

Azmi, M.M., *Studies in Early* Ḥadīth *Literature*, Beirut, 1968

—— *On Schacht's Origins of Muhammadan Jurisprudence*, Riyadh/New York etc, 1985

Bacharach, J., *A Near East Studies Handbook, 570–1974*, Seattle and London, 1974

Bosworth, C.E., *The Islamic Dynasties*, Edinburgh, 1967

Bravmann, M.M., *The Spiritual Background of Early Islam*, Leiden, 1972

Brockelmann, C., *Geschichte der Arabischen Litteratur*, i, Weimar, 1898; ii, Berlin, 1902; Supplements i–iii, Leiden, 1937–42

Brockett, A., 'The Value of the Ḥafṣ and Warsh Transmissions for the Textual History of the Qurʾān', in *Approaches to the History of the Interpretation of the Qurʾān*, ed. A. Rippin, Oxford, 1988, pp. 31–45.

Brunschvig, R., 'Polémiques médiévales autour du rite de Malik', *Andalus*, xv (1950), pp. 377–435

—— 'Averroès Juriste', in *Études d'orientalisme dédiées à la mémoire de Lévi-Provençal*, Paris, 1962, i. 35–68; reprinted in Brunschvig, *Études d'islamologie*, ed. Abdel Magid Turki, Paris, 1976, ii. 167–200

BSOAS = *Bulletin of the School of Oriental and African Studies*

Burton, J., 'Those are the high-flying cranes', *JSS*, xv (1970), pp. 246–65

—— 'The Meaning of "Iḥṣān"', *JSS*, xix (1974), pp. 47–75

—— *The Collection of the Qurʾān*, Cambridge, 1977

—— 'The Origin of the Islamic Penalty for Adultery', *Transactions of the Glasgow University Oriental Society*, xxvi (1975–6) [published 1979], pp. 16–27

—— *Abū ʿUbaid al-Qāsim b. Sallām's* K. al-nāsikh wa-l-mansūkh, E.J.W. Gibb Memorial Trust, Cambridge, 1987 (cited as Abū ʿUbayd [q.v.])

—— 'The Exegesis of Q. 2: 106 and the Islamic Theories of *Naskh*: *mā nansakh min āya aw nansahā naʾti bi khayrin minhā aw mithlihā*', *BSOAS*, xlviii (1985), pp. 452–69.

—— *The Sources of Islamic Law*, Edinburgh, 1990

—— 'Law and Exegesis: The Penalty for Adultery in Islam', in *Approaches to the Qurʾān*, ed. G.R. Hawting and Abdul-Kader A. Shareef, London, 1993, pp. 269–84

—— *An Introduction to the Hadith*, Edinburgh, 1995
Caetani, L., *Chronographia Islamica*, 3 vols., Paris, 1912
Calder, N., *Studies in Early Muslim Jurisprudence*, Oxford, 1993
Caskel, W., *Ǧamharat an-nasab: Das Genealogische Werk des Hišām ibn Muḥammad al-Kalbī*, 2 vols., Leiden, 1966
Coulson, N.J., *A History of Islamic Law*, Edinburgh, 1964
—— *Succession in the Muslim Family*, Cambridge, 1971
Crone, P., *Roman, Provincial and Islamic Law*, Cambridge, 1987
—— and Hinds, M., *God's Caliph*, Cambridge, 1986
Dixon, A.A., *The Umayyad Caliphate 65–86/684–705 (A Political Study)*, London, 1971
Doi, Abdur Rahman, *Sharīʿah: The Islamic Law*, London, 1404/1984
Dutton, Y., review of Calder's *Studies in Early Muslim Jurisprudence*, *Journal of Islamic Studies*, v (1994), pp. 102–108
—— '*ʿAmal* v. *Ḥadīth* in Islamic Law: The Case of *Sadl al-yadayn* (Holding One's Hands by One's Sides) When Doing the Prayer', *Islamic Law and Society*, iii (1996), pp. 13–40
—— 'Juridical Practice and Madinan *ʿAmal: Qaḍāʾ* in the *Muwaṭṭaʾ* of *Mālik*', forthcoming in *Journal of Islamic Studies*, x (1999)
EI = *Encyclopaedia of Islam*, 1st edn., Leiden/London, 1913–38, 2nd edn., Leiden, 1960–
Fierro, I., 'La Polémique à propos de *rafʿ al-yadayn fī l-ṣalāt* dans al-Andalus', *Studia Islamica*, lxv (1987), pp. 69–90
—— 'The Introduction of *Ḥadīth* in al-Andalus', *Der Islam*, lxvi (1989), pp. 68–93
—— 'El Derecho Mālikí en al-Andalus: Siglos II/VIII-V/XI', *Al-Qanṭara*, xii (1991), pp. 119–32
Fyzee, A.A.A., *Outlines of Muhammedan Law*, Oxford, 1949
GAL, *see* Brockelmann, *Geschichte der Arabischen Litteratur*
GAS, *see* Sezgin, *Geschichte des Arabischen Schrifttums*
GdQ, *see* Nöldeke, *Geschichte des Qorāns*, iii
Gibb, H.A.R., *Mohammedanism*, Oxford, 1949
Goitein, S.D., 'The Birth-Hour of Islamic Law?', *The Muslim World*, l (1960), pp. 23–9
Goldziher, I., *Muslim Studies*, translated from the German *Muhammedanische Studien* (Halle, 1889–90) by C.R. Barber and S.M. Stern, 2 vols., London, 1966–71
Guillaume, A., review of Schacht's *Origins*, *BSOAS*, xvi (1954), pp. 176–7
Gurāyā, Muḥammad Yūsuf, 'Historical Background of the Compilation of the *Muwaṭṭaʾ* of Mālik b. Anas', *Islamic Studies*, vii (1968), pp. 379–92
Hamidullah, *Sahifa Hammam ibn Munabbih*, 5th edn., Hyderabad, 1380/1961
Hasan, Ahmad, 'The Theory of *Naskh*', *Islamic Studies*, iv (1965), pp. 181–200
—— *The Early Development of Islamic Jurisprudence*, Islamabad, 1970
Hasan, Suhaib, *An Introduction to the Sunnah*, Al-Quran Society, London, 1990
—— *An Introduction to the Science of Hadith*, Al-Quran Society, London, 1994
Hawting, G.R., *The First Dynasty of Islam: The Umayyad Caliphate AD 661–750*, London/Sydney, 1986
—— 'The Role of Qurʾān and *Ḥadīth* in the Legal Controversy About the Rights of a Divorced Woman During Her "Waiting Period" (*ʿidda*)', *BSOAS*, lii (1989), pp. 430–45
Hodgson, M.G.S., *The Venture of Islam: Conscience and History in a World Civilization*, 3 vols., Chicago and London, 1974

Jeffery, A., *Materials for the History of the Text of the Qur'an*, Leiden, 1937
JSS = *The Journal of Semitic Studies*
Juynboll, G.H.A., *Muslim Tradition*, Cambridge, 1983
—— 'Nāfiᶜ, the *mawlā* of Ibn ᶜUmar', *Der Islam*, xx (1993), pp. 207–44
Koren, J. and Nevo, Y.D., 'Methodological Approaches to Islamic Studies', *Der Islam* lxviii (1991), pp. 87–107
Lambton, A.K.P., *Persian Grammar*, Cambridge, 1967
Lane, E.W., *Arabic-English Lexicon*, 4 vols., London/Edinburgh, 1863–1893 (lithographic reprint, 2 vols., Cambridge, 1984)
Malik, Imam, *Al-Muwatta*, translated into English by ᶜA'isha ᶜAbdarahman at-Tarjumana and Yaᶜqub Johnson, Norwich, 1982
Margoliouth, D.S., *The Early Development of Muhammedanism*, London, 1914
Motzki, H., 'The *Muṣannaf* of ᶜAbd al-Razzāq al-Ṣanᶜānī as a source of authentic *aḥādīth* of the first century A.H.', *Journal of Near Eastern Studies*, l (1991), pp. 1–21
al-Murabit, Shaykh Abd al-Qadir, *Root Islamic Education*, 2nd revised edn., London, 1993
Muranyi, M., *Materialien zur Mālikitischen Rechtsliteratur*, Wiesbaden, 1984
—— *Ein Altes Fragment Medinensischer Jurisprudenz aus Qairawān*, Stuttgart, 1985
—— *ᶜAbd Allāh b. Wahb, Leben und Werk. Al-Muwaṭṭa': Kitāb al-muḥāraba*, Wiesbaden, 1992 (cited as *Muw. Ibn Wahb* [q.v.])
Nöldeke, T., *Geschichte des Qorāns*, iii. *Die Geschichte des Qorāntexts*, 2nd ed., revised by G. Bergsträsser and O. Pretzl, Leipzig, 1926–36
Ossendorf-Conrad, B., *Das 'Kitāb al-Wāḍiḥa' des ᶜAbd al-Malik b. Ḥabīb. Edition and Kommentar zu Ms. Qarawiyyīn 809/40 (Abwāb al-ṭahāra)*, Beirut/Stuttgart, 1994 (cited as *Wāḍiḥa* [q.v.])
Ostrorog, Count Léon, *The Angora Reform*, London, 1927
Pearl, D., *A Textbook on Muslim Law*, London, 1979
Powers, D.S., *Studies in Qur'an and Ḥadīth: the Formulation of the Islamic Law of Inheritance*, Berkeley etc, 1986
Pretzl, O. (ed.), *Orthographie und Punktierung des Koran, see* al-Dānī, *al-Muqniᶜ*, ed. O. Pretzl
Rackham, O., *The History of the Countryside*, London, 1986
Raddatz, H., *Die Stellung und Bedeutung des Sufyān ath-Thaurī*, Bonn, 1967
Reinhart, A.K., 'Islamic Law as Islamic Ethics', *Journal of Religious Ethics*, xi (1983), 186–203
Rippin, A., 'Al-Zarkashī and al-Suyūṭī on the function of the "Occasion of Revelation" Material', *Islamic Culture*, liv (1985), pp. 243–58
—— 'The Function of *Asbāb al-Nuzūl* in Qur'ānic Exegesis', *BSOAS*, li (1988), pp. 1–20
Robson, J., 'Tradition, the Second Foundation of Islam', *The Muslim World*, xli (1951), pp. 22–33
—— 'The *Isnād* in Muslim Tradition', *Transactions of the Glasgow Oriental Society*, xv (1953–4) [published 1955], pp. 15–26
SALP, *see* Abbott, N., *Studies in Arabic Literary Papyri*
Schacht, J., *The Origins of Muhammadan Jurisprudence*, Oxford, 1950
—— 'The Pre-Islamic Background and Early Development of Jurisprudence', in *Law in the Middle East*, ed. M. Khadduri and H.J. Liebesny, Washington, 1955
—— 'Deux éditions inconnues du *Muwaṭṭa'*', in *Studi Orientalistici in Onore di Giorgio Levi Della Vida*, Rome, 1956, ii. 477–92

—— 'Sur quelques manuscrits de la bibliothèque de la mosquée d'al-Qarawiyyīn à Fès', in *Études d'orientalisme dédiées à la mémoire de Lévi-Provençal*, Paris, 1962, i. 271–84

—— *An Introduction to Islamic Law*, Oxford, 1964

—— 'On Abū Muṣᶜab and his *Mukhtaṣar*', *Andalus*, xxx (1965), pp. 1–14

—— 'On Some Manuscripts in Kairouan and Tunis', *Arabica*, xiv (1967), pp. 225–58

—— 'On Some Manuscripts in the Libraries of Morocco', *Hespéris Tamuda*, ix (1968), pp. 5–55

—— 'Mālik ibn Anas', *EI (2)*, vi. 262–5 [fascicule published 1987]

Sezgin, F., *Geschichte des Arabischen Schrifttums*, i, Leiden, 1967

Spies, O., 'Die Bibliotheken des Hidschas', *Zeitschrift der Deutschen Morgenländischen Gesellschaft*, xc (1936), pp. 83–120

al-Ṭabarī, *The History of al-Ṭabarī*, xx, translated by G.R. Hawting, Albany, 1989

Vesey-Fitzgerald, S., *Muhammadan Law*, London, 1931

Wansbrough, J., *Quranic Studies*, Oxford, 1977

Weiss, B., *The Search for God's Law: Islamic Jurisprudence in the Writings of Sayf al-Dīn al-Āmidī*, Salt Lake City, 1992

Zaman, I., 'The Science of *Rijāl* as a Method in the Study of Hadiths', *Journal of Islamic Studies*, v (1994), pp. 1–34

Zambaur, E. de, *Manuel de généalogie et de chronologie pour l'histoire de l'Islam*, Bad Pyrmont, 1955

Ziadeh, review of Powers' *Studies in Qur'an and Ḥadīth*, *Journal of the American Oriental Society*, cviii (1988), pp. 487–8

Indexes

Index of Legal Precepts

Purity
Wiping over leather socks 40
Tayammum 25, 125

The Prayer
The prayer in general 63, 157, 163, 225
The 'lowering of the sun' and 'darkening of the night' 62
The Madinan *adhān* 35, 36, 42, 45, 197
The *iqāma* 35, 58
Running to the prayer 57, 58, 96–7, 115, 202
Doing the prayer when one remembers 208
How to stand when doing the prayer 45, 46, 174, 198
Raising the hands during the prayer 46–7
Recitation during the prayer 25, 61, 127–8
Beginning the prayer without the *basmala* 35, 36, 45, 197
Using Ibn Masᶜūd's reading in the prayer 202
The *taslīm* at the end of the prayer 51
'Completing' the prayer 87–8
'When the prayer is finished' 89
The 'middle' prayer 57, 59, 202
The travelling prayer 163
The *ᶜīd* prayer 158, 164
The fear prayer 163, 225
The eclipse prayer 158
The prayer for rain 158
The *witr* prayer 165, 166
The prostration of thankfulness 42
The change of *qibla* 125
Ṣalāt = *duᶜā*ʾ 126–8, 130, 225

*The Qur*ʾ*an*
The 'seven *aḥruf*' 61, 201
Being in *wuḍū*ʾ to touch the Qurʾan 61, 103–4
The division of the Qurʾan for daily recitation 61
The verses of prostration 61

Zakāt
Zakāt in general 47, 63, 146–7, 149, 157, 163, 222, 223, 225
Zakāt on livestock 147, 222–3
Zakāt on horses 84, 146–8
Zakāt on crops 222
Zakāt on fresh fruit and vegetables 35, 36, 148
Zakāt on figs 216
The *niṣāb* 36, 223
Those entitled to *zakāt* 69, 70, 90, 204–5, 222
Zakāt for freeing *mukātab* slaves 90
Measuring *zakāt al-fiṭr* 35, 69–70

Fasting
Fasting in general 47
Ramaḍān superseding ᶜĀshūrāʾ 126
The fasting of a sick man 114–15
The fasting of a traveller 115, 216

'Completing' days fasted 87–8
Making up missed days 58
Breaking the fast in Ramaḍān 58, 70
Fasting *kaffāras* consecutively 57, 58, 202
Fasting during *ḥajj* 58

Iʿtikāf
In general 32
Leaving *iʿtikāf* for the Jumuʿa prayer 79, 206
The *sunna* of *iʿtikāf* 165, 166

Ḥajj
Ḥajj in general 157, 163, 225
Using perfume while in *iḥrām* 49
The *saʿy* between Ṣafā and Marwa 58, 96, 117–18, 119, 126
Rafath and *fusūq* on *ḥajj* 97–8, 129–30, 211
Argument during *ḥajj* 97, 126, 128–30
Killing game while in *iḥrām* 83–4, 89, 91, 95, 104–5, 116–17, 119
The *fidyat* (*kaffārat*) *al-adhā* 70, 93, 105
Iḥṣār 25, 92–6, 105, 164, 210
'Whatever sacrificial animal is easy' 62, 92, 93, 95, 105
The 'place of sacrifice' 94, 105
Ending *ḥajj* with a *ṭawāf* 210
'Completing' *ḥajj* and *ʿumra* 87
Doing *ḥajj* for someone else 47–8
ʿUmra being a *sunna* 164, 166

Jihād
Jihād as a theme in the Qurʾan 161
The portion for thoroughbreds and mixed-breed horses 84, 102
Using donkeys rather than horses 85
Pledges of safe conduct 49
Dealing with prisoners 219

Oaths (see also *īlāʾ* and *ẓihār* under *Divorce*)
Oaths in general 67, 68, 80
The *kaffāra* for a broken oath 70, 91

Sacrificial Animals (see also *Ḥajj*)
Sacrifices in general 158
The *ʿīd* sacrifice 226
The *ʿaqīqa* sacrifice 25, 158

Slaughtering Animals
Eating horse-meat 102–3, 116
The fat of animals slaughtered by Jews 85–6

Game (see also *Ḥajj*)
Killing game 83–4
Game of the sea 25

Inheritance
Inheritance in general 62, 71, 121, 157
Inheritance due to children 72–5, 77, 113
'Brothers' reducing a mother's portion 74
Inheritance due to a grandfather 213
Grandfathers alongside collaterals 109–13, 135
Kalāla 74, 106–14, 126, 213, 214
Debts and inheritance 75–7
Bequests in general 75–7, 121–2
Bequests to heirs 121
Bequests during late pregnancy 100–101

Marriage
Marriage in general 91, 157
The consent of a virgin 85
Marriage without a legal guardian 49–50
Marriage after *zinā* 82, 116, 124
Marriage to sisters 91, 105–6
Marriage to a wife's mother 91, 195–6
Marriage to step-daughters 118, 195–6
Marriage to Jewish and Christian women 99–100, 211
Marriage to slave-girls 98–100, 115–16, 211
Intercourse with slave-girl sisters 83, 105–6
Intercourse with one's father's slave-girls 82
Mutʿa marriage 184
Muḥṣanāt 69, 80, 92, 98, 99, 100, 106, 211–12
Nikāḥ = marriage? 82, 116, 207
The institution of the veil 125

Divorce
Divorce in general 65, 66, 67, 139, 157
The 'two arbiters' 62, 117, 215

The correct time for divorce 57, 59, 133
The validity of a forced divorce 181
Divorce is limited to three times 125, 221
Triple divorce in *tamlīk* 141–2, 152
Irrevocable divorce (*al-batta*) 140–1
The rights of a *mabtūta* divorcee 142–6
The *ʿidda* in general 62
The meaning of the word *qarʾ* 62, 132–5, 140
The *ʿidda* of *umm walads* 80–1, 91, 151, 152, 207
The *ʿidda* of widows 16, 81, 91, 106
The *ʿidda* of slave-girls 81, 91
Īlāʾ 65, 66, 68, 71, 117, 139–40, 152
Ẓihār 58, 64, 65–71, 77, 81, 91, 104, 139, 204
Liʿān 25, 64, 65, 80, 125, 126
Nisāʾ = wives or women? 65, 80, 90, 207
Azwāj = all wives 80

Suckling
Establishing foster relationship 48–9, 57, 60, 122–3, 217

Business Transactions
Defects in slaves 35
Bayʿal-khiyār 48, 198, 199
Khiyār al-majlis 48
Usury (*ribā*) 62, 63, 118, 149–51, 152, 157, 158, 224
'Usurious' substances 223
Buying a gold-embellished object with gold 165
Uncertainty (*gharar*) 63, 158, 203, 224
Qirāḍ 165, 166
Sharecropping 165

Freeing Slaves
Freeing slaves in general 158
Freeing slaves for *kaffāras* 68–9, 91
Kitāba agreements 89–90
Tadbīr 75–7, 158

Ḥudūd
Ḥudūd in general 136
The stoning penalty for adultery 57, 60, 92, 101–2, 123–4, 163, 216, 217
The penalty for *zinā* in general 50, 68, 92
The penalty for *qadhf* 50, 68, 80, 151, 152, 203, 212, 224
The penalty for theft 87, 91
Apostasy 223

Testimony
Testimony in general 80, 157
The oath of a plaintiff with only one witness 161–2, 166, 171–2

Blood-money
Blood-money in general 157, 158, 223
Retaliation for murder 85–6, 90, 119, 220
ʿAmd versus khaṭaʾ 135–6, 137, 151–2
The *kaffāra* for accidental killing 58, 69, 136, 204
The indemnity for teeth 137–9, 151
Injuries caused by *mudabbar* slaves 75–7
Qasāma 158

Miscellaneous
The *ṣāʾ* and the *mudd* 35, 36, 42, 43, 45, 197
Endowments 36, 197
Saying 'Uff!' to one's parents 114
Permission to enter 120
The validity of a forced oath of allegiance 181

Index of Legal Principles

abrogation: *see naskh*
akhbār al-āḥād 35, 36, 37, 41, 48, 49, 51–2, 57, 123, 196
ʿamal 1, 3, 4, 5, 22, 24, 25, 26, 27, 28, 29, 30, 31, 32, 55, 57, 64, 71, 77, 78, 80, 90, 91, 92, 94, 106, 113, 114, 119, 120, 122, 123, 124, 130, 133, 138, 152, 164, 168, 171, 172, 173, 175, 176, 178–80, 198, 206, 228

ʿamal versus ḥadīth 20, 41–52, 173, 175, 198, 199, 228
the authority of 37–41
the nature of 33–7
analogy: *see qiyās*
asbāb al-nuzūl 25, 64, 94, 121, 125–30

dalāla lughawiyya 82
dalāla sharʿiyya 82

ḥadīth
ʿamal versus ḥadīth: *see under ʿamal*
in general 1–5, 19, 152, 168, 178–80, 181, 185, 186, 226
individual *ḥadīths* used as a source of judgements 37, 58, 59, 66, 73, 85, 86, 88, 94, 96, 97, 103, 104, 105, 106, 122, 125, 130, 133, 134, 136, 137–9, 143, 144, 146, 171–2, 181, 195, 206
isolated *ḥadīths: see akhbār al-āḥād*
Mālik as a transmitter of 7, 12–20, 26, 30, 31, 184, 186
Mālik's family as transmitters of 11–12, 182
mursal ḥadīths 13, 17, 179, 185
mashhūr ḥadīths 196
musnad ḥadīths 13, 179, 185
mutawātir ḥadīths: *see tawātur*
the *Muwaṭṭaʾ* as an early collection of 17, 22–31, 185
Schacht's assumption of fabrication 159, 172–6
sunna versus ḥadīth: *see under sunna*
ḥaml al-muṭlaq ʿalā l-muqayyad 69, 71, 90, 104–5, 202

ijmāʿ 1, 35, 39, 42, 51, 65, 73, 90, 122, 148, 171, 179
ijmāl 63, 64, 78
ijtihād 1, 3, 29, 33, 34, 35, 36, 37, 38, 39, 40, 41, 121, 137, 157, 175, 178, 180, 221
ishtirāk 63, 64, 78, 96, 113, 135
istiḥsān 34, 159

khabar al-wāḥid: see akhbār al-āḥād

mafhūm al-mukhālafa 64, 78, 100, 114, 115–19, 203, 205
mafhūm al-muwāfaqa 64, 78, 114–15, 203
al-maṣāliḥ al-mursala 34, 117
muʾawwal texts: *see taʾwīl*
mujmal texts: *see ijmāl*
mushtarak words or phrases: *see ishtirāk*
mutawātir transmission: *see tawātur*

naskh 64, 121–5, 130, 217
naṣṣ texts 63, 64, 71, 209

qiyās 1, 4, 34, 35, 51, 52, 65, 68, 70, 73, 78, 81, 83, 84, 92, 93, 94, 100, 103, 112, 113, 114, 119, 140, 146, 148, 150, 151, 159, 179, 181

raʾy 3, 30, 33–5, 198

sabab al-nuzūl: *see asbāb al-nuzūl*
sadd al-dharāʾiʿ 34, 70
shādhdh variants (of the Qurʾan) 57–60, 96, 108, 140, 146, 201, 221
sharʿ man qablanā 85–6, 220
sunna 1–5, 19, 21, 28, 32, 33, 34, 35, 37, 39, 44, 52, 55, 57, 60, 61, 69, 73, 74, 75, 87, 91, 92, 123, 124, 148, 152, 153, 157, 160, 161–7, 178–80, 192, 227, 228, 229
sunna terms in the *Muwaṭṭaʾ* 40, 74, 120, 148, 162, 164, 165, 225, 226, 227
sunna versus ḥadīth 148, 168–77, 227

tawātur 35–6, 41, 45, 49, 57, 60, 196
taʾwīl 64
taʾwīl al-ẓāhir 78

ʿumūm 48, 65, 70, 78, 79–88, 98, 100, 114, 122, 130, 137, 148, 210
takhṣīṣ al-ʿumūm 78, 90–6, 122, 217
ʿurf 90, 207

ẓāhir meaning 49, 63, 70, 78, 79, 88, 118, 137, 143, 146
taʾwīl al-ẓāhir 78

Index of Persons

[N.B. The 'al-' of the definite article in Arabic has been ignored for indexing purposes.]

Abān ibn ʿUthmān 141, 219
Abbott, N. 24, 181, 183, 189, 193, 196
ʿAbd al-ʿAzīz [Āl Mubārak], A. 182
ʿAbd al-ʿAzīz ibn al-Mājishūn 29, 184, 192
ʿAbd al-Ḥamīd ibn ʿAbd al-Raḥmān 219
ʿAbd al-Karīm ibn Abī l-Mukhāriq 184
ʿAbd al-Karīm al-Jazarī 183
[ʿAbd al-Malik] ibn al-Mājishūn 44
ʿAbd al-Malik [ibn Marwān] 131, 136, 141, 151, 205, 210, 219
ʿAbd al-Raḥmān ibn al-Ḥakam 144
ʿAbd al-Raḥmān ibn Hurmuz al-Aʿraj 17, 183
ʿAbd al-Razzāq al-Ṣanʿānī 16, 180, 197
ʿAbd al-Wahhāb, al-Qāḍī *see* al-Qāḍī ʿAbd al-Wahhāb
ʿAbdallāh ibn Abī Bakr [... ibn Ḥazm] 43–4
ʿAbdallāh ibn Abī Ḥusayn 184
ʿAbdallāh ibn ʿAmr ibn al-ʿĀṣ 187
ʿAbdallāh ibn Muslim ibn Hurmuz 183
ʿAbdallāh ibn Qays 219
ʿAbdallāh ibn Shaddād 127
ʿAbdallāh ibn ʿUmar *see* Ibn ʿUmar
ʿAbdallāh ibn Umm Maktūm 143
ʿAbdallāh ibn Yazīd ibn Hurmuz *see* Ibn Hurmuz
ʿAbdallāh ibn al-Zubayr 128, 131, 210, 219
Abd-Allah, U.F. 13, 39–40, 50–1, 90, 170, 183, 194, 225, 227
Abū ʿĀmir 11
Abū ʿAmr ibn Ḥafṣ 143
Abū ʿAwāna 187
Abū Ayyūb al-Anṣārī 94
Abū Bakr [al-Ṣiddīq] 32, 42, 73, 107, 108, 110, 111, 127, 147, 194, 219, 223
Abū Bakr ibn ʿAbd al-Raḥmān [ibn al-Ḥārith ibn Hishām] 13, 132, 133, 139, 183
Abū Bakr [ibn ʿAmr] ibn Ḥazm 28, 147, 219, 224, 228
Abū l-Dardāʾ 44, 149, 150, 219, 223
Abū Dāwūd 1, 16, 17, 179
Abū Ḥanīfa 4, 16, 25, 47, 48, 59, 65, 66, 67, 68, 69, 70, 71, 73, 75, 79, 80, 81, 82, 86, 88, 89, 90, 92, 93, 94, 100, 102, 103, 104, 105, 109, 110, 117, 138, 139, 141, 142, 144, 146, 148, 186, 198, 202, 207, 211
Abū Hurayra 11, 17, 127
Abū l-Ḥusayn ibn Abī ʿUmar 37
Abū Isḥāq al-Isfarāyīnī 42
Abū Jaʿfar al-Manṣūr *see* al-Manṣūr
Abū Jaʿfar Yazīd ibn al-Qaʿqāʾ 199, 218
Abū Muḥammad Ṣāliḥ 203, 206
Abū Mūsā al-Ashʿarī 219
Abū Muṣʿab [al-Zuhrī] 23, 24, 25, 27, 31, 189, 190
Abū Qilāba 81
Abū Saʿīd (al-Khudrī?) 223
Abū Salama ibn ʿAbd al-Raḥmān [ibn ʿAwf] 13, 171
Abū Salama al-Mājishūn 193
Abū Suhayl Nāfiʿ ibn Abī ʿĀmir 11, 182
Abū Thawr 73, 81, 117
Abū ʿUbayd, the *mawlā* of Sulaymān ibn ʿAbd al-Malik 184
Abū ʿUbayda [ibn al-Jarrāḥ] 147, 148
Abū Yūsuf 4, 16, 35, 42–43, 50, 103, 110, 148, 164, 175, 176, 195, 197
Abū Zahra, M. 205
Abū l-Zinād [ibn Dhakwān] 13, 17
Abū l-Zubayr al-Makkī 183
Aghnides, N.P. 227
Aḥmad ibn Ḥanbal 4, 16, 18, 81, 144, 185, 206
ʿĀʾisha 48, 57, 59–60, 118, 122–3, 126, 127, 130, 132, 133, 134, 144, 145
al-Akhfash 27, 191
ʿAlī [ibn Abī Ṭālib] 14, 47, 59, 73, 81, 102, 111, 133, 195, 202, 213, 215
ʿAlī ibn al-Madīnī 17, 32
ʿAlī ibn Ziyād 23, 25, 26, 27, 30, 85, 103, 180, 188, 190

ᶜAmmār ibn Yāsir 211
ᶜAmr ibn al-ᶜĀṣ 206
ᶜAmr ibn Ḥazm 137, 138, 223
Anas [ibn Mālik] 12, 89, 118, 215
Ansari, Z.I. 170, 181, 196, 227
al-Aᶜraj *see* ᶜAbd al-Raḥmān ibn Hurmuz al-Aᶜraj
Aṣbagh ibn al-Faraj 27
ᶜĀṣim 56
ᶜAṭāᵓ ibn ᶜAbdallāh al-Khurāsānī 183
ᶜAṭāᵓ [ibn Abī Rabāḥ] 46, 89, 118, 209, 210, 215
ᶜAwn ibn Yūsuf 191
al-Awzāᶜī 16, 19, 46, 170, 187, 224
Ayyūb al-Sakhtiyānī 183
Azmi, M.M. 169, 181, 183

al-Bājī 6, 58, 59, 70, 88, 90, 104, 115, 134, 198, 206, 207, 209, 211, 217, 218
Bravmann, M.M. 164, 181
Brunschvig, R. 5, 195, 197, 203
al-Bukhārī 1, 12, 16, 127, 179, 185, 191
Burton, J. 124, 181, 216, 217, 218

Calder, N. 26, 27, 181, 191
Coulson, N.J. 159, 160, 181
Crone, P. 152, 158, 168, 181, 218

al-Dānī 56
Dāwūd al-Ẓāhirī 4, 66, 73, 144
al-Dhahabī 7, 193
Doi, A.R. 169

al-Fasawī 38
Fāṭima bint Qays 143–6, 222
Fierro, M. 198
al-Furayᶜa bint Mālik 16
Fyzee, A.A.A. 169

al-Ghāfiqī 13, 22, 183, 184
Gibb, H.A.R. 168
Goitein, S.D. 159, 160
Goldziher, I. 1, 6, 26, 169, 170, 179, 181, 189–90, 196, 218, 227, 228
Guillaume, A. 181, 226

Habbār ibn al-Aswad 94
Ḥafṣ 56, 200, 206, 224
Ḥafṣa bint ᶜAbd al-Raḥmān 49, 133
Ḥafṣa [bint ᶜUmar] 57, 59
al-Ḥajjāj ibn Yūsuf 210, 219
Ḥammād ibn Salama 187
Ḥammād ibn Zayd 15
Hammām ibn Munabbih 187
Ḥarmala ibn Yaḥyā 191
Hārūn al-Rashīd 192
Hasan, A. 170, 196, 227
Hasan, S. 169, 181
al-Ḥasan al-Baṣrī 46
al-Ḥasan al-Luᵓluᵓī 198
Hawting, G. 222
Hinds, M. 152, 218
Hishām [ibn ᶜAbd al-Malik] 28, 192
Hishām [ibn Ismāᶜīl al-Makhzūmī] 70, 205, 219
Hishām [ibn ᶜUrwa] 127
Ḥumayd ibn Qays 184
Ḥumayd al-Ṭawīl 183
Hushaym 187

Ibāḍīs 46
Ibn ᶜAbbās 59, 74, 106, 110, 111, 117, 121, 126, 127, 129, 130, 138, 205, 213, 215
Ibn ᶜAbd al-Barr 58, 184, 185, 225
Ibn ᶜAbd al-Ḥakam 31
Ibn Abī ᶜĀmir *see* Mālik ibn Abī ᶜĀmir
Ibn Abī Dhiᵓb 184, 187, 193
Ibn Abī Ḥātim 193
Ibn Abī Ḥāzim 44
Ibn Abī Zayd al-Qayrawānī 31, 197
Ibn Abī l-Zinād 44, 45, 197
Ibn al-ᶜArabī 6, 135, 185, 208, 209, 217
Ibn Bukayr 23, 27
Ibn Farḥūn 182
Ibn Ḥabīb 31, 191
Ibn Ḥajar 124
Ibn Ḥamdūn 203
Ibn Ḥanbal *see* Aḥmad ibn Ḥanbal
Ibn Ḥazm 71
Ibn Hurmuz 12, 19, 183
Ibn Isḥāq 187
Ibn al-Jazarī 199
Ibn Jurayj 29, 46, 187
Ibn Juzayy 6, 117, 211
Ibn al-Madīnī *see* ᶜAlī ibn al-Madīnī

Ibn Mahdī 18, 44
Ibn Mājah 1
Ibn al-Mājishūn *see* ᶜAbd al-ᶜAzīz ibn al-Mājishūn *and* ᶜAbd al-Malik ibn al-Mājishūn
Ibn Masᶜūd 38, 47, 73, 81, 108, 111, 118, 133, 140, 146, 185, 195, 202, 214, 215, 221, 222, 224
Ibn al-Mawwāz 31
Ibn al-Muᶜadhdhal 44
Ibn al-Mubārak 16, 187
Ibn Mujāhid 199
Ibn al-Mundhir 117
Ibn al-Musayyab *see* Saᶜīd ibn al-Musayyab
Ibn Muzayn 27, 191
Ibn Nāfiᶜ 191
Ibn Nāṣir al-Dīn 188
Ibn al-Qāsim 23, 26, 27, 31, 43, 46, 49, 65, 190, 228
Ibn Qayyim al-Jawziyya 38
Ibn Qutabya 50, 175
Ibn Rushd (al-Ḥafīd) 6, 47, 66, 82, 86, 87, 88, 100, 113, 198, 210
Ibn Rushd (al-Jadd) 51, 59, 163
Ibn Saᶜd 29–30
Ibn Shihāb [al-Zuhrī] 12–13, 14, 16, 17, 19, 28, 33, 81, 125, 132, 139, 140, 144, 184, 192
Ibn Sīrīn 46, 118, 127, 186, 215
Ibn Taymiyya 32, 35–37, 40, 195
Ibn Ṭūlūn 188
Ibn ᶜUmar 12, 16, 17, 21, 25–6, 32–33, 46, 48, 57, 59, 81, 87, 90, 96, 99, 129, 130, 131, 132, 133, 134, 139, 163, 164–5, 202, 210, 211
Ibn ᶜUyayna 16, 17, 19, 45, 129, 187
Ibn Wahb 19, 24, 27, 43, 184, 189, 190, 191
Ibn Zayd 129
Ibn Ziyād *see* ᶜAlī ibn Ziyād
Ibrāhīm al-Ḥarbī 17
Ibrāhīm ibn Abī ᶜUbla 183
Ibrāhīm al-Nakhaᶜī 46, 47, 81, 86, 185, 186
ᶜĪsā ibn Dīnār 27
Ismāᶜīlīs 46
ᶜIyāḍ 15, 22, 35–37, 39, 40, 41–45, 182, 188, 191, 197

Jabala ibn Ḥammūd 26
Jābir ibn ᶜAbdallāh al-Anṣārī 187
Jābir ibn al-Aswad 219
Jaᶜfar ibn Sulaymān 181
Jarīr ibn ᶜAbd al-Ḥamīd 187
al-Jaṣṣāṣ 6, 198, 210, 211, 217
Juynboll, G. 181, 183

Kaᶜb ibn ᶜUjra 93
Khalīl 46
Khallāf, ᶜA. 225
Khārija [ibn Zayd ibn Thābit] 13
Khawārij 124, 217

al-Layth [ibn Saᶜd] 16, 19, 31, 35, 37–9, 46, 81, 164, 166, 177, 196, 197, 216, 228

al-Mahdī 192
Mālik [ibn Anas] *passim*
Mālik ibn Abī ᶜĀmir 11, 56, 60, 182
Maᶜmar ibn Rāshid 29, 187
al-Maʾmūn 192
al-Manṣūr 29, 41, 166, 193, 195
Margoliouth, D.S. 172
Marwān [ibn al-Ḥakam] 131, 135, 138, 139, 140, 141, 144, 145, 150, 152, 219
Motzki, H. 180, 181
Muᶜādh 222
Muᶜāwiya 87, 131, 132, 135, 137, 138, 149, 150, 151, 152, 219, 228
Muḥammad ibn ᶜAbdallāh 30
Muḥammad ibn Abī Bakr [... ibn Ḥazm] 43–4
Muḥammad ibn ᶜĪsā 27
Muḥammad ibn Saḥnūn 191
Muḥammad al-ᶜUtbī *see* al-ᶜUtbī
Mujāhid 73, 129
al-Mundhir ibn al-Zubayr 49
Muqātil 224
Muranyi, M. 24, 189, 192
Muslim 1, 179, 185
Muᶜtazila 121, 124

Nāfiᶜ ibn ᶜAbd al-Raḥmān 55–6, 199, 200
Nāfiᶜ, the *mawlā* of Ibn ᶜUmar 12, 16, 33, 46, 48, 55, 184

al-Nasāʾī 1, 17
al-Nayfar, M.S. 188, 192

Ostrorog, Count 224

Powers, D.S. 124, 159, 181, 214

al-Qābisī 23
al-Qāḍī ʿAbd al-Wahhāb 41
Qālūn 55, 200
al-Qaʿnabī 23, 25, 27, 190, 191
al-Qarāfī 74, 192, 204
al-Qāsim ibn Muḥammad [ibn Abī Bakr] 13, 80, 81, 129, 132, 141, 142, 143, 144, 151
Qatāda 207

al-Rabīʿ ibn Mālik 11
al-Rabīʿ ibn Ṣabīḥ 187
Rabīʿa [ibn Abī ʿAbd al-Raḥmān] 13, 44, 45, 183, 218
Rackham, O. 174
Rāshid ibn Abī Rāshid 203, 206
Rippin, A. 126, 218
Robson, J. 168, 181, 183
Ruzayq ibn Ḥukaym *see* Zurayq ibn Ḥakīm

Saʿd ibn Abī Waqqāṣ 108
Ṣadaqa ibn Yasār 184
Sahla bint Suhayl 123
Saḥnūn 6, 26, 31, 46, 49
Saʿīd ibn Abī ʿArūba 187
Saʿīd ibn al-ʿĀṣ 87, 143–4, 219
Saʿīd ibn Jubayr 46
Saʿīd ibn al-Musayyab 13, 14, 33, 46, 79, 81, 84, 124, 133, 137, 138, 139, 193
Sālim [ibn ʿAbdallāh ibn ʿUmar] 13, 17, 33, 46, 132, 183
al-Samhūdī 182
al-Sarakhsī 6, 134, 198, 205, 210, 221, 227
Schacht, J. 1, 3, 5, 6, 24, 33, 152, 158, 159, 160, 164, 168, 169, 170–7, 181, 183, 190, 195, 196, 197, 199, 222, 226, 227, 228
'Seven *Fuqahā*ʾ' of Madina 13, 33, 130, 139, 186
Sezgin, F. 181
al-Shaʿbī 81, 186
al-Shāfiʿī 4, 5, 6, 16, 17, 27, 47, 48, 50, 52, 60, 65, 66, 67, 68, 69, 70, 71, 73, 74, 79, 80, 81, 86, 88, 89, 90, 92, 93, 94, 100, 102, 103, 104, 105, 109, 110, 117, 122, 123, 134, 136, 138, 139, 141, 142, 144, 148, 153, 168, 170, 171, 176, 179, 185, 198, 202, 207, 210, 227, 228
al-Shāṭibī 42
al-Shaybānī 4, 6, 16, 17, 23, 24–6, 27, 50, 103, 110, 124, 132, 148, 176, 179, 186, 190, 198, 202, 207, 229
Shīʿa 46, 205
Shuʿba ibn al-Ḥajjāj 16, 187
Ṣiddīq Khān 185
Subayʿa al-Aslamiyya 91, 106
Sufyān ibn ʿUyayna *see* Ibn ʿUyayna
Sufyān al-Thawrī *see* al-Thawrī
Sulaymān [ibn ʿAbd al-Malik] 147, 228
Sulaymān ibn Yasār 13, 32, 33, 132, 143, 144, 171, 193
Suwayd al-Ḥadathānī 23, 24, 25, 27, 190
al-Suyūṭī 6, 22, 125, 211

al-Ṭabarī 6, 24, 127, 128, 129, 193, 211
Ṭalḥa ibn ʿAbd al-Malik 184
Ṭalḥa ibn ʿAbdallāh ibn ʿAwf 219
Ṭāriq ibn ʿAmr 219
Ṭāwūs 122, 207
Thābit ibn al-Aḥnaf 181
al-Thawrī 16, 18, 81, 170, 187
al-Tirmidhī 1, 185

ʿUbāda ibn al-Ṣāmit 219, 223
ʿUbaydallāh ibn ʿAbd al-Karīm 44
ʿUbaydallāh ibn ʿAbdallāh [ibn ʿUtba ibn Masʿūd] 13
Ubayy 57, 58–9, 108, 215, 221
ʿUmar ibn ʿAbd al-ʿAzīz 13, 28, 30, 33, 44, 74, 81, 87, 131, 138, 141, 147, 151, 152, 171, 182, 192, 219, 224, 228
ʿUmar [ibn al-Khaṭṭāb] 11, 32, 33, 43, 44, 49, 50, 57, 58, 59, 60, 90, 94, 97, 104, 107, 108, 109, 110, 111, 113, 123, 127, 133, 135, 137, 138,

146, 147, 148, 149, 150, 163, 194, 209, 210, 213, 214, 222, 223
Umm Sharīk 143
ᶜUrwa ibn al-Zubayr 13, 117–18, 126, 127, 128, 141
Usāma ibn Zayd 143
al-ᶜUtbī 6, 31
ᶜUthmān [ibn ᶜAffān] 11, 14, 36, 37, 56, 102, 105, 106, 110, 135, 201, 206

Vesey-Fitzgerald, S. 168

al-Wāḥidī 125
al-Walīd [ibn ᶜAbd al-Malik] 138, 141, 205, 219, 221
Wansbrough, J. 124, 159, 161, 218
Warsh 55, 200, 224
Weiss, B. 203

Yaḥyā ibn ᶜAwn 191
Yaḥyā ibn Saᶜīd al-Anṣārī 13, 16
Yaḥyā ibn Saᶜīd ibn al-ᶜĀṣ 143
Yaḥyā ibn Saᶜīd al-Qaṭṭān 17
Yaḥyā ibn Yaḥyā al-Laythī 23, 25, 27, 102, 190, 217
Yaᶜqūb ibn Abī Salama 193
Yazīd ibn ᶜAbd al-Malik 80, 121, 151, 152, 219

Ẓāhirīs 66, 67, 89, 117, 141, 146
Zaman, I. 186
Zayd ibn Abī Unaysa 184
Zayd ibn ᶜAlī 187
Zayd ibn Aslam 90
Zayd [ibn Thābit] 71, 110, 111, 132, 135, 150
Zaydān, ᶜA. 225
Zaydīs 46
Ziadeh, F. 214
Ziyād ibn ᶜAbd al-Raḥmān 217
Ziyād ibn Saᶜīd 184
al-Zuhrī *see* Ibn Shihāb al-Zuhrī
Zurayq ibn Ḥakīm 87, 219
al-Zurqānī 6, 129, 141, 188